# SQL SERVER 2000

# Stored Procedure Programming

# SQL SERVER 2000

## Stored Procedure
## Programming

DEJAN **SUNDERIC**
TOM **WOODHEAD**

Osborne/**McGraw-Hill**

Berkeley   New York   St. Louis   San Francisco
Auckland   Bogotá   Hamburg   London   Madrid
Mexico City   Milan   Montreal   New Delhi   Panama City
Paris   São Paulo   Singapore   Sydney
Tokyo   Toronto

Osborne/**McGraw-Hill**
2600 Tenth Street
Berkeley, California 94710
U.S.A.

For information on translations or book distributors outside the U.S.A., or to arrange bulk purchase discounts for sales promotions, premiums, or fund-raisers, please contact Osborne/**McGraw-Hill** at the above address.

**SQL Server 2000 Stored Procedure Programming**

34567890 CUS CUS 01987654321

ISBN 0-07-212566-7


| Publisher | Proofreader |
|---|---|
| Brandon A. Nordin | Susie Elkind |
| **Vice President & Associate Publisher** | **Indexer** |
| Scott Rogers | Valerie Robbins |
| **Editorial Director** | **Computer Designers** |
| Wendy Rinaldi | Roberta Steele |
| **Project Editor** | Kelly Stanton-Scott |
| LeeAnn Pickrell | **Illustrators** |
| **Acquisitions Coordinators** | Michael Mueller |
| Tim Madrid | Beth Young |
| Monika Faltiss | **Series Design** |
| **Technical Editor** | Peter F. Hancik |
| Chris Herring | **Cover Design** |
| **Copy Editor** | Will Voss |
| Robert Campbell | |

This book was composed with Corel VENTURA™ Publisher.

Information has been obtained by Osborne/**McGraw-Hill** from sources believed to be reliable. However, because of the possibility of human or mechanical error by our sources, Osborne/**McGraw-Hill**, or others, Osborne/**McGraw-Hill** does not guarantee the accuracy, adequacy, or completeness of any information and is not responsible for any errors or omissions or the results obtained from use of such information.

Writing a book isn't easy, but living with someone who is writing
a book can be, at times, even harder. We would like to thank
our respective spouses for their patience,
understanding, and inspiration:
For Mirjana Sunderic and Ann(a) Fricker

# AT A GLANCE

# CONTENTS

# ACKNOWLEDGMENTS

We wish to thank all the people who helped to make this book a reality, in particular:

—Margaret Abbott, who helped in the preparation of about three quarters of the text

—Liang Wang, who showed us just how easy it really is to write extended stored procedures and who subsequently reviewed that portion of the book

—Snezana Milivojevic, who showed us the error of our ways in Chapter 7

—Gerry Kichok, who reviewed our rendering of SQL Server's XML capabilities in Chapter 12

# CHAPTER 1

# Introduction

Welcome to *SQL Server 2000 Stored Procedure Programming.* This book identifies and describes the key concepts, techniques, tips, tricks, and habits the professional developer needs to master in order to take full advantage of stored procedures in the SQL Server development environment.

Microsoft SQL Server is the relational database management system (RDBMS) of choice for a growing number of business organizations and professional database and application developers. The reasons for this growing popularity are quite simple:

▼ **Integration**   No other RDBMS integrates as fully and cleanly with applications and integrated development environments (IDEs) designed to run on the ubiquitous Microsoft Windows platform.

■ **Ease of use**   SQL Server provides Enterprise Manager and Query Analyzer to allow DBAs to design, develop, deploy, and manage database solutions. These interfaces automate repetitive tasks and provide simple ways to perform complex operations. SQL Server integrates seamlessly with development tools such as Visual Basic and Visual Interdev to allow developers to design and develop client/server or Internet solutions rapidly.

■ **Flexibility**   You can use different features within SQL Server to achieve similar results. (Of course, with flexibility comes choice, and choice means that the developer is responsible for choosing the most appropriate means of achieving an end. This book will help you make those choices.)

▲ **Power**   SQL Server makes large amounts of data available to large numbers of concurrent users while maintaining the security and integrity of the data. At the time of this writing, SQL Server holds the record in TPC-C benchmark tests for performance and price/performance (see www.tpc.org).

When we began working with SQL Server, reference materials relating to the development and deployment of stored procedures were rare and not particularly helpful. These materials described basic concepts, but the examples presented were often trivial and not complex enough to be applied to real-world situations in which aspects such as error handling, debugging, naming conventions, and interfaces to other applications are critical. As the legions of application developers and development DBAs migrate from Microsoft Access to SQL Server, and as SQL Server becomes the RDBMS of choice for mission-critical application development, the need for more advanced work on SQL Server stored procedures becomes even more critical.

## WHO SHOULD READ THIS BOOK

This book has been written to fill this gap, and thus it has been written with a wide audience in mind. Ideally, it will be neither the first nor the last book you read on SQL Server, but it may be the one you refer to and recommend the most. Above all, this book has been written to help professional developers get the most out of SQL Server stored procedures and produce quality work for their clients.

If you are an experienced SQL Server developer, you will find this book to be an essential reference text full of tips and techniques to help you address the development issues you encounter in the course of your day-to-day development activities.

If you have some experience with SQL Server development, but substantially more in other programming environments such as Visual Basic, you will find this book useful as a tool to orient yourself with the SQL Server environment and become proficient more quickly with SQL Server stored procedure concepts and methods.

If you are a novice SQL Server developer, the concepts, tips, and techniques you will learn in reading this book and working through the exercises will help you attain the knowledge, skills, and good habits that will make you an accomplished professional.

We hope that this book remains close to your workstation for a long time. Indeed, in the course of this book's useful life, you may in turn be all three of the users just described.

## WHAT YOU WILL FIND IN THIS BOOK

All chapters in this book (aside from the one you are reading, which is introductory in nature) provide conceptual grounding in a specific area of the SQL Server development landscape. Chapters 3 through 12 go beyond this conceptual grounding to provide the techniques and examples to help you realize the concepts within the SQL Server development environment. Chapters 2–7 and 9–12 contain exercises designed to help you apply and develop the skills learned in the chapter. You can find the solutions to the exercise in Appendix B, "Solutions."

Chapter 1, "Introduction," describes the content of this book, as well as its intended audience, and introduces you to new features available in SQL Server 2000. It also describes a sample database that we will use throughout the book to demonstrate stored procedure development.

Chapter 2, "Relational Database Concepts and the SQL Server Environment," provides a 30,000-foot overview that will help you establish a conceptual grounding in relational database management systems (RDBMSs) in general, and in SQL Server architecture in particular. It will briefly introduce the Transact-SQL language, SQL Server tools, and stored procedure design.

Chapter 3, "Stored Procedure Design Concepts," explores SQL Server stored procedure design in greater detail with particular attention paid to the different types of stored procedures, their uses, and their functionality.

Chapter 4, "Basic Transact-SQL Programming Constructs," describes Transact-SQL, the ANSI SQL-92–compliant programming language used to write scripts in SQL Server. This chapter summarizes datatypes, variables, flow control statements, and cursors in the context of SQL Server 2000.

Chapter 5, "Functions," describes the extensive set of built-in functions available in SQL Server 2000 and how to use them in various common situations.

Chapter 6, "Composite Transact-SQL Constructs—Batches, Scripts, and Transactions," describes the various ways in which you can group Transact-SQL statements for execution.

Chapter 7, "Debugging and Error Handling," provides a coherent approach to the identification and resolution of defects in code and a coherent strategy for handling errors as they occur.

Chapter 8, "Developing Professional Habits," discusses the work habits that differentiate the professional DBA from the amateur, particularly source code control and the use of naming conventions.

Chapter 9, "Special Types of Procedures," describes user-defined, system, extended, temporary, global temporary, and remote stored procedures as well as other types of procedures in Transact-SQL, such as user-defined functions, table-valued user-defined functions, after triggers, and instead-of triggers.

Chapter 10, "Advanced Stored Procedure Programming," introduces some advanced techniques for coding stored procedures such as dynamically constructed queries, optimistic locking using timestamps, and nested stored procedures.

Chapter 11, "Interaction with the SQL Server Environment," focuses on the ways in which you can use system and extended stored procedures to interact with the SQL Server environment, and discusses the ways in which user-defined stored procedures can help you leverage the existing functionality of various elements within the SQL Server environment.

Chapter 12, "XML Support in SQL Server 2000," first introduces XML as the markup language of choice for information exchange and publishing and then focuses on specific features in SQL Server 2000 that you can use to tackle XML.

Appendix A, "T-SQL and XML Datatypes in SQL Server 2000," provides you with three tables that list datatypes in use in SQL Server 2000 and the way they map.

Appendix B, "Solutions to the Exercises," provides users with solutions for the exercises that accompany the chapters.

## REQUIREMENTS

To make full use of this book, you will need access to a server running one of the following versions of SQL Server:

- ▼ **Enterprise Edition** (supports all features and scales to enterprise level; supports up to 32 CPUs and 64GB RAM)

- ■ **Standard Edition** (scales to the level of departmental or workgroup servers; supports up to 4 CPUs and 2GB RAM)

- ▲ **Evaluation Edition** (supports all features of Enterprise Edition; use is limited to 120-days; available for download over the Web)

However, you can also perform most of the activities described in this book using a stand-alone PC with Windows 98, Windows 2000, or Windows NT Workstation to run one of the following versions of Microsoft SQL Server 2000:

▼ **Personal Edition** (designed for mobile or stand-alone users and applications; does not support some advanced features such as fail-over clustering, publishing of transactional replications, OLAP Server, or Full Text Search; supports up to 2 CPUs)

■ **Developer Edition** (licensed to be used only as a development and test server, although it supports all features of Enterprise Edition)

▲ **Desktop Engine** (distributable but stripped-down version that software vendors can package and deploy with their systems; part of Microsoft Access and Visual Studio; also known as MSDE; does not contain administrative tools such as Enterprise Manager, Query Analyzer, and Books Online; does not support advanced features such as Analysis Services and replication; database size is limited to 2GB)

Although MSDE is compatible with all other versions of SQL Server 2000 and thus makes an excellent development tool in a stand-alone environment, the absence of administrative tools such as Enterprise Manager and Query Analyzer means that some of the information you find in this book will not be usable right away. We recommend that you obtain some other version (such as the Evaluation Edition).

# NEW FEATURES IN SQL SERVER 2000

SQL Server 2000 continues the design philosophy first extolled in version 7.0 and presents advances over previous versions in the following areas:

▼ Improved Web enablement

■ Improved scalability and reliability

▲ Improved development environment (faster time to market, lower Total Cost of Ownership)

## Improved Web Enablement

If you are a database or Web developer, you will find SQL Server 2000's implementation of XML both invaluable and easy to use. The addition of XML capability means that you will be able to interchange data and publish database information using XML.

SQL Server 2000 also supports secure data access from a browser through firewalls, full-text searches of formatted documents (HTML, XML), and "English" (plain language) queries.

SQL Server 2000 Analytical Services include Online Analytical Processing (OLAP) Server as well as a set of data-mining tools to allow complete integration with Microsoft Commerce Server and provide complete click-stream and Web data analysis (also known as Business Internet Analytics).

## Improved Scalability and Reliability

SQL Server is the Web's most popular database solution because Web-based e-commerce requires rapid and seamless scalability. It supports scaling up (to a more powerful server), scaling out (to more servers working concurrently) and scaling down (to nonserver operating systems such as Windows 2000 Professional, Windows NT Workstation, Windows ME, Windows 98, or even Windows CE).

When coupled with Windows 2000, SQL Server 2000 (Enterprise Edition) provides support for Symmetric Multiprocessing (SMP), so you can take advantage of up to 32 CPUs and 64 gigabytes of RAM. It can run different parts of a query on different CPUs in parallel, thus increasing the speed with which results are returned. The query optimizer uses hash and merge algorithms to improve join operations.

SQL Server 2000 provides the ability to horizontally partition workloads across multiple SQL Server installations. A group of *federated database servers* can share horizontally partitioned data. They can be (indeed, they have to be) managed independently, but they will share the workload of application requests.

Simplified configuration of fail-over clustering means that it is easier to maximize the availability of your database. You can even perform most maintenance tasks while your database remains online.

SQL Server 2000 has many improvements that support Very Large Databases (VLDB):

▼ Performance of backup and restore operations is significantly improved.

■ Bulk copy operations can be performed in parallel on the same table.

■ Multiple indexes can be performed at the same time.

▲ It now supports terabyte databases.

All these improvements make SQL Server 2000 an ideal choice for intensive line-of-business (LOB) and data warehousing solutions.

## Improved Development and Administration Environment

The speed with which the Web is driving the development of today's applications makes "time to market" a key factor in judging any development environment or effort. SQL Server 2000's improved ease of use helps you build, deploy, and manage your databased applications—whether for e-commerce, line-of-business, or data warehousing—more quickly and confidently than ever before.

SQL Server 2000 simplifies and automates performance tuning and monitoring, and it simplifies the movement of databases between instances of SQL Server. It works in conjunction with the Windows 2000 Active Directory service to allow centralized database management. It configures itself while running, automatically and dynamically, for optimal performance in an ever-changing environment. Intervention by an experienced DBA is possible but not required.

The new integrated T-SQL debugger, T-SQL templates, "instead-of" triggers, and user-defined functions will reduce development time considerably.

Microsoft's integration of Data Transformation Services (DTS) with Microsoft Message Queue Server (MSMQ) means that DTS can now access information over the Internet via FTP.

# SAMPLE DATABASE

We have created a sample database that we will use through most of this book. The subject of the Asset sample database is an asset management system within a fictional organization. Although the database is based on real-world experience within financial institutions, it is also applicable in many other environments.

The main purpose of the database is to track assets. Assets are defined as equipment, and all variations in their content, attributes, and shape are recorded as values of properties. The Inventory table tracks location, status, leasing information, and who is currently using each asset. To transfer an asset from one location to another, to assign assets to a different owner or department, to request maintenance, or to request upgrades or new assets, users of the database use orders and order items. Activities performed to complete the order are recorded in the charge log and inter-department invoices are generated. There are lookup tables used to track provinces, lease frequencies, statuses, and other details.

## Sample Database Installation

You should download this database and install it on your server before you begin to read the rest of this book. To download and install the sample Asset database:

1.  Visit **www.trigonblue.com/sp_book.htm**.

2.  Click the link to the database on the screen. When prompted, opt to save the file to disk. Remember the location to which you saved the file.

3. Unzip the contents of the zip file into the \Program Files\Microsoft SQL Server\MSSQL\Data folder of the machine on which SQL Server is installed.

4. Make sure that SQL Server is running. If necessary, run SQL Server Service Manager from Programs | MS SQL Server or use the system tray icon. If necessary, start the SQL Server service:

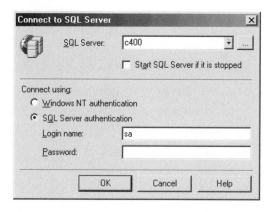

5. Run Query Analyzer (select Programs | MS SQL Server | Query Analyzer).

6. You will be prompted to connect to SQL Server. Type the server name and log in as system administrator (sa). If the password has not been set, leave the password blank (i.e., an empty string):

Query Analyzer opens a query window pointing to the master database:

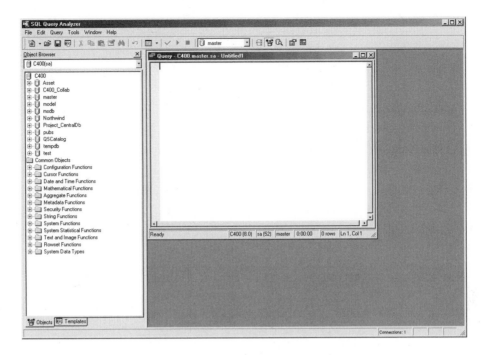

7.  Type the following text in the query window:

```
EXEC sp_attach_db 'Asset',
    'E:\Program Files\Microsoft SQL Server\MSSQL\Data\Asset_data.mdf',
    'E:\Program Files\Microsoft SQL Server\MSSQL\Data\Asset_log.ldf'
```

> If the location of the folder containing the Asset database file is different from the one shown in the command, change the command.

8.  To attach the database, select Query | Execute from the menu bar. SQL Server attaches the database. The database is now ready for use.

## Purpose and Design of the Sample Database

The Asset database is designed to track and manage assets within an organization. This database allows users to

▼  Track features of assets

■  Search for assets with specific features

■  Record the current location and status of an asset

- Track the person and organizational unit to which the asset is assigned

- Note how an asset is acquired and the cost of the acquisition

- Keep parameters concerning leases (e.g., lease payments, lease schedules, lease vendors used to obtain assets)

- Identify assets for which lease schedules have expired

- Record orders to departments in charge of services such as acquisition, disposal, servicing, and technical support

- Monitor the processing of orders

▲ Manage the costs associated with actions taken on order items

## Database Diagram

Figure 1-1 shows the physical implementation of the Asset entity relationship diagram.

### Description of Assets

The following illustration shows the tables involved in the description of each asset. Detailed information about deployed equipment and their features is essential for the proper management of current inventory as well as future upgrades and acquisitions.

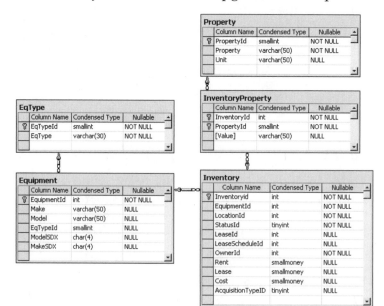

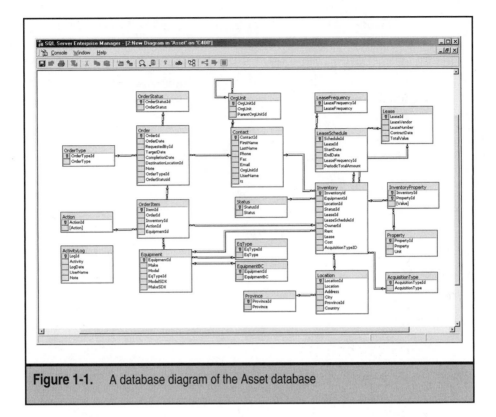

**Figure 1-1.**    A database diagram of the Asset database

Information in these asset description tables allows users to

▼ Manage a list of standard equipment deployed within the organization

■ Manage a list of attributes (properties) that can be used to describe assets

■ Manage a list of attributes for each asset

■ Obtain a summary of equipment deployed within the organization

■ Make decisions about the deployment of a software package based on the capabilities of existing equipment in the field

▲ Find obsolete pieces of equipment that need to be disposed of and replaced with new equipment

**Inventory**   The central table in the Asset database is the Inventory table. It is designed to track the assets currently deployed within an organization. The most important information about an asset indicates what kind of equipment it is. This table also stores information about the asset's current location and its status, as well as the way in which the asset was acquired and the cost of acquisition.

**Equipment**   The Equipment table stores the make and model of each type of asset. Each piece of equipment with a unique make and model has a separate record in this table. It groups equipment by equipment type. To accommodate SOUNDEX search (and illustrate the use of this SOUNDEX function), the Equipment table also has a field for precalculated SOUNDEX codes representing the makes and models of equipment.

**EqType**   This table lists types of equipment. For example, equipment types include notebook, printer, monitor, keyboard, mouse, scanner, and network hub.

**Properties**   Each asset in the database can be described with a set of attributes listed in the Properties table. This table also records a unit used to store the value of the property. For example, the properties (and units) of a monitor are size (inch), resolution (pixel), type (n/a), while an external hard disk has properties (and units) such as capacity (GB), size (inch), and adapter (n/a).

**InventoryProperty**   Each Asset in the Inventory table has a set of properties. The InventoryProperty table stores the values of each property (except for make and model, which are recorded in the Equipment table).

   For example, a Toshiba (Make) Protégé 7020 (Model) notebook (EqType) assigned to an employee has 64 (value) MB (unit) of RAM (property) and 4.3 (value) GB (unit) of HDD capacity (property) and a Pentium II 333 (value) processor (property), and so on. Another employee is using an upgraded version of the same equipment with 128 (value) MB (unit) of RAM (property) and 6.4 (value) GB (unit) of HDD capacity (property) and a Pentium II 366 (value) processor (property), and so on.

## Deployment of Assets

This set of tables keeps track of the location in which an asset is deployed and the person and organizational unit to which the asset is assigned:

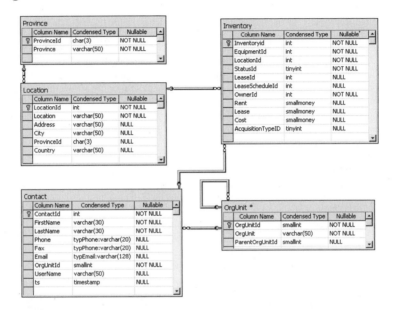

The information in these asset deployment tables allows users to

▼ Manage a list of locations within an organization

■ Manage a list of persons working within an organization

■ Retrieve contact information about persons to whom assets are assigned

■ Generate reports about assets deployed by province and organizational unit

■ Retrieve a list of assets assigned to a particular person

■ Manage relationships between organizational units

▲ Assign person(s) to organizational units

**Location** The Location table stores information about the physical location of the deployed asset. Each location has a name and an address as attributes.

**Province**    This table contains a list of provinces and states. The primary key is the abbreviation of the province/state. The presence of this table is essential for reports, which will aggregate asset deployment by location, province/state, and country.

**Contact**    This table contains a list of persons involved in the asset management process. It includes persons with assets assigned to them, persons completing and approving orders, and persons performing maintenance and support.

**Organizational Unit**    Each contact is assigned to some organizational unit within the organization. The OrgUnit table records relationships between companies, cost centers, departments, and the like. This table is designed as a recursive table: an organizational unit can be part of some other organizational unit. This quality also reflects the need for rapid changes in today's work environment due to change of ownership, restructuring, and so on.

## Leasing Tables

An important aspect of asset management is the tracking of lease information. It helps management avoid payment of penalties associated with late returns or the failure to return leased assets to the leasing vendor:

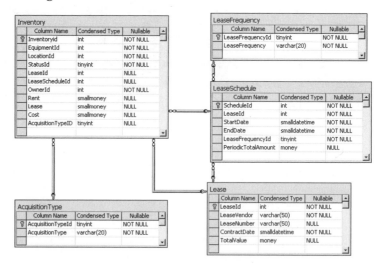

The information in the lease tables allows users to

▼ Keep track of the assets associated with each lease

■ Manage lease schedules to keep track of start, end, and duration of lease periods

■ Identify assets that need to be returned to a lease vendor

■ Generate reports on assets deployed by lease schedule and lease contract

■ Retrieve a list of assets obtained from a particular lease vendor

▲ Retrieve the total value of lease payments, lease schedules, and lease contracts

**Lease**   The Lease table contains information about lease contracts. It records the name of the lease vendor, the number of the lease that the vendor is using to track the contract, the date the contract was signed, and the total value of assets assigned to the lease.

**Lease Schedule**   Assets obtained through one lease contract might not be received on the same date. An asset might also be under a different payment regime and lease duration. Therefore, each lease contains a set of lease schedules. Each schedule is recorded in the LeaseSchedule table and is described with a start date, an end date, and the frequency of payments. This table also tracks the total value of payments per lease term.

**Lease Frequency**   LeaseFrequency is a lookup table that contains all possible values for lease frequency including monthly, semimonthly, biweekly, and weekly.

**Acquisition Type**   AcquisitionType is a lookup table that lists possible acquisition types including lease, purchase, and rent.

## Order Tables

Orders are the primary means of managing assets within the organization. Users can request new assets and the disposal of obsolete assets. They can request maintenance and technical support.

Authorized personnel can monitor orders and react to them, associate a cost with their execution, and generate invoices. The following tables are used to store information about orders:

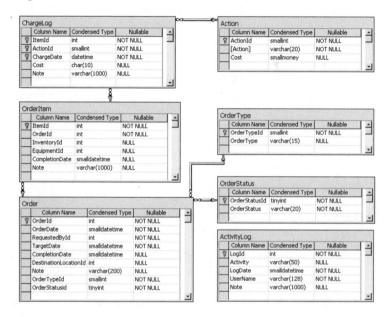

The information in these order tables allows users to

▼ Request new equipment

■ Request technical support

■ Request maintenance

■ Execute scheduled maintenance

■ Track the status of orders

■ Assign a staff member to execute the order

■ Approve the execution of orders

■ Manage a list of actions and the default costs associated with them

■ Track costs associated with each activity

■ Generate interdepartmental invoices

- Request the transfer of assets
- Request the disposal of obsolete assets
- ▲ Generate summaries and reports on performed activities

**Orders**   Users can record requests in the Order table. At that time, the order date and target date are recorded. General request requirements are recorded as an order type, and special requirements are recorded as a note. The person making the request is recorded, as well as the person approving the request and assigning the order for execution. If the order is a transfer request, the table also records a destination for the asset. Users can track the status of the order, and once it is completed, its completion date is set. At that point, one organizational unit is billed for performed actions, and once the order is paid, the payment is noted on the order and funds are assigned to the organizational unit completing the order.

**Order Items**   The OrderItem table records assets that need the intervention of authorized personnel or new equipment that needs to be purchased. Special requests are recorded in the Note field.

**Actions**   The Action table manages the list of activities needed to complete a request as well as the default cost associated with each.

**Charge Log**   Actions performed on an order item to complete an order will be recorded in the ChargeLog table. This table will be used to generate an invoice after completion of the order.

**Order Status**   The OrderStatus table is used as a lookup table to manage the status of orders. It contains statuses such as

- ▼ Ordered
- In-process
- Canceled
- Deferred
- ▲ Completed

**Order Types**   The OrderType table is used as a lookup table to store the general requirements of the order. It contains values such as

▼   Requisition

■   Transfer

■   Support

■   Scrap

▲   Repair

**Activity Log**   This table is not related specifically to the recording of orders. Rather, it is a repository for audit trail information. Most of the time it is populated by a trigger associated with some specific database change.

# SUMMARY

This chapter has provided all the information you need to use this book effectively. It has shown that the integration capability, ease of use, flexibility, and power of Microsoft SQL Server make it the relational database management system of choice for business organizations and application developers, and it has shown how the enhancements in SQL Server 2000 can help those organizations and developers meet today's technological and business challenges.

We have identified the intended audience for this book and the types and locations of information that individuals within that diverse audience can find in this book.

After reading this chapter, you should also have an understanding of the resources you will require to proceed in your quest to become an accomplished professional in the development and use of stored procedures.

Lastly, this chapter describes the sample database that we have made available to you via the Web. The sample database includes most of the examples used in this book and is essential to the effective use of this book and the successful completion of the exercises provided at the end of each chapter.

# CHAPTER 2

# Relational Database Concepts and the SQL Server Environment

You already know that SQL Server is a full-featured and powerful database management system. You may also be experienced in some or many aspects of this system. But before you proceed to become an expert in application development using SQL Server stored procedures, we should probably take a step back and look at the "big picture" to ensure that we share the same conceptual grounding.

To attain this conceptual grounding, we will start with a 30,000-ft. overview that will cover the following topics:

▼ Relational database systems and the objects that compose them

■ SQL Server architecture

■ A brief discussion of the Transact-SQL language

■ A brief introduction to SQL Server tools

▲ A quick overview of stored procedure design

This overview will be concise. It will not be the only resource you need to develop a full understanding of the ways and means of SQL Server database development. It will bring the big picture into focus, identify the components of that big picture, and describe the relationships between those components. It will serve to highlight any gaps that may exist in your knowledge, but it will be too dull an instrument to eliminate those gaps if they are too large or too pronounced.

I have written this overview to enable people in a hurry to learn the basics and then get down to working with stored procedures and building killer applications. I am going to assume that you have already had an opportunity to work with SQL Server, or some other database system, and that you understand common database concepts. The real purpose of this overview is to define the terminology that we will use as the foundation on which to build your knowledge of programming in the SQL Server environment. I will direct you to other books published by Osborne/McGraw-Hill that will help to develop your knowledge of related SQL Server conceptual and development topics:

▼ *SQL Server 2000: A Beginner's Guide* by Dušan Petkovic

▲ *SQL Server 2000 Design & TSQL Programming* by Michelle Poolet and Michael D. Reilly

# DATABASES

People often use the term "database" to describe what are really two different types of objects. The term can be associated with a physical or virtual structure used to store and manage information. It does not even matter whether it is implemented on a computer in the form of one kind of file or another, or as a set of index cards in a library. In both cases, we refer to the structure used to store information as a database.

The same word can be used in reference to a system that is used to access information and manage database storage. Of course, this usage implies that such a system is implemented as computer software. This type of database is often called a *relational database management system (RDBMS)*. Depending on the implementation, an RDBMS can also be labeled a *database server*.

## Relational Databases

One way to implement a database system on a computer is based on the concept of a *relational database system.* Such databases implement ideas first described by Codd and Date in the early 1970s. They took the name from a mathematical concept known as a *relation*, which is an ordered set of values from different domains.

## Database Objects

Data and programs in SQL Server are organized into logical components called *database objects.* Database users (administrators and developers) access and manage information in SQL Server by accessing and managing database objects.

> **NOTE:**  If you have worked with or are familiar with some object-oriented programming language or methodology, let me warn you that database objects will not comply with the definitions found in such languages.

## Tables

As with any other relational database system, the most important database objects in SQL Server are *tables*. Data in SQL Server is organized in tables, which consist of rows and columns. You can visualize SQL Server tables by thinking of the two-dimensional tables you find in spreadsheet applications such as Microsoft Excel. Usually, a table represents entities such as persons, assets, or locations. A *row* in a table corresponds to one instance of an entity (for example: one person, or one asset, or one location). Each *column* contains an attribute that describes some aspect of the entity. For example, a person can be described with columns representing first name, last name, date of birth, phone number, and other such characteristics.

The major difference between tables that comply with the relational database concept and other types of tables is that the data in a column must describe only one attribute. All values in a column must belong to only one *domain* of appropriate values. An ordered set of values that belong to different domains is called a *relation*. The collection of column definitions and other table attributes (*constraints*) belongs to a *table definition*. This information is often called *metadata* information—data about data.

There are many types of table and column attributes. *Constraints* are database objects used to enforce rules that values in columns must follow to be written to the database. Database designers can use them to specify default values, to point to a list of allowed values, or to specify a rule that needs to be satisfied. *Datatypes* are objects that specify the type of data (number, character, dates, and so on) that can be stored in a column.

## Databases

Sets of tables in SQL Server belong to *databases.* A database is an object that contains all other objects. It is stored physically in one or more *database files,* but SQL Server manages storage issues so that users do not have to be concerned with the database files themselves. Tables stored in the database can be categorized by functionality into two groups: user tables and system tables. *User tables* store application information—information about entities that database users are interested in. *System tables* store metadata information such as lists of database objects, object definitions, and database security information. There are also several *system databases,* which contain server metadata information such as the locations of other databases, definitions of maintenance tasks, configuration parameters of the server, and server security information.

## Transact-SQL Statements

RDBMS systems include special applications that enable users to issue *statements* to retrieve and change information concerning entities.

**Query Statements**   Most database applications allow the user to issue a *query statement* and view a *resultset* that contains the requested information, or to issue a *change statement* and receive a confirmation that the operation was successful. All mainstream database systems use the same standard language—*SQL (Structured Query Language)*— to describe the resultset that users want to receive from the database system. Microsoft SQL Server uses a dialect of SQL known as *Transact-SQL* or *TSQL.* All SQL dialects use the following four *basic SQL statements:* Select, Insert, Update, and Delete.

The most important Transact-SQL statement is the Select statement. It is used to describe the resultset the user wants to retrieve from the database system. The Insert statement is used to move information into tables. The purpose of the Update statement is to change information that is already stored in tables within the database. The Delete statement is used to remove records from tables.

The following statement will list all records in the Customers table:

```
select * from Customers
```

The major difference between statements in Transact-SQL and those in other programming languages is that Transact-SQL statements describe what needs to be displayed (retrieved) or changed, but not how to do it. Thus, Transact SQL is known as a *nonprocedural* language.

**DDL Statements**    Transact-SQL also contains a huge set of statements designed to create and manage database objects and other metadata information. This subset of statements is often referred to as the *Data Definition Language* (DDL).

The following statement will create a Customers table that contains six columns:

```
Create table Customers (CustomerId int,
                        CustomerName varchar(50),
                        Address varchar(50),
                        City varchar(50),
                        Phone varchar(50),
                        Fax varchar(50))
```

Each column definition also indicates the type of data the column will store.

**Groups of Statements**    Transact-SQL statements are usually issued in groups. A *script* is a set of SQL statements organized into a file. Scripts are generally created to run complex or repetitive operations such as the creation of a report, the transfer of funds from one account to another, or some database maintenance activity. A user may wish to write such a set of statements to a file for later reuse.

A *batch* is a group of one or more Transact-SQL statements that is sent to the server simultaneously. When the server receives a batch, it parses it, compiles it into an *execution plan,* and finally executes it.

**Transact-SQL Statements Organized in Database Objects**   Transact-SQL statements can also be grouped and stored in the database.

*Views* are database objects that behave like virtual tables. They are implemented as stored `Select` statements.

A *stored procedure* is a database object designed to store, for later use, a group of Transact-SQL statements that describes how some operation should be carried out. Database users (administrators and developers) can create *user-defined stored procedures*. SQL Server is delivered with a set of *system-stored procedures*, which cover all aspects of managing data, objects, and the server.

A *trigger* is a special type of procedure attached to tables and executed when a predefined change is performed on the table.

A *function* is a database object that returns a single value. Some functions are implemented as a set of Transact-SQL statements, and others are implemented as built-in functions for returning a particular value to the caller.

## Other Objects

Many other objects are also treated as database objects. *Logins* are account identifiers that allow users to be recognized by SQL Server. After users are identified, SQL Server allows them access to the databases they are authorized to use. Their logins must be recognized as *users* (another object) in those databases. Developers can create *diagrams* of tables stored in a database. Administrators can create *jobs* that are going to perform some business or maintenance operation at a scheduled time or on demand.

## Client/Server Architecture

Database users often work with specialized applications to view and modify the data in a database. Such applications are often called *client applications, client tools, front-end applications,* or *database applications*. All of these terms are descriptive of the architecture of such a system.

A *client/server system* consists of two or more programs or systems that interact to provide a user with required information or help a user to perform some action. The client application makes a request, and the server program fulfills the request:

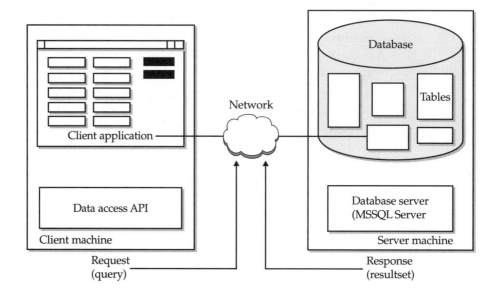

In the SQL Server environment, requests take the form of Transact-SQL statements. SQL Server processes them and returns a resultset to the client application with the required information or just a confirmation that the action was performed successfully. Many client applications or users can make requests concurrently, and SQL Server is capable of processing them in parallel.

A client application can offer a different level of comfort to a user. The simplest tools (but not the easiest to use) allow a user to enter a request in the form of a Transact-SQL statement and receive resultsets in the form of text or a table. More sophisticated tools have forms, reports, and other user-friendly screen objects.

To physically establish a connection with a database server and transfer requests and resultsets, client applications can use different *data access objects* or *data access APIs.* The most common such objects are ADO (ActiveX Database Objects), RDO (Remote Database Objects), DB-Library, ODBC, OLE DB, and DAO (Database Access Objects). Application developers use these objects, or APIs, to access database objects and data stored in them and to develop client applications in programming languages such as Visual Basic, Java, ASP, C, and C++.

This system architecture is the simplest one. The client side of such a system contains a *user interface, presentation services, business services* (the part of the application that implements business rules), and *data servicess* (the part of the system responsible for accessing the data storage). Data storage (usually a database) is located on the server. Since the components of the system are stored in two tiers—one on a workstation and the other on a server—this architecture is often called *two-tier architecture.* Because the business logic in this case is stored on the client side (workstation), this variation of two-tier architecture is often called *fat client* architecture:

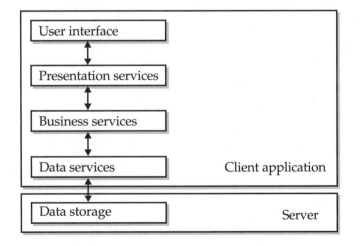

Unfortunately, such systems have many performance, security, deployment, and management issues. Some of these issues can be resolved by implementing part of the business services on the server—for example, in the form of stored procedures. Such architecture is sometimes called *fat server* or *two-and-a-half-tier architecture:*

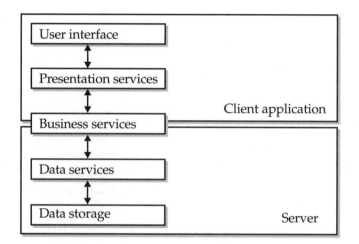

To further improve the system, application architects can use *three-tier architecture,* in which data, business, and presentation services are strictly divided into different components, or tiers:

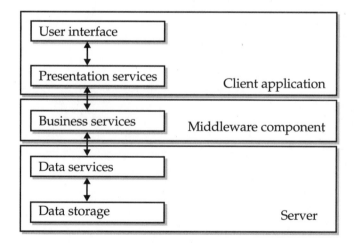

It is also possible to further divide application services, in which case it is called *multitier* or *n-tier architecture:*

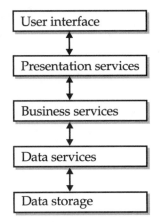

This architecture is especially convenient for Web applications, since such applications must be able to scale to thousands of users, and deployment and management requirements on such a level are very strict. The following diagram shows one variant of such architecture:

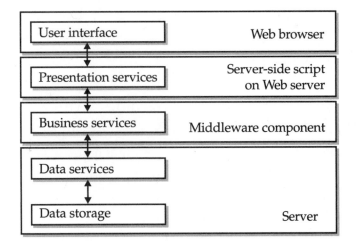

## What Are Stored Procedures?

*Stored procedures* are database objects that encapsulate collections of Transact-SQL statements on the server for later repetitive use. Although stored procedures use nonprocedural Transact-SQL statements, they are in essence procedural. They define algorithms that determine how operations should be performed.

Stored procedures are the TSQL equivalents of subroutines in other programming languages. Developers of custom database applications can use all major programming constructs while building stored procedures:

▼ Variables

■ Datatypes

■ Input/output parameters

■ Return values

■ Conditional execution

■ Loops

▲ Comments

SQL Server includes a set of *system stored procedures* designed for administering the system. Their role is to provide information, set configuration, control the environment, manage user-defined objects, and schedule and run custom tasks.

# SQL SERVER 2000 TOOLS

All versions of SQL Server except SQL Server 2000 Desktop Engine (or MSDE) are delivered with the following management tools:

▼ Service Manager

■ Enterprise Manager

■ Query Analyzer

■ DTS—Import/Export Data

- osql
- isql
- Profiler
- ▲ Client Network Utility

# Service Manager

The SQL Server database server is implemented as the following services:

- ▼ MSSQLServer
- SQLServerAgent
- MSDTC
- ▲ SQL Mail and SQLAgentMail

The RDBMS is actually implemented as the *MSSQLServer* service. It receives queries from users, executes them, sends responses to calling applications, and manages data in database files.

*SQLServerAgent* is an automation service that manages the scheduled execution of tasks and notifies administrators of problems that occur on the server.

*MSDTC* (*Microsoft Distributed Transaction Coordinator*) is a service that manages *two-phase commit* transactions spanned over multiple servers. This service ensures that changes that need to be made to data stored on different servers complete successfully.

*SQL Mail* is used to send and receive e-mail. It is possible to configure SQL Server to perform such tasks as receiving requests and returning resultsets through e-mail to notify administrators of the success status of scheduled tasks and encountered errors. SQLServerAgent also has mail capabilities, but does not use the SQL Mail service. Instead, it uses the SQLAgentMail component to send notifications. These services are available only on the Standard or Enterprise Edition of SQL Server.

On Windows NT Server and Windows 2000 Server, MSSQLServer, SQLServerAgent, and MSDTC services can be started or stopped, as can any other service, using the Services icon in Control Panel. In Windows 9*x* environments, the only way to start and stop these services is to use Service Manager. On Windows 2000, you can also use the `net start` command from the command prompt. SQL Mail service can be controlled from the Support Services node in Enterprise Manager. You will see later in this chapter how to use it.

When the Service Manager applet is running, the user can choose the current service and server using combo boxes and then use the appropriate button to start, pause, or stop the current service:

During SQL Server installation, Service Manager is set to run minimized in the system tray. The user can investigate the execution status of the current service by hovering the mouse pointer over the icon in the system tray, or by right-clicking the icon and selecting Properties from the pop-up menu.

## Query Analyzer

*Query Analyzer* is a Windows application for designing and executing Transact-SQL statements (such as queries) against a SQL Server database. This application is a descendant of isql (a text-based tool) and ISQL/W (a Windows-based tool). Before Enterprise Manager was introduced in SQL Server 6.0, administrators relied on isql to manage servers and databases and to execute queries.

Query Analyzer is designed as an MDI application that can contain one or more Query windows. Users can use Query windows to enter and execute a batch of Transact-SQL statements. A Query window contains two major components: the Query pane and the Results pane (see Figure 2-1).

The *Query pane* is a Transact-SQL syntax-sensitive editor. Because it is syntax-sensitive, users can type Transact-SQL statements in the pane and Query Analyzer will color different code components such as keywords, variables, and literals using different colors.

The *Results pane* displays the result of the code executed in the Query pane. Earlier versions of SQL Server displayed results only

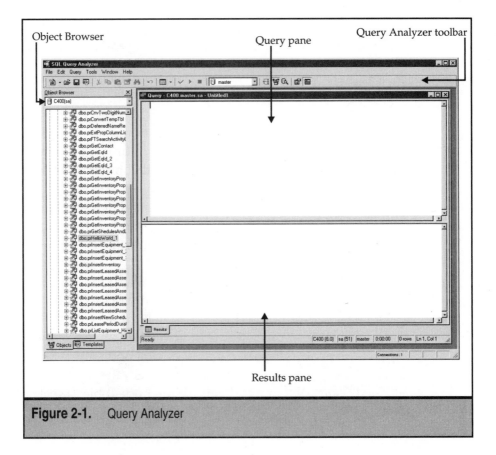

**Figure 2-1.**   Query Analyzer

in the form of text. Since SQL Server 7.0, Query Analyzer has been able to display resultsets in the form of a grid, display messages separately, and diagram the way that SQL server will execute the query (that is, the execution plan).

The *Query Analyzer toolbar* contains icons for managing the contents of the window. A noteworthy option is the DB combo box, which selects and displays the current database.

The *Object Browser* is a window that allows users to explore database objects or access predefined Transact-SQL code templates. Users can check for the existence of a database object, explore its contents (that is, view records in a table), execute, and debug objects such as stored procedures, view the structure and dependencies of an object, view and edit extended properties of the object, drag the name of a database object to the Query window or a script object to the Query window, file, or Clipboard. This very useful addition to Query Analyzer is available only in SQL Server 2000.

## Enterprise Manager

Enterprise Manager was introduced in SQL Server 6.0 as a tool to simplify server and database administration on SQL Server. It was a huge success when introduced, and over time, Microsoft has improved its functionality. Now, even all competing products include equivalent tools.

Enterprise Manager visually represents database objects stored on the server and provides tools for accessing and managing them. When it is open, you will notice two main components—the Console tree and the Details pane (see Figure 2-2).

The *Console tree* presents database and server objects in a hierarchy designed for easy navigation. It works in the same way as any other GUI tree object. Users can click the + symbol next to any node on the tree or press the right arrow key on the keyboard to expand the node. When users right-click a node, the program displays a list of menu options applicable to the node.

The *Details pane* shows details of the node (object) selected in the Console tree. If the user selects a folder with tables or stored

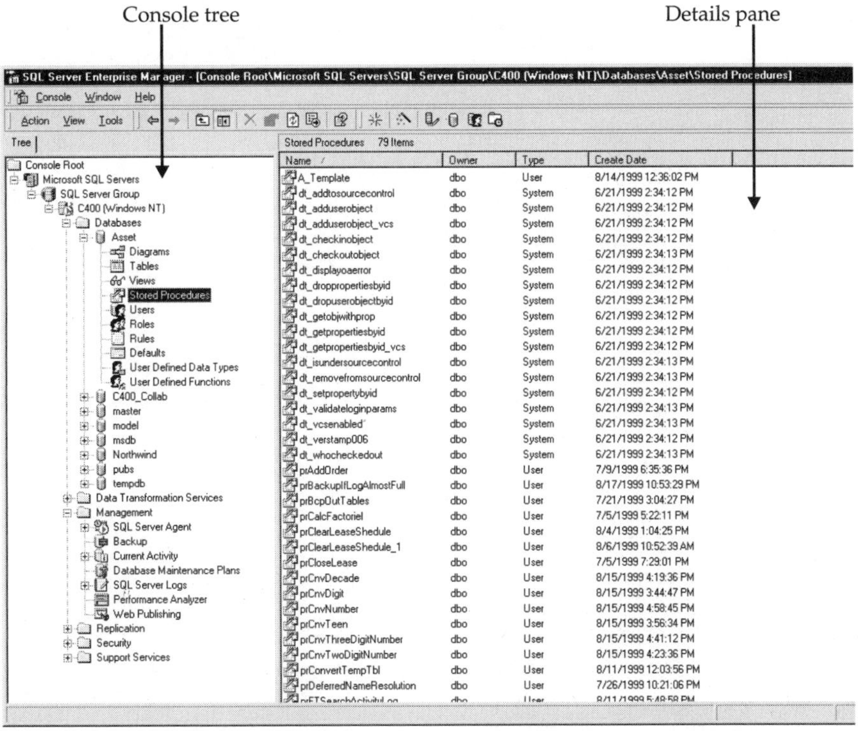

Console tree                                                    Details pane

**Figure 2-2.**   Enterprise Manager

procedures, the Details pane will list the tables or stored procedures in the current database. The behavior of the Details pane is quite similar to that of Windows Explorer.

If the user selects certain objects in the Console tree, such as a database or a server, the Details pane displays the *taskpad*—a complex report showing the state of the database or server that can also be used to manage the database or server (see Figure 2-3). Taskpads are implemented as HTML pages. Activities can be initiated by clicking links within the taskpad.

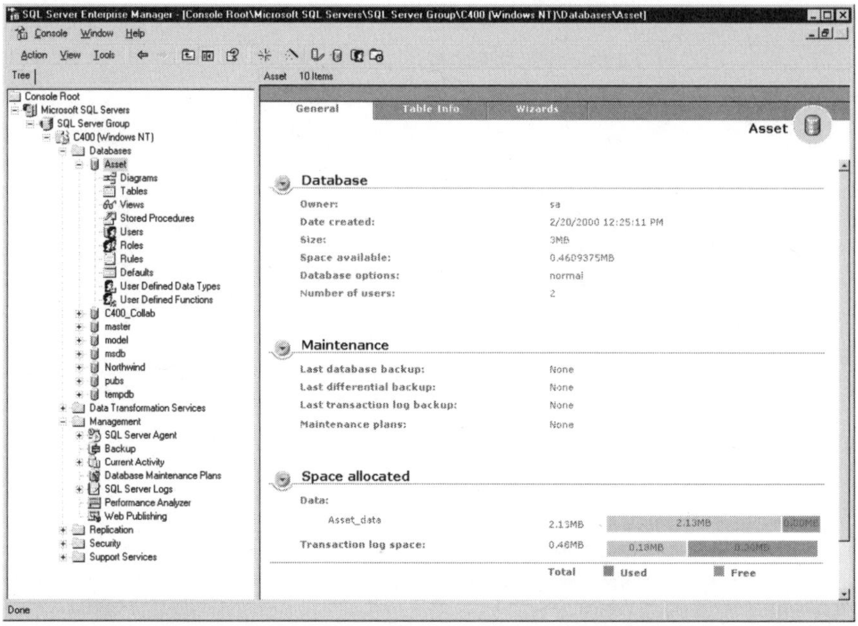

**Figure 2-3.**    The taskpad

Enterprise Manager has been developed as a Microsoft Management Console (MMC) snap-in. A *snap-in* is simply a program designed to run inside MMC. Other Back Office server management tools can also run inside MMC. This design is the reason there are two major toolbars within the Enterprise Manager interface. The top one contains options to let the user control MMC and its snap-ins. The lower one is the Enterprise Manager toolbar, and in it you will find menus and icons for administering servers and databases.

Before SQL Server 7.0, Enterprise Manager contained a query tool for executing SQL queries against a database. You now have to launch Query Analyzer from the Tools menu.

As I mentioned earlier, SQL Mail service can be controlled from the Support Services node in Enterprise Manager (see Figure 2-4).

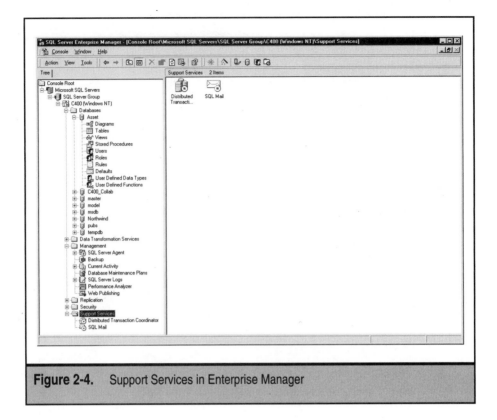

**Figure 2-4.**   Support Services in Enterprise Manager

# DTS—Import and Export Data

*Data Transformation Services* (DTS) is a component of SQL Server that
enables administrators to transfer information between servers and
databases. It is not limited to export from and import to SQL Server.
It can also be used between any ODBC- or OLE DB-compliant
databases, including Oracle, Sybase SQL Server, Access, and FoxPro,
and between other storage types such as text files, Excel
spreadsheets, and Outlook files.

The tangible part of DTS is the DTS Wizard (see Figure 2-5),
which can be started from Enterprise Manager (Data Transformation
Services) or the Windows menu (Import and Export Data). In the
screens that follow, users specify the source and target data locations
as well as the transformation to be performed on the data.

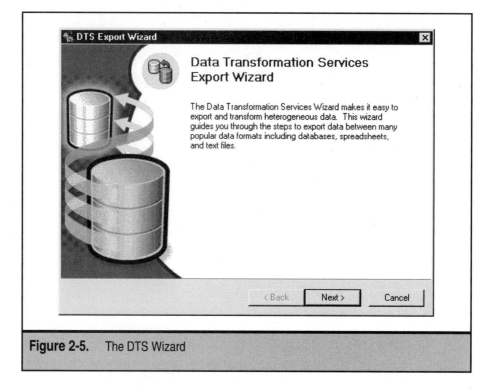

**Figure 2-5.**   The DTS Wizard

## osql and isql

Before Query Analyzer (and ISQL/W—ISQL for Windows), DBAs used a command line utility called *isql* to run Transact-SQL statements against the server (see Figure 2-6).

Tools such as isql are reminiscent of UNIX environments, and they are seldom used now that GUI applications like Query Analyzer are available.

Another tool that works from the command prompt is *osql*. It was introduced in SQL Server 7.0. The major difference between these two command line utilities lies in the API each uses to connect to SQL Server databases: osql uses ODBC to connect, and isql uses DB-Library.

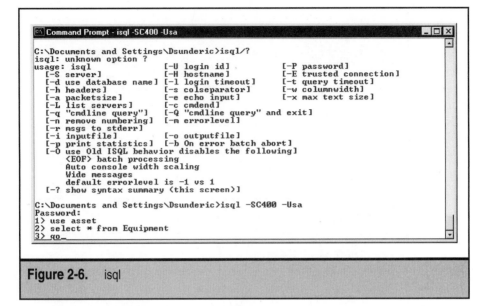

**Figure 2-6.**   isql

## SQL Server Profiler

*SQL Server Profiler* is a component of SQL Server designed to monitor activities on servers and in databases (see Figure 2-7).

Before SQL Server 2000 and SQL Server 7.0, this utility was called *SQL Trace.* Users can use this utility to capture queries against a database, the activities of a particular user application, login attempts, failures, errors, and transactions. It is often used to improve the performance of a system.

## Client Network Utility

SQL Server client tools can use different protocols to communicate with SQL Server:

▼ Named pipes

■ TCP/IP

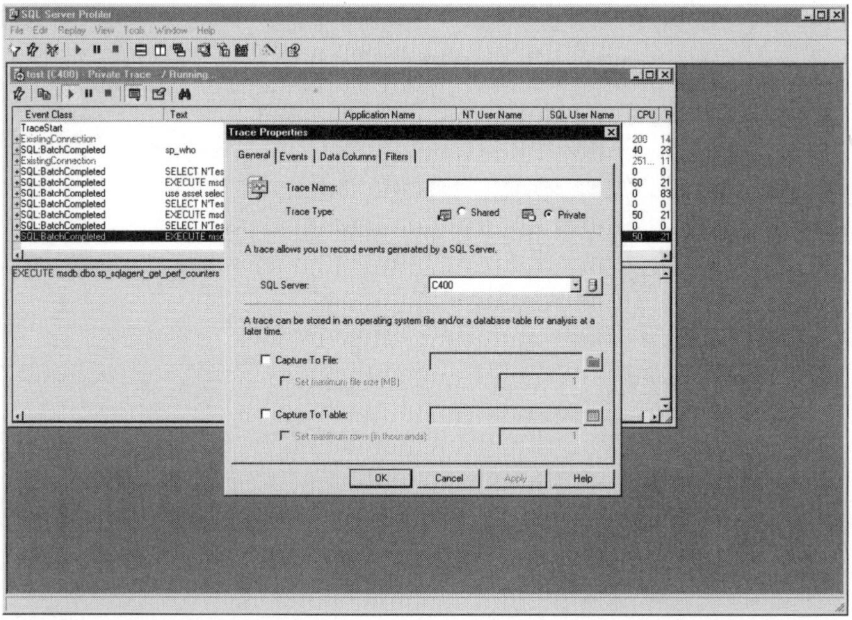

**Figure 2-7.** SQL Server Profiler

- Multiprotocol
- NWLink IPX/SPX
- AppleTalk
- Banyan VINES
- ▲ Shared memory

For each protocol, Microsoft has designed a DLL communication library that is referred to as a *Network Library* or *NetLib*.

The *Client Network Utility* is designed to select the protocol and NetLib to be used by other client tools. It is possible to specify a *default network library* and exceptions on a per-server basis:

```
SQL Server Client Network Utility                                    [x]

General | Network Libraries | DB Library Options |

  [icon]    If this client cannot use the server computer name and the default Net-Library to connect
            to SQL Server, change the default Net-Library or add a server alias with the required
            connection parameters.

Default network library:        [Named Pipes        ▼]

Server alias configurations
  | Server alias | Network library | Connection parameters |
  | dejan        | TCP/IP          | dejan,1433            |

                                                                    [ Add...   ]

                                                                    [ Remove   ]

                                                                    [ Edit...  ]

                        [   OK   ]  [ Cancel ]  [ Apply  ]  [  Help  ]
```

# The Help Subsystem and SQL Server Books Online

Traditionally, due to the nature of the environment, SQL Server client
tools (including Enterprise Manager and Query Analyzer) have been
light on context-sensitive help, but SQL Server has a subsystem that
is a great tool for browsing through its documentation—*SQL
Server Books Online.* This subsystem contains the complete set of
documentation—which used to be delivered on paper—in the
form of an online, searchable, indexed hierarchy of documents.

You can start SQL Server Books Online by selecting Start |
Programs | Microsoft SQL Server 2000 | Books Online (see
Figure 2-8). You can browse through the Contents of the hierarchy
as in Windows Explorer, or you can switch to the Index tab to see
a list of keywords or the Search tab to define search criteria. The
Favorites tab enables you to record pages that you want to refer
to later.

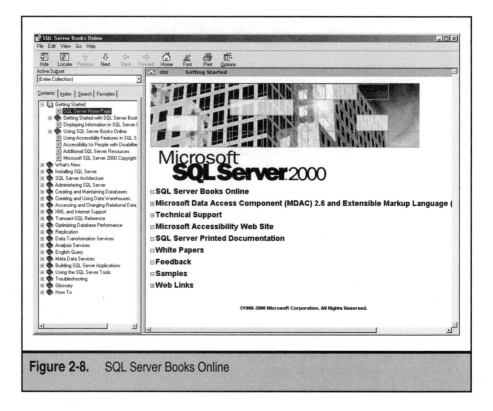

**Figure 2-8.**   SQL Server Books Online

# BASIC OPERATIONS WITH STORED PROCEDURES

This section will serve as a primer to introduce you to the concepts of executing, creating, and editing stored procedures. We will walk through the usage of the most important SQL Server client tools. Since Transact-SQL is just another programming language, we will follow a tradition first established by an unknown programmer and start with a trivial Hello World example.

## Execution of Stored Procedures from Query Analyzer

The execution of stored procedures from Enterprise Manager or Query Analyzer is very simple. Let's try it using the system stored procedure sp_who, which lists all users and processes connected to the system.

1. Run Query Analyzer (Start | Programs | Microsoft SQL Server 2000 | Query Analyzer). The Query Analyzer application will prompt you for a server, Login Name, and Password, as shown in the following illustration. If the application is unable to connect to the server, you should check whether the Microsoft SQL Server service is running and whether you correctly typed the name of the server and/or your login name and password.

```
Connect to SQL Server                           [X]

      SQL Server:   [C400                ▼] [...]
                    ☐ Start SQL Server if it is stopped

   Connect using:
      ○ Windows NT authentication
      ● SQL Server authentication
          Login name:    [sa                    ]
          Password:      [                      ]

                 [  OK  ]   [ Cancel ]   [ Help ]
```

**TIP:**  If you have not changed the server since installation, you can use **sa** as the Login Name and an empty string (blank) as the Password. The name of your machine is the name of the SQL Server.

   If you are working on the machine that has SQL Server installed, you can always use "**(local)**"or a simple dot "." to refer to the current machine as the server to which you want to connect.

2. Once you have logged in successfully, the application opens the Query window that you use to write code. In the Query pane, type the following code:

```
exec sp_who
```

3. To run the stored procedure, you can select Execute from the Query menu, click the green arrow on the toolbar, or press CTRL-E. The application will split the screen to display both query and results (see Figure 2-9).

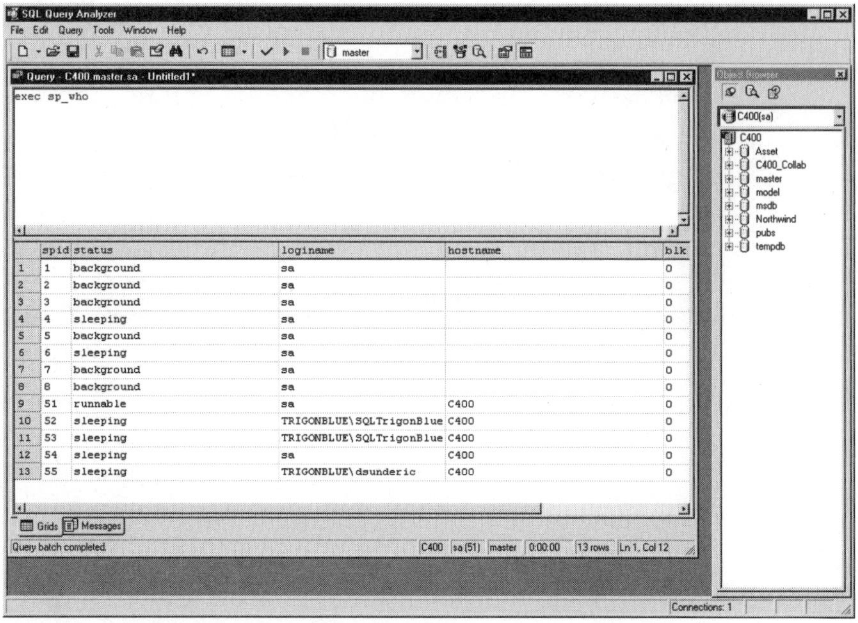

**Figure 2-9.** Execution of stored procedures from Query Analyzer

You can click the Messages tab to see whether SQL Server has returned any messages along with the result (such as the number of records, a warning, or an error). This stored procedure lists active processes on the current server and the login names of the users who started them.

4. Select Query | Results in Text and then execute the query again (Query | Execute). Query Analyzer displays the resultset in the form of text. Messages are mixed with resultsets in this case, which is the way in which Query Analyzer has always worked in past versions (see Figure 2-10).

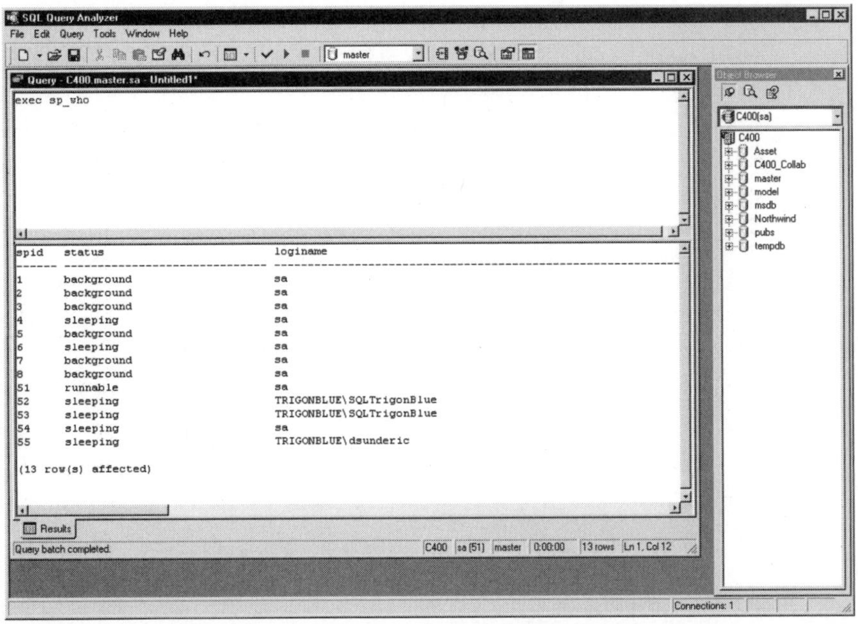

**Figure 2-10.** Results in Text

**NOTE:** Before we continue, please ensure that you have installed the sample Asset database. If you have not already installed it, go to Chapter 1 and follow the download and installation instructions.

You can also use Object Browser in Query Analyzer to list, execute, and edit stored procedures:

1. If the Object Browser is not already present on the screen, click Tools | Object Browser to display it (see Figure 2-11).

2. Open the node that contains the master database and then the node for that database's stored procedures. Right-click the stored procedure sp_who in the list. Select Open from the

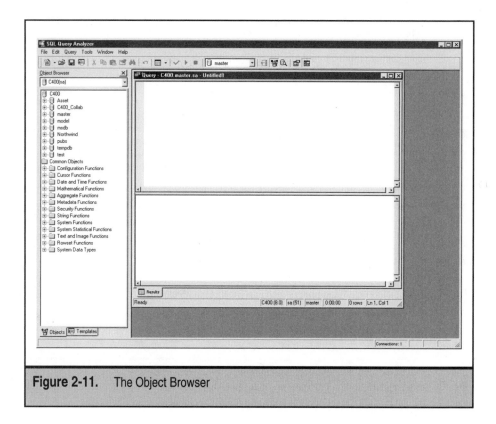

**Figure 2-11.**     The Object Browser

pop-up menu. Query Analyzer prompts you to specify
parameters and execute the stored procedure:

3. Click Execute and Query Analyzer opens a new Query window with code supporting the execution of the stored procedure. The code is executed automatically (see Figure 2-12).

# Managing Stored Procedures from Enterprise Manager

Enterprise Manager is the most important tool in the arsenal of the DBA.

1. Start Enterprise Manager (Start | Programs | Microsoft SQL Server 2000 | Enterprise Manager). In some cases, for example

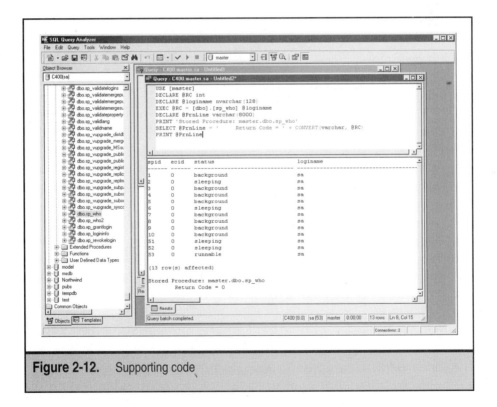

**Figure 2-12.** Supporting code

if you have never opened Enterprise Manager before, you will
have to register the first server with which you will work:

```
┌─────────────────────────────────────────────────────────┐
│ Registered SQL Server Properties                    [X]  │
├─────────────────────────────────────────────────────────┤
│ ┌ General ┐                                              │
│                                                          │
│   ╔═══╗                                                  │
│   ║   ║  Server:   [C400              ▼] [...]           │
│   ╚═══╝                                                  │
│  ┌ Connection ─────────────────────────────────────┐   │
│         ○ Use Windows NT authentication                 │
│         ● Use SQL Server authentication                 │
│             Login Name:  [sa              ]             │
│             Password:    [                ]             │
│             ☐ Always prompt for login name and password │
│  ┌ Options ────────────────────────────────────────┐   │
│     Server Group:  [📁 SQL Server Group      ▼] [...]   │
│   📂 ☑ Display SQL Server state in console              │
│       ☑ Show system databases and system objects        │
│       ☑ Automatically start SQL Server when connecting   │
│                                                          │
│          [   OK   ]   [  Cancel  ]   [  Help  ]         │
└─────────────────────────────────────────────────────────┘
```

2. Again, you need to provide the name of the server, your
   Login Name, and your Password. You can accept default
   values for the Server Group and all other Options. If the
   connection parameters are correct, Enterprise Manager will
   display a window for managing SQL Server.

3. Click the + symbol to expand the SQL Server Group branch.

4. Expand your server branch (again, click the + symbol).

5. Expand the Databases branch.

6. Expand the Asset sample database.

7. Click Stored Procedures and watch as a list of stored
   procedures is displayed in the Details pane (see Figure 2-13).

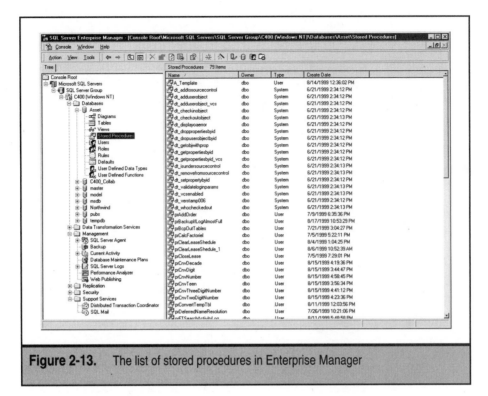

**Figure 2-13.** The list of stored procedures in Enterprise Manager

8. In this list, find a stored procedure named prGetEqId. If you right-click a stored procedure, a pop-up menu appears with options to let you perform operations such as deleting and renaming the stored procedure or creating a new stored procedure. At this point, the most interesting option on this pop-up menu is the Properties option.

9. Right-click the prGetEqId stored procedure, then select Properties on the pop-up menu. The application will open a window to allow you to view and edit the stored procedure (see Figure 2-14). See the sidebar "The Structure of Stored Procedures" for more information.

**NOTE:** Don't worry. In the following chapters, we will give you detailed descriptions of all these objects and their components.

## The Structure of Stored Procedures

We will pause a minute to explain the structure of a stored procedure. The prGetEqId stored procedure encapsulates a relatively simple `Select` statement for later use. It returns a recordset containing values from the EquipmentId column. The recordset will contain only records with the specified Make and Model.

The code of a stored procedure consists of a *header* and a *body*. The header of the stored procedure defines external attributes of the stored procedure—its *name* and a list of one or more *parameters*. The prGetEqId stored procedure has two parameters. Parameter names must start with the @ character. The developer must also define a datatype for each parameter. The header must begin with the `Create Procedure` keyword and finish with the `As` keyword.

The body of the stored procedure contains the Transact-SQL statements to be executed when the stored procedure runs. In this case, there is just one `Select` statement using the procedure parameters.

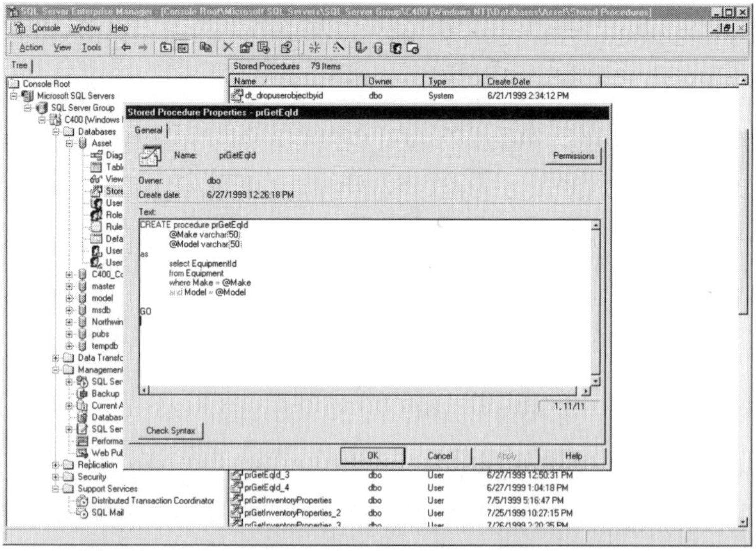

**Figure 2-14.**   Properties of a stored procedure

10. Close the Properties window.

11. Right-click any stored procedure in the list and select New Stored Procedure from the pop-up menu. Enterprise Manager displays a Properties window with a template for the stored procedure (see Figure 2-15).

12. Replace the template with the following code:

```
Create procedure prHelloWorld_1 As
    Select 'Hello world'
    Select * from Inventory
```

13. Click the Check Syntax button to verify the syntax of the procedure.

14. Click OK. The procedure is compiled and stored in the database. You will be able to see it in the list of stored procedures.

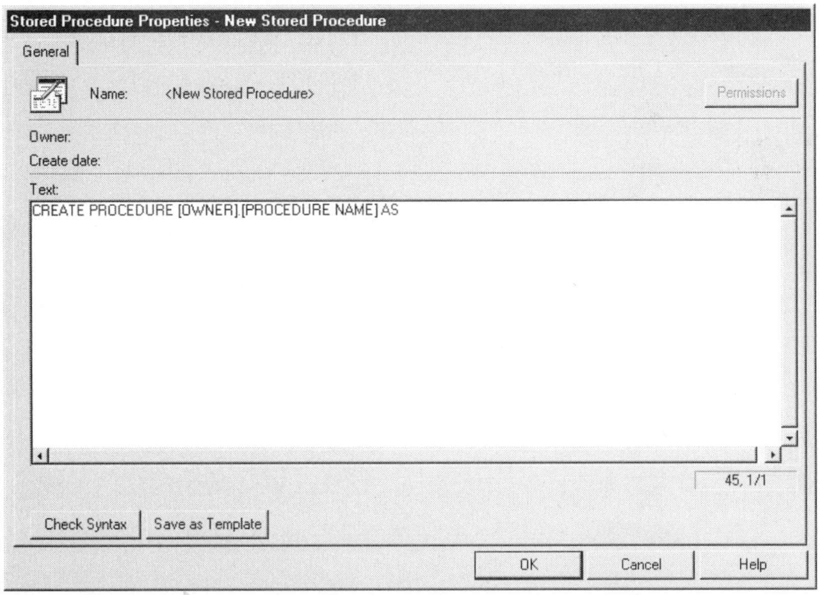

**Figure 2-15.**    A template for the New Stored Procedure

**NOTE:**   Earlier versions of Enterprise Manager did not display the stored procedure in the list automatically. The user had to refresh the screen by right-clicking the database name and selecting Refresh from the menu. This scenario still arises on occasion. For example, if you create a stored procedure (or change something in the database) using some other tool, you will need to refresh the list in Enterprise Manager.

You can switch to Query Analyzer to run the newly created stored procedure:

1.  On the Tools menu, select SQL Server Query Analyzer, switch to the Asset database, and type the following code:

```
Exec prHelloWorld_1
```

When you execute this code in the Query Analyzer, the application runs the stored procedure and displays the Hello World message and a list of records from the Inventory table.

2.  Close Query Analyzer.

## Editing Stored Procedures in Enterprise Manager

The easiest way to edit stored procedures is to use Enterprise Manager. All you need to do is to display the Properties window for the stored procedure.

1.  Verify that the Stored Procedures branch in the Asset database is still open in Enterprise Manager.

2.  Right-click the prHelloWorld_1 stored procedure and select Properties. The Properties window displays the stored procedure code.

## Editing Stored Procedures in Query Analyzer

Before Enterprise Manager was released in Microsoft SQL Server 6.0, administrators used isql (the ancestor of Query Analyzer) to do most of the work. It is still possible to edit stored procedures in the traditional way using Query Analyzer.

Traditionally, DBAs included the code for deleting (dropping) the original stored procedure and then recreating the stored procedure (with the changed code):

1. Launch Query Analyzer.

2. Make sure that you are in the Asset database.

3. Type the following code in the Query pane:

```
Drop procedure prHelloWorld_1
Go


Create procedure prHelloWorld_1
As
    Select 'Hello Dejan'
    select * from Inventory
Return 0
Go
```

4. Execute the code by selecting Execute on the Query menu.

SQL Server will first delete the existing stored procedure and then recreate it (with the new code).

The trouble with this method (dropping and then recreating) is that you also drop some attributes associated with the stored procedure (such as permissions), which also affects other dependent objects. Since Microsoft SQL Server 7.0, it is possible to use the `Alter Procedure` statement to modify an existing stored procedure without affecting permissions and other dependent objects:

```
Alter Procedure prHelloWorld_1
As
    Select 'Hello World again!'
    Select * from Inventory
Return 0

Go
```

You may have noticed the `Go` command in the previous two examples. This command is not a SQL statement. It is not even part of the TSQL language. It is a signal to Query Analyzer (and some other tools, such as isql and osql) to treat the SQL statements as one set—a batch. All statements in a batch are compiled and executed together.

In SQL Server 2000, it is possible to use Object Browser to edit stored procedures:

1.  If the Object Browser is not already present on the screen, select Tools | Object Browser to display it.

2.  Open the Asset database and then its list of stored procedures.

3.  Find and right-click prHelloWorld_1 in the list. Select Edit from the pop-up menu, and Query Analyzer displays a Query window with the code of the stored procedure in it (see Figure 2-16).

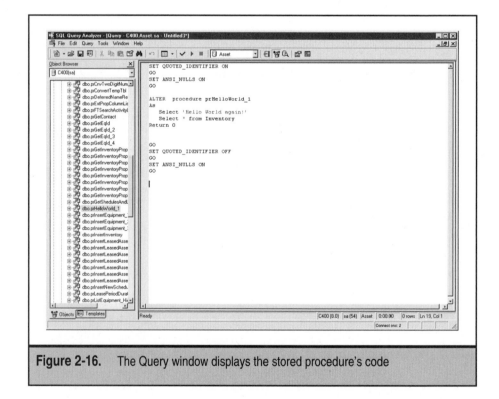

**Figure 2-16.** The Query window displays the stored procedure's code

**NOTE:** Do not be confused by the additional Set statements. They are present just to set an optimal environment for the execution of the Alter Procedure statement. You can ignore them or even delete them.

4. Once you are satisfied with changes in the code, you can simply execute it (Query | Execute).

## Syntax Errors

Sooner or later you will make a typo, and the server will react with an error. Let's deliberately cause a problem to see how the server reacts.

1. Verify that you are in Query Analyzer and that Asset is your current database. We will attempt to alter the code of prHelloWorld_1.

**NOTE:** There are two ways to type comments in the Transact-SQL language. If you type two dashes (- -), the rest of that line will be ignored by the server. Code stretched over multiple lines can be commented out by using (/*) and (*/) as delimiters at either end of the comment.

We will comment out the second line (the keyword As):

```
Alter Procedure prHelloWorld_1
--As
Select 'Hello World again!'
   Select * from Inventory
Return 0

Go
```

As soon as you execute this code, the server reports an error (see Figure 2-17). Keep in mind that SQL Server is not a perfect compiler. Some error messages that it reports may not contain sufficient details or may even be misleading. The rule of thumb is simple: check your basic syntax first.

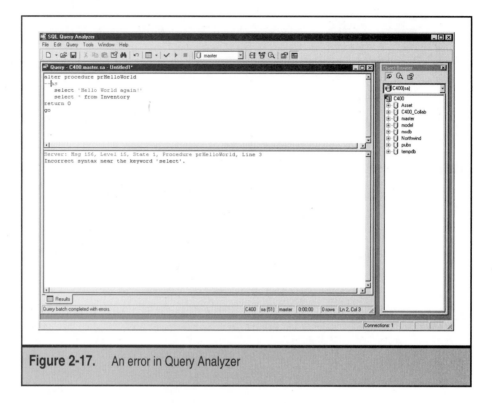

**Figure 2-17.** An error in Query Analyzer

*TIP:* If you double-click the error message in the Result pane, Query Analyzer returns the cursor to the line containing the error in the Query pane (most of the time). This is very useful when you are executing a long batch.

Another advantage the `Alter` statement has over the `Drop/Create` approach is that the stored procedure remains intact after an unsuccessful attempt such as we produced in this example.

2. You can cancel the changes or remove the dashes and attempt execution again.

## The Create Stored Procedure Wizard

Enterprise Manager contains an elaborate set of wizards that are designed to simplify database management, information transfer, replication, and physical design of database objects. Part of this set is the *Create Stored Procedure Wizard*. It can create simple stored procedures for inserting, deleting, and updating tables. To use it, follow these steps:

1. Select Tools | Wizards from the menu. Enterprise Manager displays the Select Wizard dialog.

2. Click the Database node and the program will display a list of wizards for the creation of database objects:

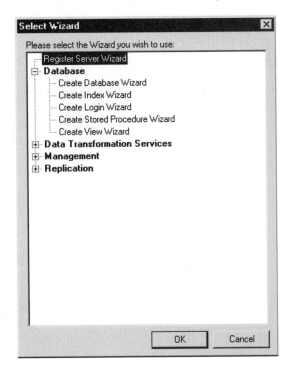

3. Select Create Stored Procedure Wizard and the program displays the wizard's start screen.

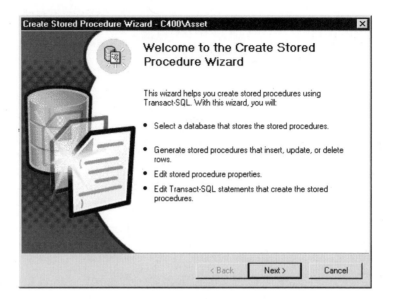

4. Click Next and the wizard prompts you to select the database:

5. Click Next and the program presents you with a list of tables in the database. The list contains three additional columns to enable you to specify which stored procedures you want to create. It is possible to create stored procedures for inserting, deleting, and updating records.

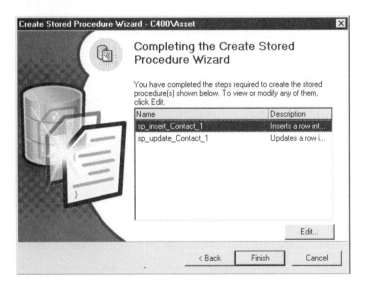

6. Mark a couple of boxes and click Next. The wizard creates stored procedures for the specified operations. To record them in the database, you need to click Finish. You can also change their names or edit their contents.

7. Select a stored procedure and click Edit. The wizard displays a list of the fields in the table. The Select column controls which fields will be included in the stored procedure. In the case of stored procedures for Update and Delete operations, it

is possible to specify which field will be used in a `Where` clause as a key to filter records.

8. Click Edit SQL and the program displays the code for the stored procedure. Here you can change generated code. It is also possible to change the generated code after the stored procedure has been recorded in the database.

▼

*TIP:*   One thing that I always do when I create a stored procedure in this way is to remove the name of the database from the statement. In a development environment, database names are often changed (for example, when you set up a test database), and the name of the database should not be hard-coded in the stored procedure. It should use objects from the current database, not from the database in which the stored procedure was created.

9.  Click OK twice to close open windows, and then click Finish to record the stored procedures in the database.

The Create Stored Procedure Wizard is not perfect, but it will help you to make your first stored procedures. Stored procedures created in this way are very simple, but performance-wise and security-wise it is much better to access data through such stored procedures than to go directly to the underlying tables.

▼

*TIP:*   I have to admit that I generate stored procedures using the wizard from time to time. If the underlying table has many columns, it is much faster to generate a stored procedure using the wizard than to type the stored procedure from scratch.

# SUMMARY

You have made your first steps in the development of stored procedures in Transact-SQL. You have seen how to

▼  Connect to SQL Server from SQL Server Query Analyzer and SQL Server Enterprise Manager

■  Execute stored procedures from Query Analyzer

■  Create stored procedures using SQL Server Enterprise Manager, SQL Server Query Analyzer, and the Create Stored Procedure Wizard

■  Edit stored procedures

■  Make and fix syntax errors

▲  Open SQL Server Books Online

# EXERCISES

1. Open SQL Server Books Online and find documentation about the sp_spaceused system stored procedure. Execute it to find out the amount of space used by the Asset database.

2. Create a stored procedure prListEquipment to return a list of equipment defined in the Equipment table of the Asset database.

3. Change the stored procedure prListEquipment so that its resultset includes equipment type in the form of text. See the following diagram:

**EqType**

| | Column Name | Condensed Type | Nullable | |
|---|---|---|---|---|
| 🔑▶ | EqTypeId | smallint | NOT NULL | ▲ |
| | EqType | varchar(30) | NOT NULL | |
| | | | | ▼ |

**Equipment**

| | Column Name | Condensed Type | Nullable | |
|---|---|---|---|---|
| 🔑 | EquipmentId | int | NOT NULL | ▲ |
| | Make | varchar(50) | NULL | |
| | Model | varchar(50) | NULL | |
| | EqTypeId | smallint | NULL | |
| | ModelSDX | char(4) | NULL | |
| | MakeSDX | char(4) | NULL | |
| | | | | ▼ |

4. Execute the stored procedure prListEquipment.

# CHAPTER 3

# Stored Procedure
# Design Concepts

Stored procedures are database objects that encapsulate collections of Transact-SQL statements on the server for later repetitive use. They are the equivalent of subroutines and functions in other programming languages.

Upon completion of this chapter you will be able to

▼ Create a stored procedure

■ Explain the elements of a stored procedure

■ List ways to return information from a stored procedure

■ Pass input parameters to a stored procedure

■ Receive output parameters from a stored procedure

■ Receive a return value from a stored procedure

■ Explain where stored procedures are stored on SQL Server

▲ Explain the compilation and reuse of stored procedures

# ANATOMY OF A STORED PROCEDURE

We can describe a stored procedure in terms of

▼ Composition

■ Functionality

▲ Syntax

## Composition

Logically, a stored procedure consists of

▼ A header *that* defines the name of the stored procedure, the input and output parameters, and some miscellaneous processing options. You can think of it as an API (application programming interface) or declaration of the stored procedure.

▲ A body that contains one or more Transact-SQL statements to be executed at runtime.

## Creating Stored Procedures

Let's look at the simplified syntax for implementing the core functionality of stored procedures:

```
CREATE PROC[EDURE] procedure_name
    [ {@parameter data_type} [= default] [OUTPUT] ] [,...n]
AS
    sql_statement [...n]
```

The following is an example of a stored procedure:

```
Create Procedure GetEquipment
    @Type varchar(50)
as
    Select *
    from Equipment
    where Type = @Type
```

This Transact-SQL statement creates a stored procedure named GetEquipment with one input parameter. During execution, GetEquipment returns a resultset containing all records from the Equipment table having a Type equal to the input parameter.

The unusual characteristic of stored procedures is their physical design. Stored procedures are actually Transact-SQL statements for creating stored procedures. In all other programming languages, procedures just list actions. They do not create anything. In this sense, stored procedures actually "create" themselves.

> **NOTE:**   Please, be patient and do not run anything against the Asset database yet.

If you try to create a stored procedure that already exists in the database, SQL Server will report an error. You can reproduce such an error if you run the same statement for creating a stored procedure twice. For example:

```
Server: Msg 2729, Level 16, State 5, Procedure GetEquipment, Line 3
Procedure 'GetEquipment' group number 1 already exists in the
database. Choose another procedure name.
```

As we have shown in Chapter 2, one way to change a stored procedure is to create it again. There are two ways to prevent the error just described. One way is to use an `Alter Procedure` statement to change the stored procedure. We will explain this technique in the next section. The traditional way to prevent this error is to delete (Drop) a stored procedure and then create it again:

```
Drop Procedure GetEquipment
go


Create Procedure GetEquipment
    @EqTypeId int
as

    Select *
    from Equipment
    where EqTypeId = @EqTypeId
go
```

If you are not sure whether a stored procedure exists, you can write a piece of code to check for its existence. If you do not, SQL Server will report an error when you try to drop a stored procedure that does not exist. This code takes advantage of the fact that SQL Server records each database object in the sysobjects table (see "Storing Stored Procedures" later in this chapter). It also uses programming constructs we have not yet introduced in this book. For now, do not worry about the details. All will become clear later.

```
if exists (select * from sysobjects
            where id = object_id('GetEquipment ')
    and OBJECTPROPERTY(id, 'IsProcedure') = 1)
drop procedure GetEquipment
GO


Create Procedure GetEquipment
    @EqTypeId int
as

    Select *
    from Equipment
    where EqTypeId = @EqTypeId
go
```

> **NOTE:**   Most of stored procedures in this book already exist in the database. If you just try to create them, SQL Server will complain. If you are sure that the code that you have typed is correct, you can drop the original stored procedure and put yours in its place. Or you can alter the original stored procedure and use your code instead.
>
> It is much better to rename your stored procedure. All stored procedures in the Asset database start with the 'pr' prefix. You could start yours, for example, with 'up' ('user procedure').
>
> I follow a similar practice when I create several versions of the same stored procedure to illustrate a point or a technique. I merely change the stored procedure's suffix by adding a version number (for instance, _1, _2).

## Altering Stored Procedures

The other way to change a stored procedure is to use the `Alter Procedure` statement:

```
Alter Procedure GetEquipment
    @EqTypeId int
as
    Select *
    from Equipment
    where EqTypeId = @EqTypeId
go
```

The syntax of this statement is identical to the syntax of the `Create Procedure` statement (except for the keyword). The main reason for using this statement is to avoid undesirable effects on permissions and dependent database objects. Earlier versions of Enterprise Manager provided a workaround for permissions problems by executing code that recreates all permissions. For more details about permissions, see Chapter 11.

The `Alter Procedure` statement preserves all aspects of the original stored procedure. The Object_id of the procedure from the sysobjects statement remains the same, and all references to the stored procedure are intact. For more details about the sysobjects table and the Object_id column, see "Storing Stored Procedures" later in this chapter.

## Limits

When you are creating or changing a stored procedure, you should keep in mind the following limits:

▼ The name of the procedure is a standard Transact-SQL identifier. The maximum length of any identifier is 128 characters.

■ Stored procedures may contain up to 1,024 input and output parameters.

▲ The body of the stored procedure consists of one or more Transact-SQL statements. The maximum size of the body of the stored procedure is 128MB.

# Functionality

One of the main purposes of a stored procedure is to return information from the SQL Server database in a usable form. There are three ways to receive information from a stored procedure:

▼ Resultset

■ Parameters

▲ Return value

## Returning Resultsets

To obtain a resultset from a stored procedure, insert a Transact-SQL statement that returns a resultset into the body of the stored procedure. You will usually insert a `Select` statement, but you could also insert a call to another stored procedure.

It is also possible to return several resultsets from one stored procedure. Such a stored procedure will simply contain several `Select` statements. You should note that some client data access methods such as RDO can access all resultsets, but others will receive just the first one or possibly even report an error.

## Input and Output Parameters

Let's add a new procedure to the Asset database:

```
Create procedure prGetEqId
     @Make varchar(50),
     @Model varchar(50)
as
     select EquipmentId
     from Equipment
     where Make = @Make
     and Model = @Model
```

This is a very simple stored procedure. It uses two input parameters to receive the Make, Model, and return identifiers of equipment that matches the specified make and model.

Physically, the stored procedure encapsulates just one Select statement. The header and body of the procedure are divided by the keyword As. The header of the stored procedure contains a list of parameters delimited with a comma (',') character. Each parameter is defined with an identifier and a datatype. Parameter identifiers must begin with the 'at' sign (@).

You can use the following statement to execute the stored procedure:

```
Execute prGetEqId 'Toshiba', 'Portege 7020CT'
```

The keyword Execute is followed by the name of the stored procedure. Since the stored procedure requires two parameters, they are provided in the form of a comma-delimited list. In this case, they are strings, so they must be delimited with single quotation marks.

The keyword Execute is not needed if the stored procedure is executed in the first statement of a batch.

```
prGetEqId 'Toshiba', 'Portege 7020CT'
```

However, I recommend you use it. It is a good habit that leads to clean code. You can use its shorter version (Exec) to save keystrokes:

```
Exec prGetEqId 'Toshiba', 'Portege 7020CT'
```

The execution will return a resultset containing just one value in one record:

```
EquipmentId
-----------
1


(1 row(s) affected)
```

Stored procedures can return output parameters to the caller. To illustrate, we will create a stored procedure similar to the previous one, but having one critical difference: this new stored procedure contains an additional parameter. The direction of the parameter is controlled by setting the keyword Output behind a datatype:

```
Create procedure prGetEqId_2
    @Make varchar(50),
    @Model varchar(50),
    @EqId int Output
as
    select @EqId = EquipmentId
    from Equipment
    where Make = @Make
    and Model = @Model
```

The Select statement does not return a resultset as the previous one did. Instead, it assigns an @EqId output parameter with the selected value.

**NOTE:** This stored procedure is not perfect. It might seem okay to you, but there is a potential problem with it. More than one piece of equipment (that is, more than one record) could correspond to the criteria. We will address this issue in detail in the chapters to follow.

In this case, we require a more complicated batch of Transact-SQL statements to execute the stored procedure. We must define the variable that will receive the output value. The parameter must be followed with the Output keyword in order to pass a value to the variable. At the end of the batch, the result of the stored procedure is displayed using the `Select` statement:

```
Declare @intEqId int
Execute prGetEqId_2 'Toshiba', 'Portege 7020CT', @intEqId output
Select @intEqId 'Equipment Identifier'
```

The batch will return the value of the output parameter:

```
Equipment Identifier
--------------------
1


(1 row(s) affected)
```

## Return Value

An alternative way to send values from a stored procedure to the caller is to use a *return value.* Each stored procedure can be finished with a `Return` statement. The statement can be followed with an *integer* value that can be read by the caller. If the return value is not explicitly set, the server will return the default value—zero (0).

Because return values are limited to integer datatypes, they are most often used to signal an error to the caller. We will examine this use later. First, let's explore its functionality on some unorthodox examples.

In the following example, the result of the selection will be assigned to the local variable and finally returned to the caller:

```
Create Procedure prGetEqId_3
     @Make varchar(50),
     @Model varchar(50)
as

Declare @intEqId int

Select @intEqId  = EquipmentId
from Equipment
```

```
where Make = @Make
and Model =.@Model
```

**Return @intEqId**

The same functionality could be achieved even without a local variable, since a `Return` statement can accept an integer expression instead of an integer value:

```
Create Procedure prGetEqId_3
    @Make varchar(50),
    @Model varchar(50)
as
    Return (select EquipmentId
            from Equipment
            where Make = @Make
            and Model = @Model)
```

To execute the stored procedure and access the returned value, we require the following lines of code:

```
Declare @intEqId int
Execute @intEqId = prGetEqId_3 'Toshiba', 'Portege 7020CT'
Select @intEqId 'Equipment Identifier'
```

Notice the difference in assigning a value. The local variable must be inserted before the name of the stored procedure. The result of the batch is the returned value:

```
Equipment Identifier
--------------------
1


(1 row(s) affected)
```

This solution, however, is not a perfect way to transfer information from a stored procedure to a caller. In the first place, it is limited by datatype. Only integers can be returned this way (including `int`, `smallint`, and `tinyint`). This method is used primarily to return status information to the caller:

```
Create Procedure prGetEqId_2
     @Make varchar(50),
     @Model varchar(50),
     @EqId int output
As
     select @EqId = EquipmentId
     from Equipment
     where Make = @Make
     and Model = @Model
Return @@Error
```

In this example, the stored procedure will potentially return an error code. @@Error is a global variable, which contains an error number in the case of failure or a zero in the case of success. To execute the stored procedure, use the following code:

```
Declare   @intEqId int,
          @intStatusCode int
Execute @intStatusCode = prGetEqId_2 'Toshiba',
                                     'Portege 7020CT',
                                     @intEqId output
Select @intEqId result, @intStatusCode ErrorCode
```

The result will look like this:

```
result        ErrorCode
-----------   -----------
1             0


(1 row(s) affected)
```

## Default Values

If the stored procedure statement has parameters, you must supply values for the parameters in your Exec statement. If a user fails to supply them, the server reports an error. It is possible, however, to assign default values to the parameters so that the user is not required to supply them. Default values are defined at the end of a parameter definition; behind the datatypes. All that is needed is an assignment (=) and a value.

Add this new procedure to the Asset database:

```
Create Procedure prGetEqId_4
    @Make varchar(50) = '%',
    @Model varchar(50) = '%'
as
    Select *
    from Equipment
    where Make Like @Make
    and Model Like @Model
```

The procedure is designed as a small search engine that accepts TSQL wild cards. You can execute this stored procedure with normal values:

```
Execute prGetEqId_4 'T%', 'Portege%'
```

The resultset will consist of records that match the criteria:

```
EquipmentId Make                    Model                   EqTypeId
----------- ----------------------- ----------------------- --------
1           Toshiba                 Portege 7020CT          1

(1 row(s) affected)
```

If one parameter is omitted, the procedure will behave, since the value that was defined as a default has been supplied.

```
Execute prGetEqId_4 'T%'
```

The server will return a resultset:

```
EquipmentId Make                    Model                   EqTypeId
----------- ----------------------- ----------------------- --------
1           Toshiba                 Portege 7020CT          1

(1 row(s) affected)
```

Even both parameters may be skipped:

```
Execute prGetEqId_4
```

The server will return all records that match the default criteria:

```
EquipmentId Make                  Model                    EqTypeId
----------- --------------------- ------------------------ --------
1           Toshiba               Portege 7020CT           1
2           Sony                  Trinitron 17XE           3


(2 row(s) affected)
```

## Passing Parameters by Name

At this point, you might wonder if it is possible to supply only the second parameter. There is a mechanism that you can use to do exactly that. In order to achieve this goal, you must type the name of the parameter and then assign a value to it. The parameter name must match its definition. It has to include everything, even the '@' sign. Once this is accomplished, it is not necessary to follow the parameter order.

This method is sometimes called *passing parameters by name*. The original method can be referred to as *passing parameters by position*. In the following example, the server will use T% for the second parameter and a default value, %, for the first one:

```
Execute prGetEqId 4 @Model = 'T%'
```

The result of the search will be:

```
EquipmentId Make                  Model                    EqTypeId
----------- --------------------- ------------------------ --------
2           Sony                  Trinitron 17XE           3


(1 row(s) affected)
```

The opportunity to skip parameters is just one reason for passing parameters by name. Even more important is the opportunity to create a method that makes code more readable and maintainable. And, if a developer makes a mistake and assigns a value to a nonexisting parameter, the error will be picked up by SQL Server. Although passing parameters by position can be a little faster, passing parameters by name is preferable.

## Syntax

The following is the complete syntax for the creation of a stored procedure:

```
CREATE PROC[EDURE] procedure_name [;number]
    [
        {@parameter data_type} [VARYING] [= default] [OUTPUT]
    ]
    [,...n]
[WITH {    RECOMPILE
        | ENCRYPTION
        | RECOMPILE, ENCRYPTION }
]
[FOR REPLICATION]
AS
    sql_statement [...n]
```

When you create a stored procedure using `With Encryption`, the code of the stored procedure is encrypted and then saved in the database. SQL Server will be able to use the encrypted version of the source code to recompile the stored procedure when needed, but none of the users (not even the system administrator) will be able to obtain it.

Keep in mind that you will not be able to change a stored procedure if you forget to preserve its code. For more details about storage and encryption of stored procedures, see "Storing Stored Procedures" later in this chapter.

As a developer, you might decide to recompile a stored procedure each time it is used. To enforce compilation, you should create the stored procedure using `With Recompile`. Recompiling for each use may improve or degrade the performance of the stored procedure: although the compilation process is extra overhead when you are executing the stored procedure, SQL Server will sometimes recompile the stored procedure differently (and more economically) based on the data it is targeting. You will find more details about compilation and reasons for recompiling a stored procedure later in this chapter.

[;*number*] is an optional integer number that can be added to the name of a stored procedure. In this way, a user can create a group of stored procedures that can be deleted with a single `Drop Procedure` statement. Procedures will have names such as

▼  prListEquipment;1

■  prListEquipment;2

▲  prListEquipment;3

This technique is an artifact of earlier versions of SQL Server for which I have never found a use.

Stored procedures that include the `For Replication` option are usually created by SQL Server to serve as a filter during the replication of databases.

An output parameter for a stored procedure can also be of the `Cursor` datatype. In such a case, the structure of resultset contained by the cursor might vary. The [`Varying`] option will notify SQL Server to handle such cases. But it is too early to talk about cursors yet. We will return to cursors in the next chapter.

All these options involve rarely used features. Some of them will be covered in more detail later in this book, but some are simply too esoteric.

# TYPES OF STORED PROCEDURES

There are many types of stored procedures:

▼  User-defined

■  System

■  Extended

■  Temporary

■  Global temporary

▲  Remote

There are also database objects, which are very similar in nature:

▼ Triggers

▲ User-defined functions

As you can infer from the name, *user-defined stored procedures* are simply plain stored procedures assembled by administrators or developers for later repetitive use. All of the examples we have discussed so far in this chapter have been such stored procedures.

Microsoft delivers a vast set of stored procedures as part of SQL Server. They are designed to cover all aspects of system administration. Internal *system stored procedures* are just regular stored procedures. Their special features result from the fact that they are stored in system databases (master and msdb) and they have the prefix sp_. This prefix is more than just a convention. It signals to the server that the stored procedure should be accessible from all databases without putting the database name as a prefix to fully qualify the name of the procedure. For example, you can use sp_spaceused to examine usage of the current database (see Figure 3-1).

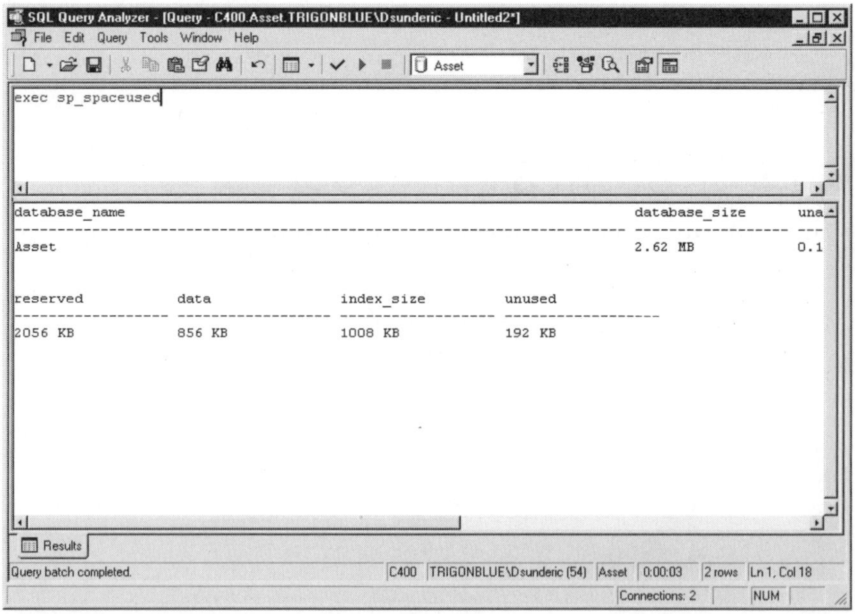

**Figure 3-1.**  Using sp_spaceused

We will examine all types of stored procedures in more detail in Chapter 9.

# COMPILATION

Transact-SQL is neither a standard programming language, nor is Microsoft SQL Server a standard environment for program execution, but the process of compiling the source code for a stored procedure and its execution bear some resemblance to the compilation and execution of programs in standard programming languages.

## The Compilation and Execution Process

When a developer executes any batch, SQL Server performs the following three steps:

▼ It parses the batch.

■ It compiles the batch.

▲ It executes the batch.

### Parsing

Parsing is a process during which the Microsoft SQL Server command parser module first verifies the syntax of a batch. If no errors are found, the Microsoft SQL Server command parser breaks the source code into logical units such as keywords, identifiers, and operators. The parser will then build an internal structure that describes the series of steps needed to perform the requested operation or to extract the requested resultset from the source data. If the batch contains a query, this internal structure is called a *query tree*, and if the batch contains a procedure, it is called a *sequence tree*.

### Compilation

In this step, a sequence tree is used to generate an execution plan. The Optimizer module analyzes the ways that information can be retrieved from the source tables. It attempts to find the fastest way that uses the smallest amount of resources (that is, processing time). It also complements the list of tasks that need to be performed (for instance, it checks security, it verifies that constraints are enforced, and it includes triggers if they need to be incorporated in processing). The result is an internal structure called an *execution plan.*

## Execution

The execution plan is then stored in the procedure cache and executed from there. Different steps in the execution plan will be posted to different modules of the relational engine to be executed: DML manager, DDL manager, stored procedure manager, transaction manager, or utility manager. Results are collected in the form of a resultset and sent to the user.

# Reuse of Execution Plans

Execution plans remain in the procedure cache for a while. If the same or some other user issues a similar batch, the relational engine will first attempt to find a matching execution plan in the procedure cache. If it exists, it will be reused. If it does not exist, Microsoft SQL Server will parse and compile a batch.

## Reuse of Query Execution Plans

A simple query can be reused only in two scenarios. First, the query text of the second query must be identical to the text of the query described by the execution plan in the cache. Everything has to match: spaces, line breaks, indentation—even case on case-sensitive servers.

The second scenario is when the query contains fully qualified database objects to reuse execution plans:

```
Select *
from Asset.dbo.Inventory
```

## Parameterized Queries

The designers of SQL Server have created two methods to improve the reuse of queries that are not designed as stored procedures:

▼   Autoparameterization

▲   The sp_executesql stored procedure

We will cover the first of these methods in the following section and the second one in Chapter 9.

## Autoparameterization

When a Transact-SQL statement is sent to SQL Server, it attempts to determine whether any of its constants can be replaced with parameters. Subsequent queries that use the same template will reuse the same execution plan.

For example, let's say that SQL Server receives the following ad hoc query:

```
SELECT FirstName, LastName, Phone, Fax, Email, OrgUnitId, UserName
FROM Asset.dbo.Contact
where ContactId = 3
```

It will try to parameterize it in the following manner and create an execution plan:

```
SELECT FirstName, LastName, Phone, Fax, Email, OrgUnitId, UserName
FROM Asset.dbo.Contact
where ContactId = @P1
```

After this, all similar queries will reuse the execution plan:

```
SELECT FirstName, LastName, Phone, Fax, Email, OrgUnitId, UserName
FROM Asset.dbo.Contact
where ContactId = 11
```

SQL Server will apply autoparameterization only when a query's template is "safe"—that is, when the execution plan will not be changed and the performance of SQL Server will not be degraded if parameters are changed.

> **NOTE:**   SQL Server might decide to create and use a different execution plan even if the query is based on the same field. For example, imagine that you are querying a table with contact information using the Country field. If your company is operating predominantly in North America, SQL Server might carry out a query for Denmark contacts based on the index on the Country field and a query for USA contacts as a table scan.

SQL Server will attempt autoparameterization on `Insert`, `Update`, and `Delete` statements too. In fact, the query must match a set of four templates in order for SQL Server to attempt autoparameterization:

```
Select {* | column-list}
From table
Where column-expression
[Order by column-list]

Insert table
Values ({constant | NULL | Default} [, ...n])

Update table
set column-name = constant
where column-expression

Delete table
Where column-expression
```

Note that a "column-expression" is an expression that involves only column names, constants, the And operator, and comparison operators: <, >, =, >=, <=, and <>.

SQL Server is more forgiving about formatting the query when autoparameterization is used, but it still does not allow changes in capitalization or changes in the way an object is qualified.

## Reuse of Stored Procedure Execution Plans

Stored procedures do not have the limitations associated with ad hoc queries, and that is the main reason stored procedures are reused more often then queries.

The reuse of execution plans is one of the main reasons why the use of stored procedures is a better solution than the use of ad hoc queries. For example, if you execute a query three times, SQL Server will have to parse, recompile, and execute it three times. A stored procedure will most likely be parsed and recompiled only once—just before the first execution.

---

**NOTE:**   Someone might argue that the time needed to compile is insignificant compared with the time needed to execute a query. That is sometimes true. But the SQL Server query engine in this version compares dozens of new processing techniques in order to select the best one to process the query or stored procedure. Therefore, the time needed to recompile a stored procedure is greater than it used to be.

---

The execution plan consists of two parts. One is reentrant and can be used concurrently by any number of processes. The other part contains the data context; that is, the parameters to be used during execution. Although this part can be reused, it cannot be used by another process concurrently, so more instances of this part will be created.

The execution plan will be removed from the procedure cache when a process called *lazywriter* concludes that the execution plan has not been used for a while, or when the execution plan's dependent database objects are changed in any of the following ways:

▼   The amount of data is significantly changed.

■   Indexes are created or dropped.

■   Constraints are added or changed.

- ■ Distribution statistics of indexes are changed.

- ▲ sp_recompile was explicitly called to recompile the stored procedure or trigger.

If a dependent database object is deleted, the stored procedure will fail during execution. If it is replaced with a new object (new ObjectId) with the same name, the execution plan does not have to be recompiled and will run flawlessly.

I was impressed with the way that lazywriter determines which execution plans are obsolete. Microsoft SQL Server 2000 contains a sophisticated emulation of the aging process. When SQL Server creates an execution plan, it assigns it a "compilation cost factor." The value of this factor depends on the expense required to create the execution plan in terms of system resources. For example, a large execution plan might be assigned a compilation cost factor of 8, while a smaller one might be assigned a factor of 2. Each time the execution plan is referenced by a connection, its age is incremented by the value of the compilation cost factor. Thus, if the compilation cost factor of the execution plan is 8, each reference to the execution plan adds 8 to its "age."

SQL Server uses the lazywriter process to decrement the age of the execution plan. The lazywriter process periodically loops through the execution plans in the procedure cache and decrements the age of each execution plan by 1. When the age of an execution plan reaches 0, SQL Server deallocates it, provided that the system is in need of the resources and no connection is currently referencing the execution plan.

## Recompiling Stored Procedures

SQL Server is intelligent enough to recompile a stored procedure when a table referenced by that stored procedure changes. Unfortunately, SQL Server does not recompile when an administrator adds an index that might help execution of the stored procedure. The stored procedure will be recompiled only when the procedure cache is flushed (which usually happens only when SQL Server is restarted).

To force compilation of a stored procedure, a DBA can use sp_recompile:

```
Exec sp_recompile prListOrders
```

This task can be very tedious if many stored procedures and/or triggers depend on a table for which an index was added. Fortunately, it is possible to name the table for which dependent objects should be recompiled:

```
Exec sp_recompile Orders
```

This statement will recompile all triggers and stored procedures that depend on the Orders table. When a stored procedure or a trigger is specified as a parameter, only that stored procedure or trigger will be recompiled. If you use a table or a view as a parameter, all dependent objects will be recompiled.

A developer might also decide to recompile a stored procedure each time it is used. A typical example is when a stored procedure is based on a query, the execution and performance of which depend on the value used as a criterion. We discussed such an example earlier in the section "Autoparameterization."

In that example, when a user requests orders from the USA, the selectivity of the index might be such that it is better for the query to do a table scan. If a user requests orders from a country that rarely appears in the particular database, the query engine might decide to use the index. To force SQL Server to evaluate these options every time, the developer should use the With Recompile option while designing the stored procedure:

```
Create Procedure prListOrders
     @Country char(3)
With Recompile
as
     Select *
     from Orders
     where Country =  @Country
```

The execution plan of a stored procedure created in this manner will not be cached on SQL Server.

It is also possible to force recompilation of a stored procedure during execution. The user/developer uses the `With Recompile` option to achieve this end:

```
Exec prListOrders 'USA' With Recompile
```

## Storing Stored Procedures

Stored procedures are persistent database objects, and Microsoft SQL Server stores them in system tables to preserve them when their execution plan is removed from the procedure cache or while SQL Server is shut down.

When the `Create Procedure` statement is executed, Microsoft SQL Server creates a new record in the sysobjects table of the current database (see Figure 3-2).

| | name | id | xtype | uid | info | status | base_schema_ver | replinfo | pare |
|---|---|---|---|---|---|---|---|---|---|
| 124 | prGetInventoryProper... | 1218103380 | P | 1 | 0 | 1610612736 | 0 | 0 | 0 |
| 125 | prDeferredNameResolution | 1250103494 | P | 1 | 0 | 1610612736 | 48 | 0 | 0 |
| 126 | prListInventoryEquipment | 1282103608 | P | 1 | 0 | 536870912 | 0 | 0 | 0 |
| 127 | prInsertLeasedAsset_1 | 1298103665 | P | 1 | 0 | 1610612736 | 16 | 0 | 0 |
| 128 | prInsertLeasedAsset_2 | 1314103722 | P | 1 | 0 | 1610612736 | 32 | 0 | 0 |
| 129 | prInsertLeasedAsset_3 | 1330103779 | P | 1 | 0 | 1610612736 | 0 | 0 | 0 |
| 130 | prInsertLeasedAsset_4 | 1346103836 | P | 1 | 0 | 1610612736 | 16 | 0 | 0 |
| 131 | prInsertLeasedAsset_5 | 1362103893 | P | 1 | 0 | 1610612736 | 112 | 0 | 0 |
| 132 | prInsertLeasedAsset_6 | 1378103950 | P | 1 | 0 | 1610612736 | 32 | 0 | 0 |
| 133 | OrgUnit | 1381579960 | U | 1 | 3 | 1610616098 | 64 | 0 | 0 |
| 134 | prInsertLeasedAsset_7 | 1394104007 | P | 1 | 0 | 1610612736 | 0 | 0 | 0 |
| 135 | PK_OrgUnit | 1397580017 | PK | 1 | 0 | 32 | 0 | 0 | 1381 |
| 136 | prClearLeaseShedule | 1410104064 | P | 1 | 0 | 1610612736 | 48 | 0 | 0 |

**Figure 3-2.**　Content of the sysobjects table

This system table contains all types of database objects; it is sometimes useful to filter it by object type using the xtype field.

The source code of the stored procedure is (usually) recorded in the syscomments system table. To see the source code, execute sp_helptext, or query the syscomments system table directly (see Figure 3-3).

The source code is stored in a field named text. The datatype of this field is `varchar(8000)`. Fortunately, this does not mean that stored procedures are limited to 8,000 characters. If the stored procedure is larger than 8,000 characters, SQL Server allocates additional records with an incremented colid field. Since this field is declared as `smallint`, a stored procedure can be 32K * 8,000 bytes ≈ 250MB long. In versions before SQL Server 2000 and SQL Server 7.0, colid was `byte` and text was `varchar(255)`, so stored procedures were limited to 255 * 255 ≈ 64KB.

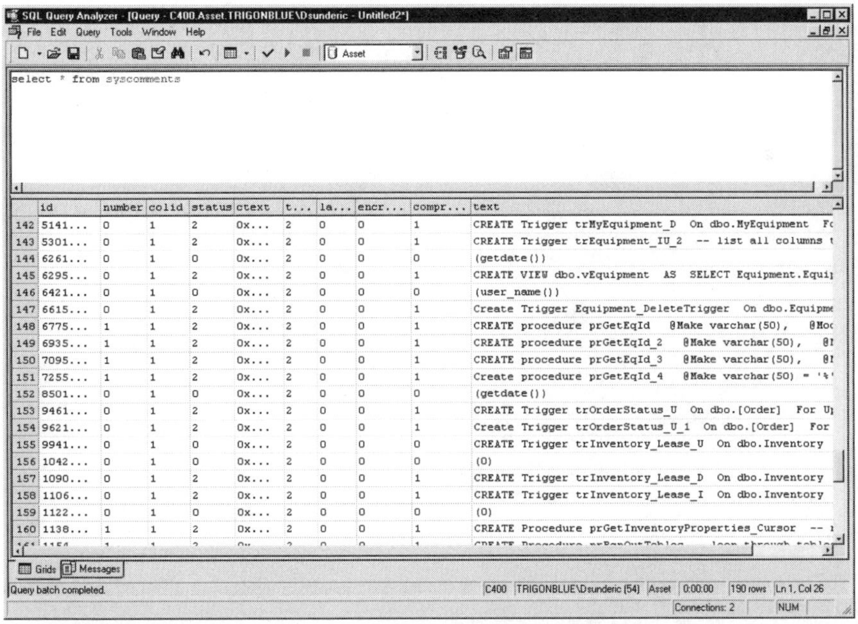

**Figure 3-3.**    Content of the syscomments table

A developer can hide the source code for a stored procedure if he or she encrypts it during creation. After he or she creates the stored procedure With Encryption, none of the users (not even the system administrator) will be able to see it on the server. Keep in mind that you can (and should) keep source code in a separate external script file.

> **NOTE:**  Before this feature was introduced in SQL Server, developers achieved the same effect by setting the syscomments..text associated with the stored procedure to null. SQL Server was able to run the stored procedure without any problem. Unfortunately, this solution caused problems during upgrades from one version of SQL Server to another. Setup programs were expecting to use the text of the stored procedures to recompile them in the new environment. To solve that problem, Microsoft has included the With Encryption clause in the statement for creating a stored procedure. Setup programs will be able to upgrade stored procedures hidden in this manner.

# MANAGING STORED PROCEDURES

SQL Server Enterprise Manager and Query Analyzer are the most important tools that the DBA will use to control the environment and manage stored procedures.

We will review the ways that you can use Enterprise Manager and Query Analyzer to:

▼  List stored procedures

■  View stored procedures

■  Rename stored procedures

■  Delete stored procedures

▲  View dependent and depending objects

## Listing Stored Procedures

The easiest way to list stored procedures in a database is to view them from Enterprise Manager. All you need to do is follow these steps:

1.  Open Enterprise Manager.

2.  Expand the server group (click +).

3.  Expand the server.

4.  Expand the database.

5.  Click the Stored Procedures node in a tree; Enterprise Manager lists the stored procedures in the Details pane (see Figure 3-4).

There are two ways to list stored procedures from Query Analyzer . We have shown how to use Object Browser in a previous chapter. The traditional way is based on Transact-SQL. SQL Server is delivered with the system stored procedure sp_stored_procedures. It lists stored procedures in the current database:

1.  Open Query Analyzer.

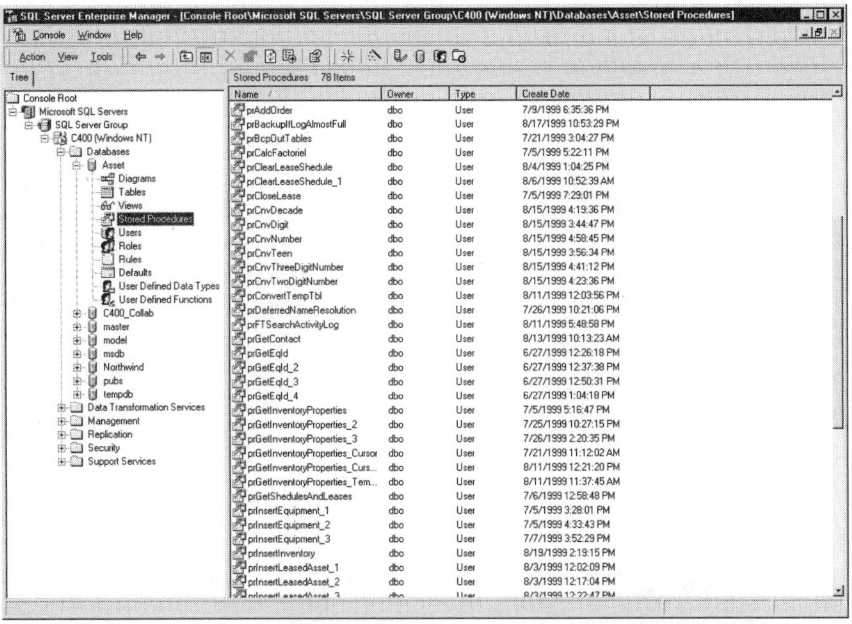

**Figure 3-4.**    Listing stored procedures in Enterprise Manager

2. Switch the current database to Asset.

3. Set Query Analyzer to display results in a grid (Query | Results In Grid).

4. Type and execute **sp_stored_procedures** (Query | Execute). The program will show the list of stored procedures in the current database (see Figure 3-5).

The stored procedure sp_stored_procedures retrieves a list of database objects from the sysobjects system table. If you want to see its contents, execute the following statement:

```
Select *
from sysobjects
```

You can see the results in Figure 3-6.

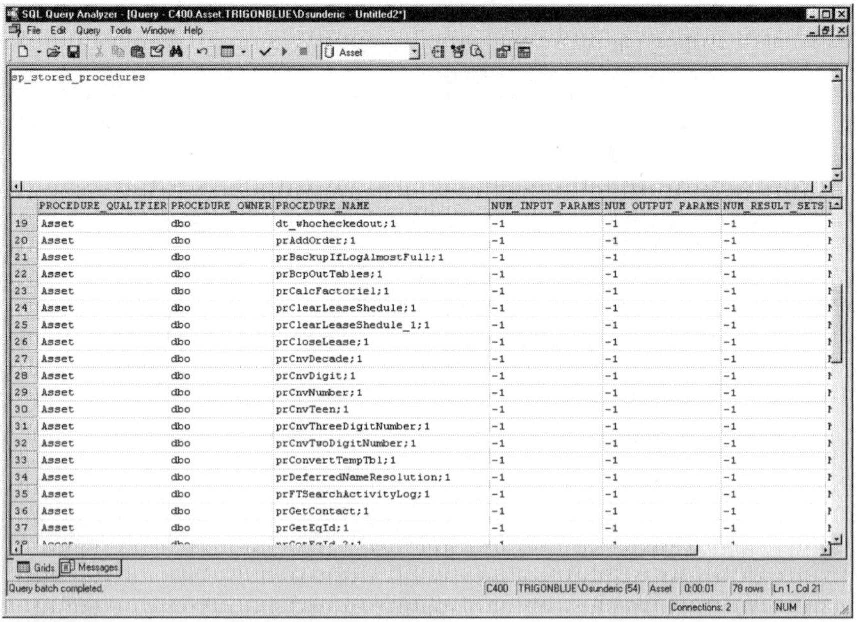

**Figure 3-5.**    Listing stored procedures in Query Analyzer

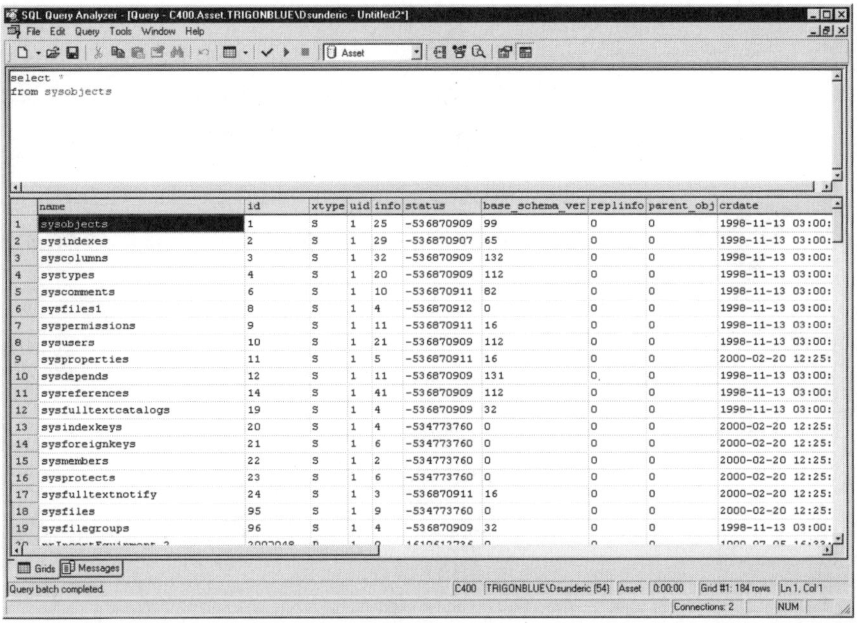

**Figure 3-6.**   A list of database objects in sysobjects

To see just user-defined stored procedures, you need to filter the database objects with xtype set to 'P':

```
Select *
from sysobjects
where xtype = 'P'
```

## Viewing Stored Procedures

We have already shown you in Chapter 2 how to display a stored procedure from Enterprise Manager. You just double-click its name and the program displays it in an editor. We have also shown that you can use Object Browser in Query Analyzer to achieve the same task. You just need to find the stored procedure in Object Browser, right-click, and then select Edit from the menu; Query Analyzer displays it in a new Query window.

It is little bit more difficult to display a stored procedure in the traditional way using Transact-SQL. You need to use the sp_help_text system stored procedure. The database that contains the stored procedure must be the current database, and you must supply the name of the stored procedure as a parameter (see Figure 3-7).

> **NOTE:** You can also use sp_helptext to view the code of other database objects such as triggers, views, defaults, and rules.

If you now want to save the code of the stored procedure, you can copy it through the Clipboard to your Query pane, or you can save Results from Query Analyzer in a text file:

1. Click the Results pane of Query Analyzer.

2. Select File | Save and specify a name for the file. Verify that the File Format is set to ANSI.

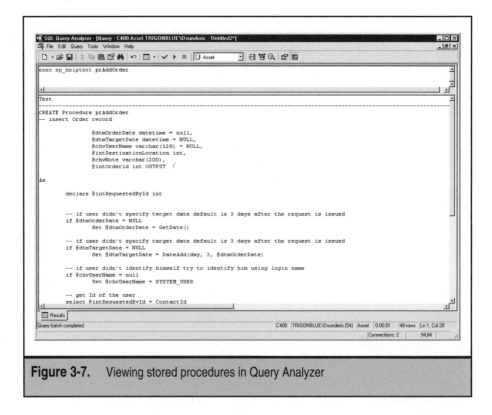

**Figure 3-7.** Viewing stored procedures in Query Analyzer

The result will be saved to an ANSI file, which you can edit in any text editor, such as Notepad. You can also open it in the Query pane:

1.  Click the Query Pane in Query Analyzer.
2.  Select File | Open and specify the name of the file.

# Renaming Stored Procedures

Enterprise Manager behaves strangely when you try to rename a stored procedure. You can click the name of the stored procedure twice, or you can right-click the stored procedure and use the pop-up menu to rename it. But if you then open the code for the stored procedure, you will see the old name for the stored procedure in the code. You need to change it there as well.

You can also use the sp_rename system stored procedure. The first parameter should be the current name of the stored procedure, the second parameter should be the new name, and the third parameter is the type of database object. To rename a stored procedure, you don't have to supply the third parameter:

```
exec sp_rename prTest, prTest2
```

Unfortunately, the previously described problem occurs again. You need to edit the code of stored procedure. Obviously, Enterprise Manager is using sp_rename to rename stored procedures.

This stored procedure can also change the names of other objects (including tables, views, columns, defaults, rules, triggers). In fact, the versatility of this stored procedure is the reason the code is not changed in the previous example. The stored procedure is designed to change the names of objects in the sysobjects table. Database objects with code such as stored procedures, views, and user-defined functions require a different strategy. It is better to drop them and create them again. Again, do not forget to change all associated objects such as permissions at the same time. The Alter statement cannot help us in this case, since we need to change the name of the stored procedure. This operation is not something that you should perform very often. It could be problematic if you did it on a production server. SQL Server contains a procedure cache—a part of the memory where it keeps compiled versions of stored procedures. You should flush the procedure cache to force all dependent stored procedures (which refer to the stored procedure by its old name) to recompile. You can use DBCC FREEPROCCACHE, or you can simply restart SQL Server and the procedure cache will be emptied.

## Deleting Stored Procedures

To delete a stored procedure from Enterprise Manager:

1. Right-click the name of the stored procedure in the list.

2. Select Delete from the pop-up menu.

It is also simple to delete a stored procedure using Object Browser in Query Analyzer:

1. Right-click the name of the stored procedure in the list.

2. Select Delete from the pop-up menu.

Drop Procedure is a Transact-SQL statement for deleting a stored procedure. To use it, you must supply the name of the stored procedure as a parameter:

```
DROP PROCEDURE prTest2
```

## Listing Dependent and Depending Objects

If you plan to perform some dramatic action such as deleting or renaming a database object, you should first investigate which objects will be affected by it. Microsoft SQL Server keeps a list of dependencies between objects in the sysdepends system table in each database.

To view this list in Enterprise Manager:

1. Right-click the name of the database object.

2. Select All Tasks.

3. Click Display Dependencies and SQL Server will display a list of dependencies:

The program displays two lists. The list to the left shows objects that reference the selected object (dependent). The list to the right shows objects that are referenced by the object (depending). In the case of prListInventoryEquipment, since no object in the database is using it, the list to the left is empty.

Use the drop-down list box at the top to change the selected object; after a short delay, the program displays its dependencies. You can also double-click any dependent or depending object and SQL Server will display a form showing its dependencies.

Select vEquipment and the program will display the following form. From this form, we can conclude that this view is based on two tables and that it is used in one stored procedure:

The system stored procedure sp_depends has a similar function. It can also return one or two resultsets—one for dependent and one for depending objects. If you execute the following statement in Query Analyzer,

```
exec sp_depends prListLeasedAssets
```

you will see a result like that in Figure 3-8.

Object Browser can also be used to display a list of dependencies:

1. Expand the node of a database object (for example, the prListLeasedAssets stored procedure).

2. Expand the Dependencies node.

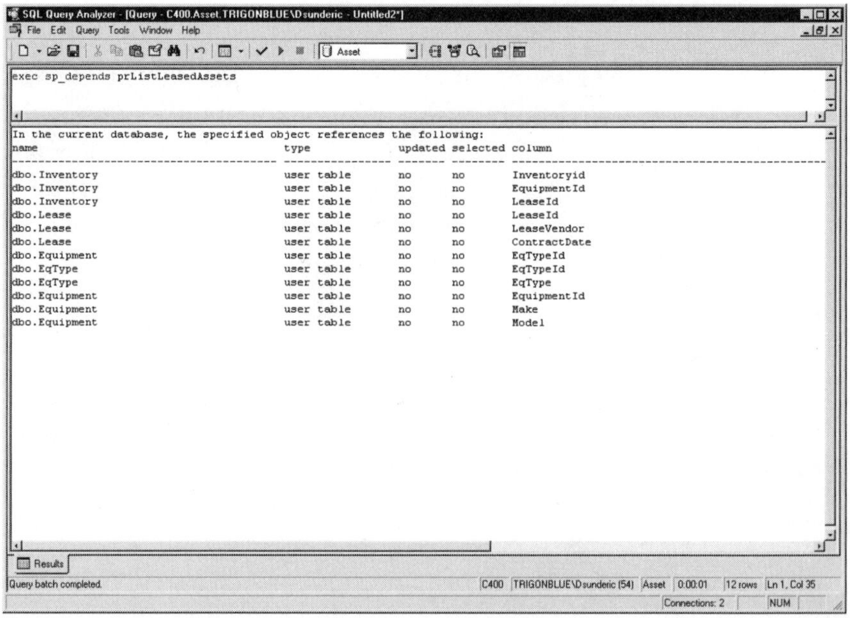

**Figure 3-8.**    Dependent and depending objects

**NOTE:**  Unfortunately, you cannot completely rely on SQL Server to get a list of dependencies. It does not update the content of the sysdepends table in all cases. You can reproduce and observe this behavior when, for example, you drop and recreate a table. However, in that case SQL Server will warn you that it cannot properly update sysdependencies. This problem has been a known issue since version 4.21. If SQL Server displays an empty list, you should open the source code and check it.

# THE ROLE OF STORED PROCEDURES IN THE DEVELOPMENT OF DATABASE APPLICATIONS

In order to properly design and use stored procedures in the development of applications, it is critical to understand their role and advantages.

## Enforcement of Data Integrity

The most important task for each database administrator is to maintain the data integrity of the database that he or she is managing. If he or she is not almost fanatical about data integrity, the results for the database will be potentially disastrous. During my career, I have encountered databases with

▼ 106 different provinces of Canada (one of them was France)

■ An Address column filled with "Guest had frozen Fish."

▲ Nine ways to write HP LaserJet III…

Stored procedures are an ideal tool to help you standardize and limit database access, and to implement validation of information and even the most complex constraints.

## Consistent Implementation of Complex Business Rules and Constraints

Transact-SQL stored procedures are powerful enough to implement even the most complex business rules, because they combine both procedural and nonprocedural approaches. Everything that is too complicated to be implemented using other constraints and that is procedural and not just relational can be implemented in the form of a stored procedure. This is a serious topic. We will expand on it in coming chapters.

## Modular Design

Stored procedures allow developers to encapsulate business functionality and provide users (mostly other programs—not end users) with a simple interface. Stored procedures behave like a black box. The user does not have to know how they are implemented, just what they do, what input is required, and what output will be generated. Humans are limited as to the amount of information that they can process, and stored procedures are a perfect way to reduce the complexity of the design process.

## Maintainability

System design is a cyclic process. Every system needs to be reviewed, changed, and improved. By hiding database structure details behind stored procedures, database administrators can reduce the need to change all other components (that is, client applications and middleware components) of the system whenever they change the database structure.

Microsoft does the same thing with system stored procedures and system tables. Although DBAs can use the contents of system tables directly in their applications, they should base their code on system stored procedures, because Microsoft reserves the right to change tables from version to version but has promised to keep the interface and functionality of stored procedures intact.

Another advantage is that stored procedures are implemented on the server and can be maintained centrally. If the business logic is implemented in the client application, a huge effort will be needed to deploy changes.

## Reduced Network Traffic

One of the major disadvantages of file-server architecture is high network traffic due to the fact that entire files are being transferred across the network. If a client/server system is well designed, the client will receive just the information it needs, which is usually just a slight portion of the database, thus significantly reducing the network traffic.

If a client/server system is implemented with even more of the processing/business logic on the server (that is, using stored procedures), even less data will be transferred back and forth through the network.

**NOTE:**    Naturally, stored procedures are not the only way to implement business logic on the server. Three-tier architecture envisions implementation of business services on a middleware server.

## Faster Execution

Stored procedures have several performance advantages over ad hoc queries. Stored procedures are cached in a compiled form on the database server, so when they need to be used, the server does not have to parse and recompile them again.

A developer can optimize a stored procedure's code so that every user will use the best possible method to perform an action.

## Enforcement of Security

One sign of a well-designed database system is that it prevents users from directly accessing the tables and forces them to use stored procedures to perform specific functions. It is also easier to manage a set of stored procedures by functionality than to manage table- and column-level permissions.

## SUMMARY

We have taken a detailed look at the world of stored procedures in this chapter. Stored procedures are database objects that encapsulate collections of Transact-SQL statements on the server for later repetitive use. As do their counterparts in other programming languages (functions and procedures), they support the use of input and output parameters and return values. Since the return value is limited to integer datatypes, parameters are mostly used to return success codes for the stored procedure.

By placing Select statement(s) inside stored procedures, developers can return one (or more) resultset(s) from a stored procedure.

To run a stored procedure, use the Execute statement. This statement must be supplied with a list of input and output parameters. Transact-SQL supports passing parameters by position and by name.

We have described how batches and stored procedures are parsed, compiled, and executed in Microsoft SQL Server. This process is similar to compilation in standard programming languages. The end result is an execution plan that is cached in the procedure cache in the hope that somebody else will need it, that it will be reused, and that there will not be a need to parse and compile it again.

Sometimes developers want to force compilation of a stored procedure. It is possible to force compilation during the creation of a stored procedure, during the execution of a stored procedure, or as needed (for example, when a new index is added to a table).

Stored procedures are saved in system tables (sysobjects and syscomments) to allow SQL Server to manipulate them and to preserve them during shutdowns or when they are removed from the procedure cache.

A developer can decide to protect his or her intellectual property and use encryption to hide a stored procedure's source code. Nobody (not even the system administrator) will be able to access this code, but SQL Server will have no problem with it, even during upgrades.

The use of Transact-SQL statements for manipulation of stored procedures and other database objects might seem outdated compared to the ease of use provided by Enterprise Manager. Unfortunately, Enterprise Manager does not provide all the functionality of Transact-SQL, and in some cases, due to errors or environmental considerations, you will not be able to use it. You do not have to use Transact-SQL statements in your everyday work, but you have to be familiar with them to be able to use them when you have to. You should try to go through a complete development cycle using both Enterprise Manager and Query Analyzer.

There is no need to learn details like the syntax of each stored procedure or statement, but you have to know that there is a stored procedure that can perform the function that you need performed, and that you will be able to find it in SQL Server Books Online.

# EXERCISES

1.  Create a stored procedure called prUpdateStatus to update the status field of a specified record in the Inventory table.

2.  Create a stored procedure called prListProperies to return a list of properties and their values for a specified Inventory item.

3.  Create a stored procedure to return a LeaseScheduleId for a specified asset.

4.  Create a stored procedure prTest_QA with a simple Select statement inside. Using just Query Analyzer, verify that it exists in the current database.

5.  Using just Query Analyzer, obtain the code of prTest_QA.

6.  Using just Query Analyzer, view dependencies of prTest_QA.

7.  Using just Query Analyzer, rename prTest_QA to sp_Test_QA.

8.  Using just Query Analyzer, delete sp_Test_QA.

# CHAPTER 4

# Basic Transact-SQL Programming Constructs

All modern relational database management systems are based on an implementation of SQL (Structured Query Language). Actually, all vendors have extended SQL into a more or less sophisticated programming language. The ANSI committee has standardized the language several times. ANSI SQL-92 is the latest incarnation. Unfortunately (or luckily—depending on your point of view), each vendor has created its own modification of this standard to extend ANSI SQL.

The language in use in Microsoft SQL Server is called Transact-SQL (TSQL). It complies with the Entry Level ANSI SQL-92 standard, and users and developers can use standard relational statements to select, update, insert, and delete records from tables.

## TSQL IDENTIFIERS

All databases, servers, and database objects in SQL Server (such as tables, constraints, stored procedures, views, columns, and datatypes) can have unique names or *identifiers*. They are usually assigned when an object is created and used from that moment on to identify the object. The identifier for the object may, if needed, be changed.

There is a set of rules for creating identifiers:

▼ Identifiers in SQL Server 2000 and SQL Server 7.0 may have between 1 and 128 characters. There are exceptions to this rule. Certain objects are limited (for instance, temporary tables can have identifiers up to only 116 characters long). Before Microsoft SQL Server 7.0, identifiers were limited to 30 characters.

■ The first character of the identifier must be a letter, underscore (_), "at" sign (@), or number sign (#). The first letter must be defined in the Unicode 2.0 standard. Among other letters, Latin letters a–z and A–Z can be used as a first character. Some characters (@ and #) have special meanings in TSQL. They act as signals to SQL Server to treat their carriers differently.

- The following characters must be letters from the Unicode 2.0 standard, or decimal digits, or one of the special characters @, #, _, or $.

- Identifiers should not match any of the Microsoft SQL Server reserved words, shown in Table 4-1.

- Identifiers cannot contain spaces or other special characters aside from @, #, _, or $.

▲ If the identifier does not comply with one of the previous rules, it must be referred to as a *delimited identifier,* and enclosed with double quotes (" ") or square brackets ([ ]), but only if the QUOTED_IDENTIFIER option is set to ON. If the QUOTED_IDENTIFIER option is set to OFF, the role of single and double quotes is reversed. Single quotes delimit identifiers, and double quotes delimit strings.

| | | | |
|---|---|---|---|
| ADD | BY | CONTAINSTABLE | DECLARE |
| ALL | CASCADE | CONTINUE | DEFAULT |
| ALTER | CASE | CONVERT | DELETE |
| AND | CHECK | CREATE | DENY |
| ANY | CHECKPOINT | CROSS | DESC |
| AS | CLOSE | CURRENT | DISK |
| ASC | CLUSTERED | CURRENT_DATE | DISTINCT |
| AUTHORIZATION | COALESCE | CURRENT_TIME | DISTRIBUTED |
| BACKUP | COLLATE | CURRENT_TIMESTAMP | DOUBLE |
| BEGIN | COLUMN | CURRENT_USER | DROP |
| BETWEEN | COMMIT | CURSOR | DUMMY |
| BREAK | COMPUTE | DATABASE | DUMP |
| BROWSE | CONSTRAINT | DBCC | ELSE |
| BULK | CONTAINS | DEALLOCATE | END |

**Table 4-1.**    Reserved Keywords

| | | | |
|---|---|---|---|
| ERRLVL | INTERSECT | PERCENT | SOME |
| ESCAPE | INTO | PLAN | STATISTICS |
| EXCEPT | IS | PRECISION | SYSTEM_USER |
| EXEC | JOIN | PRIMARY | TABLE |
| EXECUTE | KEY | PRINT | TEXTSIZE |
| EXISTS | KILL | PROC | THEN |
| EXIT | LEFT | PROCEDURE | TO |
| FETCH | LIKE | PUBLIC | TOP |
| FILE | LINENO | RAISERROR | TRAN |
| FILLFACTOR | LOAD | READ | TRANSACTION |
| FOR | NATIONAL | READTEXT | TRIGGER |
| FOREIGN | NOCHECK | RECONFIGURE | TRUNCATE |
| FREETEXT | NONCLUSTERED | REFERENCES | TSEQUAL |
| FREETEXTTABLE | NOT | REPLICATION | UNION |
| FROM | NULL | RESTORE | UNIQUE |
| FULL | NULLIF | RESTRICT | UPDATE |
| FUNCTION | OF | RETURN | UPDATETEXT |
| GOTO | OFF | REVOKE | USE |
| GRANT | OFFSETS | RIGHT | USER |
| GROUP | ON | ROLLBACK | VALUES |
| HAVING | OPEN | ROWCOUNT | VARYING |
| HOLDLOCK | OPENDATASOURCE | ROWGUIDCOL | VIEW |
| IDENTITY | OPENQUERY | RULE | WAITFOR |
| IDENTITY_INSERT | OPENROWSET | SAVE | WHEN |
| IDENTITYCOL | OPENXML | SCHEMA | WHERE |
| IF | OPTION | SELECT | WHILE |
| IN | OR | SESSION_USER | WITH |
| INDEX | ORDER | SET | WRITETEXT |
| INNER | OUTER | SETUSER | |
| INSERT | OVER | SHUTDOWN | |

**Table 4-1.** Reserved Keywords *(continued)*

As an interim migration aid, the designers of SQL Server have created an opportunity for users to run a database in four different compatibility modes (60, 65, 70, and 80), which correspond to different versions of the SQL Server (naturally, 80 corresponds to SQL Server 2000). The rules just cited are valid only if the server is running in the default 80 mode. If the server has been set to use either of the other modes, the rules are slightly different. You can find these differences easily in the SQL Server documentation. To set compatibility, use the system stored procedure sp_dbcmptlevel.

**TIP:** Users can check which identifiers are valid using the system stored procedure sp_validname.

**NOTE:** The designers of Microsoft SQL Server have assigned a special system datatype called *sysname* to control the length of identifiers.

The following are valid identifiers:

▼ Cost
■ Premium36
■ prCalcCost
■ idx_User
■ @Make
■ #Equipment
■ [First Name]
■ "Equipment ID"
■ [User]
▲ [User.Group]

**NOTE:** Although delimiters can be used to assign identifiers that are also keywords (such as GROUP) to objects, this practice is not recommended. You will save a substantial amount of time if you use regular identifiers.

# DATABASE OBJECT QUALIFIERS

The complete name of a database object consists of four identifiers concatenated in the following manner:

```
[[[server.] [database] .] [owner] .] database_object
```

Each of these identifiers must comply with the rules described in the previous section. Server, database, and owner are often referred to as *database object qualifiers.* The complete name of the object is often referred to as the *fully qualified name.* You do not have to use all qualifiers all of the time. *Server* and *database* are (naturally) the names of the server and the database in which the object is stored. When you are working in Query Analyzer, the objects you view exist in the current database of the server you are connected to. In such a case, you do not have to use the database name as part of the object name.

*Owner* is the name of the user that created the object. If the object was created by the user that created the database (or some other user that is a member of the *db_owner* fixed database role or *sysadmin* server role), SQL Server will record the owner as *dbo.* In other cases, SQL Server will assign the username of the creator as owner.

When you are accessing the object, if you do not specify the name of the owner, SQL Server will automatically try to find the object as though the current user owned it. If such an object does not exist, SQL Server will try to locate the object owned by the dbo.
For example, instead of typing

```
SQLBox.Asset.dbo.prInventoryList
```

when you are connected to the Asset database on the SQLBox server, you can use any of the following:

```
prInventoryList
dbo.prInventoryList
Asset.dbo.prInventoryList
Asset..prInventoryList
SQLBox.Asset..prInventoryList
SQLBox...prInventoryList
SQLBox..dbo.prInventoryList
```

**NOTE:** You can use periods to skip qualifiers in the middle.

# DATATYPES

*Datatypes* specify the type of information (such as number, string, picture, date) that can be stored in a column or a variable.

SQL Server had a very rich palette of available datatypes in earlier versions, but in version 7 Microsoft introduced some significant improvements. The highlight of these enhancements is the ability to store up to 8,000 characters in the varchar and char datatypes. The previous versions could handle only the standard 255 characters.

SQL Server 2000 also introduces three new datatypes: sql_variant for storing any type of data, bigint for storing eight-byte integers, and the table datatype, which can store a complete resultset.

## Groups of Datatypes

SQL Server recognizes more then two dozen *system-defined datatypes.* Apart from these datatypes, administrators are allowed to specify *user-defined datatypes* to fulfill specific needs.

The major families of system-defined datatypes are

▼ Character strings

■ Unicode character strings

■ Date and time

■ Approximate numeric

■ Exact numeric

■ Monetary

■ Binary

▲ Special

## Character Strings

Character datatypes are designed to store character strings. The three different character types vary in length and features:

▼ char

■ varchar

▲ text

The *char* datatype is used to store strings of fixed size. As noted earlier, the maximum size of this datatype is 8,000 characters, which is a significant increase over the previous 255-character limit. When a variable or a table column is assigned with a string that is shorter than its nominal size, it is padded with trailing spaces.

The *varchar* datatype stores strings of variable size. It can also be up to 8,000 characters long. When a variable or a table column is assigned with a string that is shorter than its nominal size, SQL Server does not add trailing spaces to it, but records it as is. In a table, varchar datatypes occupy two additional bytes in order to record the length of the string.

**NOTE:** Maintenance of this information requires some additional computation during I/O operation, but that time is usually countered by savings in the space required. A record using such columns will occupy less space, and more records will fit into a single page. Therefore, SQL Server will read more records when accessing data, and it is more likely that a single page contains the information that the user is looking for.

The *text* datatype is used to store huge amounts of information. One field can store up to 2GB ($2^{31}$ – 1 bytes) of information. Naturally, only a 16-byte pointer to this data is stored in the table. Therefore, additional processing overhead is involved with the use of text columns. There are special functions for processing text values.

The following command will create a table with three fields using different character string datatypes:

```
Create table Contacts(ContactId char(8),
                      Name varchar(50),
                      Note text)
```

Character constants are delimited from the rest of the Transact-SQL code with quotes. For example, the following statement will insert contact information:

```
insert into Contacts (ContactId, Name, Note)
values ('CO-92-81', 'Tom Jones', 'Tom@trigon.com')
```

## Unicode Character Strings

Microsoft SQL Server 7.0 has introduced three new character datatypes. They are equivalent to the char, varchar, and text datatypes and are called

▼  Nchar

■  Nvarchar

▲  Ntext

The main difference between these new datatypes and the older character datatypes is that the new datatypes can hold *Unicode characters,* which occupy two bytes per character. Therefore, the maximum string length that they can store is half that of the corresponding older datatypes.

The following statement will create a table with a couple of Unicode character fields:

```
Create table Contacts_2(ContactId Nchar(8),
                        Name Nvarchar(50),
                        Note Ntext)
go
```

Unicode character constants are also delimited with quotes but are prefixed with 'N':

```
insert into Contacts_2 (ContactId, Name, Note)
values (N'CO-92-81', N'Tom Jones', N'Tom@trigonblue.com')
```

**TIP:**  This 'N' prefix might look a little odd, but you will get used to it. Microsoft documentation is full of samples with Unicode constants. It was some time before I discovered the reason Microsoft uses 'N' as a prefix. It stands for "National." In fact, acceptable alternative identifiers for these datatypes are `National char`, `National char varying`, and `National text`.

## Date and Time Datatypes

SQL Server supports two datatypes for storing date and time:

▼  `datetime`

▲  `smalldatetime`

The main difference between these two datatypes is in the amount of space they occupy. `datetime` occupies eight bytes and `smalldatetime` only four. The difference in size is due to a difference in precision. The precision of `smalldatetime` is one minute, and it covers dates from January 1, 1900, through June 6, 2079, which is usually more than enough. The precision of `datetime` is 3.33 ms, and it covers dates from January 1, 1753, to December 31, 9999.

Date and time constants are written in Transact-SQL with quote delimiters (as are character strings):

```
update Contacts_2
Set DateOfBirth = '2/21/1965 10:03 AM'
where ContactId = 'CO-92-81'
```

**TIP:**  SQL Server supports many different date and time formats. The convert function accepts a parameter that controls the format of date and time functions.

If time is not specified in a constant, SQL Server automatically assigns a default value—12:00 AM (midnight). You should keep in mind that SQL Server always records time as a part of these datatypes. Thus, if you want to select all contacts born on a particular day, you should *not* use something like this:

```
select *
from Contacts_2
where DateOfBirth = '2/21/1965'
```

This statement would extract records with DateOfBirth set to midnight of that day. Such a solution might be acceptable if all other applications recording values in the field also make the same mistake. A proper solution would be

```
select *
from Contacts
where DateOfBirth >= '2/21/1965' and DateOfBirth < '2/22/1965'
```

## Integer Numbers

Integer numbers are values without a decimal point. Traditionally, SQL Server supports one-, two-, and four-byte integers. SQL Server 2000 introduces an eight-byte integer. The *bit* datatype is used to store 1 or 0 to represent logical true and false values. This is the only datatype that cannot store NULL as a value.

| Datatype | Storage Size (bytes) | Minimum | Maximum |
|---|---|---|---|
| int | 4 | –2,147,483,648 (2G) | 2,147,483,647 (2G – 1) |
| smallint | 2 | –32768 (–32K) | 32767 (32K – 1) |
| tinyint | 1 | 0 | 255 ($2^8 - 1$) |
| bigint | 8 | –9,223,372,036,854,775,808 ($-2^{63}$) | 9,223,372,036,854,775,807 ($2^{63}-1$) |
| bit | 1 bit | 0 | 1 |

The great thing about the `int` datatypes is that they can store huge numbers in a small space. For this reason, they are often used for key values. If `int` is the primary key, a table can store up to four billion records.

**TIP:** We are still waiting for a computer that can handle four billion records. But lately, data warehousing systems are getting bigger and bigger, and there are some implementations of distributed databases that can use integers higher than two billion.

The following statement will create a table with a couple of integer fields:

```
CREATE TABLE Inventory_2 (
    InventoryId int,
    GTIN bigint ,
    LocationId smallint ,
    StatusId tinyint ,
    AcquisitionTypeID tinyint,
    Operational bit)
```

Naturally, integer constants do not need delimiters:

```
update Inventory_2
Set StatusId = 3,
    Operational = 0
Where InventoryId = 3432
```

## Approximate Numbers

Decimal numbers are often stored in `real` and `float` datatypes, also known as *single* and *double precision.* Their advantage is that they do not occupy much space but can hold large ranges of numbers. The only trouble is that they are not exact.

The precision of `real` numbers is up to 7 digits, and the precision of `float` numbers is up to 15 digits. For this reason, they are ideal for science and engineering (where, for example, you may not care about a couple of meters when you are measuring the distance between the Earth and the Moon), but they are not adequate for the financial industry (where a company budget has to be exact to the last cent).

To record the number 234,000,000,000 in mathematics, you can use $234 \times 10^9$, and in Transact-SQL you can use 234E9. This technique is known as *scientific notation*. The number after E is called the *exponent*, and the number before E is called the *mantissa*. This notation can be used to store small constants, too. In mathematics, 0.000000000234 can be written as $0.234 \times 10^{-9}$ or in Transact-SQL as 0.234E-9.

SQL Server uses the IEEE 754 standard to store these numbers. When a `float` or `real` variable or column is assigned a number, SQL Server first converts the decimal number to its binary representation. This conversion is the reason these values are very close, but only approximately equal to the decimal version. This is why they are referred to as *approximate numbers*. Therefore, you should not rely on the equivalence of two such numbers. You should limit their use in Where clauses to < and > operators and avoid the use of the = operator.

```
Create table Patient (PatientId int,
                      FullName varchar(30),
                      Weight real,
                      Height real,
                      ADP smallint,
                      BDZ tinyint)
go
```

Naturally, delimiters are not needed with `float` and `real` constants:

```
insert into Patient (PatientId, FullName, Weight, Height, ADP, BDZ)
values (834021, 'Tom Jones', 89.5, 188.5, 450, 11)
```

## Exact Numbers

The `decimal` or `numeric` datatype does not lose digits when storing numbers. Unfortunately, it requires much more space than the `real` and `float` datatypes. When a `decimal` column or a variable is defined, the developer has to specify its scale and precision.

*Precision* is the number of digits in the number, and *scale* is the number of digits behind the decimal point. For example, the number 123456.789 has a precision of 9 and a scale of 3.

SQL Server can store `decimal` numbers with a maximum precision of 38. Naturally, scale is related to precision and can be less than or equal to precision.

```
Create table Patient (PatientId int,
                      FullName varchar(30),
                      Weight decimal(5,2),
                      Height decimal(5,2),
                      ADP smallint,
                      BDZ tinyint)
go
```

`Decimal` constants do not need delimiters either:

```
insert into Patient (PatientId, FullName, Weight, Height, ADP, BDZ)
values (834021, 'Tom Jones', 89.5, 188.5, 450, 11)
```

## Monetary Datatypes

The `money` and `smallmoney` datatypes are a compromise between the precision of `decimal` numbers and the small size of `real` numbers. `Smallmoney` occupies four bytes and uses the same internal structure as do `int` numbers. The last four digits are treated as digits behind the decimal point. For this reason, they can store numbers ranging from –214,768.3648 to 214,768.3647. The `money` datatype uses the same structure for storing information as the `bigint` datatype. It occupies eight bytes for storage, so its values must be range from –922,337,203,685,477.5808 to +922,337,203,685,477.5807:

```
CREATE TABLE Inventory_2 (
    Inventoryid bigint,
    EquipmentId int ,
    LocationId smallint ,
    StatusId tinyint ,
    AcquisitionTypeID tinyint,
    Rent smallmoney,
    LeaseCost smallmoney)
go
```

Monetary constants can be preceded by $ or one of 17 other currency symbols (you can see them listed in SQL Server Books Online):

```
update Inventory_2
Set Rent = $0,
LeaseCost = $119.95
Where InventoryId = 3432
```

## *Binary* Datatypes

binary datatypes are used to store strings of bits. SQL Server supports three basic binary datatypes, the attributes of which are similar to character datatypes:

▼ binary

■ varbinary

▲ image

binary and varbinary datatypes can store up to 8,000 bytes of information, and image can store up to 2GB of data:

```
CREATE TABLE MyTable (
    Id int,
    BinData varbinary(8000),
    Diagram image)
go
```

binary constants are written as hexadecimal representations of bit strings and prefixed with "0x" (zero and x):

```
Update MyTable
Set BinData = 0x82A7210B
where Id = 121131
```

**TIP:**   I doubt that you will often use binary datatypes. The image datatype is sometimes used to store binary files such as pictures, documents, or sound files, but these are not generally the types of information that should be kept in a relational database as opposed to a file system. It is recommended that you store just the path to those files in a database table.

## The *Timestamp* Datatype

The timestamp is a datatype not designed to store date or time information, but a binary value that serves as a version number of the record. It is used to implement optimistic locking. You can find more details about this subject in Chapter 10. Only one field in a table can be defined as the timestamp value. It occupies eight bytes.

## The *Uniqueidentifier* Datatype

The uniqueidentifier datatype stores 16-byte binary values. These values are often called *Global Unique Identification numbers* (GUID). When a system generates a new GUID value, it is guaranteed that the same value cannot be produced again, neither on the same computer nor on any other computer in the world. GUIDs are generated using the identification number of the network card and a unique number obtained from the computer's clock. Manufacturers of network cards guarantee that the identification number of a network card will not be repeated in the next 100 years.

A uniqueidentifier constant is usually presented as

▼ **character string**   '{BB7DF450-F119-11CD-8465-00AA00425D90}'

▲ **binary constant**   0xaf16a66f7f8b31d3b41d30c04fc96f46

However, you will rarely type such values. In Transact-SQL, GUIDs should be generated using the NEWID function. There is also an API function that can produce a GUID value.

## The *Variant* Datatype

The sql_variant datatype is based on the same idea as the variant datatype in Visual Basic. It is designed to allow a single variable, column, or parameter to store values in different datatypes. Internally, variant objects record two values:

▼ The actual value

▲ The metadata describing the variant: base datatype, maximum size, scale, precision, and collation

The following statement creates a lookup table that can store values of different types:

```
Create table Lookup(
    LookupGroupId tinyint,
    LookupId smallint,
    LookupValue sql_variant)
Go
```

Before SQL Server 2000, I had to use more than one field to store lookup values of different datatypes.

The following statements illustrate how you can insert different types of values in one column:

```
Insert Lookup (LookupGroupId, LookupId, LookupValue)
Values (2, 34, 'VAR')
Insert Lookup (LookupGroupId, LookupId, LookupValue)
Values (3, 22, 2000)
Insert Lookup (LookupGroupId, LookupId, LookupValue)
Values (4, 16, '1/12/2000')
Insert Lookup (LookupGroupId, LookupId, LookupValue)
Values (4, 11, $50000)
```

A sql_variant object can store values of any datatype *except:*

▼ text

■ ntext

■ image

■ timestamp

▲ sql_variant

But there are more serious restrictions on their use:

▼ sql_variant columns *cannot* be part of *primary* or *foreign keys.*

■ sql_variant columns *can* be used in *indexes* and *unique keys* as long as their values are shorter than 900 bytes.

■ sql_variant columns *cannot* have an identity property.

- sql_variant columns *cannot* be part of a computed column.

- Developers *must use functions for converting datatypes* when assigning values from sql_variant objects to objects of other datatypes.

- The comparison of sql_variant objects has complex rules and is prone to errors.

- sql_variant values are automatically converted to nvarchar(4000) when accessed from client applications using OLE DB Provider for SQL Server 7.0 or the SQL Server ODBC Driver from SQL Server version 7.0. If stored values are longer then 4,000 characters, SQL Server will return just the first 4,000 characters.

- sql_variant values are automatically converted to varchar(255) when accessed from client applications using the SQL Server ODBC Driver from SQL Server version 6.5 or earlier, or using DB-Library. If stored values are longer then 255 characters, SQL Server will return just the first 255 characters.

- sql_variant columns are not supported in the Like predicate.

- sql_variant columns do not support full-text indexes.

- sql_variant objects cannot be concatenated using the '+' operator, even if the stored values are strings or numeric. The proper solution is to convert values before concatenation.

▲ Some functions (AVG, IDENTITY, ISNUMERIC, POWER, RADIANS, ROUND, SIGN, STDEV[P], SUM, VAR[P]) do not support sql_variant parameters.

*TIP:* You should be very conservative in using the sql_variant datatype. Its use has serious performance and design implications.

### The *Cursor* Datatype

This is a special kind of datatype that can contain references to cursors. You will see later in this chapter that cursors are programming constructs that are designed to allow operations on records one at a time. It is not possible to define a column of this type. It can be used only for variables and stored procedure output values.

### The *Table* Datatype

The table datatype is used to store a recordset for later processing. In some ways, this datatype is similar to a temporary table. It was introduced in SQL Server 2000. You cannot use this type to define a column. It can only be used as a *local variable* to *return the value of a function.*

> **NOTE:**   You will find more information about table variables later in this chapter, and information about functions in Chapters 5 and 9.

## Datatype Synonyms

In some cases, developers can use different identifiers to refer to a datatype. For example, the char datatype can be referenced as character and varchar as character varying. Some of these synonyms are based on ANSI SQL-92 standard requirements.

> **NOTE:**   Appendix A contains a table with a list of datatypes and their descriptions, ranges, sizes, and sample constants.

## User-Defined Datatypes

The user can define custom datatypes in the database. These new types are based on system-defined datatypes and are accessible only in the database in which they are defined. You can define them from the user interface or using a stored procedure as illustrated here:

```
Exec sp_addtype Phone, varchar(20), 'NOT NULL'
Exec sp_addtype typPostalCode, varchar(7), 'NULL'     -- in Canada
```

The first parameter is the name of the new datatype, the second one is the system-defined datatype that it represents, and the third one defines null-ability of the datatype. When the command is executed, the server will add the type to the *systype* table of the current database. New types can be based on any system-defined type except `timestamp`.

**TIP:** A fascinating aspect of user-defined datatypes is that you can change them in one step across the database. This feature is very useful during the development stage of a database. During production, tables contain data and it is not possible to run a script and create them all from scratch.

**NOTE:** The designers of Microsoft SQL Server have included one special datatype with the server—*sysname.* It is used to control the length of Transact-SQL identifiers. When the server is working in default mode, the length of this type is set to 128 characters. When the compatibility level is set to 65 or 60, the length is shortened to 30 characters.

# VARIABLES

Variables in Transact-SQL are the equivalent of variables in other programming languages, but due to the nature of Transact-SQL language, their use and behavior are somewhat different.
There are two types of variables in Transact-SQL:

▼ Local variables

▲ Global variables

# Local Variables

The major difference between the two types of variables is their scope. The scope of local variables is batch. This restriction implicitly includes a single stored procedure. It is a significant limitation. However, several workarounds can be used as solutions to this problem.

A stored procedure cannot access variables defined in other stored procedures. One way to pass values to and from stored procedures is to use parameters. Keep in mind that you are passing only the values associated with the variables, not references as you can in some other programming languages.

Another way to transfer value between stored procedures or between batches is the use of more permanent database objects such as tables or temporary tables.

Let's review basic operations with local variables.

## Declaring Variables

Before you can do anything with a local variable, you need to declare it. Declaration consists of the reserved word `Declare` and a list of variables followed by a datatype.

The names of variables must comply with the rules for identifiers. Limitations include the following:

▼  The name of the variable must begin with the "at" sign (@).

▲  The second character must not be an "at" sign (@). It can be any other character allowed for identifiers:

```
Declare @LastName varchar(50)
```

It is possible to define several variables in a single `Declare` statement. You just need to separate them with commas:

```
Declare    @LastName varchar(50),
           @FirstName varchar(30),
           @BirthDate smalldatetime
```

You can also define variables based on user-defined datatypes:

```
Declare @OfficePhone phone
```

**NOTE:**  You cannot define the null-ability of the variable, as you can with table columns. This does not mean that variables cannot contain null values. In fact, before assignment, the value of each variable is null. It is also possible to explicitly set the value of each variable to null.

## Assigning Values with the *Select* Statement

There are several ways to assign a value to a local variable. Before SQL Server 7.0, the only way to do this was to use a modification of the `Select` statement:

```
Select @LastName = 'Smith'
```

It is also possible to assign several variables in the same statement:

```
Select    @LastName = 'Smith',
          @FirstName = 'David',
          @BirthDate = '2/21/1965'
```

**NOTE:**  It is necessary to assign a value of an appropriate datatype to the variable; however, there are some workarounds. In some cases, the server will perform an implicit conversion from one datatype to another. SQL Server includes a set of functions for this purpose. CONVERT and CAST can be used to change the datatype of the value (see Chapter 5).

Quite often, variables are assigned values from the resultset of the `Select` statement:

```
Select    @Make = Equipment.make,
          @Model = Equipment.Model,
          @EqType = Equipment.EqType
From EqType INNER JOIN Equipment
    ON EqType.EqTypeId = Equipment.EqTypeId
Where EquipmentId = 2
```

There are some potential problems associated with this approach. The question is: How will the server assign values if the resultset contains multiple records, or no records?

If more than one record is returned in the resultset, a variable will be assigned the values from the *last* record. The only trouble is that we cannot predict which record will be the last because this position depends on the index that the server uses to create the resultset.

It is possible to create workarounds to exploit these facts (that is, to use hints to specify an index or use minimum and/or maximum functions to assign extreme values). The recommended solution, however, is to narrow the search criteria so that only one record is returned.

The other behavior that might cause unexpected results is the case in which a resultset does not return any records. It is a common belief and expectation of many developers that the variable will be set to null. This is absolutely incorrect. The content of the variable *will not be changed* in this case.

Observe the following example, or try to run it against the Asset database:

```
Declare    @make varchar(50),
           @model varchar(50),
           @EqType varchar(50)


Select     @Make = 'ACME',
           @Model = 'Turbo',
           @EqType = 'cabadaster'


Select     @Make = make,
           @Model = Model,
           @EqType = EqType.EqType
From EqType INNER JOIN Equipment
    ON EqType.EqTypeId = Equipment.EqTypeId
Where EquipmentId = -1

Select @make make, @model model, @EqType EqType
```

Since the Equipment table does not have a record with the identifier set to –1, the variables will keep their original value. Only if the values of the variables were not previously set will they continue to contain a null value.

The variable can be assigned with any Transact-SQL expression such as a constant, or a calculation, or even a complete Select statement that returns a single value:

```
Select     @Make = make,
           @Model = Model,
           @EquipmentName = Make + ' ' + Model,
           @EqType = (select EqType
                      from EqType
                      where EqTypeId = Equipment.EqTypeId)
From Equipment
Where EquipmentId = 2
```

There is one combination of statements and expressions that will result in a syntax error. It is not possible to return a resultset from the Select statement and to assign a variable in the same Select statement:

```
Select     make,
           @Model = Model
From Equipment
Where EquipmentId = 2
```

## Displaying the Values of Variables

The value of a variable can be displayed to the user using a Select or a Print statement:

```
Select @LastName
Print @FirstName
```

It is possible to include a local variable in a resultset that will be returned to the user:

```
Select     make "Selected make",
           Model "Selected Model",
```

```
        @Model "Original model"
From Equipment
Where EquipmentId = 2
```

## Assigning Values with the *Set* Statement

In SQL Server 2000 and SQL Server 7.0, the syntax of the Set statement has been expanded to support the assignment of local variables. In earlier versions, it was possible to use the Set statement only to declare cursor variables. Today, Microsoft is proclaiming this as a preferred method for assigning variables:

```
Set @LastName = 'Johnson'
```

There is just one problem with the Set statement—it is not possible to assign several values with one statement. You will be forced to write code like this:

```
Set        @Make = 'ACME'
Set        @Model = 'Turbo'
Set        @EqType = 'cabadaster'
```

## Assigning Values in the *Update* Statement

The ability to set the values of local variables in an Update statement is a feature that is buried deep in the oceans of SQL Server Books Online. It is an element that was designed to solve concurrency issues when code needs to read and update a column concurrently.

```
Update Inventory
Set @mnsCost = Cost = Cost * @fltTaxRate
Where InventoryId = @intInventoryId
```

# Global Variables

Global variables constitute a special type of variable. The server maintains the values in these variables. They carry information specific to the server or a current user session. They can be examined from anywhere, whether from a stored procedure or a batch. In the

SQL Server 7.0 and SQL Server 2000 documentation, Microsoft refers to them as *scalar functions,* meaning that they return just one value. Since you can still find references to global variables in some documentation, and since we would like to use some of them in this chapter, we will review them both here and in the next chapter, which is dedicated to functions.

Global variable names begin with an "@@" prefix. You do not need to declare them, since the server constantly maintains them.

Let's review the principal global variables.

## @@identity

This is a function or global variable that you will use frequently. It is also a feature that generates many of the questions on Usenet newsgroups.

One column in each table can be defined as the `identity` column, and the server will automatically generate a unique value in it. This is a standard technique in Microsoft SQL Server for generating *surrogate keys* (keys whose values are just numbers and do not carry any information). Usually, such columns will be set to assign sequential numbers:

```
Create table Eq (EqId int identity(1,1),
                 Make varchar(50),
                 Model varchar(50),
                 EqTypeId int)
```

The `@@identity` global variable will allow the user to find out which value was generated by the server. It is important to read the value as soon as possible (that is, in the next Transact-SQL statement). Otherwise, it might happen that you initiate, for example, another stored procedure or a trigger that inserts a record to a different table with an identity column. In such a case, SQL Server overwrites the number stored in `@@identity` with the new value. In the following example, a record will be inserted and a new identifier will immediately be read:

```
Declare @intEqId int
Insert into Eq(Make, Model, EqTypeId)
Values ('ACME', 'Turbo', 2)
Select @intEqId = @@identity
```

If one Transact-SQL statement inserts several records into a table with an identity column, @@identity will be set to the value from the last record:

```
Declare @intEqId int
Insert into Equipment(Make, Model, EqTypeId)
    Select Make, Model, EqTypeID
    From NewEquipment
Select @intEqId = @@identity
```

You will use this function very often. One of the most common types of stored procedures that you will write will just insert a record and return its new key to the caller.

### @@error

After each Transact-SQL statement, the server sets the value of this variable to an integer value:

▼ 0—if the statement was successful

▲ Error number—if the statement has failed

This global variable is the foundation of all methods for error handling in the Microsoft SQL Server environment. It is essential to examine the value of this variable before any other Transact-SQL statement is completed because the value of the @@error will be reset. Even if the statement is only a simple Select statement, the value of the @@error variable will be changed after it. In the following example, let's assume that an error will occur during the Update statement. @@error will contain the error code only until the next statement is executed; even the command for reading the @@error value will reset it. If it was completed successfully, SQL Server will set @@error to 0. The only way to preserve the @@error value is to immediately read it and store it in a local variable. Then it can be used for error handling.

```
Update Equipment
Set EqTypeId = 3
Where EqTypeId = 2
Select @intErrorCode = @@error
```

If it is necessary to read more than one global variable immediately after a statement, all such variables should be included in a single `Select` statement:

```
Declare    @intEqId int,
           @intErrorCode int
Insert into Equipment(Make, Model, EqTypeId)
Values ('ACME', 'Turbo', 2)
Select     @intEqId = @@identity,
           @intErrorCode = @@Error
```

The `@@error` variable will be set to an error number only in the case of errors, not in the case of warnings. Supplementary information that the server posts regarding errors or warnings (that is, severity, state, and error messages) are not available inside a stored procedure or a batch. Only the error number is accessible from a stored procedure or a batch. Further components of error messages can be read only from the client application.

You will find more details about use of the `@@error` function in the section about error handling in Chapter 7.

## @@rowcount

After each Transact-SQL statement, the server sets the value of this variable to the total number of records affected by it. It can be used to verify the success of selected operations.

```
select Make, Model, EqTypeid
into OldEquipment
from Equipment
where EqTypeid = 2

if @@rowcount = 0
    Print "No rows were copied!"
```

**NOTE:** Certain statements (like the `if` statement) will set `@@arowcount` to 0, and certain statements (like `Declare`) will not affect it.

ROWCOUNT_BIG is a function introduced in SQL Server 2000. It returns the number of affected records in the form of a `bigint` number.

**TIP:** When you try to update an individual record, SQL Server will not report an error if your `Where` clause specifies a criterion that does not qualify any (or qualifies too many) records. SQL Server will not update anything, and you might, for example, think that the operation was successful. You can use @ @`rowcount` to identify such cases.

## *Table* Variables

SQL Server 2000 introduces the `table` datatype. A statement declaring a `table` variable initializes the variable as an empty table with a specified structure. As a table definition, such a statement includes definitions of columns with their datatype, size, precision, optional primary key, unique and check constraints, and indexes. All elements have to be defined during the declaration. It is not possible to alter or add them later.

The following batch declares a `table` variable, inserts rows in it, and returns them to the user:

```
Declare @MyTableVar table
    (Id int primary key,
    Lookup varchar(15))

Insert @MyTableVar values (1, '1Q2000')
Insert @MyTableVar values (2, '2Q2000')
Insert @MyTableVar values (3, '3Q2000')

Select * from @MyTableVar
Go
```

Because of their nature, `table` variables have certain limitations:

▼ Table variables can only be part of the `Select`, `Update`, `Delete`, `Insert`, and `Declare Cursor` statements.

■ Table variables can be used as a part of the `Select` statement everywhere tables are acceptable, except as the destination in a `Select...Into` statement:

```
Select LookupId, Lookup
Into @TableVariable        -- wrong
From Lookup
```

■ Table variables can be used in `Insert` statements except when the `Insert` statement collects values from a stored procedure:

```
Insert into @TableVariable     -- wrong
    Exec prMyProcedure
```

■ Unlike temporary tables, `table` variables always have a *local scope*. They can be used only in the batch, stored procedure, or function in which they are declared.

■ The scope of cursors based on `table` variables is limited to the scope of the variable (the batch, stored procedure, or function in which they are defined).

▲ Table variables are considered to be nonpersistent objects, and therefore they will not be rolled back after a `Rollback Transaction` statement.

# FLOW CONTROL STATEMENTS

Flow control statements from TSQL are rather rudimentary as compared with similar commands in other modern programming languages such as Visual Basic or C++. Their use requires knowledge and some skill to overcome their lack of user friendliness. However, on a positive note, they allow the creation of very complex procedures.

This section covers the use of the following Transact-SQL statements and programming constructs:

▼   Comments

■   Statement block

■   If

■   While

■   Break

■   Continue

■   GoTo

▲   WaitFor

# Comments

Developers can mark comments inside the source code of a batch or a stored procedure so that they are ignored during compilation and execution by SQL Server. It is a common practice to accompany source code with remarks that will help readers to understand the programmer's intentions.

Comments can also be a piece of Transact-SQL source code that the developer does not want to execute for a particular reason (usually while developing or debugging). Such a process is usually referred to as *commenting out* the code.

## Single-Line Comments

There are two methods to indicate a comment. A complete line or part of the line can be marked as a comment if the user places two hyphens (- -) at the beginning. The remainder of the line will become a comment. The comment will be finished at the end of line:

```
-- This is a comment. Whole line will be ignored.
```

You can place the comment in the middle of a Transact-SQL statement. In the following example we will comment-out the last column:

```
Select LeaseId, LeaseVendor --, LeaseNumber
From Lease
Where ContractDate > '1/1/1999'
```

This type of comment can be nested in another comment defined with the same or a different method:

```
-- select * from Equipment -- Just for debugging
```

This commenting method is compatible with the SQL-92 standard.

## Multi-Line Comments—/* ... */

The second commenting method is native to SQL Server. It is suitable for commenting out blocks of code that can span multiple lines. Such a comment must be divided from the rest of the code with a pair of delimiters: (/*) and (*/):

```
/*
This is a comment.
All these lines will be ignored.
*/


/* List all equipment. */
select * from Equipment
```

Comments do not have a length limit. It is best to write as much as is necessary to adequately document the code.

SQL Server documentation forbids the nesting of multi-line comments. In different versions and in different tools this may or may not generate a syntax error:

```
/* This is a comment.
/* Query Analyzer will understand the following delimiter
as the end of the first comment. */
    This will generate a syntax error in some cases. */
Select * from Equipment
```

If you type this code in Query Analyzer, the program will not color the last line of explanation as a comment. (I am not sure you will be able to see a difference on the paper.) However, during the execution in Query Analyzer, the third line of the comment is ignored and will return a resultset without reporting a syntax error (see Figure 4-1).

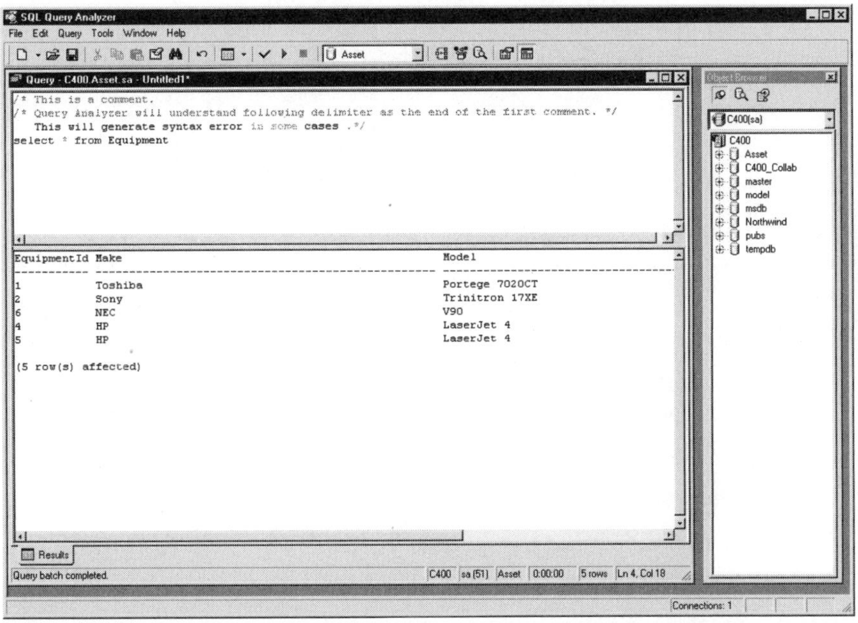

**Figure 4-1.**  Problems with comments

Single-line comments can be nested inside multi-line comments:

```
/*
-- List all equipment.
Select * from Equipment
*/
```

In Chapter 6, when we discuss batches, we will illustrate the requirement that multi-line comments not span two or more batches.

## Documenting Code

Again, your comments will be of benefit to other developers who may read your code, and they will be better still if you make their presence in the code as obvious as possible. It is a favorable, although

not required, practice to accompany comment delimiters with a full
line of stars, or to begin each commented line with two stars:

```
/******************************************************************
** File: prInsertEquipment.sql
** Name: prInsertEquipment
** Desc: Insert equipment and equipment type
**       (if not present).
**
** Return values: ErrorCode
**
** Called by:   middleware
**
** Parameters:
** Input                                   Output
** ----------                              -----------
** Make                                    EqId
** Model
** EqType
**
** Auth: Dejan Sunderic
** Date: 1/1/2000
*******************************************************************
** Change History
*******************************************************************
** Date:        Author:     Description:
** --------     --------    ------------------------------------
** 11/1/2000    DS          Fixed:49. Better error handling.
** 11/2/2000    DS          Fixed:36. Optimized for performance.
*******************************************************************/
```

Inserting two stars at the beginning of each line serves two purposes:

▼ They are a visual guide for your eye. If you comment out code
this way, you will not be in doubt whether a piece of code is
functional or commented out.

▲ They will force SQL Server to report a syntax error if
somebody makes an error (for example by nesting comments
or by spanning comments over multiple batches).

The preceding example is based on part of a SQL script for creating a stored procedure generated by Visual InterDev. It is very useful to keep track of all these items explicitly, especially Description and Change History. It is a personal choice to be more elaborate in describing stored procedures, but if you are, your comments can be used as instant design documentation.

Occasionally, developers believe that this type of header is sufficient code documentation, but you should consider commenting your code throughout. It is important to comment not *how* things are being done, but *what* is being done. We recommend that you write your comments to describe what a piece of code is attempting to accomplish, then write the code itself. In this way, you create design documentation that eventually becomes code documentation.

# Statement Blocks—*Begin ... End*

The developer can group several Transact-SQL statements by using Begin ... End statements in a logical unit. Such units are then typically used in flow-control statements to execute a group of Transact-SQL statements together. Flow-control statements like If, Case, and While can incorporate a single statement or a statement block to be executed when certain conditions are met.

```
Begin
      Transact-SQL statements
End
```

There must be one or more Transact-SQL statements inside a block. If there is only one statement inside, you could remove the Begin and End keywords. Begin and End must be used as a pair. Alone, they are meaningless. If a compiler does not find a matching pair, it will report a syntax error.

Begin and End can also be nested, but this practice is prone to errors. However, if you are cautious and orderly, there should not be a problem. An excellent way to avoid such problems is to indent the code:

```
Begin

    Insert Order(OrderDate, RequestedById,
                 TargetDate, DestinationLocation)
    Values(@OrderDate, @ContactId,
           @TargetDate, @LocId)

    Select    @ErrorCode = @@Error,
              @OrderId = @@Identity

    if @ErrorCode <> 0
    begin
        RaiseError('Error occurred while inserting Order!', 16,1)
        Return @@ErrorCode
    end
End
```

## Conditional Execution—the *If* Statement

The If statement is the most common flow control statement. It is used to examine the value of a condition and to change the flow of code based on the condition. First, let us review its syntax.

```
If boolean_expression
    {Transact-SQL_statement | statement_block}
[else
    {Transact-SQL_statement | statement_block}]
```

When the server encounters such a construct, it examines the value of the Boolean expression. If this value is True (1), it executes the statements or the statement block that follows it. The Else component of the statement is optional. It includes a single statement or a statement block that will be executed if the Boolean expression returns a value of False (0).

**NOTE:**   The most common mistake made by users of Visual Basic or other programming languages is to place a delimiter to finish the statement (i.e.,"endif"). Note also that the Boolean expression must not be followed by "then" (another VB artifact).

The following code sample tests the value of the @ErrorCode variable. If the variable does not contain a zero, the server inserts a record in the Order table and then records the value of the identity key and any error that may have occurred in the process.

```
If @ErrorCode <> 0
Begin
    Insert Order(OrderDate,  RequestedById,
            TargetDate, DestinationLocation)
    Values(@dtOrderDate,   @intContactId,
            @dtTargetDate, @intLocId)

    Select    @intErrorCode = @@Error,
              @intOrderId = @@Identity
End
```

Let us take a look at a more complex case. The following stored procedure will insert a record in the equipment table and return the ID of the record to the caller. Unfortunately, the user supplies the equipment type in text form. The stored procedure must then find out if such an equipment type exists in the database and insert it if it does not.

```
Create Procedure prInsertEquipment_1
-- store values in equipment table.
-- return identifier of the record to the caller.
    (
        @chvMake varchar(50),
        @chvModel varchar(50),
        @chvEqType varchar(30)
    )
As
declare    @intEqTypeId int,
           @intEquipmentId int

-- read Id of EqType
Select @intEqTypeId
From EqType
Where EqType = @chvEqType
```

```
-- does such eqType already exists in the database
If  @intEqTypeId IS NOT NULL
    --insert equipment
    Insert Equipment (Make, Model, EqTypeId)
    Values (@chvMake, @chvModel, @intEqTypeId)
Else
    --if it does not exist
    Begin
        -- insert new EqType in the database
        Insert EqType (EqType)
        Values (@chvEqType)

        -- get id of record that you've just inserted
        Select @intEqTypeId = @@identity

        --insert equipment
        Insert Equipment (Make, Model, EqTypeId)
        Values (@chvMake, @chvModel, @intEqTypeId)
    End
Select @intEquipmentId = @@identity


-- return id to the caller
return @intEquipmentId
```

There are a few items that could be changed in this stored procedure, but the importance of this example is to illustrate a use of the Else statement.

One item that could be improved upon is the process of investigating the EqType table with the Exists keyword. Its use here is similar to its use in the Where clause:

```
If [NOT] Exists(subquery)
    {Transact-SQL_statement | statement_block}
[else
    {Transact-SQL_statement | statement_block}]
```

Such a statement tests for the presence of the records in the subquery.

The stored procedure prInsertEquipment can be modified to use the `Exists` keyword:

```
. . .
If  Exists (Select EqTypeId From EqType Where EqType = @chvEqType)
. . .
```

Naturally, if you use the `Not` operator, the encapsulated statement will be executed if the subquery does not return records:

```
Alter Procedure prInsertEquipment_2
-- store values in equipment table.
-- return identifier of the record to the caller.
    (
        @chvMake varchar(50),
        @chvModel varchar(50),
        @chvEqType varchar(30)
    )
As
declare    @intEqTypeId int,
        @intEquipmentId int



-- does such eqType already exists in the database
If  Not Exists (Select EqTypeId From EqType Where EqType = @chvEqType)
    --if it does not exist
    Begin
        -- insert new EqType in the database
        Insert EqType (EqType)
        Values (@chvEqType)

        -- get id of record that you've just inserted
        Select @intEqTypeId = @@identity
    End
else
    -- read Id of EqType
    Select @intEqTypeId
    From EqType
    Where EqType = @chvEqType

--insert equipment
Insert Equipment (Make, Model, EqTypeId)
Values (@chvMake, @chvModel, @intEqTypeId)
```

```
Select @intEquipmentId = @@identity

-- return id to the caller
Return @intEquipmentId
```

If statements can be nested. In fact, both If and Else can be nested:

```
Create Procedure prInsertEquipment_3
-- store values in equipment table.
-- return identifier of the record to the caller.
    (
        @chvMake varchar(50),
        @chvModel varchar(50),
        @chvEqType varchar(30),
        @intEquipmentId int
    )
As
declare @intEqTypeId int,
        @ErrorCode int

-- does such eqType already exists in the database
If  Not Exists (Select EqTypeId From EqType Where EqType = @chvEqType)
    --if it does not exist
    Begin
        -- insert new EqType in the database
        Insert EqType (EqType)
        Values (@chvEqType)

        -- get id of record that you've just inserted
        Select @intEqTypeId = @@identity,
            @ErrorCode = @@Error
        If @ErrorCode <> 0
            begin
                Select 'Unable to insert Equipment Type. Error: ',
                    @ErrorCode
                Return 1
            End
    End
Else
    Begin
        -- read Id of EqType
```

```
            Select @intEqTypeId
            From EqType
            Where EqType = @chvEqType
            Select @ErrorCode = @@Error

            If @ErrorCode <> 0
               begin

                   Select 'Unable to get Id of Equipment Type. Error: ',
                          @ErrorCode
                       Return 2
               End
     End


--insert equipment
Insert Equipment (Make, Model, EqTypeId)
Values (@chvMake, @chvModel, @intEqTypeId)

Select @ErrorCode = @@Error
If @ErrorCode <> 0
    Begin
         Select 'Unable to insert Equipment. Error: ', @ErrorCode
         Return 3
    End

-- return id to the caller
Select @intEquipmentId = @@identity

Return 0
```

There is no limit to the number of levels. However, this capability should not be abused. The presence of too many levels is a sure sign that a more in-depth study should be made concerning code design.

# Looping—the *While* Statement

Transact-SQL contains only one statement that allows looping:

```
While Boolean_expression
    {sql_statement | statement_block}
    [Break]
```

```
{sql_statement | statement_block}
[Continue]
```

If the value of the Boolean expression is `True` (1), the server will execute one or more encapsulated Transact-SQL statement(s). From inside the block of statements, this execution can be controlled with the `Break` and `Continue` statements. The server will interrupt the looping when it encounters a `Break` statement. When the server encounters a `Continue` statement, it will ignore the rest of the statements and restart the loop.

> **NOTE:**   Keep in mind that loops are primarily tools for third-generation languages. In such languages, code was written to operate with records one at a time. Transact-SQL is a fourth-generation language and is written to operate with sets of information. It is possible to write code in Transact-SQL that will loop through records and perform operations on a single record, but you pay for this feature with severe performance penalties. However, there are cases when such an approach is necessary.

It is not easy to find bona fide examples to justify the use of loops in Transact-SQL. Let us investigate a stored procedure that calculates the factorial of an integer number:

```
Create Procedure prCalcFactorial
-- calculate factorial
-- 1! = 1
-- 3! = 3 * 2 * 1
-- n! = n * (n-1)* . . . 5 * 4 * 3 * 2 * 1
    @N tinyint,
    @F int OUTPUT
As

Set @F = 1

while @N > 1
begin
    set @F = @F * @N
    Set @N = @N - 1
end

return 0
```

Another example could be a stored procedure that returns a list of properties assigned to an asset in the form of a string:

```
Create Procedure GetInventoryProperties
/*
Return comma-delimited list of properties that are describing asset.
i.e.: Property = Value Unit;Property = Value Unit;Property = Value
 Unit;Property = Value Unit;Property = Value Unit;...
*/
    (
        @intInventoryId int,
        @chvProperties varchar(8000) OUTPUT
    )

As

declare @intCountProperties int,
        @intCounter int,
        @chvProperty varchar(50),
        @chvValue varchar(50),
        @chvUnit varchar(50)

Create table #Properties(
        Id int identity(1,1),
        Property varchar(50),
        Value varchar(50),
        Unit varchar(50))

-- identify Properties associated with asset
insert into #Properties (Property, Value, Unit)
    select Property, Value, Unit
    from InventoryProperty inner join Property
    on InventoryProperty.PropertyId = Property.PropertyId
    where InventoryProperty.InventoryId = @intInventoryId

-- set loop
select @intCountProperties = Count(*),
       @intCounter = 1,
       @chvProperties = ''
from #Properties

-- loop through list of properties
while @intCounter <= @intCountProperties
```

```
begin
    -- get one property
    select @chvProperty = Property,
        @chvValue = Value,
        @chvUnit = Unit
    from #Properties
    where Id = @intCounter

    -- assemble list

    set @chvProperties = @chvProperties + '; '
                    + @chvProperty + '='
                    + @chvValue + ' ' +  @chvUnit

    -- let's go another round and get another property
    set @intCounter = @intCounter + 1
end

drop table #Properties
return 0
```

## Unconditional Execution—the *GoTo* Statement

The GoTo statement forces the server to continue the execution from a *label*:

```
GoTo label
...
label:
```

The *label* has to be within the same stored procedure or batch. It is not important whether the *label* or the GoTo statement is defined first in the code. The *label* can even exist without the GoTo statement to which it is pointing. Naturally, the server will report an error if it encounters a GoTo statement that points to a nonexistent label.

The following stored procedure uses the GoTo statement to interrupt further processing and display a message to the user when an error occurs:

```
Create Procedure prCloseLease
-- Clear Rent, ScheduleId, and LeaseId on all assets associated
```

```
-- with specified lease.

    @intLeaseId int
As
    -- delete schedules
    Update Inventory
    Set Rent = 0,
        LeaseId = null,
        LeaseScheduleId = null
    Where LeaseId = @intLeaseId
    If @@Error <> 0 Goto PROBLEM


    -- delete schedules
    Delete from LeaseSchedule
    Where LeaseId = @intLeaseId
    If @@Error <> 0 Goto PROBLEM


    -- delete lease
    Delete from Lease
    Where LeaseId = @intLeaseId
    If @@Error <> 0      Goto PROBLEM
    Return 0


PROBLEM:
    Select 'Unable to remove lease from the database!'
Return 1
```

## To *GoTo* or Not to *GoTo*—That Is the Question

The use of the GoTo statement is a very controversial issue. For
example, if a language contains an If statement and a GoTo statement,
all other flow-control statements are optional. On the other hand,
extensive use of the GoTo statement leads to unmanageable code
often referred to as "spaghetti code" (see Figure 4-2).

A stigma became attached to the GoTo statement shortly after
Edsger Dijkstra published a paper entitled "Go To Statement
Considered Harmful" in *Communications of the ACM* in 1968.
He observed that the number of GoTo statements in a body
of code is inversely proportional to the quality of the code.

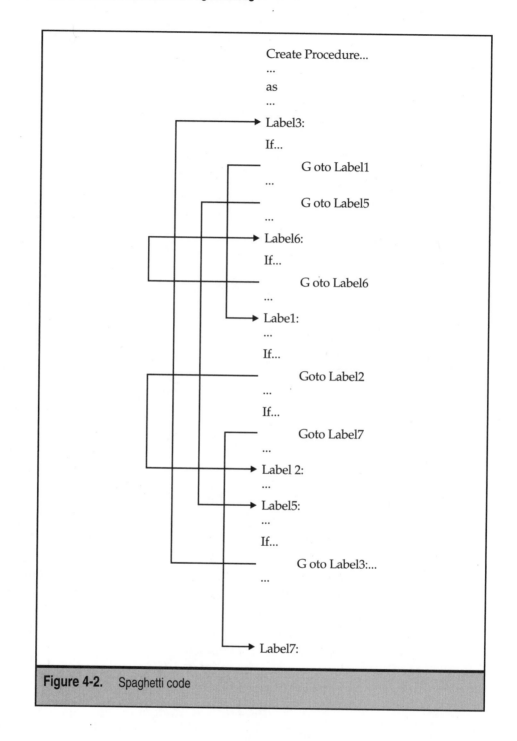

**Figure 4-2.** Spaghetti code

Intense discussions followed for many years and brought to light the following points:

▼ Code that does not contain a GoTo statement is easier to read and understand. Code that uses GoTo statements is also difficult to format in a manner that emphasizes its logical structure.

■ The use of GoTo statements sometimes leads the compiler to produce a slower and larger executable.

■ The use of GoTo statements tends to spread like termites. If their use is allowed in the environment, pretty soon they will appear both where they should and where they should not.

■ Code that does not contain GoTo statements is easier to debug and test.

▲ The use of GoTo statements contradicts the principles of structured programming.

The question is: Should the GoTo statement be used? In my opinion, the overuse of GoTo statements is more a symptom than a cause of low-quality code. In some cases, their use is justified, but the developer must be sure that such is the case and that it is not possible to produce a better solution using other programming constructs.

For example, the following loop can be implemented using GoTo, but I recommend that you use While instead:

```
Create Procedure prLoopWithGoTo
-- just an example how to implement loop using If and Goto
As
declare    @MaxCounter int,
           @Counter int

Select     @MaxCounter = Max(EquipmentId),
           @Counter = 1
from Equipment

LOOP:
if @Counter < @MaxCounter
begin
```

```
        -- some work
        Select @Counter -- this line is meaningless:
                         -- we need to do something to demonstrate loop

        set @Counter = @Counter + 1
        GoTo LOOP
  end
```

The point of this example is not merely to replace the GoTo statement in a mechanical manner. The point is that use of the While statement produces code that is much easier to read. Thus, replacing GoTo with While is a change for the better.

Some database administrators base their error-handling practices on the use of the GoTo statement. There is an example of this type of code in the stored procedure prCloseLease shown in the previous section. This solution is not a perfect one. You will see several other error-handling solutions in Chapter 7.

## Scheduled Execution—the *WaitFor* Statement

There are two ways to schedule the execution of a batch or stored procedure in SQL Server. One way is based on the use of *SQL Server Agent* (a tool formerly known as Task Scheduler). The other way is to use the WaitFor statement. The WaitFor statement allows the developer to specify the time when, or a time interval after which, the remaining Transact-SQL statements will be executed:

```
WaitFor {Delay 'time' | Time 'time'}
```

There are two variants to this statement. One specifies the delay (time interval) that must pass before the execution can continue. The time interval specified as a parameter of the statement must be less than 24 hours. In the following example, the server will pause for one minute before displaying the list of Equipment:

```
WaitFor Delay '00:01:00'
    Select * from Equipment
```

The other variant is more significant. It allows the developer to schedule a time when the execution is to continue. The following example runs a full database backup at 11:00 P.M.:

```
WaitFor Time '23:00'
    Backup Database Asset To Asset_bkp
```

There is one problem with this Transact-SQL statement. The connection remains blocked while the server waits to execute the statement. Therefore, it is much better to use SQL Server Agent than the `WaitFor` statement to schedule jobs.

# CURSORS

Relational databases are designed to work with sets of information (records). In fact, the purpose of the `Select` statement, as the most important statement in SQL, is to define a set of records. In contrast, end-user applications display information to the user record by record (or maybe in small batches). To close the gap between these conflicting requirements, RDBMS architects have invented a new class of programming constructs—*cursors*.

Many types of cursors are implemented in various environments using different syntax, but all cursors work in a similar fashion:

1. A cursor first has to be defined and its features have to be set.

2. The cursor must be populated.

3. The cursor then has to be positioned (*scrolled*) to a record or block of records that need to be retrieved (*fetched*).

4. Information from one or more current records is fetched, and then some modification can be performed or some action can be initiated based on the fetched information.

5. Optionally, steps 3 and 4 are repeated.

6. Finally, the cursor must be closed and resources released.

Cursors can be used on both server and client sides. SQL Server and the APIs for accessing database information (OLE DB, ODBC, DB-Library) all include sets of functions for processing cursors.

SQL Server supports three classes of cursors:

▼  Client cursors

■  API Server cursors

▲  Transact-SQL cursors

The major difference between Transact-SQL cursors and other types of cursors is their purpose. Transact-SQL cursors are used from stored procedures, batches, functions, or triggers to repeat custom processing for each row of the cursor. Other kinds of cursors are designed to access database information from the client application. We will review only Transact-SQL cursors.

## Transact-SQL Cursors

Processing in Transact-SQL cursors has to be performed in the following steps:

1.  Use the `Declare Cursor` statement to create the cursor based on the `Select` statement.

2.  Use the `Open` statement to populate the cursor.

3.  Use the `Fetch` statement to change the current record in the cursor and to store values into local variables.

4.  Do something with the retrieved information.

5.  If needed, repeat steps 3 and 4.

6.  `Close` the cursor. Most of the resources (memory, locks…) will be released.

7.  `Deallocate` the cursor.

**NOTE:** Transact-SQL cursors do not support processing blocks of records. Only one record can be fetched at a time.

It is best to show this process through an example. We will rewrite the stored procedure that we used to illustrate the use of the `While` statement. The purpose of this stored procedure is to collect the properties of a specified asset and return them in delimited format (Property = Value Unit;). The final result should look like this:

```
CPU=Pentium II;RAM=64 MB;HDD=6.4 GB;Resolution=1024x768;Weight=2 kg;
```

Here is the code for the new instance of the stored procedure:

```
Alter Procedure prGetInventoryProperties_Cursor
/*
Return comma-delimited list of properties that are describing asset.
Property = Value unit;Property = Value unit;Property = Value unit;
Property = Value unit;Property = Value unit;Property = Value unit;...
*/
    (
        @intInventoryId int,
        @chvProperties varchar(8000) OUTPUT,
        @debug int = 0
    )

As

declare    @intCountProperties int,
           @intCounter int,
           @chvProperty varchar(50),
           @chvValue varchar(50),
           @chvUnit varchar(50),
           @insLenProperty smallint,
           @insLenValue smallint,
           @insLenUnit smallint,
           @insLenProperties smallint

Set @chvProperties = ''

Declare @CrsrVar Cursor

Set @CrsrVar = Cursor For
    select Property, Value, Unit
    from InventoryProperty inner join Property
    on InventoryProperty.PropertyId = Property.PropertyId
    where InventoryProperty.InventoryId = @intInventoryId

Open @CrsrVar

Fetch Next From @CrsrVar
Into @chvProperty, @chvValue, @chvUnit

While (@@FETCH_STATUS = 0)
```

```
Begin

    Set @chvUnit = Coalesce(@chvUnit, '')

    If @debug <> 0
        Select @chvProperty Property,
               @chvValue [Value],
               @chvUnit [Unit]

    -- check will new string fit
    Select @insLenProperty = DATALENGTH(@chvProperty),
           @insLenValue = DATALENGTH(@chvValue),
           @insLenUnit = DATALENGTH(@chvUnit),
           @insLenProperties = DATALENGTH(@chvProperties)


    If @insLenProperties + 2 + @insLenProperty + 1 +
       @insLenValue + 1 + @insLenUnit > 8000
    Begin
        Select 'List of properties is too long (> 8000 char)!'
        Return 1
    End

    -- assemble list
    Set @chvProperties = @chvProperties + @chvProperty + '='
                       + @chvValue + ' ' +  @chvUnit + '; '
    If @debug <> 0
        Select @chvProperties chvProperties

    Fetch Next From @CrsrVar
    Into @chvProperty, @chvValue, @chvUnit

End

Close @CrsrVar
Deallocate @CrsrVar

Return 0
```

The stored procedure will first declare a cursor:

```
Declare @CrsrVar Cursor
```

The cursor will then be associated with the collection of Properties related to the specified asset:

```
Set @CrsrVar = Cursor For
    Select Property, Value, Unit
    From InventoryProperty inner join Property
    On InventoryProperty.PropertyId = Property.PropertyId
    Where InventoryProperty.InventoryId = @intInventoryId
```

Before it can be used, the cursor needs to be opened:

```
Open @CrsrVar
```

The content of the first record can then be fetched into local variables:

```
Fetch Next From @CrsrVar
Into @chvProperty, @chvValue, @chvUnit
```

If the fetch was successful, we can start a loop to process the complete recordset:

```
While (@@FETCH_STATUS = 0)
```

After the values from the first record are processed, we read the next record:

```
    Fetch Next From @CrsrVar
    Into @chvProperty, @chvValue, @chvUnit
```

Once all records have been read, the value of `@@fetch_status` is set to −1 and we exit the loop. We need to close and deallocate the cursor and finish the stored procedure.

```
Close @CrsrVar
Deallocate @CrsrVar
```

Now, let's save and execute this stored procedure:

```
Declare @chvRes varchar(8000)
Exec prGetInventoryProperties_Cursor 5, @chvRes OUTPUT
Select @chvRes Properties
```

SQL Server will return the following:

```
Properties
----------------------------------------------------------------------
---------------------------
CPU=Pentium II ; RAM=64 MB; HDD=6.4 GB; Resolution=1024x768 ; Weight
=2 kg; Clock=366 MHz;
```

# Cursor-Related Statements and Functions

Let's review statements and functions that you need to utilize to control cursors.

### The *Declare Cursor* Statement

This statement declares the Transact-SQL cursor and specifies its behavior and the query on which it is built. It is possible to use syntax based on the SQL-92 standard or native Transact-SQL syntax. We will display only the simplified syntax. If you need more details, refer to SQL Server Books Online.

```
Declare cursor_name Cursor
For select_statement
```

The name of the cursor is an identifier that complies with the rules set for local variables.

### The *Open* Statement

The Open statement executes the Select statement specified in the Declare Cursor statement and populates the cursor:

```
Open { { [Global] cursor_name } | cursor_variable_name}
```

### The *Fetch* Statement

The Fetch statement reads the row specified in the Transact-SQL cursor.

```
Fetch    [  [ Next | Prior | First | Last
                | Absolute {n | @nvar}
```

```
          | Relative {n | @nvar}
     ]
     From
]
{ { [Global] cursor_name } | @cursor_variable_name}
[Into @variable_name[,...n] ]
```

This statement can force the cursor to position the current record at the Next, Prior, First, or Last record. It is also possible to specify the Absolute position of the record or a position Relative to the current record.

If the developer specifies a list of global variables in the Into clause, those variables will be filled with values from the specified record.

If the cursor has just been opened, you can use Fetch Next to read the first record.

## @@fetch_status

@@fetch_status is a function (or global variable) that returns the success code of the last Fetch statement executed during the current connection. It is often used as an exit criterion in loops that fetch records from a cursor.

| Success Code | Description |
|---|---|
| 0 | Fetch was completely successful. |
| −1 | Fetch statement tried to read a record outside the recordset (last record was already read) or fetch statement failed. |
| −2 | Record is missing (for example, somebody else has deleted the record in the meantime). |

## @@cursor_rows

As soon as the cursor is opened, the @@cursor_rows function (or global variable) is set to the number of records in the cursor (you can use this variable to loop through the cursor also).

### The *Close* Statement

This statement closes an open cursor, releases the current recordset, and releases locks on rows held by the cursor:

```
Close { { [Global] cursor_name } | cursor_variable_name }
```

This statement must be executed on an opened cursor. If the cursor has just been declared, SQL Server will report an error.

### The *Deallocate* Statement

After the Close statement, the structure of the cursor is still in place. It is possible to open it again. If you do not plan to use it any more, you should remove the structure as well:

```
Deallocate { { [Global] cursor_name } | @cursor_variable_name}
```

## Problems with Cursors

Cursors are a valuable but dangerous tool. Their curse is precisely the problem they are designed to solve—the differences between the relational nature of database systems and the record-based nature of client applications.

First of all, cursors are procedural and thus contradict the basic idea behind the SQL language—that is, to define what is needed in a result, not how to get it.

Performance penalties are an even larger problem. Regular SQL statements are set-oriented and much faster. Some types of cursors lock records in the database and prevent other users from changing them. Other types of cursors create an additional copy of all records and then work with them. Both approaches have performance implications.

Client-side cursors and API Server cursors are also not the most efficient way to transfer information between server and client. It is much faster to use a "fire hose" cursor, which is actually not a cursor at all. You can find more details about "fire hose" cursors in *Hitchhiker's Guide to Visual Basic and SQL Server, 5th edition* by William Vaughn (Microsoft Press).

# The Justified Uses of Cursors

The rule of thumb is to avoid the use of cursors whenever possible. However, in some cases such avoidance is not possible.

Cursors can be used to perform operations that cannot be performed using set-oriented statements. It is acceptable to use cursors to perform processing based on statements, stored procedures, and extended stored procedures, which are designed to work with one item at a time. For example, the sp_addrolemember system stored procedure is designed to set an existing user account as a member of the SQL Server role. If you can list users that need to be assigned to a role, you can loop through them (using a cursor) and execute the system stored procedure for each of them.

Excessive processing based on a single row (for example, business logic implemented in the form of an extended stored procedure) can also be implemented using a cursor. If you implement such a loop in a stored procedure instead of in a client application, you can reduce network traffic considerably.

Another example could be the export of a group of tables from a database to text files using bcp. The bcp is a command prompt program that can work with one table at a time. To use it within a stored procedure, you need to execute it using the xp_cmdshell extended stored procedure, which can run just one command at a time:

```
Create Procedure prBcpOutTables
--loop through tables and export them to text fields
    @debug int = 0
As


Declare    @chvTable varchar(128),
           @chvCommand varchar(255)


Declare @curTables Cursor


-- get all USER-DEFINED tables from current database
Set @curTables = Cursor FOR
    select name
```

```
            from sysobjects
            where xType = 'U'

Open @curTables

-- get first table
Fetch Next From @curTables
Into @chvTable

-- if we successfully read the current record
While (@@fetch_status = 0)
Begin

        -- assemble DOS command for exporting table
        Set @chvCommand = 'bcp "Asset..[' + @chvTable
                        + ']" out C:\sql7\backup\' + @chvTable
                        + '.txt -c -q -Sdejan -Usa -Pdejan'
        -- during test just display command
        If @debug <> 0
            Select @chvCommand chvCommand

        -- in production execute DOS command and export table
        If @debug = 0
            Execute xp_cmdshell @chvCommand, NO_OUTPUT

        Fetch Next From @curTables
        Into @chvTable

End

Close @curTables
Deallocate @curTables

Return 0
```

If you execute this stored procedure (without specifying the @debug parameter), SQL Server will execute the following sequence of command prompt commands to export tables:

```
bcp "Asset..[AcquisitionType]" out C:\sql7\backup\AcquisitionType.txt -c -q -Sdejan -Usa -Pdejan
bcp "Asset..[MyEquipment]" out C:\sql7\backup\MyEquipment.txt -c -q -Sdejan -Usa -Pdejan
bcp "Asset..[Equipment]" out C:\sql7\backup\Equipment.txt -c -q -Sdejan -Usa -Pdejan
bcp "Asset..[EqType]" out C:\sql7\backup\EqType.txt -c -q -Sdejan -Usa -Pdejan
bcp "Asset..[ActivityLog]" out C:\sql7\backup\ActivityLog.txt -c -q -Sdejan -Usa -Pdejan
bcp "Asset..[OrderType]" out C:\sql7\backup\OrderType.txt -c -q -Sdejan -Usa -Pdejan
bcp "Asset..[OldEquipment]" out C:\sql7\backup\OldEquipment.txt -c -q -Sdejan -Usa -Pdejan
bcp "Asset..[Property]" out C:\sql7\backup\Property.txt -c -q -Sdejan -Usa -Pdejan
bcp "Asset..[OrderStatus]" out C:\sql7\backup\OrderStatus.txt -c -q -Sdejan -Usa –Pdejan
....
```

*TIP:*   In Chapter 10, we will demonstrate another method for looping through a set of records using the `While` statement. Personally, I seldom use cursors; I prefer to use the method demonstrated in Chapter 10.

# SUMMARY

After reading this chapter, you should be able to

▼  Define regular and delimited identifiers.

■  Select the appropriate datatype.

■  Declare a variable.

■  Assign a value to the variable using a `Select`, `Set`, or `Update` statement.

■  Display the value of the variable to a user.

■  Use global variables.

■  Use the `@@identity` variable to read the value of a key field.

▲  Read the value of the `@@error` variable to determine if a statement was successful.

Transact-SQL is not a feature-rich programming language, but its statements, if well harnessed, will arm the developer to code even the most complex algorithms.

We have demonstrated how the developer can use comments to document code and make it more understandable. We have learned the rules that are of the utmost importance in the formulation of comments. We have seen how to implement conditional executions using an `If` statement and how to use the `While` statement to implement a loop. We have learned how to schedule executions using the `WaitFor` statement and the risks involved in overusing the `GoTo` statement.

Cursors are a powerful feature designed to bridge the gap between the relational aspect of database systems and the navigational aspect of client applications. We have seen that the use of cursors creates some performance and structural problems in stored procedures, and we have concluded that they should be used with caution and only for problems that cannot be resolved with set operations.

# EXERCISES

1. Which datatypes can store strings and what are the differences among them?

2. Is it better to use `decimal` or `real` variables to store monetary values?

3. When variables are assigned with a `Select` statement that returns a recordset instead of a single record, which values will be assigned to the variables?

4. What values will be assigned to the variable when a `Select` statement returns an empty recordset?

5. Create two stored procedures—prStoreOrder, which will insert an order and return an Order number, and prStoreOrderItem, which will insert the item of the order.

6. Create a stored procedure that creates a temporary table with just one integer field. The stored procedure should then insert numbers from 1 to 100 into the table and at the end, return those numbers as a resultset to the caller.

7. Stored procedure sp_spaceused can return information about the space used by a database object. Collect the names of all tables in the Asset database using:

```
select name from sysobjects where xtype = 'U'
```

and then loop through them to display space information to users.

8. Create a stored procedure that lists orders scheduled for today with a status set to 1.

9. Create a stored procedure that lists orders and displays three character abbreviations of order status and type (that is, Ordered ⇨ Ord, Canceled ⇨ Cnl, Deferred ⇨ Dfr, and so on).

10. Create a stored procedure that will return a recordset with the field names of the specified table. The stored procedure should have only one input parameter—table name.

11. Explain the problems associated with the use of cursors.

12. Stored procedure sp_spaceused can return information about the space used by a database object. Collect the names of all tables in the Asset database using

```
select name from sysobjects where xtype = 'U'
```

Use a cursor to loop through the table names to display space information to users.
This exercise is equivalent to exercise 7. Compare the solutions.

13. Create two stored procedures that will return a resultset in the form of a denormalized Inventory table (see Figure 4-3). All fields in the Inventory table that are links to other lookup tables should be replaced with values from those lookup tables.

Each stored procedure should use a different method to obtain information:

▼  Select statement with join

▲  Looping with cursor

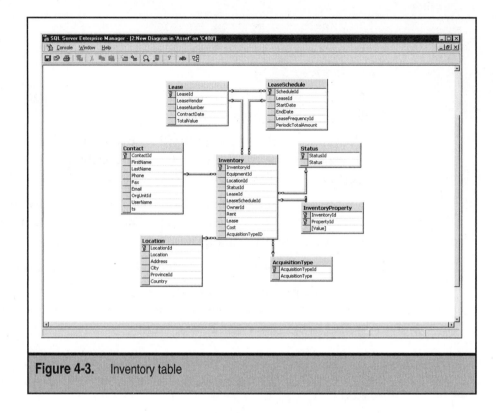

**Figure 4-3.** Inventory table

# CHAPTER 5

## Functions

Microsoft has done a fantastic job providing database administrators with an extensive and coherent set of built-in functions for SQL Server. Users of SQL Server 2000 are now also able to create their own functions. We will cover the design of user-defined functions in Chapter 9 and focus here on the use and attributes of built-in functions.

## USING FUNCTIONS

Functions are Transact-SQL syntax elements that are used to evaluate a list of parameters and return a single value to the caller. The usual syntax for calling a function is

```
Function_name ([parameter] [,...n])
```

For example, a sine function has the following syntax:

```
SIN(float_expression)
```

To display the sine of 45 degrees you can use:

```
SELECT SIN(45)
```

Some functions have more than one parameter, and some do not require parameters at all. For example, the GETDATE function returns the current date and time on the system clock to the caller. We will use the GETDATE function to present the most common ways to use functions in Transact-SQL.

### In Selection and Assignment

Functions can be a value or a part of a value to be assigned or selected as a recordset. In the following example, two variables are populated using values stored in a selected record and a third variable is populated using a function:

```
Select    @chvMake = Make,
          @Model = Model,
          @dtsCurrentDate = GETDATE()
```

```
from Equipment
where EqId = @intEqId
```

This use is not limited to the Select statement. Values can be assigned in the Set statement, displayed in the Print statement, stored in a table using Update and Insert, or even used as parameters for other functions.

```
Create Procedure prInsertNewSchedule
    @intLeaseId int,
    @intLeaseFrequencyId int
As

    Insert LeaseSchedule(LeaseId, StartDate,
                    EndDate, LeaseFrequencyId)
    Values (    @intLeaseId,                   GETDATE(),
                DATEADD(Year, 3, GETDATE()), @intLeaseFrequencyId)


return @@Error
```

This procedure inserts the current date (using the GETDATE function) in the StartDate column. The EndDate column is calculated using the DATEADD function, which uses the GETDATE function as one parameter. It is used to set the end date three years from the current date.

## In Filtering Criteria

Functions are often used in the Where clause of Transact-SQL statements among the filtering criteria:

```
SELECT Inventory.InventoryId
FROM LeaseSchedule INNER JOIN Inventory
    ON LeaseSchedule.ScheduleId = Inventory.LeaseScheduleId
WHERE (LeaseSchedule.EndDate < GETDATE())
AND (Inventory.Rent <> 0)
```

This Select statement selects the lease schedules that have reached end of term.

## In Expressions

In general, you can use a function in any place in which you can use an expression. For example, an `If` statement requires a Boolean expression, the result of which will determine further execution steps:

```
If @dtmLeaseEndDate < GETDATE()
    Begin
        . . .
    end
```

## As Check and Default Constraints

Functions can be used inside `Check` and `Default` constraints:

```
CREATE TABLE [dbo].[Order] (
    [OrderId] [int] IDENTITY (1, 1) NOT NULL ,
    [OrderDate] [smalldatetime] NOT NULL ,
    [RequestedById] [int] NOT NULL ,
    [TargetDate] [smalldatetime] NOT NULL ,
    [CompletionDate] [smalldatetime] NULL ,
    [DestinationLocationId] [int] NULL
) ON [PRIMARY]

GO


ALTER TABLE [dbo].[Order] WITH NOCHECK ADD
        CONSTRAINT [DF_Order_OrderDate] DEFAULT (GETDATE()) FOR [OrderDate],
        CONSTRAINT [PK_Order] PRIMARY KEY  CLUSTERED
    (
        [OrderId]
    )  ON [PRIMARY]
GO
```

In this case, the Order table automatically sets the OrderDate field to the current date if the user omits to supply its value.

## Instead of Tables

Since SQL Server 2000 has a new `table` datatype, it is also possible for a function to return a recordset. Microsoft documentation refers to such functions as *table-valued functions*. These functions can be used in situations in TSQL where tables are expected. In the following example, the result of the function is used to join with another table (EqType) to produce a new resultset:

```
Select *
from dbo.NewEquipment(DATEADD(month, -1, GetDate()) NewEq
inner join EqType
on NewEq.EqTypeId = EqType.EqTypeId
```

To reference a table-valued function, you must specify the object owner along with the function name (*owner.function*). The only exception to this rule is in the use of built-in table-valued functions. In this case, you must place two colons (::) in front of the function name. For example, the `fn_EXTENDEDPROPERTY` function lists properties of the database object (see Figure 5-1). For more details about extended properties, refer to Chapter 10.

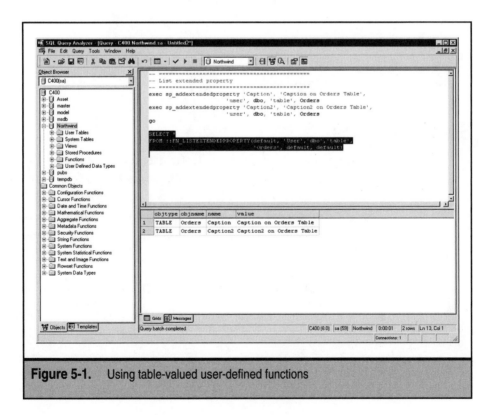

**Figure 5-1.**    Using table-valued user-defined functions

# TYPES OF FUNCTIONS

Depending on the way that functions are created, functions in SQL Server 2000 can be divided into two groups:

▼ Built-in

▲ User-defined

*Built-in functions* are delivered as a part of the Transact-SQL language. They are implemented as part of SQL Server. *User-defined functions* allow users to define their own Transact-SQL functions. Users can design them by combining other Transact-SQL statements. Unfortunately, SQL Server 7.0 does not support user-defined functions. We will examine the details of the design of user-defined functions in Chapter 9.

We can identify three major groups of functions according to the result that is returned:

▼ Scalar

■ Rowset

▲ Aggregate

## Scalar Functions

Most of the time when we refer to functions, we are thinking of the scalar type. The name of this type refers to the fact that these functions return only one value.

Considering their functionality but not necessarily their return values, we can divide scalar functions into the following groups:

▼ System

■ Date and time

■ String

■ Mathematical

■ Metadata

■ Security

- Text and image
- Cursor
- Configuration
▲ System statistical

We will not be able to cover in detail all functions defined in Microsoft SQL Server. We will simply discuss the most important of them. You can find complete documentation of all functions in SQL Server Books Online.

## System Functions

System functions return information related to the Microsoft SQL Server environment. They are used to return object names and identifiers, current user, current database, session, application, and login; to investigate the datatype of an expression; and to perform conversions between datatypes.

Let's examine some of the most important system functions and look at some examples.

**Conditional Expression—*CASE***   In other programming languages, CASE is usually a flow-control programming construct. In earlier versions of SQL Server documentation, CASE is usually classified as an expression. Since SQL Server 7.0, it is classified as a function, which is mathematically more correct. However, all of these classifications are more or less true.

The CASE function/expression enables the user to evaluate an expression and to return the value associated with the result of the expression. For example, the CASE function/expression in the following stored procedure returns the approximate number of days associated with a leasing schedule:

```
Create Procedure prLeasePeriodDuration
-- return approximate number of days associated with lease frequency
    @inyScheduleFrequencyId tinyint,
    @insDays smallint OUTPUT
As
Declare @chvScheduleFrequency varchar(50)
```

```
Select @chvScheduleFrequency = ScheduleFrequency
From ScheduleFrequency
where ScheduleFrequencyId = @inyScheduleFrequencyId

select @insDays =
CASE @chvScheduleFrequency
         When 'monthly' then 30
         When 'semi-monthly' then 15
         When 'bi-weekly' then 14
         When 'weekly' then 7
         When 'quarterly' then 92
         When 'yearly' then 365
     END
return
```

The CASE function/expression works much like a Select statement with nested If statements. In fact, most of the time you can write equivalent code using nested If statements.

There are two types of CASE function/expressions:

▼ Simple CASE function/expressions

▲ Searched CASE function/expressions

A *simple CASE function/expression* has the following syntax:

```
CASE input_expression
    WHEN when_expression THEN result_expression
        [...n]
    [
        ELSE else_result_expression
    ]
END
```

The previous example used this kind of CASE function/expression. SQL Server attempts to match the *input_expression* with one of the *when_expression*s. If it is successful, it returns the *result_expression* associated with the first matching *when_expression*. An Else clause is also part of the CASE function/expression. If the value of the *input_expression* is not equal to either of the *when_expression*s, the function returns the value of the *else_result_expression*.

A *searched CASE function/expression* is very similar. The only difference is that it does not have an *input_expression.* The complete criteria are inside the When clause in the form of a Boolean expression:

```
CASE
    WHEN Boolean_expression THEN result_expression
        [...n]
    [
        ELSE else_result_expression
    ]
END
```

SQL Server returns the *result_expression* associated with the first *Boolean_expression,* which is True. If all *Boolean_expressions* are false, SQL Server returns the *else_result_expression.*

In the following example, a searched CASE function/expression has to be used because the *Boolean_expression*s have different operators (= and Like):

```
Create Procedure prListLeaseInfo
-- list all lease contract information
As

Select LeaseVendor [Lease Vendor],
        LeaseNumber [Lease Number],
        CASE -- some vendors have id of sales reps
            -- incorporated in lease numbers
            When LeaseVendor = 'Trigon FS'
                    THEN SUBSTRING( LeaseNumber, 5, 12)
            When LeaseVendor Like 'EB%'
                    THEN SUBSTRING( LeaseNumber, 9, 8)
            When LeaseVendor Like 'MMEX%'
                    THEN SUBSTRING( LeaseNumber, 7, 6)
            When LeaseVendor = 'DAFS'
                    THEN SUBSTRING( LeaseNumber, 8, 11)
            Else 'Unknown'
        end [Lease Agent],
        ContractDate [Contract Date]
        from Lease
```

**TIP:** Although both examples use CASE functions/expressions as a part of the Select statement, keep in mind that you can use it anywhere that you can place an expression. This flexibility might come in very handy in some situations.

**Getting Information About Data**   You can use numerous functions to return information about data, the most important of which are

▼  ISDATE

■  ISNUMERIC

■  DATALENGTH

■  SQL_VARIANT_PROPERTY

▲  BINARY_CHECKSUM

ISDATE is a function that you can use to determine whether a character value or expression contains a valid date. It is particularly useful when you are forced to read data from text files. If the result of this function is 1 (true), SQL Server guarantees that you will be able to convert the data to date and time datatypes. ISDATE uses the following syntax:

```
ISDATE(expression)
```

In the following stored procedure, SQL Server verifies that Lease Data (received as a string) can be converted to a datetime value. It then stores this result with the rest of the parameters in the Lease table:

```
Create Procedure prLoadLeaseContract
-- insert lease contract information and return id of lease

        @chvLeaseVendor varchar(50),
        @chvLeaseNumber varchar(50),
        @chvLeaseDate varchar(50),
        @intLeaseId int OUTPUT
As
Declare @intError int

-- test validity of date
if ISDATE(@chvLeaseDate) = 0
begin
     Raiserror ("Unable to Convert to date.", 16, 1)
     return 1
```

```
end

insert into Lease(LeaseVendor, LeaseNumber, ContractDate)
values (@chvLeaseVendor, @chvLeaseNumber,
        Convert(smalldatetime, @chvLeaseDate))

select    @intError = @@Error,
          @intLeaseId = @@identity

return @intError
```

You can use the ISNUMERIC function to determine whether it is possible to convert a character value or expression into one of the numeric datatypes (int, smallint, tinyint, real, float, money, smallmoney, decimal, or numeric). ISNUMERIC uses the following syntax:

```
ISNUMERIC(expression)
```

The DATALENGTH function returns the number of bytes used to contain a value. This information is particularly useful when processing character datatypes of variable length.

> **NOTE:** DATALENGTH returns the number of bytes, not the number of characters. For example, each character in the Nvarchar datatype or any of the other Unicode datatypes uses two bytes.

The DATALENGTH function uses the following syntax:

```
DATALENGTH(expression)
```

For example, if you assign a string value to a variable, and that value is too long, SQL Server will not report an error. It will simply truncate the value and assign it. The following stored procedure was originally designed without verifying that the list of properties will fit into the output variable. Since SQL Server 2000 and SQL Server 7.0 support data lengths of as much as 8,000 characters using the varchar datatype, it is unlikely that you will exhaust the available storage very often.

However, experienced developers do not rely on such expectations (just think of the Y2K problem).

This stored procedure uses the DATALENGTH function to evaluate whether the resulting string is longer then 8,000 characters before the strings are concatenated:

```
Alter Procedure prGetInventoryProperties
-- return comma-delimited list of properties describing asset.
-- i.e.: Property = Value unit;Property = Value unit;Property
-- = Value unit;

    (
            @intInventoryId int,
            @chvProperties varchar(8000) OUTPUT
    )

As

declare @intCountProperties int,
        @intCounter int,
        @chvProperty varchar(50),
        @chvValue varchar(50),
        @chvUnit varchar(50),
        @insLenProperty smallint,
        @insLenValue smallint,
        @insLenUnit smallint,
        @insLenProperties smallint

Create table #Properties(
        Id int identity(1,1),
        Property varchar(50),
        Value varchar(50),
        Unit varchar(50))

-- identify Properties associated with asset
insert into #Properties (Property, Value, Unit)
        select Property, Value, Unit
```

```
        from InventoryProperty inner join Property
        on InventoryProperty.PropertyId = Property.PropertyId
        where InventoryProperty.InventoryId = @intInventoryId

-- set loop
select    @intCountProperties = Count(*),
          @intCounter = 1,
          @chvProperties = ''
from #Properties

-- loop through list of properties
while @intCounter <= @intCountProperties
begin
     -- get one property
     select @chvProperty = Property,
            @chvValue = Value,
            @chvUnit = Unit
     from #Properties
     where Id = @intCounter

     -- check will new string fit
     select @insLenProperty = DATALENGTH(@chvProperty),
            @insLenValue = DATALENGTH(@chvValue),
            @insLenUnit = DATALENGTH(@chvUnit),
            @insLenProperties = DATALENGTH(@chvProperties)

     if @insLenProperties + 2 + @insLenProperty
           + 1 + @insLenValue + 1 + @insLenUnit > 8000
     begin
          select 'List of properties is too long '
                  + '(over 8000 characters)!'
          return 1
     end

     -- assemble list
     set @chvProperties = @chvProperties + '; '
                        + @chvProperty + '='
```

```
                                + @chvValue + ' '
                                + @chvUnit

        -- let's go another round and get another property
        set @intCounter = @intCounter + 1
    end

drop table #Properties
return 0
```

The `SQL_VARIANT_PROPERTY` function supports the `sql_variant` datatype introduced in SQL Server 2000. It returns specified *property* information about data stored in or obtained from the *expression* parameter. It is possible to request one of the following properties:

▼ BaseType

■ Precision

■ Scale

■ TotalBytes

■ Collation

▲ MaxLength

This function uses the following syntax:

```
SQL_VARIANT_PROPERTY(expression, property)
```

The property parameter must be specified in the form of a string:

```
SELECT    SQL_VARIANT_PROPERTY(Lookup,'BaseType'),
          SQL_VARIANT_PROPERTY(Lookup,'Precision'),
          SQL_VARIANT_PROPERTY(Lookup,'Scale')
FROM      Lookup
WHERE     LookupGroupId = 16
AND       LookupId = 4
```

The `BINARY_CHECKSUM` function has been introduced in SQL Server 2000. It calculates the binary checksum of a specified expression or set of table columns. It is designed to detect changes in a record. This function uses the following syntax:

```
BINARY_CHECKSUM(*|expression[,...n])
```

The following stored procedure compares the binary checksum of columns containing new information with the checksum of columns already stored in the table; if the values do not match, the new data will be inserted into the table:

```
CREATE Procedure prUpdateEquipment
-- Check if values were changed in the meanwhile
-- Update values in equipment table.
        @intEquipmentId int,
        @chvMake varchar(50),
        @chvModel varchar(50),
        @intEqTypeId int,
        @debug int = 0
As
declare @intNewEquipmentBC int

set @intNewEquipmentBC = BINARY_CHECKSUM(@chvMake,
                                          @chvModel,
                                          @intEqTypeId)
if @debug <> 0
     Select @intNewEquipmentBC NewBC
if @debug <> 0
        select EquipmentBC OldBC
        from EquipmentBC
        where EquipmentId = @intEquipmentId

if not exists (Select EquipmentBC
                from EquipmentBC
                where EquipmentId = @intEquipmentId)
    insert EquipmentBC (EquipmentId, EquipmentBC)
        select @intEquipmentId,
              BINARY_CHECKSUM(Make, Model, EqTypeId)
        from Equipment
```

```
                          where EquipmentId = @intEquipmentId

    -- Check if values were changed in the meanwhile
    if @intNewEquipmentBC <> (Select EquipmentBC
                                from EquipmentBC
                                where EquipmentId = @intEquipmentId)
begin
    if @debug <> 0
        select 'Information will be updated.'

    -- update information
    update Equipment
    Set  Make = @chvMake,
         Model = @chvModel,
         EqTypeId = @intEqTypeId
    where EquipmentId = @intEquipmentId

    if exists(select EquipmentId
              from    EquipmentBC
              where   EquipmentId = @intEquipmentId)
        update EquipmentBC
        Set EquipmentBC = @intNewEquipmentBC
        where EquipmentId = @intEquipmentId
    else
        insert EquipmentBC (EquipmentId, EquipmentBC)
        values (@intEquipmentId, @intNewEquipmentBC)
end
return
```

**NOTE:** BINARY_CHECKSUM is case-sensitive. It evaluates columns/expressions differently depending on the case (uppercase/lowercase) used in the column or expression. This might seem unusual, since most SQL Server behavior depends on the code page that you select during installation. If the default is selected, SQL Server ignores the case of characters when matching them. The nature of the algorithm used to implement the BINARY_CHECKSUM function is such that it cannot work that way.

> *TIP:* BINARY_CHECKSUM is a much-needed tool for Data Warehousing projects. It allows DBAs to detect and handle the problem of "slowly changing dimensions type 2 and 3."

**Functions for Handling NULL Value**   SQL Server is equipped with a set of three functions to help ease the pain of using NULLs in your database system:

```
NULLIF(expression, expression)
ISNULL(check_expression, replacement_value)
COALESCE(expression [,...n])
```

NULLIF returns NULL if two expressions in the function return the same value. If the expressions are not equivalent, the function returns the value of the first expression.

This function can be useful when calculating the average of columns with values that have special meaning. For example, let's assume that the author of the Asset database has created constraints or stored procedures such that a user can leave the value of the Inventory.Rent column as either null or zero (0) when equipment is not leased. In this case, the AVG function for calculating the average of the column will eliminate records containing null from the average but keep records with zero. It is not that the AVG function is implemented improperly, but that our design can be improved. It is possible to implement a workaround using the NULLIF function:

```
select    AVG(Rent) "average without nulls",
          AVG(NULLIF(Rent, 0)) "average without nulls and zeros"
from Inventory
```

An average calculated in this way will be different from an average calculated in the standard way:

```
average without nulls average without nulls and zeros
-------------------- -------------------------------
100.0000                150.0000
(1 row(s) affected)


Warning: Null value eliminated from aggregate.
```

The ISNULL function examines the *check_expression*. If its value is NULL, the function returns the *replacement_value*. If the value of the *check_expression* is not NULL, the function returns the *check_expression*.

Let's suppose you want to calculate an average based on the total number of computers in the Inventory table. You can use the ISNULL value to replace NULL values during the calculation:

```
select AVG(Rent) "without nulls",
       AVG(ISNULL(rent, 0)) "with nulls as zeros"
from Inventory
```

The average price of computers that counts nulls as zeroes is less than the average that ignores computers with the price set to NULL.

```
without nulls       with nulls as zeros
-----------------   --------------------
100.0000            75.0000


(1 row(s) affected)


Warning: Null value eliminated from aggregate.
```

The last line is a warning that refers to the way AVG is calculated.

> **NOTE:** The name of this function is confusing, especially if you are a Visual Basic programmer as well. It cannot be used to test whether the value of an expression is null. You should use these operators instead:
>
> If *expression* IS NULL
> If *expression* IS NOT NULL

The COALESCE function is often used to coalesce (unite) values that are split into several columns. The result of the function is the first non-null expression. This function uses the following syntax:

```
COALESCE(expression [,...n])
```

In the following example, we coalesce (unite) values from three columns (Rent, Lease, and Cost) into one value (Acquisition Cost). Only one of those values in a single record is not null, and COALESCE will return it:

```
SELECT Inventory.Inventoryid,
      Equipment.Make + ' ' + Equipment.Model Equipment,
      AcquisitionType.AcquisitionType,
      COALESCE(Inventory.Rent, Inventory.Lease, Inventory.Cost) [Cost]
FROM Inventory INNER JOIN AcquisitionType ON
      Inventory.AcquisitionTypeID = AcquisitionType.AcquisitionTypeId
              INNER JOIN Equipment
          ON Inventory.EquipmentId = Equipment.EquipmentId
```

The result will contain just one column showing the cost of acquisition:

```
Inventoryid Equipment                           AcquisitionType Cost
----------- ----------------------------------- --------------- ---------
5           Toshiba Portege 7020CT              Purchase        1295.0000
6           Toshiba Portege 7020CT              Rent             200.0000
8           Toshiba Portege 7020CT              Lease             87.7500
10          Toshiba Portege 7020CT              Lease             99.9500
```

**Conversion Functions**   The CAST and CONVERT functions are used to convert the information in one datatype to another specified datatype explicitly. There is just one small difference between these two functions: CONVERT allows the user to specify the format of the result. Their syntax is

```
CAST(expression AS data_type)
CONVERT (data_type[(length)], expression [, style])
```

In this case, the *expression* is any value or expression that you want to convert, and the *data_type* is the new datatype. For example, the following statement concatenates two strings and an error number and displays them as one string:

```
Select "Error ["+Cast(@@Error as varchar)+"] has occurred."
```

The result is an error number integrated with a sentence, which might be useful in an error handling situation:

```
-----------------------------------------------------
Error [373] has occurred.
```

In the CONVERT function, *style* refers to the formatting style used in the conversion of date and time (datetime, smalldatetime) or numeric (money, smallmoney, float, real) expressions to strings (varchar, char, nvarchar, nchar). For example, the following command displays the current date in default and German style:

```
select GetDate() standard, CONVERT(varchar, GetDate(), 104) German
```

The result is

```
standard                    German
-------------------------   ------------------------------
1999-07-11 11:45:57.730     11.07.1999
```

Table 5-1 lists formatting styles that you can use when converting datetime to character or character to datetime information.

| Style with 2-Digit Year | Style with 4-Digit Year | Standard | Format |
|---|---|---|---|
| – | 0 or 100 | Default | mon dd yyyy hh:miAM (or PM) |
| 1 | 101 | USA | mm/dd/yy |
| 2 | 102 | ANSI | yy.mm.dd |
| 3 | 103 | British/French | dd/mm/yy |
| 4 | 104 | German | dd.mm.yy |
| 5 | 105 | Italian | dd-mm-yy |
| 6 | 106 | – | dd mon yy |
| 7 | 107 | – | mon dd, yy |
| 8 | 108 | – | hh:mm:ss |
| – | 9 or 109 | Default + milliseconds | mon dd yyyy hh:mi:ss:mmmAM (or PM) |
| 10 | 110 | USA | mm-dd-yy |

**Table 5-1.**    Formatting Styles for *Datetime* Information

| Style with 2-Digit Year | Style with 4-Digit Year | Standard | Format |
|---|---|---|---|
| 11 | 111 | Japan | yy/mm/dd |
| 12 | 112 | ISO | yymmdd |
| - | 13 or 113 | Europe default + milliseconds | dd mon yyyy hh:mm:ss:mmm(24h) |
| 14 | 114 | – | hh:mi:ss:mmm(24h) |
| – | 20 or 120 | ODBC canonical | yyyy-mm-dd hh:mi:ss(24h) |
| – | 21 or 121 | ODBC canonical (with milliseconds) | yyyy-mm-dd hh:mi:ss.mmm(24h) |
| – | 130 | Kuwaiti | dd/mm/yyyy hh:mi:ss.mmmAM |
| – | 131 | Kuwaiti | dd mm yyyy hh:mi:ss.mmmAM |

**Table 5-1.**   Formatting Styles for *Datetime* Information *(continued)*

In the following example, we format a monetary value:

```
Select    $12345678.90,
          CONVERT(varchar(30), $12345678.90, 0),
          CONVERT(varchar(30), $12345678.90, 1),
          CONVERT(varchar(30), $12345678.90, 2)
```

The result is

```
------------- -------------- --------------- -------------
12345678.9000 12345678.90    12,345,678.90    12345678.9000
```

The following table lists formatting styles that you can use when converting monetary values to character information:

| Value | Output |
|---|---|
| 0 (default) | 2 digits behind decimal point<br>No commas every three digits<br>i.e.: 1234.56 |
| 1 | 2 digits behind decimal point<br>Commas every three digits<br>i.e.: 1,234.56 |
| 2 | 4 digits behind decimal point<br>No commas every three digits<br>1234.5678 |

The following table lists formatting styles that you can use when converting float or real values to character information:

| Value | Output |
|---|---|
| 0 (default) | In scientific notation, when needed<br>6 digits maximum |
| 1 | 8 digits always in scientific notation |
| 2 | 16 digits always in scientific notation |

**TIP:** Microsoft recommends using the CAST function whenever the formatting power of CONVERT is not required, because CAST is compatible with the ANSI SQL-92 standard.

When you specify the target datatype of variable length as a part of the CAST or CONVERT functions, you should include its length, too. If you do not specify length, SQL Server assigns a default length of 30. Therefore, the previous example could be written as

```
Select    $12345678.90,
          CONVERT(varchar, $12345678.90, 0),
```

```
CONVERT(varchar, $12345678.90, 1),
CONVERT(varchar, $12345678.90, 2)
```

You need to use conversion functions when you

▼ Supply a Transact-SQL statement or function with a value in a specific datatype

■ Set the format of a date or number

▲ Obtain a value that uses an exotic datatype

In some cases, the program automatically (that is, behind the scenes) converts the value if the required datatype and the supplied datatype are compatible. For example, if some function requires a char parameter, you can supply even a datetime parameter and SQL Server will perform an *implicit conversion* of the value. In the opposite direction, you must use an *explicit conversion*—that is, you must use conversion functions. If it is not possible to convert data to a certain datatype, SQL Server raises an error.

*TIP:*  You can find a table in SQL Server Books Online that lists which datatypes can be converted to other datatypes and which kind of conversion (explicit or implicit) is required.

**Information About the Current Session**    The following functions return information associated with the current session (for instance, how did you log on to the server, what is your user name in the database, what is the name of the server, what permissions do you have in the current database).

| Function | Description |
|----------|-------------|
| APP_NAME | Name of the application that opened the session |
| HOST_ID | ID of the computer hosting the client application |
| HOST_NAME | Name of the computer hosting the client application |

| | |
|---|---|
| PERMISSIONS | Bitmap that specifies permissions on a selected column, a database object, or the current database |
| CURRENT_USER | Name of the database user (same as USER_NAME) |
| SESSION_USER | Name of the database user who owns the current session |
| SYSTEM_USER | Name of the server login that owns the current session. If the user has logged on to the server using Microsoft Windows NT Authentication, this function returns the Windows NT login |
| USER_NAME | Name of the database user (same as CURRENT_USER) |

The following stored procedure uses the SYSTEM_USER function to identify the person adding an order to the system:

```
Create Procedure prAddOrder
-- insert Order record

    @dtmOrderDate datetime = null,
    @dtmTargetDate datetime = NULL,
    @chvUserName varchar(128) = NULL,
    @intDestinationLocation int,
    @chvNote varchar(200),
    @intOrderid int OUTPUT

As

    declare     @intRequestedById int

    -- If user didn't specify order date
    -- default is today.
    if @dtmOrderDate = NULL
        Set @dtmOrderDate = GETDATE()

    -- If user didn't specify target date
```

```
-- default is 3 days after request date.
if @dtmTargetDate = NULL
    Set @dtmTargetDate = DATEADD(day, 3, @dtmOrderDate)

-- if user didn't identify himself
-- try to identify him using login name
if @chvUserName = null
    Set @chvUserName = SYSTEM_USER

-- get Id of the user
select @intRequestedById = ContactId
from Contact
where UserName = @chvUserName

-- if you can not identify user report an error
If @intRequestedById = null
    begin
        RAISERROR('Unable to identify user in Contact table!',
                  1, 2)
        return 1
    end

-- and finally create Order
Insert into [Order](OrderDate, RequestedById, TargetDate,
                    DestinationLocationId,  Note)
Values (@dtmOrderDate, @intRequestedById, @dtmTargetDate,
        @intDestinationLocation,   @chvNote)

set @intOrderid = @@identity
```

```
return 0
```

**Functions for Handling Identity Values**   *Identity* columns are used
in SQL Server tables to generate unique identifiers for each record
automatically. Numbers that are generated in this manner are based
on two values—*identity seed* and *identity increment*. SQL Server starts
assigning identity values from an identity seed, and every row is
given a value that is greater than the previous one by the value
specified in the identity increment (or less than that value if you
use a negative increment value).

In Chapter 4, we covered the use of the `@@identity` function/global variable. It returns the last value generated by SQL Server while inserting record(s) into the table with an identity value:

```
Declare @intEqId int
Insert into Equipment(Make, Model, EqTypeId)
Values ('ACME', 'Turbo', 2)
Select @intEqId = @@identity
```

The `IDENT_SEED` and `IDENT_INCR` functions return to the user the values of the seed and the increment for the selected table or view:

```
Select IDENT_SEED('Inventory'), IDENT_INCR('Inventory')
```

The `IDENTITY` function allows a user to generate identity values while using the `SELECT ... INTO` command. Let me remind you that this command selects records and immediately inserts them into a new table. Without it, developers are forced to create a new table with an identity column and then insert the selected records into the table. With it, everything can be achieved in one step:

```
SELECT     IDENTITY(int, 1,1) AS ID,
           Property.Property,
           InventoryProperty.Value,
           Property.Unit
INTO #InventoryProperty
FROM InventoryProperty INNER JOIN Property ON
     InventoryProperty.PropertyId = Property.PropertyId
WHERE (InventoryProperty.InventoryId = 12)
```

## Date and Time Functions

This set of functions is designed to process data and time values and expressions.

**Get (Current) Date**   `GETDATE` is the function that you will probably use more often than any other date and time function. It is designed to return the system time in datetime format.

We have already demonstrated the use of this function in the first section of this chapter, "Using Functions."

**Extracting Parts of Date and Time**    From time to time, you will need to extract just one component of the date and time value. The basic functionality necessary to achieve this end is implemented in the following three functions:

```
DAY(date)
MONTH(date)
YEAR(date)
```

These functions require expressions of the datetime or smalldatetime datatype, and they all return the corresponding integer value.

The DATEPART and DATENAME functions provide similar functionality, but they are more flexible:

```
DATEPART(datepart, date)
DATENAME(datepart, date)
```

The user can specify which component of the date to obtain by supplying a *datepart* constant from Table 5-2 (you can use either the full name or the abbreviation).

| Datepart—Full | Datepart—Abbreviation |
|---|---|
| Millisecond | ms |
| Second | ss, s |
| Minute | mi, n |
| Hour | hh |
| weekday | dw |
| Week | wk, ww |
| dayofyear | dy, y |
| Day | dd, d |
| Month | mm, m |
| Quarter | qq, q |
| Year | yy, yyyy |

**Table 5-2.**    Dateparts and Abbreviations Recognized by SQL Server

DATEPART will then return the index value of the *datepart*, and DATENAME will return the string that contains the appropriate name. Naturally, DATENAME is not meaningful in some cases (for example, year, second) and SQL Server will return the same number as it does for DATEPART.

```
SELECT     GETDATE(),
           DATENAME(month, GetDate()) AS 'Month Name',
           DATEPART(yyyy, GetDate()) AS 'Year'
```

Notice that the first parameter is not a character parameter. You cannot fill it using an expression or variable.

### Date and Time Calculations

Transact-SQL contains two functions for performing calculations on date and time expressions:

```
DATEADD(datepart, number, date)
DATEDIFF(datepart, startdate, enddate)
```

DATEADD can be used to add a *number* of *datepart* intervals to a specified *date* value. DATEDIFF returns the number of *datepart* intervals between a *startdate* and an *enddate*. Both of these functions use a value from Table 5-2, shown in the previous section, to specify *datepart*. The following stored procedure lists due dates for the lease:

```
Alter Procedure prListTerms
-- return list of due days for the leasing
    @dtsStartDate smalldatetime,
    @dtsEndDate smalldatetime,
    @chvLeaseFrequency varchar(20)
As
set nocount on

declare @insDueDates smallint -- number of intervals

-- calculate number of DueDates
select @insDueDates =
    CASE @chvLeaseFrequency
        When 'monthly'
            then DATEDIFF(month, @dtsStartDate, @dtsEndDate)
```

```
            When 'semi-monthly'
                    then 2 * DATEDIFF(month, @dtsStartDate, @dtsEndDate)
            When 'bi-weekly'
                    then DATEDIFF(week, @dtsStartDate, @dtsEndDate)/2
            When 'weekly'
                    then DATEDIFF(week, @dtsStartDate, @dtsEndDate)
            When 'quarterly'
                    then DATEDIFF(qq, @dtsStartDate, @dtsEndDate)
            When 'yearly'
                    then DATEDIFF(y, @dtsStartDate, @dtsEndDate)
      END

-- generate list of due dates using temporary table
Create table #DueDates (ID int)

while @insDueDates >= 0
begin
      insert #DueDates (ID)
      values (@insDueDates)

      select @insDueDates = @insDueDates - 1
end

-- display list of Due dates
select ID+1, Convert(varchar,
      CASE
            When @chvLeaseFrequency = 'monthly'
                    then DATEADD(month,ID, @dtsStartDate)
            When @chvLeaseFrequency = 'semi-monthly'
            and ID/2 =  CAST(ID as float)/2
                    then DATEADD(month, ID/2, @dtsStartDate)
            When @chvLeaseFrequency = 'semi-monthly'
            and ID/2 <> CAST(ID as float)/2
                    then DATEADD(dd, 15,
                                    DATEADD(month, ID/2, @dtsStartDate))
            When @chvLeaseFrequency = 'bi-weekly'
                    then DATEADD(week, ID*2, @dtsStartDate)
```

```
            When @chvLeaseFrequency = 'weekly'
                 then DATEADD(week, ID, @dtsStartDate)
            When @chvLeaseFrequency = 'quarterly'
                 then DATEADD(qq, ID, @dtsStartDate)
            When @chvLeaseFrequency = 'yearly'
                 then DATEADD(y, ID, @dtsStartDate)
      END , 105) [Due date]
from #DueDates
order by ID

-- wash the dishes
drop table #DueDates

return 0
```

***TIP:***   Execute and investigate carefully this stored procedure (see Figure 5-2). Or even better, try to create it yourself. You will learn a lot from the problems that you encounter.

## String Functions

Microsoft SQL Server supports an elaborate set of string functions. (Who would expect such a thing from a tool developed in C? ;))

**Basic String Manipulation**    The LEN function uses the following syntax:

```
LEN(string_expression)
```

This function returns the length of a string *in characters*. The input parameter can be any kind of string expression. DATALENGTH, a similar system function, returns the *number of bytes* occupied by the value.

```
declare @chvEquipment varchar(30)
set @chvEquipment = 'Toshiba Portege 7020CT'
select Len(@chvEquipment)
```

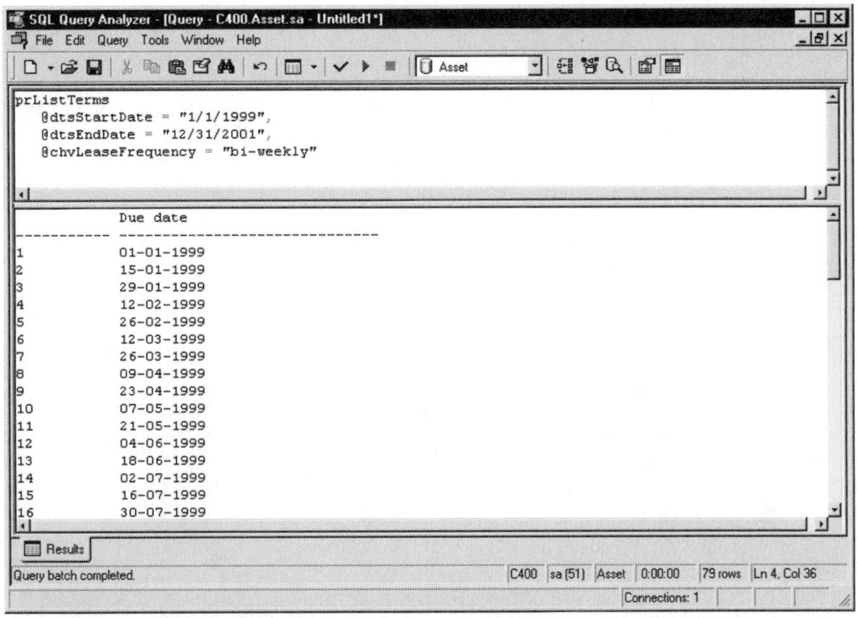

**Figure 5-2.** Executing prListTerms

The result is

```
----------

          22
```

The following two functions return the number of characters from the left or right side of the string:

LEFT(*character_expression*, *integer_expression*)
RIGHT(*character_expression*, *integer_expression*)
Earlier versions of Microsoft SQL Server contained only the RIGHT function.

```
declare @chvEquipment varchar(30)
set @chvEquipment = 'Toshiba Portege 7020CT'
select Left(@chvEquipment, 7) Make, Right(@chvEquipment, 14) Model
```

The result of this batch is

```
Make     Model
-------  --------------
Toshiba  Portege 7020CT
```

Before the introduction of the LEFT function, developers had to implement its functionality using the SUBSTRING function:

```
SUBSTRING(expression, start, length)
```

The SUBSTRING function takes a set (*length*) of characters from the string (*expression*) starting from a specified (*start*) character. The *expression* can be any character, text, image, or binary datatype. Because of this datatype flexibility, the *length* and *start* parameters are based on the number of *bytes* when the *expression* is of the text, image, binary, or varbinary datatypes, rather than on the number of characters. In the case of Unicode datatypes, one character occupies two bytes. If you specify an odd number, you may get unexpected results in the form of split characters.

The following batch extracts part of a string:

```
declare @chvEquipment varchar(30)
set @chvEquipment = 'Toshiba Portege 7020CT'
select SUBSTRING(@chvEquipment, 9, 7)
```

The resultset is

```
-------
Portege
```

The CHARINDEX function returns the index of the first occurrence of a string (*expression1*) within a second string (*expression2*):

```
CHARINDEX(expression1, expression2 [, start_location])
```

There is an optional parameter that allows you to specify the start location for the search:

```
Create Procedure prSplitFullName
-- split full name received in format 'Sunderic, Dejan'
```

```
-- into last and first name
-- default delimiter is comma and space ', ',
-- but caller can specify other
      @chvFullName varchar(50),
      @chvDelimiter varchar(3) = ', ',
      @chvFirstName varchar(50) OUTPUT,
      @chvLastName varchar(50) OUTPUT
As
set nocount on

declare @intPosition int

Set @intPosition = CHARINDEX(@chvDelimiter, @chvFullName)

If @intPosition > 0
begin
    Set @chvLastName = LEFT(@chvFullName, @intPosition - 1)
    Set @chvFirstName = RIGHT(@chvFullName,
        LEN(@chvFullName) - @intPosition - LEN(@chvDelimiter) )
end
else
    return 1

return 0
```

All of these string functions might look to you like a perfect tool for searching table columns, but there is just one problem with this application. If you apply a conversion function inside the `Where` clause of a `Select` statement, SQL Server does not use the index to query the table. Instead, it performs a table scan—even if the index exists. For example, you should not use the CHARINDEX function to identify records with a particular string pattern:

```
select *
from Equipment
where CHARINDEX('Portege', Model) > 0
```

The `Like` operator with wildcard characters is a much better choice if the string that you are looking for is at the beginning of the field:

```
select *
from Equipment
where Model like 'Portege%'
```

**String Conversion**   The following two functions remove leading and trailing blanks from a string:

```
LTRIM(character_expression)
RTRIM(character_expression)
```

In the following query, we use both of them at the same time:

```
select LTRIM(RTRIM('    Dejan Sunderic   '))
```

The following functions convert a string to its uppercase or lowercase equivalent:

```
UPPER(character_expression)
LOWER(character_expression)
```

Use the `STR` function to convert numeric values to strings:

```
STR(float_expression[, length[, decimal]])
```

The *length* parameter is an integer that specifies the number of characters needed for the result. This parameter includes everything: sign, digit, and decimal point. If needed, the function rounds the value and then converts it. If you do not specify a length, the default length is 10 characters, and the default decimal length is 0 (that is, the number will be converted to an integer).

SQL Server provides a number of functions for converting character types:

```
CHAR(integer_expression)
ASCII(character_expression)
NCHAR(integer_expression)
UNICODE(character_expression)
```

The `CHAR` and `NCHAR` functions return characters with the specified integer code according to the ASCII and Unicode standards:

```
select NCHAR(352) + 'underi' + NCHAR(263)
```

Depending on fonts, operating systems, language settings, and other criteria, you may get proper or improper results from this expression (see Figure 5-3).

There is another interesting use of the CHAR function. You can use it to insert control characters into output. For example, you can add tabulators (9) or carriage returns (13). In the past, this was a very important way to format output.

The ASCII and UNICODE functions perform the opposite operation. They return the integer that corresponds to the first character of an expression (see Figure 5-4).

The following two functions generate a string of a specified length (*integer_expression*) and fill it with spaces or a specified character:

```
SPACE(integer_expression)
REPLICATE(character_expression, integer_expression)
```

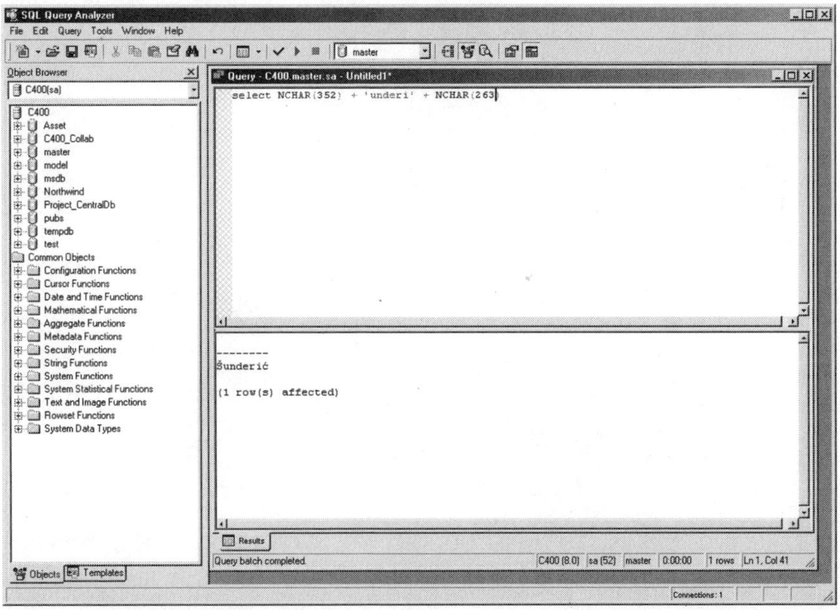

**Figure 5-3.**    Using Unicode characters

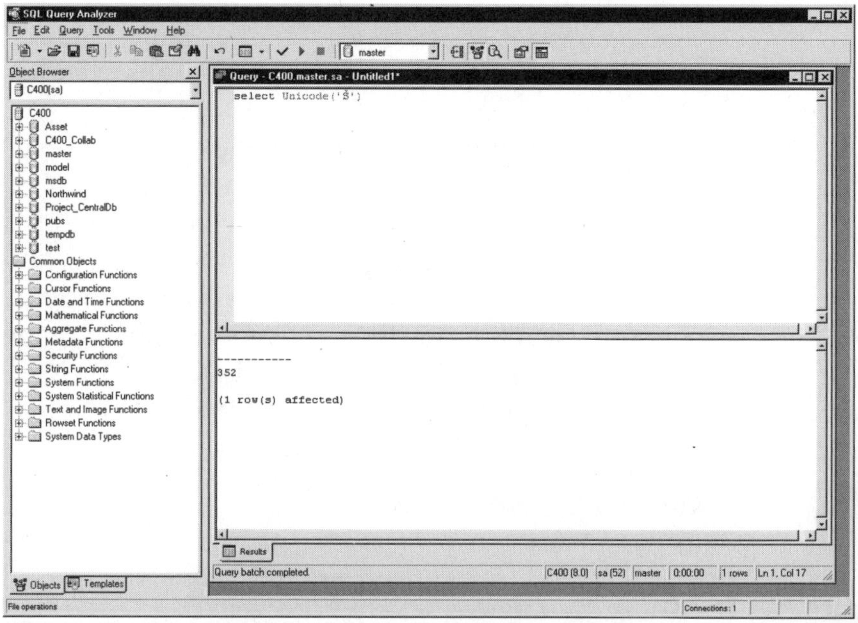

**Figure 5-4.** Identifying Unicode characters

For example

```
select SPACE(4) + REPLICATE('*', 8)
```

This statement returns a useless result, but then, these functions were used at one time primarily to format output:

```
-----------
    ********
```

Use the STUFF function to stuff a string:

```
STUFF(character_expression1, start, length, character_expression2)
```

No, this is not meant for stuffing a turkey... SQL Server removes a *length* of *character_expression1*, beginning at a specified *start* point, and replaces it with *character_expression2*. The specified length does not have to match that of *character_expression2*:

```
select STUFF('Sunderic, Dejan', 9, 2, Char(9))
```

This query replaces the comma and space in the target string with a tabulator:

```
------------------

Sunderic     Dejan
```

**Advanced String Manipulation**   The PATINDEX function is similar to the CHARINDEX function:

```
PATINDEX('%pattern%', expression)
```

The major difference is that it allows the use of wildcard characters in the search pattern.

```
Set @intPosition = PATINDEX('%,%', @chvFullName)
```

Again, if you use this function to search against a table column, SQL Server ignores the index and performs a table scan.

> **TIP:**   In earlier versions of SQL Server, PATINDEX was the only reasonable (although not very fast) way to query the contents of text columns and variables. Since version 7, SQL Server has had a new feature—Full-Text Search—that allows linguistic searches against all character data and works with words and phrases instead of with character patterns. Basically, Microsoft has included Index Server in the standard and Enterprise editions of SQL Server 7.0 and 2000.

The SOUNDEX function is an implementation of the Soundex name search algorithm used since the 1880s by the National Archives in the U.S. to index U.S. censuses:

```
SOUNDEX(character_expression)
```

The idea behind this algorithm is that words that have the same consonants usually sound similar.

The function returns a four-character SOUNDEX code that starts with the first letter of the word and is followed by three numbers. These numbers represent the second, third, and fourth consonants in the string. Vowels and the letters 'h' and 'y' are ignored. If a word contains fewer than four consonants, the code is padded with zeros. Conversion stops immediately when the program encounters a nonalphabetic character:

```
select SOUNDEX('Dejan'), SOUNDEX('Dan'),
       SOUNDEX('dayan'), SOUNDEX('David')
```

These names will be evaluated as the following constants:

```
----- ----- ----- -----
D250  D500  D500  D130
```

You are probably wondering how is it possible to represent all the consonants in the English alphabet with nine digits. In fact, in this algorithm, all consonants are mapped to seven digits. In some cases, this function is very successful (that is, it will recognize similarities between Richardson and Richards), but in some cases it fails miserably:

```
select SOUNDEX('Cline'), SOUNDEX('Klein')
```

It is true that these two names are spelled differently, but they are often pronounced the same. Unfortunately, the SOUNDEX function does not match them:

```
----- -----
C450  K450
```

Irish folk are out of luck too, because conversion will stop at the first nonalphabetical character in a string:

```
select SOUNDEX("O'Brien"), SOUNDEX("O'Hara")
```

The result starts with the first letter in the string(O) and is padded with three zeros (0):

```
----- -----
O000  O000
```

As with some other string functions that perform conversions, it is not recommended that you apply the SOUNDEX function against a table column in a Where clause. SQL Server will neglect to use the index and perform a table scan instead:

```
select *
from Equipment
where SOUNDEX(Model) = SOUNDEX('Portege')
```

A better solution is to precalculate a SOUNDEX code and store it in a separate column (that is, ModelSDX). If that column has an index, SQL Server will use it to speed up the query:

```
select *
from Equipment
where ModelSDX = SOUNDEX('Portege')
```

Another problem with this function is that it cannot properly handle names consisting of multiple parts. Such names are very common in multicultural environments such as Canada—or the Internet.

The DIFFERENCE function uses the same SOUNDEX algorithm to compare two string expressions:

```
DIFFERENCE(character_expression, character_expression)
```

It returns the number of consonants that match. Therefore, the possible results are numbers between 0 (worst) and 4 (best). For example:

```
select SOUNDEX('Dejan'),
       SOUNDEX('Dan'),
       DIFFERENCE('Dejan', 'Dan')
```

In this case, only one consonant is different:

```
----- ----- -----------
D250  D500  3
```

## Mathematical Functions

Although its primary function is not solving algebra problems, Microsoft SQL Server supports the following basic mathematical functions:

| Function | Description |
| --- | --- |
| ABS(*numeric_expression*) | Returns the absolute (positive) value of the expression. |
| ACOS(*numeric_expression*) | Returns an angle in radians of which the cosine is given (also ARCCOSINE). |
| ASIN(*numeric_expression*) | Returns an angle in radians of which the sine is given (also ARCSINE). |
| ATAN(*numeric_expression*) | Returns an angle in radians for a given tangent (also ARCTANGENT). |
| ATN2(*numeric_expression*, *numeric_expression*) | Returns an angle in radians of which the tangent is between the two given tangents. |
| CEILING(*numeric_expression*) | Returns the smallest integer greater than or equal to the given numeric expression. |
| COS(*numeric_expression*) | Returns the cosine of the specified angle (angle is in radians). |
| COT(*numeric_expression*) | Returns the cotangent of the specified angle (angle is in radians). |

| Function | Description |
| --- | --- |
| DEGREES (*numeric_expression*) | Converts the given angle in radians into degrees. |
| EXP (*numeric_expression*) | Returns the exponential value of a given numeric expression. |
| FLOOR (*numeric_expression*) | Returns the largest integer less than or equal to the given numeric expression. |
| LOG (*numeric_expression*) | Returns the natural logarithm for the given numeric expression using the base-2 system. |
| LOG10 (*numeric_expression*) | Returns the base-10 logarithm. |
| PI () | Returns the constant value of PI (3.14159265358979). |
| POWER (*numeric_expression*, *p*) | Returns the value of the given numeric expression to the specified power ($p$). |
| RADIANS (*numeric_expression*) | Converts degrees to radians. |
| RAND (*seed*) | Calculates a random floating-point number between 0 and 1. |
| ROUND (*numeric_expression*, *length*, [*function*]) | Returns a numeric expression rounded to the specified length or precision. |
| SIGN (*numeric_expression*) | Returns the positive, zero, or negative sign of the given expression. |

| Function | Description |
| --- | --- |
| SIN(*numeric_expression*) | Returns the sine of the specified angle (angle is in radians). |
| SQUARE(*numeric_expression*) | Returns the square of the given expression. |
| SQRT(*numeric_expression*) | Returns the square root of the given expression. |
| TAN(*numeric_expression*) | Returns the trigonometric tangent of the given angle (angle is in radians) |

## Metadata Functions

These functions are like a drill that you can use to obtain information about a database and database objects.

| Function | Description |
| --- | --- |
| COL_LENGTH(*table*, *column*) | Returns the length of the column. |
| COL_NAME(*table_id*, *column_id*) | Returns the name of the column specified by Table Identification Number and Column Identification Number. |
| COLUMNPROPERTY(*id*, *column*, *property*) | Returns information about a column or stored procedure parameter. |
| DATABASEPROPERTY(*database*, *property*) | Returns the value of the named database property for a given database and property name. |

| Function | Description |
| --- | --- |
| DATABASEPROPERTYEX(*database*, *property*) | Returns the value of the named database property for a given database and property name. The returned value is of the sql_variant datatype. This function is available only in SQL Server 2000. |
| DB_ID(*database*) | Returns the database identification number for the given database. |
| DB_NAME(*database_id*) | Returns the database name for a given database identification number. |
| FILE_ID(*file_name*) | Returns the identification number for a logical filename in the current database. |
| FILE_NAME(*file_id*) | Returns the logical filename for the given file identification number. |
| FILEGROUP_ID(*filegroup_name*) | Returns the identification number for the given filegroup name. |
| FILEGROUP_NAME(*filegroup_id*) | Returns the filegroup name for the given filegroup identification number. |

| Function | Description |
| --- | --- |
| FILEGROUPPROPERTY(filegroup_name, property) | Returns the filegroup property value for the given filegroup name and property name. |
| FILEPROPERTY(file_name, property) | Returns the value of the given property for the given filename. |
| FULLTEXTCATALOGPROPERTY (catalog_name, property) | Returns information about full-text catalog properties. |
| FULLTEXTSERVICEPROPERTY (property) | Returns information about a full-text service property. |
| INDEX_COL(table, index_id, key_id) | Returns the indexed column name. |
| INDEXPROPERTY (table_id, index, property) | Returns the value of the given property for a given table identification number and index name. |
| OBJECT_ID(object) | Returns the identification number of the given object. |
| OBJECT_NAME(object_id) | Returns the database object name for the given object identification number. |
| OBJECTPROPERTY(ID, property) | Returns information about the specified property for a given object's identification number. |

| Function | Description |
| --- | --- |
| `@@@PROCID` | Returns the identification number of the current stored procedure. |
| `TYPEPROPERTY(type, property)` | Returns information about the datatype. |

## Security Functions

SQL Server 7.0 has introduced many improvements in the area of security. The most important of these is the introduction of the "role" concept. Roles in SQL Server correspond to roles in MS Transaction Server and groups in Windows NT.

In earlier versions of SQL Server, users could belong to only one group. This restriction led to problems when a developer wanted to implement more complex security rules. The result was often a security hierarchy of groups, where each "higher" group could perform all activities that "lower" groups could perform. Unfortunately, this model does not always correspond to the requirements of a particular business environment. Some implementations involved a considerable number of groups, all of which had to be managed.

In SQL Server 2000 and SQL Server 7.0, one user can be associated with many roles. Thus, you can assign a set of permissions to a role and then assign each user a set of required roles.

Security functions return information about users, roles, and their assignments:

| Function | Description |
| --- | --- |
| `IS_MEMBER(group | role)` | Indicates whether the current user is a member of a Windows NT group or SQL Server role. |
| `IS_SERVERROLEMEMBER(role[, login])` | Indicates whether the current user is a member of the specified server role. |

| Function | Description |
|---|---|
| `SUSER_ID([login])` | Returns the user's login identification number. |
| `SUSER_NAME([user_id])` | Returns the user's login identification name. |
| `SUSER_SID([login])` | Returns the user's security identification number. |
| `SUSER_SNAME([user_sid])` | Returns the login identification name for the user's security identification number. |
| `USER_ID([user])` | Returns the database user's identification number. |
| `USER` | Returns the database user name. |

## Text and Image Functions

SQL Server does not have an elaborate set of text and image functions, since you should generally not keep your documents or pictures inside the database. The proper place for these files is in the file system. You should keep only descriptions of and pointers (that is, the path) to those files in the database itself.

| Function | Description |
|---|---|
| `PATINDEX(%pattern%, expression)` | Returns the starting position of the first occurrence of the pattern. |
| `TEXTPTR(column)` | Returns the text pointer value. |
| `TEXTVALID(column, text_pointer)` | Validates the given text pointer. |

## Cursor Functions

These functions are designed to return status information about cursors and cursor operations.

| Function | Description |
|---|---|
| @@@CURSOR_ROWS | Returns the number of rows that are in the last cursor opened in the connection. |
| CURSOR_STATUS({'local', 'cursor_name'} CURSOR_STATUS {'global', 'cursor_name'} CURSOR_STATUS {'variable', 'cursor_variable'}) | Determines whether a procedure returned a cursor and result set for the given parameter. |
| @@@FETCH_STATUS | Returns status of the last cursor fetch statement. |

## Configuration Functions

These functions return information about different settings and constants for the SQL Server implementation:

| Function | Description |
|---|---|
| @@@CONNECTIONS | Returns the number of connections since SQL Server was started. |
| @@@DATEFIRST | Returns the value of the SET DATEFIRST parameter that indicates the specified first day of each week. |
| @@@DBTS | Returns the value of the timestamp datatype. |
| @@@LANGUAGE | Returns the name of the language that is currently in use by SQL Server. |

| Function | Description |
|---|---|
| @@@LANGID | Returns the language ID for the language that is currently in use by SQL Server. |
| @@@LOCK_TIMEOUT | Returns the lock time-out setting (milliseconds). |
| @@@MAX_CONNECTIONS | Returns the maximum number of simultaneous connections allowed on SQL Server. |
| @@@MAX_PRECISION | Returns the level of precision used by decimal and numeric datatypes on the server. |
| @@@OPTIONS | Returns information about current SET options. |
| @@@NESTLEVEL | Returns the nesting level for the current stored procedure. |
| @@@REMSERVER | Returns the name of a remote server. |
| @@@SPID | Returns the server process ID for the current process. |
| @@@SERVERNAME | Returns the name of the server. |
| @@@SERVICENAME | Returns the name of the registry key under which SQL Server is running. |
| @@@TEXTSIZE | Returns the current value of the TEXTSIZE option specified by the SET statement (maximum length in bytes of text and image data in the Select statement). |
| @@@VERSION | Returns date, processor type, and version of Microsoft SQL Server. |

A stored procedure can call or execute another stored procedure. Such stored procedures are said to be "nesting." SQL Server 7.0 and SQL Server 2000 have a limit of 32 stored procedure nesting levels. Earlier versions could nest up to 16 stored procedures.

The @@NESTLEVEL global variable keeps track of the number of nesting levels and can be used before executing a stored procedure to determine whether the number of nesting levels will cause the stored procedure to fail.

> **TIP:** Although the number of nesting levels is limited, there is no limit on the number of stored procedures that can be *called* from a single stored procedure. You can use this capability to construct a workaround if you ever encounter a problem with this issue. You will seldom have this problem, but the function has value as a debugging tool. You should not bother to test this value before each procedure call.

## System Statistical Functions

SQL Server maintains statistics about its performance and execution from the moment that it is started. The following functions are designed to obtain statistical information:

| Function | Description |
| --- | --- |
| @@@CPU_BUSY | Returns the time the CPU spent performing a task since SQL Server was last started. Time is in milliseconds. |
| @@@IDLE | Returns the time (in milliseconds) that SQL Server has been idle since it was started. |
| @@@IO_BUSY | Returns the time (in milliseconds) that SQL Server spent performing input and output operations since it was started. |
| @@@PACK_RECEIVED | Returns the number of input packets read from the network. |
| @@@PACK_SENT | Returns the number of output packets written to the network. |
| @@@PACKET_ERRORS | Returns the number of network packet errors since SQL Server was started. |

| Function | Description |
|---|---|
| @@@TIMETICKS | Returns the number of microseconds per tick. |
| @@@TOTAL_ERRORS | Returns the number of read/write errors since SQL Server was started. |
| @@TOTAL_READ | Returns the number of disc reads without cache reads by SQL Server since it was started. |
| @@@TOTAL_WRITE | Returns the number of disc writes by SQL Server since it was started. |

## Aggregate Functions

These functions perform an operation on a set of fields and return a single value. Their use is relatively limited. They can be used in the following situations:

▼   The selection list of the Select statement

■   A Having clause

▲   A Compute clause

| Function | Description |
|---|---|
| AVG( [ALL \| DISTINCT] expression) | Returns the average value in the group. |
| COUNT( [ALL \| DISTINCT] expression \|*) | Counts the number of items in the group. |
| COUNT_BIG( [ALL \| DISTINCT] expression \|*) | Counts the number of items in the group. The result is returned in the form of a bigint number. This function is available only in SQL Server 2000. |

| Function | Description |
|---|---|
| GROUPING(*Column_Name*) | Creates an additional column with a value of 1 when a row is added by the CUBE or ROLLUP operator or 0 if it is not the result of a CUBE or ROLLUP operator. |
| MAX(*expression*) | Returns the maximum value in the expression. |
| MIN (*expression*) | Returns the minimum value in the expression. |
| SUM(*expression*) | Returns the sum of the expression's values. |
| STDEV(*expression*) | Returns the statistical standard deviation for the values in the expression. |
| STDEVP(*expression*) | Returns the statistical standard deviation for the population for the values in the expression. |
| VAR(*expression*) | Returns the statistical variance of the values in the expression. |
| VARP(*expression*) | Returns the statistical variance for the population for the values in the expression. |

Except for the COUNT function, all aggregate functions remove records that have null in the specified field from the set.

```
select AVG(Rent) [Average Rent] from Inventory
```

As you can see, SQL Server will even print a warning about nulls:

```
Average Rent
------------
```

```
200.0000

(1 row(s) affected)

Warning: Null value eliminated from aggregate.
```

You apply COUNT on a specific field:

```
select COUNT(Rent) [Rentals] from Inventory
```

SQL Server will count only records that do not have null in the Rent field:

```
Rentals
------------
241

(1 row(s) affected)

Warning: Null value eliminated from aggregate.
```

You can apply COUNT on all fields:

```
select COUNT(*) [Assets] from Inventory
```

SQL Server counts all records in the table:

```
Assets
------------
7298

(1 row(s) affected)
```

# Rowset Functions

Functions from this set are unusual in that they return a complete recordset to the caller. They cannot be used (as scalar functions) in any place where an expression is acceptable. They can be used in Transact-SQL statements only in situations where the server expects a table reference. An example of such a situation is the From clause of the Select statement. These functions were introduced in Microsoft SQL Server 7.0.

The OPENQUERY function is designed to return a recordset from a linked server. It can be used as a part of Select, Update, Insert, and Delete Transact-SQL statements. The Query parameter must contain a valid SQL query in the dialect of the linked server, since the query will be executed (as-is—as a pass-through query) on the linked server. This function uses the following syntax:

```
OPENQUERY(linked_server, 'query')
```

**NOTE:**   Linked servers are OLE DB data sources that are registered on the local SQL Server. After registration, the local server knows how to access data on the remote server. All that is needed in your code is a reference to the name of the linked server.

You can register a linked server to be associated with the Northwind.mdb sample database either from Enterprise Manager or using the following code:

```
EXEC sp_addlinkedserver
    @server = 'Northwind_Access',
    @provider = 'Microsoft.Jest.OLEDB.4.0',
    @srvproduct = 'OLE DB Provider for Jet',
    @datasrc = 'c:\program files\Microsoft '
            + 'Office2000\Office\Samples\northwind.mdb'
Go
```

Then, you can use the OPENQUERY function to return records from the linked server:

```
SELECT *
FROM OPENQUERY(Northwind_Access, 'SELECT * FROM Orders')
```

OPENROWSET is very similar to the OPENQUERY function:

```
OPENROWSET(
'provider_name',
{'datasource';'user_id';'password' | 'provider_string' },
{ [catalog.][schema.]object | 'query'}
)
```

It is designed for connecting to a server that is not registered as a linked server. Therefore, the developer must supply both the connection parameters and the query to use it. There are several options for defining the connection, such as OLE DB, ODBC, and OLE DB for ODBC, along with two options for specifying a resultset: a pass-through query or a valid name for a database object.

The following query joins one table from the remote SQL Server with two tables on the local SQL Server:

```
SELECT a.au_lname, a.au_fname, titles.title
FROM OPENROWSET('MSDASQL',
    'DRIVER={SQLServer};SERVER=Toronto;UID=sa;PWD=pwd',
    pubs.dbo.authors) AS a
        INNER JOIN titleauthor
        ON a.au_id = titleauthor.au_id
            INNER JOIN titles
            ON titleauthor.title_id = titles.title_id
```

**TIP:** Although this code will work fine, if you plan repetitive use of some data source, you should consider registering it as a linked server. In this way, you can join data residing on different servers and different databases. Depending on the features of the OLE DB provider, you can also use this function to delete, update, or insert information on other servers.

## SUMMARY

We have described a large number, perhaps an overwhelming number, of SQL Server functions. If you think there are just too many functions defined in Transact-SQL, or that you will never remember them all, don't worry. We described all of these functions to give you an idea of the possibilities. It is first of all important to have a sense of what is achievable and what is not, and then you can easily consult documentation and work out the details. As with many other human pursuits, knowing something is often not as important as knowing where to find out about something.

A more frequent problem is that the function that you need does not exist in Transact-SQL. Sometimes you will be able to find a system stored procedure or extended stored procedure with the functionality you require.

# EXERCISES

1.  Create a `Select` statement that returns the quarter from the current date in the following format: '3Q2000'.

2.  Create a table called ExpectedShippingDate that contains the following fields:

    ■ ExpectedShippingDateId (offset from the starting date)

    ■ ExpectedShippingDate

    ■ ExpectedShippingDateOfMonth

    ■ ExpectedShippingMonth

    ■ ExpectedShippingYear

    ■ ExpectedShippingQuarter

    The table should be filled with one record for each date since 1/1/2000. Create a stored procedure Setup_ExpectedShippingDate to fill it.

3.  Create a table to store contact information. The last column should contain a binary checksum value so that later you can see if the record has changed.

# CHAPTER 6

## Composite Transact-SQL Constructs—Batches, Scripts, and Transactions

Transact-SQL statements can be grouped and executed together in a variety of ways. They can be

▼ Recompiled as a part of a stored procedure, user-defined function, or trigger

■ Written and executed individually or in groups from client utilities in the form of batches

■ Grouped and stored in external script files that can be opened and executed from various client utilities

▲ Grouped in transactions that succeed completely or fail completely

After completing this chapter you will understand

▼ The concept of a batch

■ How to set a batch explicitly

■ How a batch functions when errors are present

■ The effects of deferred name resolution on batch execution

■ Which Transact-SQL statement has to be alone in a batch

■ How to use variables, comments, and database objects in a batch

■ What a script is

■ How to generate scripts to generate database objects

■ What a transaction is

■ What types of transactions MS SQL Server supports

■ How to set transactions explicitly

■ How to create nested transactions

■ Restrictions on use

▲ Common mistakes and how to avoid them

It is not necessary to run examples from the text against the Asset database, but if you do, you must first make sure that the database contains the following table:

```
Create Table Part(PartId int identity,
                  Make varchar(50),
                  Model varchar(50),
                  Type varchar(50))
```

We will use this table to demonstrate the many features of batches. Some of the changes are destructive, so we will not use existing tables such as Equipment, which we may need for other purposes later. Just run the statement against the database using Query Analyzer.

# BATCHES

A *batch* is a set of Transact-SQL statements that are sent to and executed by SQL Server simultaneously. The most important characteristic of a batch is that it is parsed and executed on the server as an undivided entity. In some cases, batches are set implicitly. For example, if you decide to execute a set of Transact-SQL statements from Query Analyzer, the program will treat that set as one batch and do so invisibly:

```
Insert Into Part (Make, Model, Type)
Values ('Toshiba', 'Portege 7010CT', 'notebook')

Insert Into Part (Make, Model, Type)
Values ('Toshiba', 'Portege 7020CT', 'notebook')

Insert Into Part (Make, Model, Type)
Values ('Toshiba', 'Portege 7030CT', 'notebook')
```

Some tools, such as Query Analyzer, osql, and isql, use the Go command to divide Transact-SQL code into explicitly set batches. In the following example, the code for dropping a stored procedure is in one batch and the code for creating a new stored procedure is in another. The batch is explicitly created using the Go command:

```
If Exists (Select * From sysobjects
           Where id = object_id(N'[dbo].[prPartList]')
           And OBJECTPROPERTY(id, N'IsProcedure') = 1)
    Drop Procedure [dbo].[prPartList]
```

```
Go

Create Procedure prPartList
As
     Select * from Part
Return 0
Go
```

In Query Analyzer, you can highlight (that is, select with the mouse) part of the code and execute it. Query Analyzer treats the selected piece of code as a batch and sends it to the server. It ignores the rest of the code (see Figure 6-1).

In other utilities and development environments, batches may be divided in some other manner. In ADO, OLEDB, ODBC, and DB-Library, each command string prepared for execution (in the respective object or function) is treated as one batch.

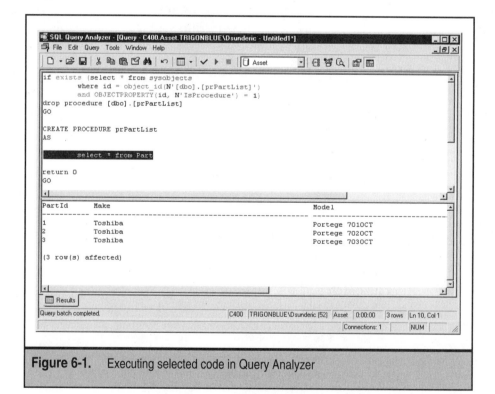

**Figure 6-1.** Executing selected code in Query Analyzer

# Using Batches

*Batches* reduce the time and processing associated with transferring statements from client to server, as well as that associated with parsing, compiling, and executing Transact-SQL statements. If a developer decides to execute a set of 100 insert commands against a database, it is preferable to group them in one batch rather than send them to the server as 100 separate statements. The overhead involved in sending 100 separate statements and receiving 100 separate results is very high. Network traffic will be increased unnecessarily, and the whole operation will be slower for the user.

# Batches and Errors

The fact that the batch is compiled as an undivided entity has interesting implications for syntax errors. Results will vary according to whether the syntax error occurs in a statement or in the name of a database object. If a DBA writes a batch with a statement that contains a syntax error, the whole batch will fail to execute.

Consider the following batch:

```
Insert into Part (Make, Model, Type)
Values ('Toshiba', 'Portégé 7020CT', 'Notebook')
Selec * from Part
```

It consists of two commands. The second contains a syntax error—a missing letter in the `Select` keyword. If you execute this batch in Query Analyzer, SQL Server will not compile or execute but will return the following error:

```
Server: Msg 170, Level 15, State 1, Line 3
Line 3: Incorrect syntax near 'Selec'
```

If you make a typo in the name of the database object (for instance, in a table or column name), the situation is very different. Note that the name of the table in the following `Insert` statement is incorrect:

```
Insert into art (Make, Model, Type)
Values ('Toshiba', 'Portege 7020CT', 'Notebook')
Select * from Part
```

In this example, the application will notice an error and stop execution as soon as it encounters it:

```
Server: Msg 208, Level 16, State 1, Line 1
Invalid object name 'art'.
```

SQL Server executes the batch in three steps: it parses, compiles, then executes. In the first phase, SQL Server verifies batch syntax. It focuses on the sequence of keywords, operators, and identifiers. The first batch used a statement with a typo in a keyword. SQL Server picked up the error during the parsing phase.

The error in the second batch (an invalid object name) was picked up during execution. To further demonstrate this fact, let's investigate the following example, where the error is in the second statement:

```
Insert into Part (Make, Model, Type)
Values ('Toshiba', 'Portege 7020CT', 'Notebook')
Select * from art
```

In this case, the application behaves differently:

```
(1 row(s) affected)

Server: Msg 208, Level 16, State 1, Line 1
Invalid object name 'art'.
```

Both commands are parsed and compiled, then the first command is executed, and finally the second command is canceled. Users with experience on earlier versions of Microsoft SQL Server will remember that such a scenario would produce very different results in those earlier versions.

Microsoft SQL Server versions 2000 and 7.0 have a feature called *deferred name resolution*. It allows the server to compile Transact-SQL statements even when underlying objects do not yet exist in the database. This feature can prove to be very useful when you are transferring objects from one database or server to another. You do not have to worry about dependencies and the order in which objects are created. Unfortunately, the introduction of this feature also has some strange secondary effects. In the case of the last example:

▼  The server has successfully compiled a batch, since the name resolution is not part of the compilation.

■  The first command was executed without a problem.

▲  When a problem was encountered in the second command, the server canceled all further processing and returned a runtime error.

Keep this problem in mind when writing batches. Developers in modern programming languages like Visual Basic or Visual C++ usually employ sophisticated error-handling strategies to avoid situations like this. Transact-SQL also contains programming constructs for error handling. We will explore them in the next chapter.

The situation could be worse. Particular runtime errors (for example, constraint violations) do not stop execution of the batch. In the following case, we attempt to use an `Insert` statement to insert a value in the identity column.

> **NOTE:**  Identity columns are a feature used by SQL Server to generate unique, sequential numbers for each record inserted in a table. It is equivalent to the AutoNumber datatype in Microsoft Access. Naturally, you should not attempt to specify values in such columns.

```
Select PartId, Make + ' ' + Model Part from Part
Insert into Part (PartId, Make, Model, Type)
Values (1, 'IBM', 'Thinkpad 390D', 'Notebook')
Select PartId, Make + ' ' + Model Part from Part
Go
```

The result is a "partial failure":

```
PartId       Part
----------- ----------------------------------------------------
1            Toshiba Portege 7020CT


(1 row(s) affected)
```

```
Server: Msg 544, Level 16, State 1, Line 1
Cannot insert explicit value for identity column in table
'Part' when IDENTITY_INSERT is set to OFF.
PartId       Part
-----------  ----------------------------------
1            Toshiba Portege 7020CT
```

(1 row(s) affected)

In some cases "partial success" may be tolerable, but in the real world it is generally not acceptable.

Let's investigate a case in which several batches are written, divided by a Go statement, and executed together. Although the user has issued a single command to execute them, the client application will divide the code into batches and send them to the server separately. If an error occurs in any batch, the server will cancel its execution. However, this does not mean that execution of the other batches is canceled. The server will try to execute the next batch automatically.

In some cases this may be useful, but in most it may not be what the user expects to happen. In the following example, a user tries to delete one column from the Part table. One way to perform this action (very popular until DBAs got spoiled with fancy tools like Enterprise Manager or the Alter Table ... Drop Column statement) would be to

▼   Create a temporary table to preserve the information that is currently in the Part table.

■   Copy information from the Part table to the temporary table.

■   Drop the existing Part table.

■   Create a Part table without the irrelevant columns.

■   Copy the preserved information back to the Part table.

▲   Drop the temporary table.

A code to implement this functionality could be created in a set of five batches:

```
Create Table TmpPart (PartId int identity,
                      Make varchar(50),
                      Model varchar(50),
                      Type varchar(50))
Go


Insert into TmpPart (PartId, Make, Model, EqTypeId)
Select PartId, Make, Model, EqTypeId from Part
Go


Drop Table Part
Go


Create Table Part (PartId int identity,
                   Make varchar(50),
                   Model varchar(50))
Go


Insert into Part (PartId, Make, Model)
Select PartId, Make, Model from TmpPart
Go


Drop Table TmpPart
Go
```

In theory, this set of batches would work perfectly. However, there is just one problem—the developer didn't take errors into account. For example, if a syntax error occurs in the first batch, a temporary table will not be created, Part information will not be preserved in it, and when the code drops the table, the information will be lost. To observe a method that experienced developers use to handle errors, read the next chapter.

# DDL Batches

Data Definition Language (DDL) is that part of Transact-SQL dedicated to the creation of database objects. For internal reasons, some DDL statements must stand alone in the batch, including the following statements:

▼ Create Procedure

■ Create Trigger

■ Create Default

■ Create Rule

■ Create View

■ Set Showplan_Text

▲ Set Showplan_All

If these statements are combined with other statements in a batch, the batch will fail.

## Self-Sufficient Content

During compilation, the batch is converted into a single execution plan. For this reason, the batch must be self-sufficient. In the real world, this concept has vast implications for the scope of database objects, variables, and comments.

**Scope of Objects**    Some DDL statements can be inside batches together with other commands, but keep in mind that the resulting object will not be accessible until the batch is completed. For example, it is not possible to add new columns to the table and to access those new columns in the same batch. Therefore, the following batch will fail:

```
Alter Table Part ADD Cost money NULL
select PartId, Cost from Part
Go
```

The Select statement is not able to access the Cost column, and the whole batch will fail:

```
Server: Msg 207, Level 16, State 3, Line 1
Invalid column name 'Cost'.
```

Therefore, the batch has to be divided in two:

```
Alter Table Part ADD Cost money NULL
Go
Select PartId, Cost from Part
Go
```

However, a workaround with the `Execute` statement will not work either:

```
Exec ('ALTER TABLE Part ADD Cost money NULL')
Select PartId, Cost from Part
Go
```

**Scope of Variables**    All (local) variables referenced in a batch must also be declared in that batch. The following code will result in the failure of the second batch:

```
Declare @Name as varchar (50)
Go
Select @Name = 'Dejan'
Go
```

**Scope of Comments**    Comments must be started and finished within the same batch. Ignoring this requirement will result in some very interesting outcomes, because Go commands are preprocessed on the client side, before the code is sent to the server. Take a look at the comment in the following sample:

```
Select * From Part
Go
Update Part
Set Type = 'desktop'
Where Type = 'PC'
/*
Go

Update Part
Set Type = 'Notebook'
Where Type = 'Laptop'
Go
```

```
Select * from Part
Go
Update Part
Set Type = 'desktop'
Where Type = 'computer'
Go
*/
Select * from Part
Go
```

To developers of other programming languages, this might look perfectly legal. Query Analyzer will even change the color of the code that is commented out. Unfortunately, this code is a complete disaster. Due to errors, the server will cancel execution of parts that the user expects to run and execute other parts that are commented out:

```
PartId       Make           Model              Type
-----------  -------------  -----------------  ------------------
1            Toshiba        Portege 7020CT     Laptop
(1 row(s) affected)


Server: Msg 113, Level 15, State 1, Line 2
Missing end comment mark '*/'.


(1 row(s) affected)

PartId       Make           Model              Type
-----------  -------------  -----------------  ------------------
1            Toshiba        Portege 7020CT     Notebook
(1 row(s) affected)


Server: Msg 170, Level 15, State 1, Line 4
Line 4: Incorrect syntax near '/'.
```

Query Analyzer will ignore the comments and send everything between the Go commands as separate batches.

The first batch is the only batch that behaves in accordance with the administrator's intention. The second batch fails because the comments are not complete:

```
Update Part
Set Type = 'desktop'
Where Type = 'PC'
/*
```

The third batch is executed because the server is not aware of the administrator's intention to comment it out:

```
Update Part
Set Type = 'Notebook'
Where Type = 'Laptop'
```

The fourth batch is also executed, because the server is not aware of the administrator's intention to comment it out:

```
Select * from Part
```

The fifth batch is also executed:

```
Update Part
Set Type = 'desktop'
Where Type = 'computer'
```

The last batch fails:

```
*/
Select * from Part
```

**TIP:** Comments must be started and finished within the same batch.

If the administrator wants to comment out the Go command, he must use two dashes as a comment marker at the beginning of the row:

```
--Go
```

# SCRIPTS

A *script* is usually defined as a collection of Transact-SQL statements (in one or more batches) in the form of an external file. Client tools, such as Query Analyzer, isql, osql, and Enterprise Manager, usually have support for managing script files.

Scripts are usually stored in plain text files with a .sql extension. This makes them manageable from any text editor as well as from many sophisticated tools, such as the Microsoft application for code control, Visual SourceSafe.

Query Analyzer has the usual features (File | Open, Save) of any text editor. isql and osql are command line utilities that allow the user to specify script files with code to be executed against the server.

## Database Scripting

One of the most exciting features in Enterprise Manager for both junior and senior administrators is the ability to perform reverse engineering on the database. The result of this process is a script with DDL statements, which can be used to re-create all database objects. This script can be used to

▼ Explore user and system database objects

■ Back up source code

■ Establish a source control process

▲ Transfer the complete database (or just some objects) to another server (and/or another database)

The process of database scripting is very simple. The user selects a database in Enterprise Manager and runs Tools | Generate SQL Script. The program prompts the user to specify the objects to be scripted:

On the Formatting tab, the user can decide in which format each database object is to be generated. A small preview template helps users make the right choice among several options:

The Options tab allows the user to specify options for supporting objects such as indexes, triggers, constraints, logins, users, roles, and permissions. The ability to specify a character set is very important for multilanguage environments.

```
Generate SQL Scripts - C400\Asset                              ☒

  General | Formatting | Options |

  ┌ Security scripting options ──────────────────────────────────────────
  │          ☐ Script database
  │ (icon)   ☐ Script database users and database roles
  │          ☐ Script SQL Server logins (Windows NT and SQL Server logins)
  │          ☐ Script object-level permissions
  ┌ Table scripting options ─────────────────────────────────────────────
  │          ☐ Script indexes
  │ (icon)   ☐ Script full-text indexes
  │          ☐ Script triggers
  │          ☐ Script PRIMARY keys, FOREIGN keys, defaults and check constraints
  ┌ File options ────────────────────────────────────────────────────────
  │          ┌ File format ─────────────┐  ┌ Files to generate ──────────┐
  │ (icon)   │ ○ MS-DOS text (OEM)      │  │ ⦿ Create one file           │
  │          │ ○ Windows text (ANSI)    │  │ ○ Create one file per object│
  │          │ ⦿ International text      │  │                             │
  │          │    (Unicode)             │  │                             │
  │          └──────────────────────────┘  └─────────────────────────────┘

                              ┌──────┐  ┌────────┐  ┌──────┐
                              │  OK  │  │ Cancel │  │ Help │
                              └──────┘  └────────┘  └──────┘
```

**TIP:** If you want to be able to open a script file from regular editors (that do not support Unicode) such as Notepad, you should select Windows Text (ANSI) as your file format.

The reason you are generating script and the use that you have planned for it will influence the decision to generate a single file (for example, when you want to transfer the object) or one file per object (for example, when you want to use scripts to establish source code control).

**TIP:** Use database scripting to explore the sample databases delivered with this book and the sample and system databases published with SQL Server. Exploration of other styles and methods in coding will help you to gain knowledge and build experience.

## THE TRANSACTION CONCEPT

Even from the very name of the Transact-SQL language, you can conclude that *transactions* play a major role in SQL Server. They are an important mechanism for enforcing the consistency and integrity of the database.

Transactions are the smallest units of work in SQL Server. To qualify a unit of work as a transaction, it must satisfy the four criteria often referred to as the *ACID* test (Atomicity, Consistency, Isolation, Durability):

▼   **Atomicity**   All data changes must be completed successfully, or none of them will be written permanently to the database.

■   **Consistency**   After a transaction, the database must be left in a consistent state. All rules must be applied during processing to ensure data integrity. All constraints must be satisfied. All internal data structures must be left in an acceptable state.

■   **Isolation**   Changes to the database made by a transaction must not be visible to other transactions until the transaction is complete. Before the transaction is committed, other transactions should see the data only in the state it was in before the transaction.

▲   **Durability**   Once a transaction is completed, changes must not revert even in the case of a system failure.

## Autocommit Transactions

In fact, every Transact-SQL statement is a transaction. When it is executed, it either finishes successfully or is completely abandoned. To illustrate this, let's try to delete all records from EqType table. Take a look at the following diagram:

A foreign key relationship exists between the EqType and Equipment tables. The foreign key will prevent the deletion of records in the EqType table that are referenced by records in the Equipment table.

Let's try to delete them anyway. You can see the result of such an attempt in Figure 6-2.

Two `Select` statements that will count the number of records in EqType are placed around the `Delete` statement. As expected, the `Delete` statement is aborted because of the foreign key. The count of records before and after the `Delete` statement is the same, which confirms that all changes made by the `Delete` statement were canceled. So the database remains in the state that it was in before the change was initiated.

If there were no errors, SQL Server would automatically commit the transaction (that is, it would record all changes) to the database. This kind of behavior is called *autocommit*.

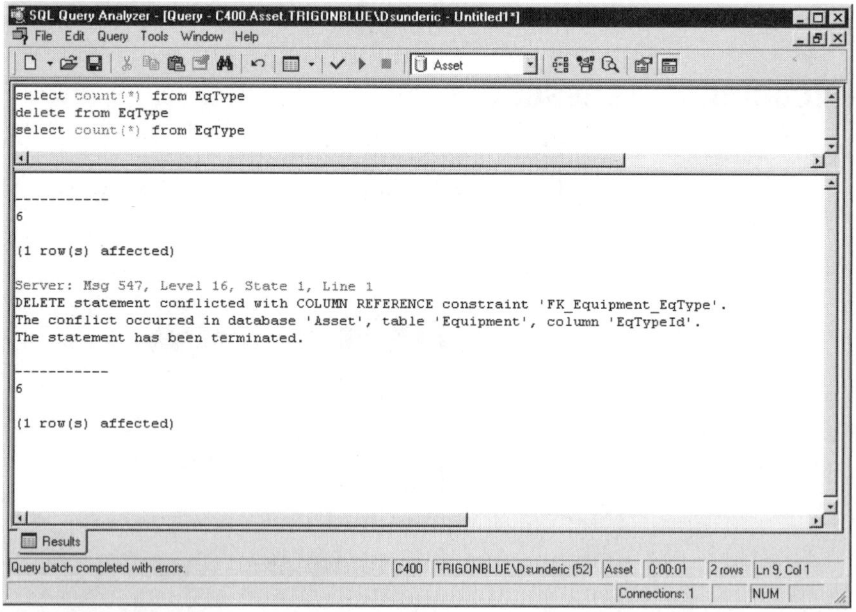

**Figure 6-2.**    Complete failure of attempt to delete records

In this case, SQL Server deleted records one after the other from the EqType table until it encountered a record that could not be deleted because of the foreign key relationship, at which point the operation was canceled.

# Explicit Transactions

The most popular and obvious way to use transactions is to give explicit commands to start or finish the transaction. Transactions started in this way are called *explicit transactions*. Developers can group two or more Transact-SQL statements into a single transaction using the following statements:

▼  `Begin Transaction`

■  `Rollback Transaction`

▲  `Commit Transaction`

If anything goes wrong with any of the grouped statements, all changes need to be aborted. The process of reversing changes is called *rollback* in SQL Server terminology. If everything is in order with all statements within a single transaction, all changes are recorded together in the database. In SQL Server terminology, we say that these changes are *committed* to the database.

We will demonstrate the use of these processes on the prClearLeaseSchedule stored procedure. Its main purpose is to set monthly lease amounts to zero for each asset associated with an expired lease schedule. It also sets the total of the lease amounts to zero. These two suboperations must be performed simultaneously to preserve the integrity of the database.

```
Create Procedure prClearLeaseShedule
-- Set value of Lease of all equipment
-- associated with expired Lease Schedule to 0.
-- Set total amount of Lease Schedule to 0.

      @intLeaseScheduleId int
As
```

```
Begin Transaction


-- Set value of Lease of all equipment
-- associated with expired Lease Schedule to 0
Update Inventory
Set Lease = 0
Where LeaseScheduleId = @intLeaseScheduleId

If @@Error <> 0 goto PROBLEM



-- Set total amount of Lease Schedule to 0
Update LeaseSchedule
Set PeriodicTotalAmount = 0
Where ScheduleId = @intLeaseScheduleId
If @@Error <> 0 goto PROBLEM

Commit Transaction
Return 0

PROBLEM:
Print ' Unable to eliminate lease amounts from the database!'
Rollback Transaction
Return 1
```

Before the real processing starts, the Begin Transaction statement notifies SQL Server to treat all of the following actions as a single transaction. It is followed by two Update statements. If no errors occur during the updates, all changes are committed to the database when SQL Server processes the Commit Transaction statement, and finally the stored procedure finishes. If an error occurs during the updates, it is detected by if statements and execution is continued from the PROBLEM label. After displaying a message to the user, SQL Server rolls back any changes that occurred during processing.

# Implicit Transactions

The third transaction mode is called the *implicit transaction*. To use this mode, you set a connection using the Set Implicit_Transactions On statement. Any of the following statements will serve as an implicit start to a transaction:

- ▼ Alter Table
- ■ Create
- ■ Delete
- ■ Drop
- ■ Fetch
- ■ Grant
- ■ Insert
- ■ Open
- ■ Revoke
- ■ Select
- ■ Truncate Table
- ▲ Update

To finish the transaction, a developer must use the Commit Transaction or Rollback Transaction statement. After that, any of the specified commands will start another transaction.

# Transaction Processing Architecture

An explanation of how transactions are implemented in Microsoft SQL Server will give you some insight into many processes.

Every change to the database is recorded in a transaction log before it is written to the appropriate tables. In SQL Server 2000 and SQL Server 7.0, transaction logs are implemented in separate files (or a set of files) with the extension .ldf. All modifications are written to this file chronologically. The records in this transaction log can later be used to roll back the transaction (thus providing Atomicity), or to commit the changes to the database (thus providing Durability). Two types of records can be stored in transaction logs:

▼ Logical operations performed (for instance, insert, delete, start of transaction)

▲ Before and after images of the changed data (that is, copies of data before and after the change is made)

The transaction log mechanism helps to resolve many issues:

▼ If a client application loses its connection before a transaction is finished, SQL Server will detect a problem and roll back changes (thus providing Consistency).

▲ If the machine loses power during processing, SQL Server will recover the database when services are restored. All transactions that were recorded in the transaction log in an undivided manner (that is, as part of a complete transaction set) are rolled forward (written to data tables) as if nothing unusual has happened (Durability). All transactions that were not completed before the problem occurred are rolled back (deleted) from the database.

The transaction log plays an important role in the implementation of backups in SQL Server. When a user starts a *full backup*, SQL Server records a complete snapshot of the data tables in backup files. At that point, SQL Server marks the current position in the transaction log and continues to record all changes to the database in the transaction log. Transactions logged during the process are also recorded as part of the full backup. When the backup is complete, SQL Server makes another mark in the transaction log. At the time of the next backup, a *transaction log backup* will suffice. To restore the database, an administrator first uses the full backup and then one or more transaction log backups that have been run since the full backup. SQL Server runs through the transaction log and applies changes to the data tables.

# Nested Transactions

SQL Server allows you to nest transactions. Basically, this feature means that a new transaction can start even though the previous one is not complete:

```
Begin transaction

...

    Begin transaction

    ...

    Commit transaction

...

Commit transaction
```

Usually this situation occurs when one stored procedure containing a transaction calls another stored procedure that also contains a transaction. In the following example, prCompleteOrder completes an order by setting its completion date and changing the status of the order, and then looping through associated order items and calling prCompleteOrderItem to complete each of them; prCompleteOrderItem sets the completion date of an order item to the last ChargeLog date associated with that OrderItem. Both of these procedures contain a transaction:

```
Alter Procedure prCompleteOrder_1
-- complete all orderItems and then complete order
@intOrderId int,
@dtsCompletionDate smalldatetime

As
set nocount on

Declare @intErrorCode int,
        @i int,
        @intCountOrderItems int,
        @intOrderItemId int

Select @intErrorCode = @@Error
```

```
If @intErrorCode = 0
    Begin Transaction

-- complete order
If @intErrorCode = 0
Begin
     Update [Order]
     Set CompletionDate = @dtsCompletionDate,
         OrderStatusId = 4 -- completed
     Where OrderId = @intOrderId

     Select @intErrorCode = @@Error
End



-- loop through OrderItems and complete them
If @intErrorCode = 0
Begin
     Create Table #OrderItems(
          id int identity(1,1),
          OrderItemId int)

     Select @intErrorCode = @@Error
End



-- collect orderItemIds
If @intErrorCode = 0
Begin
     Insert Into #OrderItems(OrderItemId)
          Select ItemId
          From OrderItem
          Where OrderId = @intOrderId
          Select @intErrorCode = @@Error
End
```

```
If @intErrorCode = 0
Begin
      Select @intCountOrderItems = Max(Id),
            @i = 1
      From #OrderItems

      Select @intErrorCode = @@Error
End

while @intErrorCode = 0 and @i <= @intCountOrderItems
Begin
      If @intErrorCode = 0
      Begin
            Select @intOrderItemId = OrderItemId
            From #OrderItems
            Where id = @I
            Select @intErrorCode = @@Error
      End

      If @intErrorCode = 0
            Exec @intErrorCode = prCompleteOrderItem_1 @intOrderItemId

If @intErrorCode = 0
            Set @i = @i + 1
End

If @intErrorCode = 0 and @@trancount > 0
      Commit Transaction
Else
      Rollback Transaction
return @intErrorCode
Go


Alter Procedure prCompleteOrderItem_1
-- Set CompletionDate of OrderItem to date
```

```
-- of last ChargeLog record associated with OrderItem.
    @intOrderItemId int
As
set nocount on
Declare @intErrorCode int
Select @intErrorCode = @@Error


If @intErrorCode = 0
    Begin Transaction


-- Set CompletionDate of OrderItem to date
-- of last ChargeLog record associated with OrderItem.
If @intErrorCode = 0
Begin
    update OrderItem
    Set CompletionDate = (Select Max(ChargeDate)
                            from ChargeLog
                            where ItemId = @intOrderItemId)
    Where ItemId = @intOrderItemId

    Select @intErrorCode = @@Error
End


If @intErrorCode = 0 and @@trancount > 0
Commit Transaction
Else
    Rollback Transaction
Return @intErrorCode
```

In the case of nested transactions, no `Commit` statements except the outer one will save changes to the database. Only after the last transaction is committed will all changes to the database become permanent. Up to that point, it is still possible to roll back all changes.

The interesting question is how SQL Server knows which transaction is the last one. It keeps the number of opened transactions in the @@trancount global variable for each user connection. When SQL Server encounters a Begin Transaction statement, it increments the value of the @@trancount, and when SQL Server encounters a Commit Transaction statement, it decrements the value of the @@trancount. Therefore, the only effect of a nested (internal) Commit Transaction statement is a change to the @@trancount value. Only the outer Commit Transaction statement (when @@trancount = 1) stores changes in data tables rather than in the transaction log.

Figure 6-3 shows an academic example that does not contain any real processing, but that demonstrates the effect of nested stored procedures on the @@trancount global variable.

An interesting inconsistency to observe is in the behavior of the Rollback Transaction statement. No matter how many transaction levels deep execution extends, the Rollback Transaction statement will cancel all changes caused by all transactions (and bring the @@trancount value down to zero).

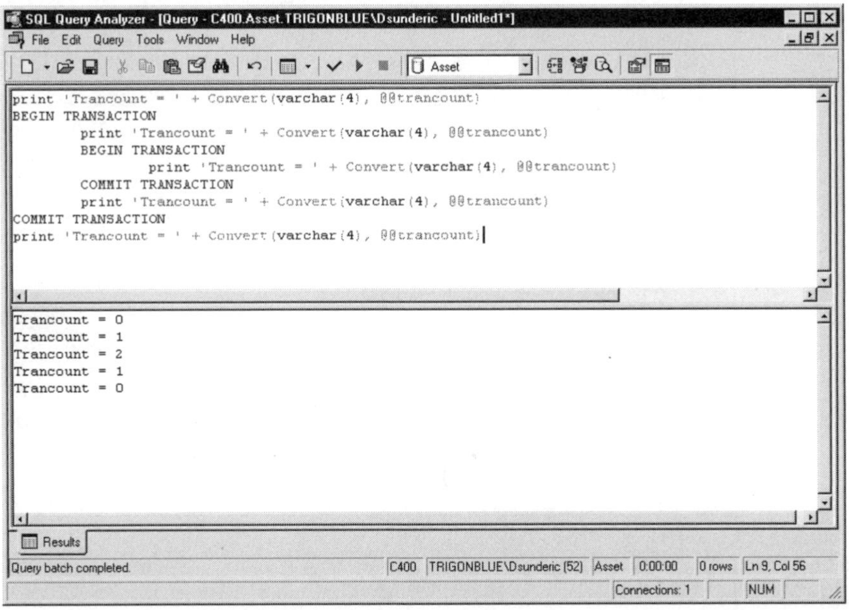

**Figure 6-3.**   Effect of transactional statements on @@trancount

In fact, if you execute an additional `Rollback Transaction` statement after the first one, SQL Server will report an error (see Figure 6-4).

> **TIP:** I have to admit that I had many problems with this issue at one time. Be careful.

To prevent this error, you need to test for the value of the `@@trancount` variable before you execute the `Rollback Transaction` statement. A simple way to test for this value could work something like this:

```
if @@trancount > 0
Rollback Transaction
```

You will find a much better solution in Chapter 7.

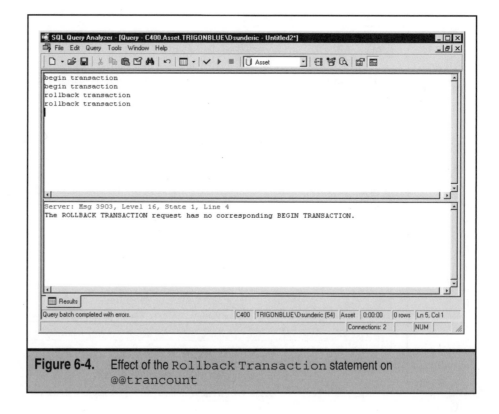

**Figure 6-4.** Effect of the `Rollback Transaction` statement on `@@trancount`

## Named Transactions

Transaction statements can be named. The name must be a valid SQL Server identifier (that is, no more than 128 characters), but SQL Server will read only the first 32 characters:

```
Begin Tran[saction] [transaction_name|@transaction_name_variable]
Commit Tran[Saction] [transaction_name|@transaction_name_variable]
Rollback [Tran[saction] [transaction_name|@transaction_name_variable]]
```

I know that this sounds like a perfect tool for resolving some issues with nested transactions. Unfortunately, in nested transactions, only the names of outer transactions are recorded by SQL Server. If you try to roll back any of the inner transactions, errors occur. Figure 6-5 provides an academic demonstration of such an attempt.

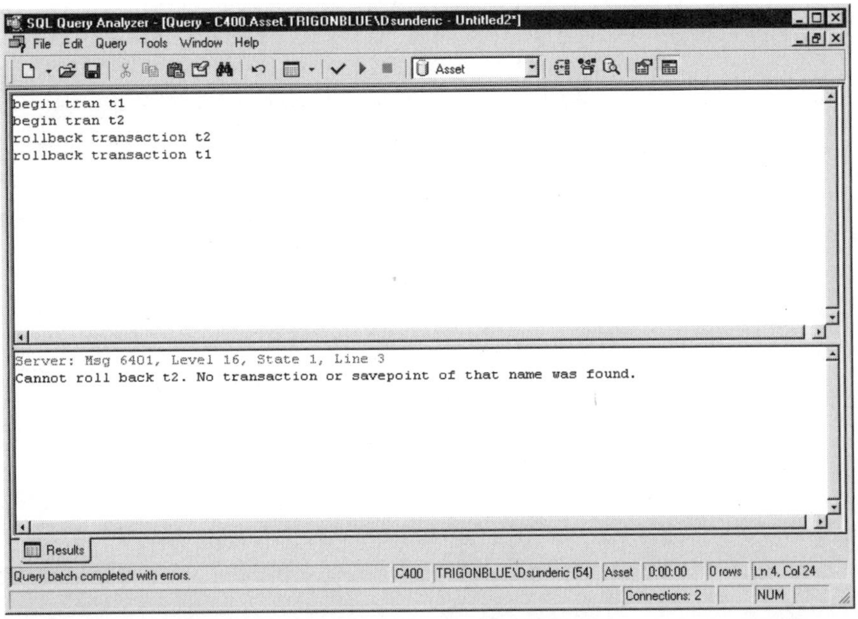

**Figure 6-5.** Named transactions

**TIP:** From Figure 6-5, you can see that you need to know the name of the outer transaction that has called all other stored procedures/transactions. This is not a practical requirement, especially when your stored procedure will be called from more than one stored procedure. Therefore, I recommend that you do not use transaction names.

## Savepoints

SQL Server contains a mechanism for canceling part of a transaction. This statement may seem to contradict the basic idea of a SQL Server transaction as I have explained it, but it can be justified in some cases (for example, in the case of bad connections or if an operation has a low probability of success). The mechanism is known as a *savepoint*.

To mark a savepoint in a transaction, use the following statement:

```
Save Tran[saction] {savepoint_name|@savepoint_variable}
```

The savepoint's name is also a SQL Server identifier, but SQL Server reads only the first 32 characters.

Savepoints do not save anything to the database. They just mark the point to which you can roll back a transaction. Resources (like locks) also stay in place after a `Save Transaction` statement. They are released only when a transaction has been completed or canceled.

The following procedures are designed to store an order and set of order items in a database. The prScrapOrderSaveItem stored procedure uses savepoints to roll back the insertion of a particular item.

```
Create Procedure prScrapOrder
-- save order information.

    @dtsOrderDate smalldatetime,
    @intRequestedById int,
    @dtsTargetDate smalldatetime,
    @chvNote varchar(200),
    @insOrderTypeId smallint,
    @inyOrderStatusId tinyint
As
```

```
    Set nocount on

    Insert [Order](OrderDate,    RequestedById,
                   TargetDate,   Note,
                   OrderTypeId,  OrderStatusId)
    Values (@dtsOrderDate,       @intRequestedById,
            @dtsTargetDate,      @chvNote,
            @insOrderTypeId,     @inyOrderStatusId)

Return @@identity
Go

Create Procedure prScrapOrderSaveItem
-- Saves order item.
-- If error occurs, this item will be rolled back,
-- but other items will be saved.

-- demonstration of use of Save Transaction
-- must be called from sp or batch that initiates transaction
     @intOrderId int,
     @intInventoryId int,
     @intOrderItemId int OUTPUT
As
    Set nocount on
    Declare    @intErrorCode int,
               @chvInventoryId varchar(10)

    -- name the transaction savepoint
    Set @chvInventoryId = Convert(varchar, @intInventoryId)

    Save Transaction @chvInventoryId

    -- Set value of Lease of all equipment associated
    -- with expired Lease Schedule to 0
    Insert OrderItem (OrderId, InventoryId)
    Values (@intOrderId, @intInventoryId)
```

```
        Select @intOrderItemId = @@identity,
               @intErrorCode = @@Error

        If @intErrorCode <> 0
        Begin
             Rollback Transaction @chvInventoryId
             Return @intErrorCode
        End

Return 0
Go
```

The following script demonstrates how an application using these stored procedures must initiate a transaction:

```
Declare    @intOrderId int,
           @intOrderItemId int

Begin Tran

Exec @intOrderId = prScrapOrder @dtsOrderDate = '1/10/1999',
                        @intRequestedById = 1,
                        @dtsTargetDate = '1/1/2000',
                        @chvNote = NULL,
                        @insOrderTypeId = 3, -- scrap
                        @inyOrderStatusId = 1 -- ordered
Exec prScrapOrderSaveItem @intOrderId,
                        11,
                        @intOrderItemId OUTPUT
Exec prScrapOrderSaveItem @intOrderId,
                        5,
                        @intOrderItemId OUTPUT
Exec prScrapOrderSaveItem @intOrderId,
                        7,
                        @intOrderItemId OUTPUT

Commit Tran
```

*TIP:* I have to tell you that, personally, I never use this mechanism. It is neither controllable nor flexible enough for my taste.

# Locking

Let me remind you of the requirements represented by the so-called ACID test. The Isolation requirement means that changes to the database made by a transaction are not visible to other transactions that are themselves in an intermediate state at the time of that transaction's completion, and that before the transaction is committed, other transactions can see data only in the state it was in before the transaction.

To satisfy the Isolation requirement, SQL Server uses *locks*. A lock is a restriction placed on the use of a resource in a multiuser environment. It prevents other users (that is, processes) from accessing or modifying data in the resource. SQL Server automatically acquires and releases locks on resources in accordance with the actions a user performs. For example, while the user is updating a table, nobody else can modify or even see records that are already updated. As soon as all updates connected to the user action are completed, the locks are released and the records become accessible.

There is just one problem with this process. Other users have to wait for the resource to become available again—they are *blocked*. Such blocking can lead to performance problems or even cause a process to crash. It is a tradeoff between data integrity and performance. SQL Server is intelligent enough to handle most problems, and it does a great job in preventing problems. It is also possible for a developer or an administrator to control the locking mechanism using *transaction isolation levels* and *optimizer hints*. I will describe these features later in this chapter.

Locks can have different levels of granularity. They can be acquired on

▼  Rows

■  Pages

■  Keys

- Ranges of keys
- Indexes
- Tables
▲ Databases

SQL Server automatically acquires a lock of the appropriate granularity on a resource. If it finds out during execution that a lock is no longer adequate, it dynamically changes the lock's granularity.

Locks are acquired by connection. Even if two connections are initiated from the same application, one can block the other.

The type of lock acquired by SQL Server depends on the effect that the change statement will have on the resource. For example, different locks are applied for the `Select` statement and the `Update` statement. There are five lock types:

▼ *Shared* (read) locks are usually acquired for operations that do not modify data (that is, read operations). Another transaction can also acquire a lock on the same record, and thus the lock is shared. The shared lock is released when the transaction moves on to read another record.

- *Exclusive* (write) locks are acquired for statements that modify data (such as `Insert`, `Update`, and `Delete`). Only one exclusive lock on a resource can be held at a time. An exclusive lock can be acquired only after other locks on the resource (including shared locks) are released.

- *Update* locks resemble shared locks more than they do exclusive locks. They are used to notify SQL Server that a transaction will later modify a resource. They prevent other transactions from acquiring exclusive locks. Update locks can coexist with shared locks. Just before the resource is modified, SQL Server promotes the update lock to an exclusive lock.

- *Intent* locks are set on an object of higher granularity to notify SQL Server that a process has placed a lock of lower granularity inside the object. For example, if a transaction places a lock on a page in a table, it will also place an intent lock on the table. The intent lock means that SQL Server does not have to scan the whole table to find out if a process has placed a lock on some page or record inside, in order to place a table lock for another transaction. In fact, there are three different types of intent locks: IS (intent share), IX (intent exclusive), and SIX (shared with intent exclusive).

▲ *Schema* locks prevent the dropping or modifying of a table or index while it is in use. There are two types of schema locks. Sch-S (schema stability) locks prevent table or index drops. Sch-M (schema modification) locks ensure that other transactions cannot access the resource while it is being modified.

## Transaction Isolation Levels and Hints

A developer or administrator can change the default behavior of SQL Server using *transaction isolation levels* or *lock hints.* Transaction isolation levels set locking on the connection level, and lock hints on the statement level. SQL Server can work on four different transaction isolation levels:

▼ *Serializable* is the highest level in which transactions are completely isolated. The system behaves as though the transactions are occurring one after another. This level of isolation may lead to some performance issues.

■ *Repeatable Read* level forces SQL Server to place shared locks and hold them until the transaction is completed.

■ *Read Committed* is the default level in SQL Server. SQL Server places shared locks when reading.

▲ *Read Uncommitted* is the lowest level of isolation in SQL Server. It ensures that physically corrupt data is not read. SQL Server will not place shared locks, and it will ignore exclusive locks. You will have the fewest performance issues when using this level, but you will also likely have many data integrity problems.

Isolation level is specified in the Set statement. For example

```
Set Transaction Isolation Level Repeatable Read
```

Locking hints change the behavior of the locking manager as it processes a single Transact-SQL statement. They overwrite behavior set by the transaction isolation level. The following table describes hints that can be used to control locking:

| Hints | Description |
| --- | --- |
| Holdlock or Serializable | Holds a shared lock until a transaction is completed. The lock will not be released when the resource is no longer needed, but when the transaction is completed. |
| Nolock | This hint applies only to Select statements. SQL Server will not place shared locks, and it will ignore exclusive locks. |
| Updlock | Uses update instead of shared locks while reading a table. |
| Rowlock | Specifies the granularity of locks at the row level. |
| Paglock | Specifies the granularity of locks at the page level. |
| Tablock | Specifies the granularity of locks at the table level. |
| Tablockx | Specifies the granularity of locks at the table level and the type of lock to be exclusive. |
| Readcommitted | Equivalent to the default isolation level (Read Committed). |

| | |
|---|---|
| Readpast | This hint is applicable only in `Select` statements working under the `Read Committed` isolation level. Resultsets created with this hint will not contain records locked by other transactions. |
| Readuncommitted | Equivalent to `Read Uncommitted` isolation level. |
| Repeatableread | Equivalent to `Repeatable Read` isolation level. |

Locking hints can be used in `Select`, `Insert`, `Update`, or `Delete` statements. They are part of the `From` clause. For example, the following command will hold a lock until the transaction is completed:

```
Select *
From Inventory With (HOLDLOCK)
Where InventoryId = @intInventoryId
```

The next example demonstrates the use of hints in an `Update` statement and the use of more than one hint in a statement:

```
Update Inventory With (TABLOCKX, HOLDLOCK)
Set StatusId = 4
Where StatusId = @intStatusId
```

## Distributed Transactions

Microsoft Distributed Transaction Coordinator (MS DTC) is a component that allows users to span transactions over two or more servers.

Servers in this scenario are called *resource managers,* and MS DTC performs the function of transaction coordinator. In fact, all those resource managers do not even have to be Microsoft servers. They just have to be compatible with MS DTC. For example, it is possible to execute a single transaction against databases on Microsoft SQL Server and Oracle.

When transactions are distributed over different resource managers, different mechanisms have to be applied by the transaction coordinator to compensate for problems that might occur in such an environment. A typical problem is network failure. For example, everything might be executed properly by individual resource managers, but if the transaction coordinator is not informed, the result is the same as if one of the resource managers had failed. The transaction will be rolled back.

One mechanism for dealing with such problems is called two-phase commit (2PC). As the name implies, it consists of two phases:

▼ Prepare phase

▲ Commit phase

The prepare phase starts when a transaction manager receives a request to execute a transaction. It notifies the resource managers and informs them of the work that needs to be done. The resource managers perform all changes and even write everything from the transaction log in memory to the disk. When everything is completed, each resource manager sends a message indicating success or failure status to the transaction coordinator.

The commit phase starts when the transaction coordinator receives messages from resource managers. If the resource managers successfully complete the preparation phase, the transaction coordinator sends a Commit command to the resource managers. Each of them makes the changes permanently to the database and reports the success of the operation to the transaction coordinator. If any of the resource managers reports failure during the preparation phase, the transaction coordinator will send a Rollback command to all resource managers.

From a developer's point of view, distributed transactions are very similar to regular transactions. The major difference is that the developer needs to use the following statement to start the transaction:

```
Begin Distributed Tran[saction]  [transaction_name]
```

Transactions are completed with regular Commit or Rollback statements. The following stored procedure updates two tables in a local database and then updates information in a remote database using a remote stored procedure:

```
Alter Procedure prClearLeaseShedule_distributed
-- Set value of Lease of all equipment associated to 0
-- Set total amount of Lease Schedule to 0.
-- notify lease company that lease schedule is completed
    @intLeaseScheduleId int
As
    Declare @chvLeaseNumber varchar(50),
            @intErrorCode int


    -- Verify that lease has expired
    If GetDate() <       (Select EndDate
                    From LeaseSchedule
                    Where ScheduleId = @intLeaseScheduleId)


        Raiserror ('Specified lease schedule has not expired yet!', 16,1)
    If @@Error <> 0
    Begin
        Print 'Unable to eliminate lease amounts from the database!'
        Return 50000
    End


    -- get lease number
    Select @chvLeaseNumber = Lease.LeaseNumber
    From Lease
    Inner Join      LeaseSchedule
    On Lease.LeaseId = LeaseSchedule.LeaseId
    Where (LeaseSchedule.ScheduleId = @intLeaseScheduleId)


Begin Distributed Transaction

    -- Set value of Lease of all equipment associated to 0
    Update Inventory
    Set Lease = 0
    Where LeaseScheduleId = @intLeaseScheduleId
    If @@Error <> 0 Goto PROBLEM
```

```
        -- Set total amount of Lease Schedule to 0
        Update LeaseSchedule
        Set PeriodicTotalAmount = 0
        Where ScheduleId = @intLeaseScheduleId
        If @@Error <> 0 Goto PROBLEM


        -- notify lease vendor
Exec @intErrorCode = lease_srvr.LeaseShedules..prLeaseScheduleComplete
                    @chvLeaseNumber, @intLeaseScheduleId


        If @intErrorCode <> 0 GoTo PROBLEM

        Commit Transaction
        Return 0

PROBLEM:
        print 'Unable to complete lease schedule!'
        Rollback Transaction
Return 50000
```

Apart from a reference to the remote stored procedure, the only thing that the developer needed to do was to use the `Distributed` keyword to start the transaction. Everything else was managed by MS DTC.

# Typical Errors

Transactions are a powerful weapon in the hands of a programmer, but improper use can cause substantial damage. I will try to forewarn you of some typical problems.

## A Never Ending Story

The worst thing that you can do is to open a transaction and then forget to close it. All changes sent to the database through that connection will become part of that transaction; resources normally released at the end of a transaction are held indefinitely; other users cannot access resources; and eventually, your server chokes.

## Spanning a Transaction over Batches

A transaction can span batches. SQL Server counts transactions over the connection, so it is "legal" to issue two batches like this over one connection:

```
Begin Transaction
update Inventory
set Lease = 0
where LeaseScheduleId = 141
Go

update LeaseSchedule
Set PeriodicTotalAmount = 0
where ScheduleId = 141
Commit Transaction
Go
```

However, I cannot think of any justification for doing so, and you significantly increase the probability of error. For example, you could easily forget to finish the transaction.

## Named Transactions and Savepoints

Transaction names and savepoint names do not bring much value to your solutions, but they do bring additional risks. There are too many rules that you need to keep in mind. It is best not to use them at all.

## Rollback Before Begin

Sometimes you might set your error handling so that all errors that occur in a stored procedure are treated in the same way. Naturally, you will include a statement to roll back the transaction. If an error occurs before the transaction starts, the stored procedure will jump to the error handling code and another error will occur:

```
Create Procedure prClearLeaseShedule_1
-- Set value of Lease of all equipment associated
-- with expired Lease Schedule to 0
-- Set total amount of Lease Schedule to 0.

    @intLeaseScheduleId int
As

    -- Verify that lease has expired
    If GetDate() < (select EndDate
                from LeaseSchedule
                where ScheduleId = @intLeaseScheduleId)
        raiserror ('Specified lease schedule has not expired yet!', 16,1)

-- If error occurs here,
-- server will execute Rollback before transaction is started!
if @@Error <> 0 goto PROBLEM

Begin Transaction

    -- Set value of Lease of all equipment associated
    -- with expired Lease Schedule to 0
    update Inventory
    set Lease = 0
    where LeaseScheduleId = @intLeaseScheduleId
    if @@Error <> 0 goto PROBLEM

    -- Set total amount of Lease Schedule to 0
    update LeaseSchedule
    Set PeriodicTotalAmount = 0
    where ScheduleId = @intLeaseScheduleId
    if @@Error <> 0 goto PROBLEM

    commit transaction
    return 0
```

PROBLEM:

```
print 'Unable to eliminate lease amounts from the database!'
     rollback transaction
return 1
```

## Multiple Rollbacks

Unlike Commit statements, only one Rollback statement is required to close a set of nested transactions. In fact, if more than one Rollback statement is executed, SQL Server will raise another error.

## Long Transactions

SQL Server places locks on data that have been modified by a transaction to prevent other users from further changing the data until the transaction is committed. This feature can lead to problems if a transaction takes "too long" to complete.

*NOTE:* There is no exact definition of "too long." The longer a transaction works, the greater the likelihood that problems will occur.

Some of the problems that might occur if a long transaction is present in the database include the following:

▼  Other users are blocked. They will not be able to access and modify data.

■  The transaction log fills up. (SQL Server 2000 and SQL Server 7.0 will automatically increase the size of transaction log, but you could fill your disk as well.)

▲  Most of the time, transaction log work is performed in memory. If all available memory is used before the transaction is complete, SQL Server will start saving changes to disk, thus reducing the overall performance of the server.

> ***TIP:*** You should be particularly aware of concurrency problems because they are the problems most likely to happen. While you are developing applications, you will probably work alone (or in a small group) on the server, but the situation will change drastically when you place 50, 250, or 5,000 concurrent users on the production server.

## SUMMARY

Before continuing the exploration of stored procedures, we had to make a sojourn to review other methods of grouping Transact-SQL statements. The advantages and disadvantages of batches and scripts have led the designers of SQL Server to implement stored procedures as a prominent feature for DBAs.

Batches are sets of Transact-SQL statements that are sent to SQL Server simultaneously. It is possible to set a batch explicitly in Query Analyzer and other tools by using the Go command or by highlighting a part of the code that needs to be executed. If SQL Server encounters a syntax error during parsing of the batch, further processing of that batch is stopped. Processing of other batches may continue.

A script is an ordinary text file, usually with a .sql extension, that contains Transact-SQL statements. It is possible to generate a script with all the DDL statements needed to re-create a complete database and all the objects inside it. Script files can be opened and executed from SQL Server client utilities such as Query Analyzer, isql, and osql.

Transactions are one of the most important concepts in SQL Server. Their use is required to keep a database consistent. Even if a developer is not explicitly using transactions, SQL Server treats each Transact-SQL statement as a separate transaction.

The use of transactions can become complicated if a developer decides to nest them. Special care is required to handle the different behaviors of the Commit and Rollback statements. It is also possible to name transactions, but this practice introduces a new level of complexity that needs to be managed and therefore is not recommended. Savepoints allow developers to roll back a part of a transaction. This practice is not consistent with the basic concept that a transaction should be either completely committed or completely rolled back. However, in some cases, solutions based on Savepoint can be helpful.

SQL Server uses locks to enforce different levels of isolation between transactions. Administrators and developers can set levels for connection or specify which lock will be used inside the Transact-SQL statement.

# EXERCISES

1. Create a database script for the Asset database.

2. Create a database script for a single stored procedure in the Asset database. Add a line of comment into the script and execute it.

3. What is the problem with the following script?

```
select *
from Eq
/*
Go
delete Eq
where EqId > 100
Go
*/
select *
from EqType
```

How can you fix it?

4. How do the `Rollback Transaction` and `Commit Transaction` statements affect `@@trancount`?

5. Create a table with bank account information and then a stored procedure for transferring funds from one account to another. The stored procedure should contain transaction processing.

6. Is it okay to span transaction over multiple batches?

# CHAPTER 7

# Debugging and Error Handling

Debugging and error handling seem like such negative topics. By admitting debugging as a necessary phase of development and error handling as a required practice, we seem to admit to weakness in our abilities as developers. But we are not the computers themselves: we cannot account for all contingencies when we write code. So, to find the error of our ways after the fact, we need a coherent approach to the identification and resolution of defects in our code and a coherent strategy for handling errors in our code as they occur.

# DEBUGGING

The process of debugging is an integral part of both the development and stabilization phases of software production.

## What Is a "Bug"?

You have probably heard errors and defects found in software referred to as "bugs." This word has found its way into our everyday language and reality so that we now seem to regard the bug as normal and inevitable—like death and taxes. However, not many people know how this term actually entered the language.

It happened in the dim, distant technological past when computers occupied whole rooms (if not buildings). On one occasion, technicians were investigating a malfunction on such a computer. Much to their surprise, they found the cause of the circuit malfunction to be a large moth that had been attracted by the heat and glow of the machine's vacuum tubes. Over time, all computer-related errors (particularly the ones that were difficult to explain) came to be known as bugs.

Sometimes we anthropomorphize bugs—give them human attributes. They can seem in turn capricious and malicious, but the bugs we experience in application and database development are not related to mythological folk such as gremlins. Bugs are very real, but their causes are inevitably human. Computers bear no malice toward users or developers, compilers do not play practical jokes, and operating systems are not being stubborn when they refuse to operate as expected. No, when you encounter an error, you can be sure that it was you or another programmer who caused it. What you need to do is find the offending code and fix it, but to find bugs efficiently and painlessly, you need to establish a debugging process—a formal routine with well-defined steps and rules.

# The Debugging Process

The objectives of the debugging process are to identify and resolve the defects present in a software product. This process consists of two phases:

1. Identification
2. Resolution

## Identification

The identification phase consists of two primary activities:

1. Stabilize the error.
2. Find the source of the error.

**Stabilize the Error**     In most cases, identifying the error consumes 95 percent of your debugging time, whereas fixing it often requires just a few minutes. The first step in identifying an error is to stabilize (or isolate) the error. You must make the error repeatable. What this means is that you must find a test case that causes the error to recur predictably. If you are not able to reproduce the error, you will not be able to identify its cause nor will you be able to fix it.

But we need to qualify the test case in another way. It is not enough to create a test case that will cause the error to occur predictably. You must also strive to simplify the test case in order to identify the minimum circumstances under which the error will occur. Refining the test case is certainly the most difficult aspect of debugging, and cultivating this skill will greatly enhance your debugging efficiency, while removing a large part of the frustration. Stabilizing the error answers the question, "What is the error?" With this knowledge in hand, we can go on to answer the question, "Why does the error occur?"

**Find the Source of the Error**    After you identify the minimum circumstances under which the error will occur, you can proceed to find the source of the error. If your code is properly structured and well written, this search should not be a difficult task. You can apply a variety of tools at this point:

▼   Your brain (first and foremost)

■   SQL Server

▲   TSQL Debugger

*Use your brain:* The most important debugging tool at your disposal is your brain. If you can follow the program's execution and understand its logic, you will be able to understand the problem as well. When you have learned everything your test cases can teach you, you can create a hypothesis, then prove it through further testing.

*SQL Server:* Some errors will be clearly reported by SQL Server. Be sure that your client application picks up and displays all error messages reported by the server. Also, try using Query Analyzer to execute your stored procedures without the client application. Naturally, you should take care to use the same parameters that were passed from the client application when you produced the error.

*TSQL Debugger:* An integral part of Visual Studio is TSQL Debugger. It enables you to set breakpoints in your code and pause the execution to investigate and change the contents of the local variables, the global variables, and the input and output parameters. The TSQL Debugger lets you step through the code of your stored procedures and triggers. It is fully integrated with many development environments and lets you move from Visual Basic, JavaScript, C++, or any other client code into a Transact-SQL statement code. Query Analyzer in SQL Server 2000 also contains a TSQL Debugger. It has features similar to the one in Visual Studio.

## Resolution

Resolving defects in your code is usually much easier then finding those defects, but do not take this phase too lightly. At this point in the development cycle, when the product shipping date is looming large, you may be tempted by the "quick fix." Resist this temptation: it often causes developers to introduce new errors while fixing the old ones. It is seldom an issue of carelessness or incompetence, but rather of increased pressure to fix and ship a product.

The resolution phase consists of two primary activities:

1. Develop the solution in a test environment.

2. Implement the solution in the production environment.

**Develop the Solution in a Test Environment**     To consistently resolve defects in your code, you need to assemble two critical ingredients:

▼   A test environment

▲   Source code control

*Test environment:* SQL Server is especially susceptible to errors generated in haste to solve a problem, because a stored procedure is compiled and saved as a single action. If you are trying to resolve defects on the production system, you are performing brain surgery *in vivo.*

Although it is possible to perform fixes in a production environment, it is always much better to step back, spend adequate time understanding the problem, and then attempt to solve the problem outside of the production environment.

If a test environment does not exist or if the existing test environment is outdated, you may be tempted to "save time" with a "quick and dirty" fix. Before you go down this path, however, you should consider the resources that would be required to reverse the changes made if you happen to make a mistake. Anything you do, you should be able to undo quickly and easily.

Let it be understood, loud and clear: you need a test environment!

*Source code control:* Keep source code of your procedures and database objects. Source code control gives you a snapshot of your application at critical nodes in the development cycle and allows you to "turn back the clock." It gives you the ability to reverse changes if you find they have introduced new problems or failed to solve the existing one. Visual SourceSafe, which we will examine in the next chapter, is a perfect tool for this function.

Source code control works best if you take a patient approach to debugging. You should save versions often to help you identify the source of errors when they occur. It is a poor practice to make multiple changes per version. Old and new errors tend to overlap and lead you to incorrect conclusions.

**Implement the Solution in the Production Environment**    Once you are satisfied with the change, you should implement it in the production environment. Then test. Then test again. You should not assume that it will work in the production environment because it worked in the test environment. If, after stringent testing, everything is still functioning properly, you should then look for other places in the code and database structure where similar errors may be situated.

# Debugging Tools and Techniques

Modern development environments contain sophisticated tools to help you debug your applications. The TSQL Debugger in Visual Studio and TSQL Debugger in Query Analyzer are such tools and will help you to identify and fix problems in your code. We will first examine TSQL Debugger in Visual Studio and then in Query Analyzer. However, even if your development environment does not support the TSQL Debugger, there are techniques you can employ to achieve the same results. We will discuss them later in this chapter.

## TSQL Debugger in Visual Studio

TSQL Debugger is a dream tool for developers working in Visual Studio to find errors in a Microsoft SQL Server environment, but there is a downside: TSQL Debugger from Visual Studio is difficult to install and configure. This difficulty arises from the nature of the environment and the complexity of the components required for debugging.

Debugger was initially released as a part of Visual C++ 4.2. Now it is a component of the Enterprise Edition of all Visual Studio tools (such as Visual Basic and Visual InterDev).

**Requirements**   Before you continue, make sure that your development environment fulfills the following requirements:

1. Microsoft SQL Server 7.0 or 2000 (or Microsoft SQL Server 6.5 with Service Pack 2 or later) must be installed. At the time of publication, TSQL Debugger was not compatible with Desktop Engine (MSDE).

2. Microsoft SQL Server must be running on Windows NT 4.0 Server or Windows 2000 Server or higher.

3. You must have the Enterprise Edition of one Visual Studio development tool such as Visual Basic or Visual InterDev.

4. Client-side tools must be installed on workstations with Windows 9x, Windows NT 4.0, or Windows 2000.

**Configuration**   TSQL Debugger is a complex tool that relies on the synchronous behavior of many components. Because all of these components are delivered with different versions of various programs, the biggest challenge that you face is to force all of these components to work together. You can achieve this end by following these configuration steps:

1. Install debugging components on your SQL Server machine.

2. Set up a valid user account (not a system account).

3. Verify that DCOM is properly configured.

*Install debugging components:* The installation of debugging components is different for each development tool. First, check the documentation provided with the development tool for details. When you install the development tool, it is a good idea to use the Custom Setup option to make sure that the SQL Server Debugging components are installed.

In Visual Studio 6.0, the setup program is in the Sqldbg_ss folder on Disc 2. You may need to reinstall SQL Server Debugging if the Application Event Log contains error messages referring to missing DLLs containing "SDI" in their names. For example:

```
17750: Cannot load the DLL SDI, or one of the DLLs it references.
Reason: 126 (The specified module could not be found.).
```

You should check the Application Event Log for messages like this one if your debugger is not working.

With some development tools, you need to perform an additional step to enable the TSQL Debugger. For example, in Visual Basic you need to access the Add In Manager and select TSQL Debugger To Be Loaded.

*Set up a valid user account (not a system account):* SQL Server can run as a service under the virtual LocalSystem account or under a real user account with adequate privileges. For debugging purposes, it must run under a real user account. To set up a user account under Windows 2000:

1. Open the Control Panel and then Administrative Tools.

2. Open the Services applet.

3. Select the MSSQLServer service and then right-click.

4. When context menu appears on the screen, select Properties.

5. The program will display the Properties dialog box. Switch to the Log On tab (see Figure 7-1).

6. Select This Account and type the user name in the text box.

7. Type the password for the account in the Password text box.

8. Type the password again in the Confirm Password text box, and then click OK to close the dialog box.

9. Right-click the MSSQLServer service again, and choose Restart from the menu.

**TIP:** I am using an Administrator account. This account was created by the system during Windows NT setup, but it is not a "system account."

*Verify that DCOM is properly configured:* SQL Server uses DCOM to communicate between the client workstation and the database server during debugging.

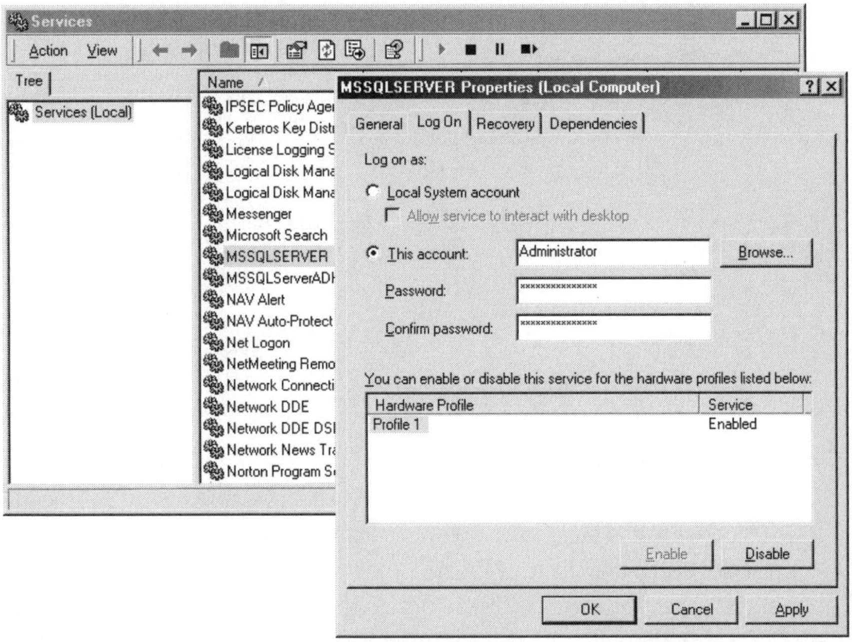

**Figure 7-1.**    Setting Services

*TIP:*  If both TSQL Debugger and SQL Server are running on the same machine during debugging, you will not need to configure DCOM.

When Microsoft SQL Server is installed on a server machine, all DCOM settings are configured to support DCOM for cross-machine debugging. However, due to security issues, administrators occasionally have restricted access to the server through DCOM. If you have followed all of the instructions in your development tool's documentation and your debugger is still not working, check DCOM configuration:

1.  Run dcomcnfg.exe from the Command Prompt. The Distributed COM Configuration Properties window appears.

2. Open the Default Security tab.

3. In Default Access Permissions, click Edit Default.

4. If the Everyone group already has Allow Access permission, your DCOM configuration is okay. If not, add the user that you plan to use (apply *domain\user* format).

5. Assign Allow Access permission to the new user.

6. If the System group does not have Allow Access permission, add it.

**SQL Server Debugging Interface**    Microsoft developers have defined a DLL with a set of functions to be called before each Transact-SQL statement. This tool is called the SQL Server Debugging Interface (SDI). The core of SDI is a pseudo-extended stored procedure called sp_sdidebug. It is defined in the sysobjects table as an extended stored procedure, although it is not based on an external DLL file. Its name includes the prefix "sp" so that it can be accessed from all databases as a system stored procedure. When the debugger executes this stored procedure, it loads the DLL, which provides access to SQL Server internal state information.

**NOTE:**    SDI adds substantial overhead and makes the machine run more slowly. For this reason, you should never use TSQL Debugger on a production machine.

**Using TSQL Debugger in Visual Studio**    Let's demonstrate the use of TSQL Debugger from Visual InterDev.

The major difference between debugging stored procedures and debugging within other programming languages is that you do not need to run the application to debug a single procedure.

1. Open Data View in Visual InterDev.

2. Open Stored Procedures and right-click the stored procedure prGetInventoryProperties_3.

3.  When you click Debug, TSQL Debugger starts the procedure
    and prompts you for input parameters (see Figure 7-2).
    Use the Value combo box to select <DEFAULT> or Null or
    type something appropriate.

4.  Click OK.
    TSQL Debugger opens the source code of the procedure
    and pauses on the first executable statement. A small yellow
    arrow on the left border marks the position of the statement to
    be executed next. The commands in the Debug menu become
    enabled, as do two more windows that enable you to examine
    the state of the environment, as shown in Figure 7-3.

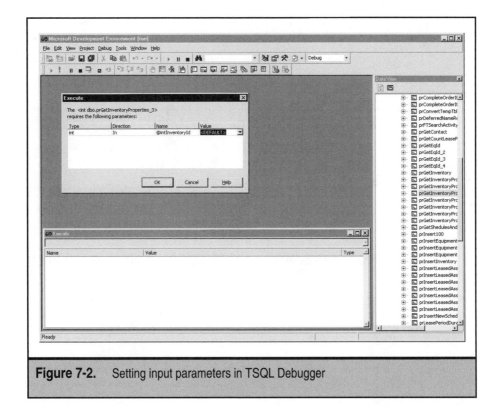

**Figure 7-2.**    Setting input parameters in TSQL Debugger

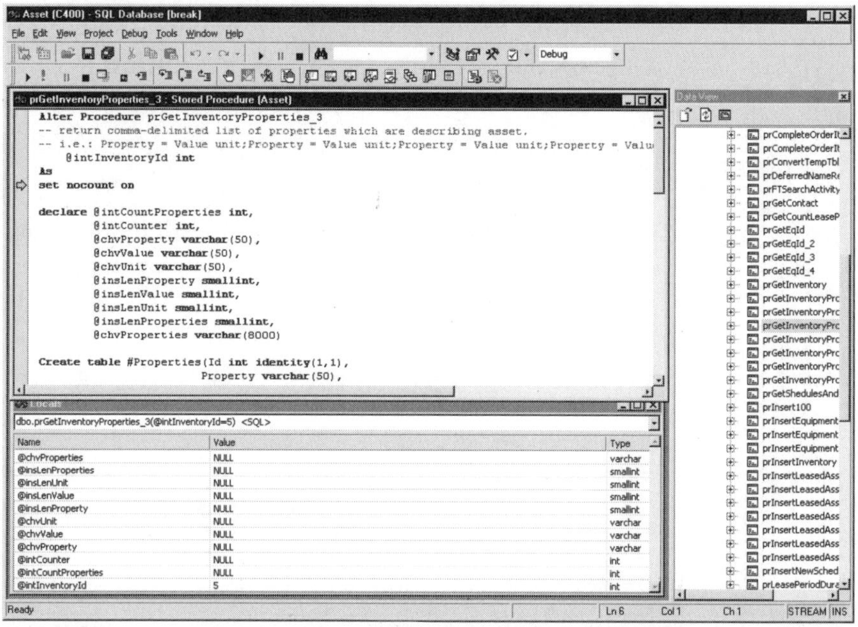

**Figure 7-3.** TSQL Debugger

- The Locals window allows you to scroll through the local variables and parameters of the stored procedure and to see its current contents and datatype:

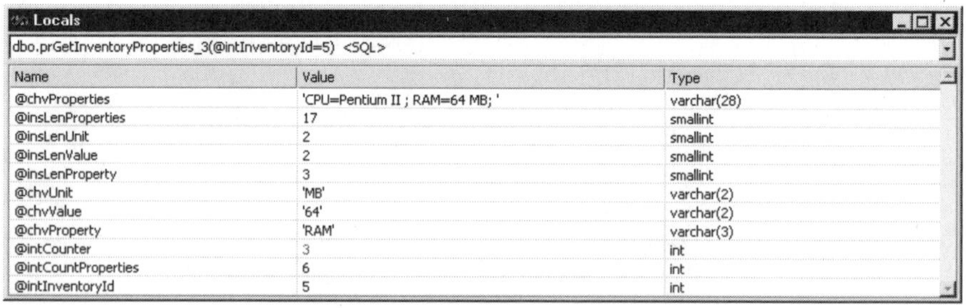

As the stored procedure's code is executed, the values of variables change. To help you follow the execution, TSQL Debugger colors the values of variables that were changed in the previous statement. The Locals window allows you to change values of variables interactively during execution of the code. This window has more than one tab, but only this one has meaning in TSQL Debugger. The other tabs are used to debug client applications.

■ The Watch window has a similar function. You can type, or drag from the code, a Transact-SQL expression to be evaluated in this window. This feature is useful when you want to investigate the values of expressions in if, while, case, and other similar statements. The Watch window also contains an Output tab, which displays resultsets returned by the Select statement and messages sent from the Print statement.

5. Click the Debug menu. The majority of commands available on the Debug menu target execution control. Most of the time you will use the Step Into or Step Over commands to step through a stored procedure. These commands execute one Transact-SQL statement at a time. The difference between them is in the way they behave when they encounter a nested stored procedure.

■ If you choose Step Into, TSQL Debugger opens the code of the nested stored procedure and lets you step through it.

■ If you choose Step Over, the nested stored procedure is treated as any other Transact-SQL statement and is executed in a single step.

■ The Step Out command enables you to execute the rest of the nested stored procedures without pause and halts only when the stored procedure is completed in the calling stored procedure.

■ A useful option on the Debug menu is Run To Cursor, which enables you to position the cursor somewhere in the code and to execute everything to that point in a single step. In essence, this command lets you set a temporary breakpoint.

**NOTE:**  Breakpoints are markers in a code that serve to stop execution when certain conditions are met. In TSQL Debugger, the only such condition is when the execution has reached the position of the breakpoint. In Visual Basic, Visual C++, and other tools, the condition can be met when a variable changes value, when a breakpoint has been reached a selected number of times, or when a Boolean expression is true.

6. Next, right-click a line of code containing an executable Transact-SQL statement, then choose Insert Breakpoint on the Debug menu.
    SQL Server marks that position with a big red dot on the left border. The breakpoint makes it unnecessary to step through the code. Just run it and it will stop at the position that interests you. From this point, you can either explore variables or continue to step through the code, as shown in Figure 7-4.

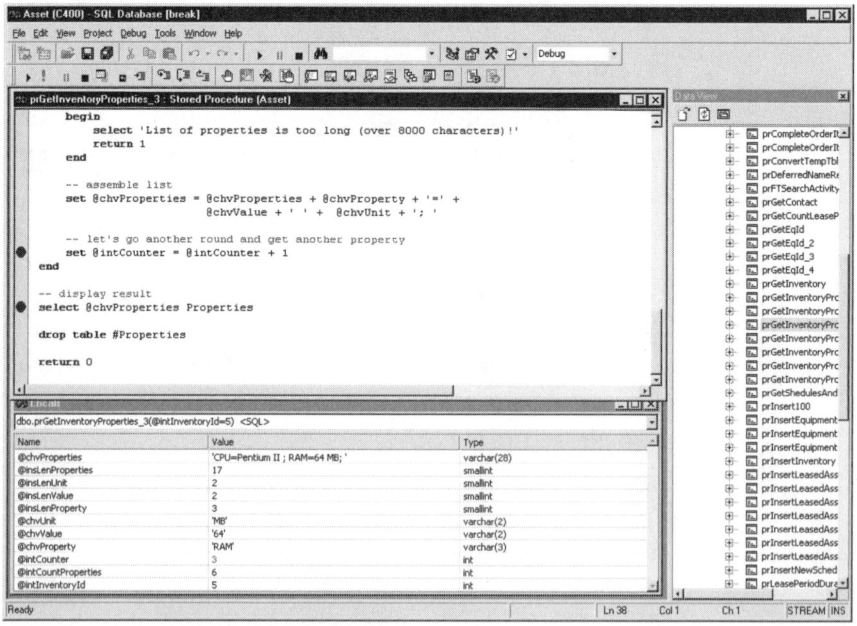

**Figure 7-4.**    Breakpoints in TSQL Debugger

If you want to continue until another breakpoint is reached, use the Start command.

One of my favorite features in the Visual Basic debugger is the ability to continue execution from the position of the cursor. Unfortunately, due to the architecture of the tool, the Set Next Step command is not available in TSQL Debugger.

## TSQL Debugger in Query Analyzer

Query Analyzer in SQL Server 2000 also contains a TSQL Debugger. It seems that Microsoft has decided to resolve their support nightmare with the setup and configuration of TSQL Debugger in Visual Studio. The Debugger tool in Query Analyzer is much more robust, as well as easier to configure.

**Requirements**    The requirements for using the TSQL Debugger in Query Analyzer are quite simple:

1. You must have Microsoft SQL Server 2000 installed, any version other than the Desktop Engine or Desktop Edition.

2. Microsoft SQL Server 2000 must be running on Windows NT 4.0 Server or Windows 2000 Server (or higher).

3. Client-side tools must be installed on workstations with Windows 98, Windows ME, Windows NT 4.0, or Windows 2000.

**Configuration**    TSQL Debugger setup is quite simple. Just make sure that you select the Debugger Interface from among the Development Tools during SQL Server setup. If you did not select it during the initial setup, you can simply run setup again and add this component.

**Using TSQL Debugger in Query Analyzer**    TSQL Debugger in Query Analyzer has features similar to the Visual Studio Debugger, although the interface is a little different. The interface is quite intuitive. To use it, follow these steps:

1. Open Query Analyzer and connect to the database.

2. Use Object Browser or Object Search to find a target stored procedure.

3. Right-click the stored procedure and choose Debug from the pop-up menu. Query Analyzer prompts you to supply parameters for the stored procedure:

```
┌─────────────────────────────────────────────────────────┐
│ Debug Procedure                                      [×]  │
├─────────────────────────────────────────────────────────┤
│ Procedures:      [dbo.prGetInventoryProperties_3      ▼] │
│                                                           │
│ Databases:       [                                    ▼] │
│                                                           │
│ Parameters:              Data type:                       │
│ [@intInventoryId    ]    [int                         ] │
│                                                           │
│                          Direction:                       │
│                          [Input                        ] │
│                                                           │
│                          Value:          ☐ Set to null   │
│                          [5                            ] │
│ ☑ Auto roll back                                         │
│        [  Execute  ]    [  Close  ]    [  Help  ]        │
└─────────────────────────────────────────────────────────┘
```

4. Click each parameter in the Parameters list and type the value. When you are done, select Execute and SQL Server launches the T-SQL Debugger window (see Figure 7-5).

TSQL Debugger opens the source code for the procedure and pauses on the first executable statement. A small yellow arrow on the left border marks the position of the statement to be executed next. You will not be able to edit the stored procedure's code, but you can use buttons on the window's toolbar to step through the stored procedure, and you can use the panels in the lower part of the window to investigate local and global variables and view the callstack and the result of the procedures.

The left section of the middle portion of the window allows you to monitor and even set values for local variables and parameters of the stored procedure.

The middle section allows you to monitor values of global variables. Naturally, all values are not initially present, but you

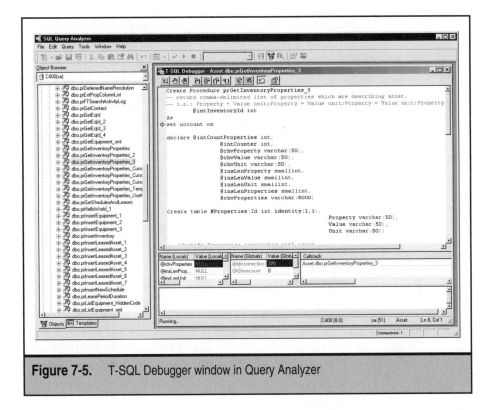

**Figure 7-5.** T-SQL Debugger window in Query Analyzer

can type them yourself. The right section lists (nested) procedures in the order in which they are called. The lower part of the window displays the result as it would be in the Results pane of the Query window.

The buttons on the toolbar of the T-SQL Debugger window control the execution of the code. Most of the time you will use the Step Into or Step Over buttons. These commands have the same effect as those in Visual Studio—they allow you to execute one Transact-SQL statement at a time. Again, the difference between them is in the way they behave when they encounter a nested stored procedure (a procedure that is executed from the procedure that we are debugging). If you choose Step Into (F11), TSQL Debugger opens the code of the nested stored procedure and lets you step through it. If you choose Step Over (F10), the nested stored procedure is treated as any other Transact-SQL statement and is executed in a single step.

The Step Out (SHIFT-F11) command enables you to execute the rest of the nested stored procedures without pause and halts only when the stored procedure is completed in the calling stored procedure. Run To Cursor (CTRL-F10) enables you to position the cursor somewhere in the code and to execute everything to that point in a single step.

It is also possible to use breakpoints in Query Analyzer. As we explained earlier, *breakpoints* are markers in code that serve to stop execution when certain conditions are met. In TSQL Debugger, the only such condition is when the execution has reached the position of the breakpoint. To set (or remove) a breakpoint, a user can click a line of code and then click the Toggle Breakpoints button (or press F9). Again, the program marks the breakpoint with a big red dot at the beginning of the line. Then, the user can simply run the procedure using the Go button (F5). It is not necessary to step through the code. The program stops execution when it encounters a breakpoint.

**NOTE:**  T-SQL Debugger in Query Analyzer has one small limitation—it is not possible to open more then one T-SQL Debugger. Only one stored procedure can be debugged at a time (along with the procedures that are nested in it).

## Poor Man's Debugger

You can debug your stored procedures even if you do not have TSQL Debugger (that is, if your environment does not comply with all the requirements).

Before debuggers became part of the programming environment, developers used simple techniques to print the contents of variables and follow the execution of code. Some programming languages include commands (for instance, Assert in Visual Basic 6.0) that are active only during debugging. In others, you simply add print commands during the development stage and comment them out before releasing the code into production.

In Transact-SQL, I use a very simple technique that allows me to view the contents of the variables and recordsets when I am testing a stored procedure from Query Analyzer. I add one additional parameter with the default set to 0 to the stored procedure.

```
@debug int = 0
```

In the stored procedure, at all important points, I add code that tests the value of the @debug variable and displays the values of selected variables or resultsets:

```
if @debug <> 0
      select    @chvProperty Property,
                @chvValue [Value],
                @chvUnit [Unit]
. . .


if @debug <> 0
      select * from #Properties
```

I do not use the Print statement for this purpose because

▼  It does not support the display of resultsets.

■  In older versions, it was impossible to concatenate a string inside a Print statement.

▲  Some utilities handle messages from the Print statement differently than they do the resultset from the Select statement.

In the following example, you can see a stored procedure that is designed to support this kind of testing:

```
Alter Procedure prGetInventoryProperties_2
-- Return comma-delimited list of properties
-- which are describing asset.
-- i.e.: Property=Value unit;Property=Value unit;...        (
          @intInventoryId int,
          @chvProperties varchar(8000) OUTPUT,
          @debug int = 0
      )

As
```

```
set nocount on

declare    @intCountProperties int,
           @intCounter int,
           @chvProperty varchar(50),
           @chvValue varchar(50),
           @chvUnit varchar(50),
           @insLenProperty smallint,
           @insLenValue smallint,
           @insLenUnit smallint,
           @insLenProperties smallint

declare @chvProcedure sysname
set @chvProcedure = 'prGetInventoryProperties_2'

if @debug <> 0
    select '**** '+ @chvProcedure + 'START ****'

Create table #Properties(Id int identity(1,1),
                         Property varchar(50),
                         Value varchar(50),
                         Unit varchar(50))

-- identify Properties associated with asset
insert into #Properties (Property, Value, Unit)
    select Property, Value, Unit
    from InventoryProperty inner join Property
    on InventoryProperty.PropertyId = Property.PropertyId
    where InventoryProperty.InventoryId = @intInventoryId

if @debug <> 0
    select * from #Properties

-- set loop
select @intCountProperties = Count(*),
       @intCounter = 1,
```

```
        @chvProperties = ''
from #Properties

-- loop through list of properties
while @intCounter <= @intCountProperties
begin
    -- get one property
    select    @chvProperty = Property,
              @chvValue = Value,
              @chvUnit = Coalesce(Unit, '')
    from #Properties
    where Id = @intCounter

    if @debug <> 0
        select    @chvProperty Property,
                  @chvValue [Value],
                  @chvUnit [Unit]

    -- check will new string fit
    select @insLenProperty = DATALENGTH(@chvProperty),
           @insLenValue = DATALENGTH(@chvValue),
           @insLenUnit = DATALENGTH(@chvUnit),
           @insLenProperties = DATALENGTH(@chvProperties)

    if @insLenProperties + 2
      + @insLenProperty + 1
      + @insLenValue + 1
      + @insLenUnit > 8000
    begin
        select 'List of properties is too long '
        + '(over 8000 characters)!'
        return 1
    end

    -- assemble list
    set @chvProperties = @chvProperties + @chvProperty
```

```
                        + '=' + @chvValue + ' ' +  @chvUnit + '; '
            if @debug <> 0
                select @chvProperties chvProperties

            -- let's go another round and get another property
            set @intCounter = @intCounter + 1
    end

    drop table #Properties

    if @debug <> 0
        select '**** '+ @chvProcedure + 'END ****'

    return 0
```

**Execution in a Test Environment**   To debug or test a stored procedure, I execute the stored procedure from Query Analyzer with the @debug parameter set to 1.

```
declare @chvResult varchar(8000)
exec prGetInventoryProperties
    @intInventoryId = 5,
    @chvProperties = @chvResult OUTPUT,
    @debug = 1


select @chvResult Result
```

Naturally, you can pass parameters either by name or by position. The result of the execution will be an elaborate printout like the one shown in Figure 7-6.

**Execution in the Production Environment**   In production, the stored procedure is called without a reference to the @debug parameter. Here, SQL Server assigns a default value to the parameter (0), and the stored procedure is executed without debug statements.

```
exec prGetInventoryProperties
        @intInventoryId = 5,
        @chvProperties = @chvResult OUTPUT
```

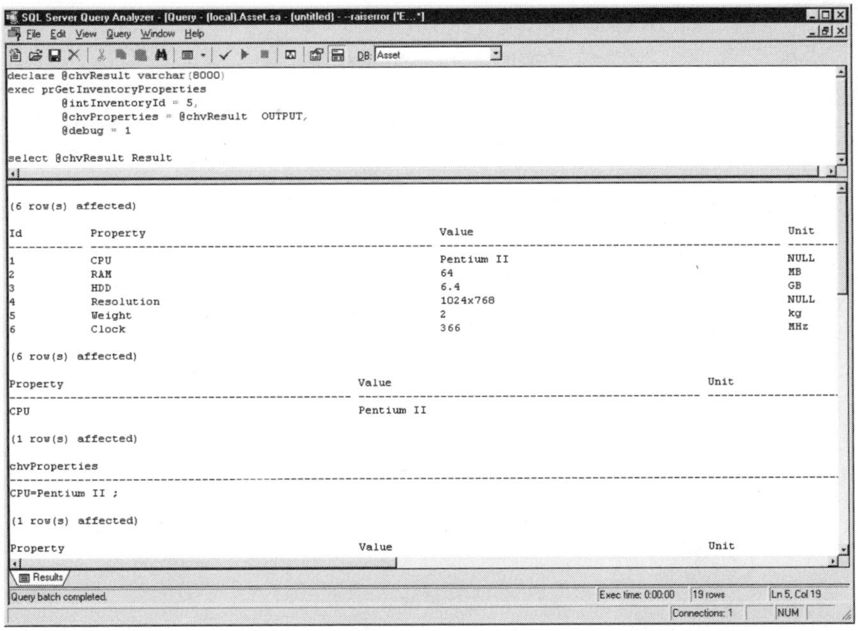

**Figure 7-6.** Poor Man's Debugger

**Nested Stored Procedures**   Two tricks can help you debug a set of nested stored procedures (that is, when a stored procedure calls another stored procedure). It is a useful practice to display the name of the stored procedure at the beginning and end of the stored procedure.

```
declare @chvProcedure sysname
set @chvProcedure = 'prGetInventoryProperties_2'

if @debug <> 0
    select '**** '+ @chvProcedure + 'START ****'
...
if @debug <> 0
    select '**** '+ @chvProcedure + 'END ****'

return 0
```

When you call a nested stored procedure, you need to pass the value of the @debug parameter to it as well. In this way, you will be able to see its debugging information.

```
exec prGetInventoryProperties @intInventoryId,
                              @chvProperties OUTPUT,
                              @debug
```

## Typical Errors

You should keep the following issues in mind when you are writing your code and testing Transact-SQL programs:

▼ NULLS

■ Assignment of variable from resultset

■ No records affected

■ Wrong size or datatype

■ Default length

■ Rollback of triggers

■ Warnings and lower-priority errors

■ Nested comments

■ Deferred name resolution

■ Cursors

▲ Overconfidence

### NULLs

Many errors are a result of the inadequate treatment of NULL values in Transact-SQL code. Developers often forget that local variables or table columns might contain NULLs. If such a value becomes part of any expression, the result will also be NULL.

The proper way to test the value of an expression for NULLs is to use the IS NULL or IS NOT NULL clauses. Microsoft SQL Server treats the use of = NULL as another way to type IS NULL, but <> NULL is not the equivalent of IS NOT NULL. The result of such an expression is always simply NULL. It will never be true, and stored procedures will always skip statements after the If statement when you use the <> NULL clause.

```
If @intInventoryId IS NULL
...
If @intInventoryId = NULL
...
If @intInventoryId IS NOT NULL
...
If @intInventoryId <> NULL   -- WRONG!!!
...
```

## Assignment of Variable from Resultset

Earlier, we discussed assigning the value(s) for a variable(s) using the resultset of the Select statement. This technique is fine when the resultset returns precisely one record. However, if the resultset returns more than one record, the variable(s) are assigned using the value(s) from the last record in recordset. Not perfect, but in some cases, you can live with it. It is sometimes difficult to predict which record will be returned as last in the recordset. It depends on the query and the index that SQL Server has used.

A more serious problem occurs when the recordset is empty. The values of the variables are changed in this case, and the code is vulnerable to several mistakes. If you do not expect the resultset to be empty, your stored procedure will fail. If you expect the values of the variables to be NULL, your stored procedure will function correctly only immediately after it is started (that is, in the first iteration of the process). In such a case, the local variables are not yet initialized and will contain NULLs. Later, when variables are initialized, their values will remain unchanged. If you are testing the contents of the variables for NULLs to find out if the record was selected, you will just process the previous record again.

## No Records Affected

Developers sometimes assume that SQL Server will return errors if a Transact-SQL statement affects no records. Unfortunately, this error is semantic rather than syntactic and SQL Server will not detect it.

In order to determine such an error, use the `@@rowcount` function rather than the `@@error` function:

```
declare @intRowCount int
declare @intErrorCode int

update Inventory
Set StatusId = -3
where AssetId = -11

select @intRowCount = @@rowCount,
       @intErrorCode = @@Error

if @@rowCount = 0
begin
     select "Record was not updated!"
     --return 50001
end
```

## Wrong Size or Datatype

I can recall one occasion when a colleague of mine spent two days going through a complicated data conversion process to find out why his process was consistently failing. In one of the nested stored procedures, I had declared the variable as `tinyint` instead of `int`. During the testing phase of the project, everything worked perfectly, because the variable was never set to a value higher than 255. However, a couple of months later in production, the process started to fail as values climbed higher.

Similar problems can occur if you do not fully understand the differences between similar formats (for example, `char` and `varchar`, `money` and `smallmoney`), or if you fail to synchronize the sizes of datatypes (for instance, char, varchar, numeric, and other datatypes of variable size).

## Default Length

A similar problem can occur when a developer does not supply the length of the variable datatype and SQL Server assigns a default length.

For example, the default length of the varchar datatype is 30. Most of the time SQL Server reports an error if the length is omitted, but not in all cases. In the Convert function, for example, the user need only specify the datatype:

```
Convert(varchar, @intPropertyId)
```

If the resulting string is short enough, you will not have any problems. I recall a colleague who employed this method for years without any problems, and then....

Unfortunately, other statements and functions behave as expected. If you declare a variable and assign it like so:

```
Declare @test varchar
Set @test = '123456789012345678901234567890'
Select datalength(@test), @test
```

SQL Server will allocate just one byte to the string and return the following:

```
----------- ----
1           1


(1 row(s) affected)
```

## Rollback of Triggers

In different versions of SQL Server, triggers react differently in rollback transaction statements. When a trigger is rolled back in SQL Server 7.0 or SQL Server 2000, the complete batch that initiated the trigger fails and the execution continues from the first statement of the next batch.

Version 4.2 behaves in a similar manner. In version 6.0, processing continues in the trigger, but the batch is canceled. In version 6.5, the processing continues in both the trigger and the batch. It was the responsibility of the developer to detect errors and cascade out of the process.

## Warnings and Lower Priority Errors

Warnings do not stop the execution of a stored procedure. In fact, you cannot even detect them from within the SQL Server environment.

Low-level errors, which are detectable using the @@error function, do not abort the execution either. Unfortunately, there are also errors that abort processing completely, so that the error handlers in stored procedures do not process the error.

## Nested Comments

Only single line comments (--) can be nested. Nested multiline comments (/* */) may be treated differently by different client tools.

I recommend that you put one or two stars (**) at the beginning of each line that is commented out. In this manner, the problem will be obvious if the comments are nested and SQL Server starts to compile part of the code that you consider to be commented out.

```
/**********************************************************
**     select *
**     from #Properties
**********************************************************/
```

## Deferred Name Resolution

It is possible (in Microsoft SQL Server 7.0 and Microsoft SQL Server 2000) to create database objects (such as stored procedures and triggers) that refer to other database objects that do not exist within the database. In previous versions, such attempts were treated as syntax errors. This feature helps tremendously when you need to generate a database structure and objects using script. Unfortunately, that introduces a number of risks. If you make a typo in the name of the table from which you want to retrieve records, SQL Server will not report a syntax error during compilation but will report a runtime error during execution.

```
Create Procedure prDeferredNameResolution
As
    set nocount on
    select 'Start'
    select * from NonExistingTable
    select 'Will execution be stopped?'
return
```

If you attempt to run this stored procedure, SQL Server will return the following:

```
-----
Start

Server: Msg 208, Level 16, State 1,
Procedure prDeferredNameResolution, Line 7
Invalid object name 'NonExistingTable'.
```

The execution will be stopped. Even an error handler written in Transact-SQL will not be able to proceed at this point.

## Cursors

Be very cautious when you use cursors. Test the status after each fetch; place error handling after each command; do not forget to close and deallocate the cursor when you do not need it any more. There are many rules and regulations for using cursors, and some of them might seem trivial, but even the smallest mistake can halt the execution of your code.

## Overconfidence

The overconfidence that comes with routine may be your worst enemy. If you perform the same or similar tasks over and over again, you can lose focus and skip basic steps. Do not put code into production before it is thoroughly tested; do not place bug fixes directly into production; use error handling even if the code seems straightforward and the chance for error slight.

# ERROR HANDLING

A developer's effective use of error handling procedures is often an excellent indicator of his or her seniority in that particular programming language. Those of us who deal with a C or Visual Basic environment are accustomed to a whole set of feature-rich error handling objects, procedures, and functions. Compared with them, TSQL seems rather inadequate. The developer can employ only one global variable and a few procedures for setting or raising errors. However, the apparent inadequacy of the tool set cannot justify sloppy solutions.

In this section, we will discuss the concept of error handling and offer a coherent methodology for its implementation. We will also discuss some alternative techniques involving the XACT_ABORT and Raiserror statements.

## Using Error Handling

Since TSQL is so laconic (critics may say feature poor), development DBAs commonly express themselves in a very concise manner. DBAs frequently write ad hoc scripts for one-time use or manual execution, and they thus neglect the need for consistent error handling.

Logic that is fine in standard languages like Visual Basic or C frequently does not work in TSQL. For example, an error may occur in TSQL, but if TSQL does not consider it fatal, processing will continue. Also, if the error is fatal, all processing will stop. The process does not react: it is just killed.

## Why Bother?

For many, the question is why be concerned with implementing error handling at all? Let us review this question through the following example:

```
Create Procedure prInsertLeasedAsset_1
-- Insert leased asset and update total in LeaseSchedule.
-- (demonstration of imperfect solution)
            (
        @intEquipmentId int,
        @intLocationId int,
        @intStatusId int,
        @intLeaseId int,
        @intLeaseScheduleId int,
        @intOwnerId int,
        @mnyLease money,
        @intAcquisitionTypeID int
        )
As
set nocount on

begin transaction

-- insert asset
insert Inventory(EquipmentId,      LocationId,
                 StatusId,         LeaseId,
                 LeaseScheduleId,  OwnerId,
                 Lease,            AcquisitionTypeID)
values (         @intEquipmentId, @intLocationId,
                 @intStatusId,     @intLeaseId,
                 @intLeaseScheduleId,@intOwnerId,
                 @mnyLease,        @intAcquisitionTypeID)

-- update total
update LeaseSchedule
Set PeriodicTotalAmount = PeriodicTotalAmount + @mnyLease
where LeaseId = @intLeaseId

commit transaction

return
```

This may seem a trivial example, and it is true that in all probability nothing would go wrong, but let's imagine an error occurs on the `Update` statement. The error could be for any reason—overflow, some constraint, or inadequate permission, for example. As explained earlier, transactions do not roll back on their own when an error occurs. Instead, SQL Server simply commits everything that was changed when it encounters the `Commit Transaction` statement as if nothing unusual had happened. Unfortunately, from that moment on, the total of the lease schedule will have the wrong value.

## Tactics of Error Handling

Some DBAs recognize the importance of this issue and place error handling in critical positions in their code. The result would be something like the following:

```
Create Procedure prInsertLeasedAsset_2
-- Insert leased asset and update total in LeaseSchedule.
-- (demonstration of not exactly perfect solution)
    (
        @intEquipmentId int,
        @intLocationId int,
        @intStatusId int,
        @intLeaseId int,
        @intLeaseScheduleId int,
        @intOwnerId int,
        @mnyLease money,
        @intAcquisitionTypeID int
    )
As
set nocount on

begin transaction

-- insert asset
insert Inventory(EquipmentId,     LocationId,
                 StatusId,        LeaseId,
                 LeaseScheduleId, OwnerId,
```

```
                     Lease,              AcquisitionTypeID)
values (             @intEquipmentId, @intLocationId,
                     @intStatusId,      @intLeaseId,
                     @intLeaseScheduleId,@intOwnerId,
                     @mnyLease,          @intAcquisitionTypeID)
If @@error <> 0
Begin
    Print 'Unexpected error occurred!'
    Rollback transaction
    Return 1
End


-- update total
update LeaseSchedule
Set PeriodicTotalAmount = PeriodicTotalAmount + @mnyLease
where LeaseId = @intLeaseId


If @@error <> 0
Begin
    Print 'Unexpected error occurred!'
    Rollback transaction
    Return 1
End


commit transaction


return 0
```

This kind of solution contains substantial repetition—especially if your business logic requires more than two Transact-SQL statements to be implemented. A more elegant solution is to group codes into a generic error handling procedure:

```
Create Procedure prInsertLeasedAsset_3
-- Insert leased asset and update total in LeaseSchedule.
-- (demonstration of not exactly perfect solution)
    (
          @intEquipmentId int,
          @intLocationId int,
```

```
                    @intStatusId int,
                    @intLeaseId int,
                    @intLeaseScheduleId int,
                    @intOwnerId int,
                    @mnyLease money,
                    @intAcquisitionTypeID int
        )
As
set nocount on

begin transaction

-- insert asset
insert Inventory(EquipmentId,      LocationId,
                    StatusId,         LeaseId,
                    LeaseScheduleId, OwnerId,
                    Lease,            AcquisitionTypeID)
values (          @intEquipmentId, @intLocationId,
                    @intStatusId,     @intLeaseId,
                    @intLeaseScheduleId,@intOwnerId,
                    @mnyLease,        @intAcquisitionTypeID)
If @@error <> 0 GOTO ERR_HANDLER

-- update total
update LeaseSchedule
Set PeriodicTotalAmount = PeriodicTotalAmount + @mnyLease
where LeaseId = @intLeaseId
If @@error <> 0 GOTO ERR_HANDLER

commit transaction

return 0

ERR_HANDLER:
    Print 'Unexpected error occurred!'
    Rollback transaction
    Return 1
```

This is better, but it does not deal with all of the issues that need to be handled.

A typical error that beginners in TSQL make is to check the value of a global variable and then try to return or process it. Such an attempt is usually the result of a good intention such as wanting to notify the user of an error that has occurred.

```
Create Procedure prInsertLeasedAsset_4
-- Insert leased asset and update total in LeaseSchedule.
-- (demonstration of not exactly perfect solution)
        (
                @intEquipmentId int,
                @intLocationId int,
                @intStatusId int,
                @intLeaseId int,
                @intLeaseScheduleId int,
                @intOwnerId int,
                @mnyLease money,
                @intAcquisitionTypeID int
        )
As
set nocount on


begin transaction


-- insert asset
insert Inventory(EquipmentId,      LocationId,
                 StatusId,         LeaseId,
                 LeaseScheduleId,  OwnerId,
                 Lease,            AcquisitionTypeID)
values (         @intEquipmentId,  @intLocationId,
                 @intStatusId,     @intLeaseId,
                 @intLeaseScheduleId,@intOwnerId,
                 @mnyLease,        @intAcquisitionTypeID)
If @@error <> 0 GOTO ERR_HANDLER

-- update total
```

```
update LeaseSchedule
Set PeriodicTotalAmount = PeriodicTotalAmount + @mnyLease
where LeaseId = @intLeaseId
If @@Error <> 0 GOTO ERR_HANDLER

commit transaction

return 0

ERR_HANDLER:
    Print 'Unexpected error occurred: '
          + Convert(varchar, @@Error) -- this will
                                      -- not work,
                                      -- as expected
    Rollback transaction
    Return @@Error
```

Although something like this could work in Visual Basic, for example, in this case the stored procedure will return 0 as an error number. SQL Server sets the value of the `@@Error` variable after each statement. It treats each statement separately, so the value of `@@Error` is set to 0 subsequently when the `If` statement is (successfully) executed. Thus the `Print` statement displays 0 as an error number, and eventually the stored procedure will also return 0.

## A Coherent Error Handling Methodology

Let's discuss a single coherent error handling methodology. The fundamental idea is that *all* SQL statements within a stored procedure should be covered by this error handling solution. Any time an unexpected error occurs, a stored procedure should stop further processing. When the current stored procedure stops processing, so should the stored procedures that called it.

The basic feature of this solution is to follow all SQL statements with a statement that reads the contents of the `@@Error` variable, along with an `If` statement, which checks whether the previous command completed successfully.

```
Create Procedure prInsertLeasedAsset_5
-- Insert leased asset and update total in LeaseSchedule.
        (
                @intEquipmentId int,
                @intLocationId int,
                @intStatusId int,
                @intLeaseId int,
                @intLeaseScheduleId int,
                @intOwnerId int,
                @mnyLease money,
                @intAcquisitionTypeID int
        )
As
set nocount on

Declare @intErrorCode int
Select @intErrorCode = @@Error

begin transaction

If @intErrorCode = 0
begin
    — insert asset
    insert Inventory(EquipmentId,      LocationId,
                     StatusId,         LeaseId,
                     LeaseScheduleId,  OwnerId,
                     Lease,            AcquisitionTypeID)
        values (         @intEquipmentId, @intLocationId,
                         @intStatusId,    @intLeaseId,
                         @intLeaseScheduleId,@intOwnerId,
                         @mnyLease,       @intAcquisitionTypeID)
    Select @intErrorCode = @@Error
end

If @intErrorCode = 0
begin
    — update total
```

```
        update LeaseSchedule
        Set PeriodicTotalAmount = PeriodicTotalAmount + @mnyLease
        where LeaseId = @intLeaseId
        Select @intErrorCode = @@Error
end

If @intErrorCode = 0
      COMMIT TRANSACTION
Else
      ROLLBACK TRANSACTION

return @intErrorCode
```

If an error occurs, the If statements prevent further execution of the business logic and pass an error to the end of the procedure. Changes will be rolled back, and the stored procedure returns the value of the @intErrorCode variable to the calling stored procedure or script. If an error occurs, this variable may be used to notify the calling procedure that there was a problem.

## Nested Stored Procedures

The calling stored procedure might have the same error handling system in place. In such a case, calls to the stored procedures should treat the returned values as error codes:

```
. . .
If @ErrorCode = 0
Begin
      execute @intErrorCode = MyStoredProcedure @parm1, @param2...
End
```

The method works like a cascade that stops all further processing in a whole set of nested stored procedures.

## Interfacing to Other Environments

This error handling structure is very useful even in cases when a stored procedure is called from another programming environment, such as Visual Basic or Visual C++. The return value of a stored

procedure can be retrieved, and an error can be handled on that
level as well.

```
conn.Open "provider=sqloledb;data source=sqlserver;" + _
"user id=sa;password=;initial catalog=Asset"

With cmd
    Set .ActiveConnection = conn
    .CommandText = "prInsertLeasedAsset_5"
    .CommandType = adCmdStoredProc
    .Parameters.Refresh
    .parameters(1).Value =  4
    .parameters(2).Value =  1
    .parameters(3).Value =  1
    .parameters(4).Value =  1
    .parameters(5).Value =  1
    .parameters(6).Value =  1
    .parameters(7).Value = 99.95
    .parameters(8).Value =  1
    Set rs = .Execute()
    lngReturnValue = .Parameters(0).Value
end with
If lngReturnValue <> 0 Then
    MsgBox "Procedure have failed!"
    Exit Sub
Else
    MsgBox "Procedure was successful"
end if
```

## Other Global Variables

Cases should be handled with the same Select statement that
reads @@Error when you wish to read the value of some other
global variables immediately after the statement. You often
require such a technique when you are using identity columns.

```
insert Inventory(EquipmentId,    LocationId,
                 StatusId,       LeaseId,
                 LeaseScheduleId, OwnerId,
```

```
                             Lease,              AcquisitionTypeID)
          values (          @intEquipmentId, @intLocationId,
                            @intStatusId,     @intLeaseId,
                            @intLeaseScheduleId,@intOwnerId,
                            @mnyLease, .       @intAcquisitionTypeID)
          Select @intErrorCode = @@Error,
                @intInventoryId = @@identity
```

## Transaction Processing

You can integrate transaction processing perfectly with this solution. Review Chapter 5 to remind yourself why Rollback and Commit must be treated differently.

At the beginning of a stored procedure or transaction, the developer should add the following code:

```
Declare @intTransactionCountOnEntry int
If @intErrorCode = 0
Begin
    Select @intTransactionCountOnEntry = @@TranCount
    BEGIN TRANSACTION
End
```

At the end of the procedure (and/or transaction), the developer should complete the transaction:

```
If @@TranCount > @intTransactionCountOnEntry
Begin
    If @intErrorCode = 0
        COMMIT TRANSACTION
    Else
        ROLLBACK TRANSACTION
End
```

The solution will also perform well in the case of nested stored procedures. All procedures are rolled back using the same cascading mechanism.

The local variable @TransactionCountOnEntry is used to track the number of opened transactions upon entry into a stored procedure. If the number is unaffected within the stored procedure, there is no reason either to Commit or Rollback within the procedure. The finished stored procedure looks like this:

```
Alter Procedure prInsertLeasedAsset_6
-- Insert leased asset and update total in LeaseSchedule.
          (
          @intEquipmentId int,
          @intLocationId int,
          @intStatusId int,
          @intLeaseId int,
          @intLeaseScheduleId int,
          @intOwnerId int,
          @mnyLease money,
          @intAcquisitionTypeID int,
          @intInventoryId int OUTPUT
          )
As
set nocount on

Declare @intErrorCode int,
        @intTransactionCountOnEntry int

Select @intErrorCode = @@Error

If @intErrorCode = 0
Begin
    Select @intTransactionCountOnEntry = @@TranCount
    BEGIN TRANSACTION
End

If @intErrorCode = 0
begin
    -- insert asset
    insert Inventory(EquipmentId,     LocationId,
                     StatusId,        LeaseId,
                     LeaseScheduleId, OwnerId,
                     Lease,           AcquisitionTypeID)
      values (       @intEquipmentId, @intLocationId,
```

```
                              @intStatusId,      @intLeaseId,
                              @intLeaseScheduleId,@intOwnerId,
                              @mnyLease,          @intAcquisitionTypeID)
         Select @intErrorCode = @@Error,
                @intInventoryId = @@identity
    end


    If @intErrorCode = 0
    begin
         -- update total
         update LeaseSchedule
         Set PeriodicTotalAmount = PeriodicTotalAmount + @mnyLease
         where LeaseId = @intLeaseId
         Select @intErrorCode = @@Error
    end


    If @@TranCount > @intTransactionCountOnEntry
    Begin
         If @@Error = 0
             COMMIT TRANSACTION
         Else
             ROLLBACK TRANSACTION
    End


    return @intErrorCode
```

## XACT_ABORT

SQL Server does, in fact, have an equivalent to the On Error Go To command used by Visual Basic. The SET XACT_ABORT statement forces SQL Server to roll back the complete transaction and stop further processing on the occurrence of any error.

```
create Procedure prInsertLeasedAsset_7
-- Insert leased asset and update total in LeaseSchedule.
-- (demonstration of imperfect solution)
```

```
                    (
                    @intEquipmentId int,
                    @intLocationId int,
                    @intStatusId int,
                    @intLeaseId int,
                    @intLeaseScheduleId int,
                    @intOwnerId int,
                    @mnyLease money,
                    @intAcquisitionTypeID int
                    )
As
set nocount on
SET XACT_ABORT ON
begin transaction

-- insert asset
insert Inventory(EquipmentId,      LocationId,
                 StatusId,         LeaseId,
                 LeaseScheduleId,  OwnerId,
                 Lease,            AcquisitionTypeID)
values (         @intEquipmentId, @intLocationId,
                 @intStatusId,     @intLeaseId,
                 @intLeaseScheduleId,@intOwnerId,
                 @mnyLease,        @intAcquisitionTypeID)

-- update total
update LeaseSchedule
Set PeriodicTotalAmount = PeriodicTotalAmount + @mnyLease
where LeaseId = @intLeaseId

commit transaction

return (0)
```

Unfortunately, this solution presents a problem. This statement will also completely stop execution of the current batch. The error can still be detected and handled from the client application, but inside the Transact-SQL code, SQL Server will treat it as a fatal error.

## Raiserror

An important tool for implementing error handling is the RAISERROR statement. Its main purpose is to return a message to the user. Open Query Analyzer and execute the following statement:

```
Raiserror ('Error occurred!', 0, 1)
```

The server will display an error message in the Result pane (see Figure 7-7).

The numbers specified as second and third parameters indicate the severity and state of the error.

Naturally, this statement does more than return this meager result. It also sets the value of the @@error global variable (function) to the number of the error that you have raised. If you do not specify a number (as we did not in the previous example), SQL Server will assign an error number of 50000 to it.

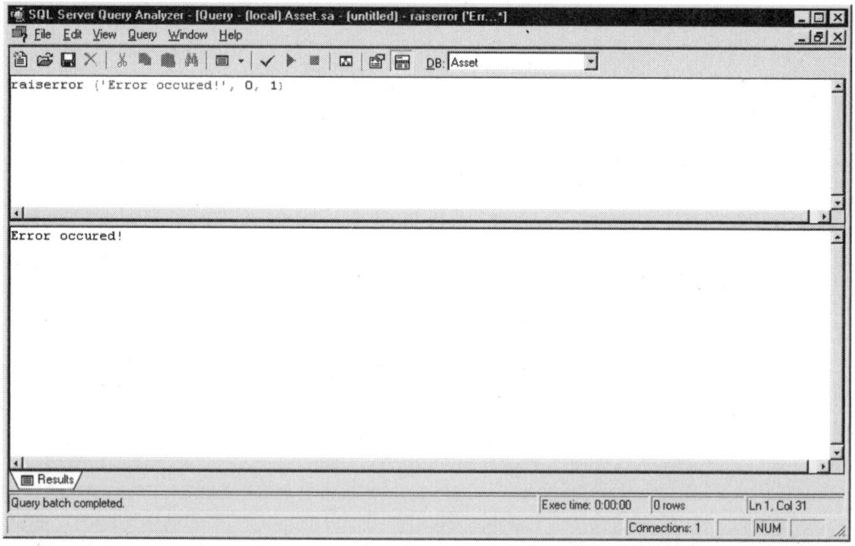

**Figure 7-7.**    Using Raiserror

You can also display errors that are predefined in SQL Server if you reference them by their numbers, and you can also define your own errors using the sp_addmessage system stored procedure:

```
Exec sp_addmessage 50001,
                    16,
                    'Unable to update Total of LeaseSchedule'
```

Then you can display this message using the following statement:

```
Raiserror (50001, 16, 1)
```

The server will return the following:

```
Server: Msg 50001, Level 16, State 1, Line 1
Unable to update Total of LeaseSchedule
```

You can set the state and severity of the error and/or record the error in the SQL Server Error Log, and even in the Windows NT Error Log:

```
Raiserror (50001, 16, 1) WITH LOG
```

# SUMMARY

Some developers consider debugging the most difficult part of the development process. However, a systematic approach, common sense, and modern debugging tools can significantly reduce the effort required to solve errors.

This chapter has presented an overview of bugs and the process of debugging in general. We have presented a systematic approach to the debugging process. We have discussed the configuration and use of TSQL Debugger. We have discussed debugging without TSQL Debugger and looked at some of the most common errors found in Transact-SQL.

We have demonstrated two solutions for handling errors inside Transact-SQL code. You should choose one and make a habit of using it. Personally, I do not like to use XACT_ABORT because I can exercise more control by investigating the @@error function.

Critics might object to this solution, because it adds a significant amount of code to the script, and they might add that the solution would be improved if the developer could "hide" error handling to emphasize the statements that are performing the "real" processing. But the real value of this error handling solution is that it is a coherent solution that permits the code in stored procedures to work in a uniform manner and lets developers know what to expect when the unexpected occurs.

So, until Microsoft creates something new....

# EXERCISES

1. Add debugging code in the following stored procedure:

```
Alter Procedure prSpaceUsedByTables_1
-- loop through table names in current database
    -- display info about amount of space used by each table
As
Set nocount on
declare @MaxCounter int,
        @Counter int,
        @TableName sysname

Create table #Tables (
    Id int identity(1,1),
    TableName sysname)

-- collect table names
insert into #Tables(TableName)
    select name
    from sysobjects
    where xtype = 'U'

-- prepare loop
Select    @MaxCounter = Max(Id),
          @Counter = 1
from #Tables
```

```
while @Counter <= @MaxCounter
begin
     -- get table name
     select @TableName = TableName
     from #Tables
     where Id = @Counter

     -- display space used
     exec sp_spaceused  @TableName
     set @Counter = @Counter + 1
end


drop table #Tables
```

2. Execute the stored procedure through Query Analyzer to review debugging information.

3. Run the stored procedure through TSQL Debugger to try debugging.

4. What is the problem with the following code snippet?

```
update LeaseSchedule
Set PeriodicTotalAmount = PeriodicTotalAmount + @mnyLease
where LeaseId = @intLeaseId
If @@Error <> 0
begin
     Print 'Unexpected error occurred: '
          + Convert(varchar, @@Error)
     Rollback transaction
     Return @@Error
end
```

5. Change the stored procedure from exercise 5 in Chapter 5 so that it complies with the error handling solution proposed in this chapter.

6. Take the stored procedure from exercise 7 in Chapter 4 and wrap it in the error handling solution described in this chapter.

# CHAPTER 8

## Developing Professional Habits

This chapter discusses two critical aspects of application development:

▼ Source code control

▲ Naming conventions

The very ideas of "control" and "convention" may be anathema to some inexperienced developers who view themselves as unconventional characters outside the control of standard social constructs. For experienced professionals, however, using source code control and consistent naming conventions are not onerous tasks but ingrained habits and second nature. Nothing differentiates the professional from the amateur like these two habits.

# THE CONCEPT OF SOURCE CODE CONTROL

*Source code control* (or *version control*) is typically introduced in development environments where more than one developer needs to work with the same piece of code. If automated tools for source code control are not employed, developers must contend with the following issues:

▼ Manual integration of source code changes

■ Manual management of older versions of source code

▲ Greater risk of errors due to lack of constraints

Microsoft provides a source code control package as an integral part of its development tool set under the name Visual SourceSafe. This package allows developers to control their most valuable asset—source code. You can also use the Visual SourceSafe database to manage other file types such as Web content, documentation, and test data, but our focus in this chapter is on how to use Visual SourceSafe to manage the development cycle.

# Introduction to Microsoft Visual SourceSafe

Microsoft's primary purpose in developing Visual SourceSafe as a part of its Visual Studio suite of development tools was to provide a project-oriented means of storing and organizing code that would allow developers to spend more time developing their projects than managing them. The emphasis is on ease of use and integration with a wide range of development tools. SQL Server 7.0 developers can benefit greatly from this ease of use and integration, not only with regard to source code, but also as a means of organizing all related files such as project documentation and test data.

As with SQL Server, there are different ways of implementing Visual SourceSafe. It is essentially a client/server application, but if you are an independent developer, your development workstation will likely also be your NT Server, SQL Server, and Visual SourceSafe Server. Of course, if you are an independent developer, you may be wondering what need you have for source code control. I will discuss this issue later in the chapter. For now you can take my word that source code control is just as important for the solo developer working on a simple project as it is for the large development team working on a complex, component-based project.

If you are a member of a development team, the Visual SourceSafe client will allow you to work on local copies of code while preventing other members of your team from overwriting your changes while you have the code "checked out" from the Visual SourceSafe Server. The benefit of this simple concept is obvious, but you have to work with and become comfortable with Visual SourceSafe before its many other benefits will become just as obvious. After you have posted your source code, you can

▼ "Get" the current version of all files.

■ "Check-out" a copy of a file that needs to be changed. Visual SourceSafe will prevent all other developers from changing the file until it is returned ("checked-in") to the Visual SourceSafe database.

- See differences between a local (changed) version of a source code file and the latest version recorded in the Visual SourceSafe database.

- Label current versions of all files as code that belongs to a particular release of a software product.

- Retrieve any older version of a particular file or a complete set of project files.

- See changes between any two versions of a source code file.

- Deploy a project (on some development platforms such as the Web).

- Share common files between separate projects.

▲ Make a single backup copy of the complete source code and all supporting files.

## Administering the Visual SourceSafe Database

Before you can use Visual SourceSafe, you need to create users and assign privileges to them.

When you install Visual SourceSafe, you create just two users: *Admin* and *Guest.* The Admin user has all privileges on the database and can also create other users. The Guest user is initially limited to read-only access to source code files. Both users are created with their password set to an empty string (that is, blank). Since this state constitutes a threat to your source code, your first step should be to set the Admin password.

To set the Admin password:

1. Open Visual SourceSafe Administrator (Select Start | Programs | Microsoft Visual Studio 6.0 | Microsoft Visual SourceSafe | Visual SourceSafe 6.0 Admin).

2. Select Admin in the Administrator window.

3. Select Change Password on the Users menu. The Change Password dialog appears (see Figure 8-1).

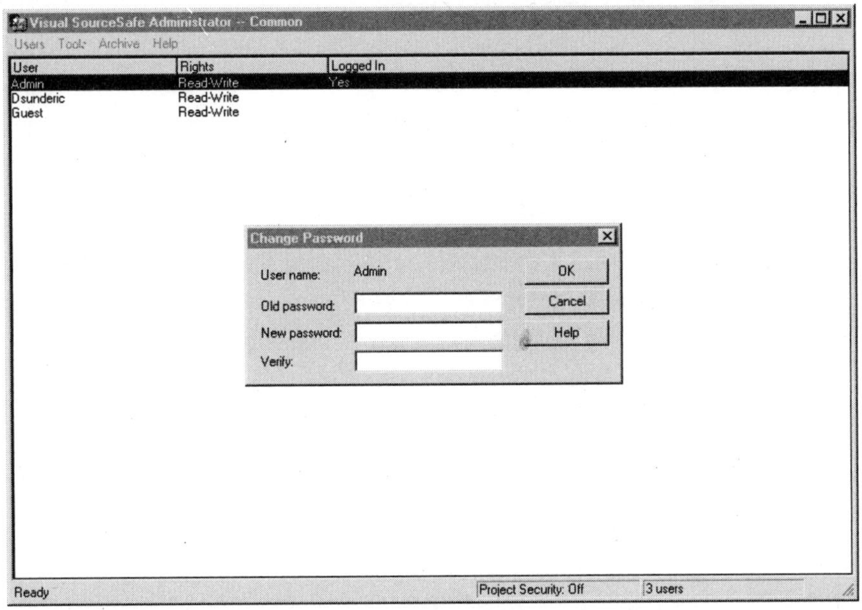

**Figure 8-1.**   Visual SourceSafe Administrator

4.  Leave the Old Password field blank. (Remember, the initial password is an empty string.)

5.  Type the string you want to use as the Admin password in the New Password field.

6.  Type the string again in the Verify field, then click OK.

Now, let's create another user:

1.  Choose Add User on the Users menu.

2.  Specify a user name and password, verify the password, and leave the Read-Only box unchecked, since you want to give the new user both Read and Write permissions to the Visual SourceSafe database.

**TIP:** If the Visual SourceSafe user name and password match the operating system user name and password, the user will not have to type them each time she opens Visual SourceSafe on the local system. Visual SourceSafe will pick them up automatically.

**NOTE:** With Visual SourceSafe, you can assign more refined permission levels such as Add, Rename, Delete, Check In, Check Out, Destroy, and Read. To activate this wide-ranging control, click Tools | Options | Project Security and check the Enable Project Security option.

## Adding a Database to Visual SourceSafe

To demonstrate the implementation of source code control in a database project, you will add code from your sample Asset database in Visual InterDev 6.0.

1. Open the Asset database project in Visual InterDev.

2. Open the Data View.

3. Right-click the data connection (see Figure 8-2).

4. Select Add to Source Control on the pop-up menu and Visual InterDev will prompt you to create a new project in the Visual SourceSafe database:

---

**Enable Source Control**

You are about to add the Database connection 'Asset' to source control. The source control database location is relative to your SQL Server database.

Example: C:\VSS\srcsafe.ini

This process may take several minutes.

Source control database location:
iles\Microsoft Visual Studio\Common\VSS\srcsafe.ini

Source control project name:
asset

Comment:

OK   Cancel   Help

---

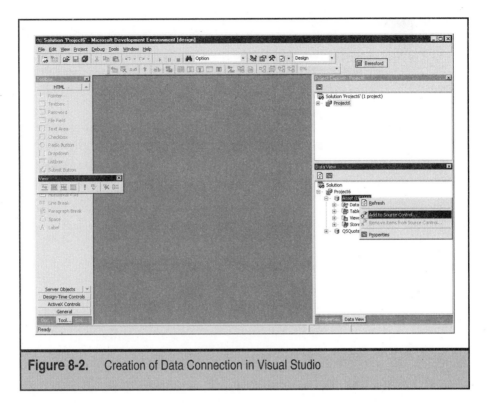

**Figure 8-2.**    Creation of Data Connection in Visual Studio

5. Type the location of your Visual SourceSafe database (that is, the location of the srcsafe.ini file).

Since Visual SourceSafe should be installed on the same machine as SQL Server, the location of the Source Safe database that you need to specify in this text box should be relative to the server machine. If you are developing from a workstation that is separate from the "development" server, you have to be careful how you enter the location of the Visual SourceSafe database. You should use the server's absolute path (for example: C:\Program Files\Microsoft Visual Studio\Common\VSS) regardless of whether you have that drive mapped on your workstation using another drive letter such as S:.

**NOTE:** On my machine, the Visual SourceSafe database is located in the C:\Program Files\Microsoft Visual Studio\Common\VSS folder. My computer, in this case, is a development workstation, as well as the SQL Server and Visual SourceSafe server.

6. Name the project and type a comment to describe the project if you want. The application will then prompt you for your Visual SourceSafe user name (Login ID) and password.

7. Type the user name and password you created earlier in this chapter and click OK to close this dialog and post the Asset database to Visual SourceSafe.

Visual SourceSafe creates a project and locks all stored procedures. You can see a small lock icon beside each stored procedure in Data View (see Figure 8-3).

**NOTE:** From this moment, you must check out a stored procedure before you can change it. Unfortunately, this solution does not prevent another developer from using some other tool to change a stored procedure directly in the database. Visual SourceSafe only works through consensus. Loose cannons can still wreak havoc on your development ship.

## Managing Stored Procedures

When stored procedures are locked, you can open them for viewing in the editor, but Visual InterDev will prevent you from changing them until you check them out:

1. Right-click a procedure and select Open. Visual InterDev opens a copy of the procedure but marks it "read-only."

2. Try to change its code and save it. Visual InterDev will prevent you from saving it.

Now, let's change a stored procedure:

1. Right-click a procedure and select Check Out from the pop-up menu.

2. Visual InterDev will first compare the version in Visual SourceSafe with the version in the SQL Server database.

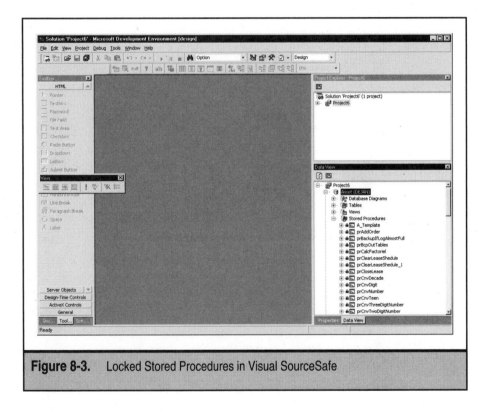

**Figure 8-3.**   Locked Stored Procedures in Visual SourceSafe

If the versions do not match, the application will display a warning and prompt you to specify the version that you want to use:

3. You can select either the database or the Visual SourceSafe version, or you can decide to post the database version to Visual SourceSafe. Naturally, you should first check the differences between them.

4. Select one of these options. Visual InterDev displays a checkmark beside the stored procedure in Data View to indicate that the stored procedure is checked out (see Figure 8-4).

Now you can open and edit the stored procedure, and Visual InterDev will allow you to save the changes. When you save the changed stored procedure, Visual InterDev will store it in the SQL Server database, but the stored procedure remains checked out. The assumption is that you are working on your development (or test) server and that you need time to test changes. Once you are satisfied with the stored procedure, you can use the Check In option to save it in Visual SourceSafe.

To edit a stored procedure:

1. Right-click the stored procedure to open it.

2. Find the RAISERROR statement, and change its severity from 1 to 16 (or make some other trivial change).

3. Select Save on the File menu to save your changes.

4. Right-click the stored procedure and select Check In from the pop-up menu.

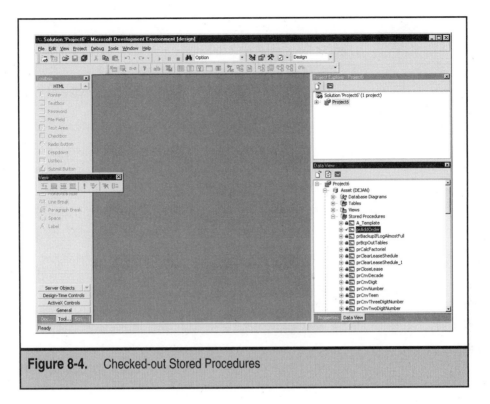

**Figure 8-4.**   Checked-out Stored Procedures

5.  The application will prompt you for a comment. Take the time to indicate what changes you made. This will be incredibly helpful if some detective work is required later.

```
Check In to Source Control                    [×]

Comment for 'dbo.prAddOrder':
Changed severity of the error message|



                        OK          Cancel
```

6.  Click OK. Visual InterDev will save the changes in Visual SourceSafe and lock the stored procedure. The stored procedure is now ready to be checked out by another member of the development team, or for implementation as part of a cohesive version.

> **NOTE:** When I first started to use Visual SourceSafe, the directions implied by the terms "Check Out" and "Check In" sounded inverted to me. Just think of Visual SourceSafe as an actual safe from which you are taking your code and into which you subsequently return your code after you are done with it.

7. Now, go back and check out the same stored procedure again.

8. Open it and reverse your previous changes (change the severity of the RAISERROR statement from 16 to 1, or reverse whatever other trivial change you made).

9. Save the stored procedure. (You can open the stored procedure from Enterprise Manager to verify its contents.)

10. Let's assume that you are not satisfied with these changes and that you want to abandon them. (You have tested them and the result is not what you expected.) All you need to do is to select Undo Check Out. The Visual SourceSafe Server will lock the stored procedure again and use the existing copy from Visual SourceSafe to reverse the changes to the database. (Again, you can open the stored procedure from Enterprise Manager to verify its contents.)

## Visual SourceSafe Explorer

The full power of Visual Source Safe can only be realized through one special tool—Visual SourceSafe Explorer. Let's look at this tool:

1. Open Visual SourceSafe Explorer (Start | Programs | Microsoft Visual Studio 6.0 | Microsoft Visual SourceSafe 6.0 | Visual SourceSafe 6.0).

2. Expand the Asset project (that is, click the + symbol beside it) and drill down until you reach Stored Procedures (see Figure 8-5).

We will examine some of the most interesting features of the Visual SourceSafe Explorer, particularly history, labels, and versions.

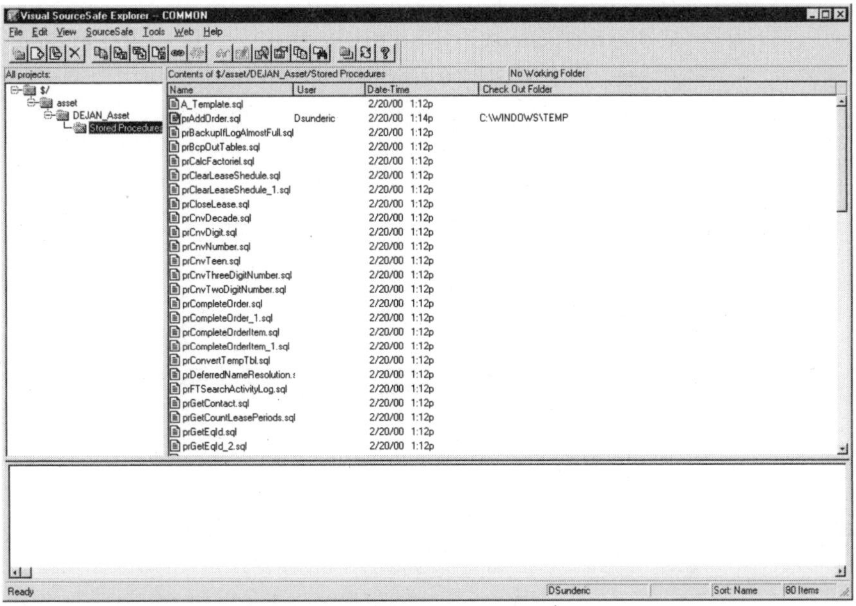

**Figure 8-5.**    Visual SourceSafe Explorer

## Stored Procedures in Visual SourceSafe

Bear in mind that Visual SourceSafe was not originally designed to work with an environment like SQL Server. In fact, version 7.0 is the first version of Microsoft SQL Server with which you can use Visual SourceSafe. Some commands and concepts will not fit perfectly.

Visual SourceSafe is designed to work with source code in the form of ASCII text files. Stored procedures are database objects. In order to save stored procedures in Visual SourceSafe, Visual InterDev has to create and manage temporary script files behind the scenes. Unfortunately, some commands are file-oriented and will not work as expected in the SQL Server environment. For example, if you try to rename a file with a stored procedure, Visual SourceSafe will not change the name of the stored procedure, but only the name of the script file.

## History

Visual SourceSafe keeps an audit trail of changes on a stored procedure. To view this history of changes:

1.  Right-click the stored procedure that you edited earlier in this chapter.

2.  Select Show History from the pop-up menu.

3.  Visual SourceSafe prompts you to define the history details you would like to display:

4.  In this case, accept the defaults and click OK.

Visual SourceSafe will display a list of the different versions of the stored procedure, along with the name of the user responsible for each action:

Now you have several options. If you select one version, you can View the code in an ASCII viewer. You can also see Details of the selected version such as comments and timestamp. The Get button lets you obtain a version of the stored procedure in a text file.

You can also temporarily or permanently set one of the previous versions to be a current one. The Pin function is usually applied as a temporary measure to test the behavior of an older version of a procedure. If you find that changes you made in your code are introducing more problems than they are solving, you can use the Rollback function to return to an earlier version of the code. All newer versions will be deleted.

My favorite option is Diff. It compares two versions of a file.

1.  Select two versions of a stored procedure (for example, version 2 and version 3) in the History window. You can select multiple versions by pressing the CTRL key and then clicking them.

2.  Click the Diff button. The Difference Options dialog appears:

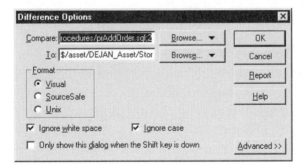

3.  This dialog lets you specify parameters for comparing files. If you wish to ignore case and white space, click OK to accept the defaults; Visual SourceSafe displays a window in which the differences between the two versions are highlighted (see Figure 8-6).

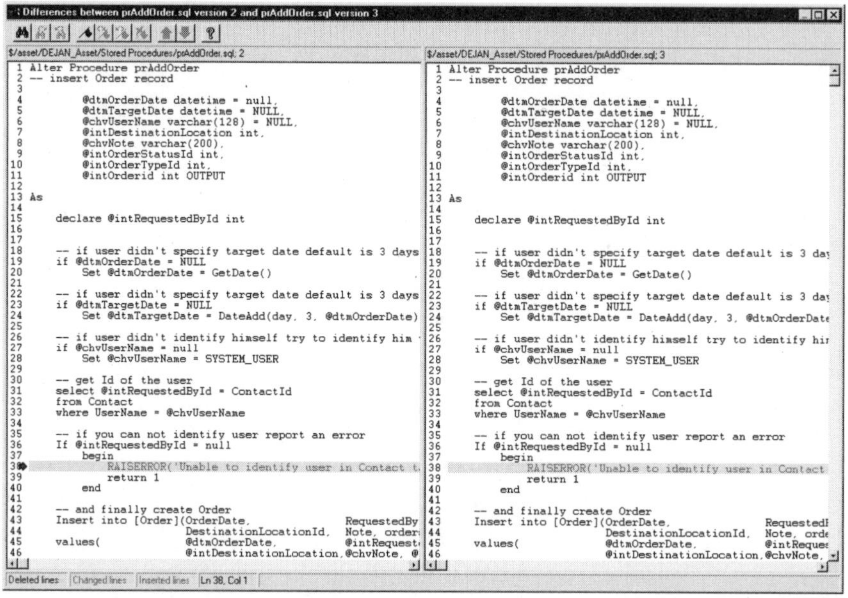

**Figure 8-6.** File Differences in Visual SourceSafe Explorer

## Labels and Versions

You have probably realized by now that the term "version" in Visual SourceSafe does not actually correspond to the concept of version (or release) that we generally think of when we consider software. A Visual SourceSafe version actually corresponds to a change in the source code. You should use Labels in Visual SourceSafe to implement the equivalent of a release.

You can apply the Label option from the main window of the Visual SourceSafe Explorer. You can select one or more files and/or one or more projects (folders). When you apply the Label option (File | Label), the Label dialog appears and prompts you to specify the text of the label (your official release number, for example):

The current versions of all selected files will be labeled. Later, you can use these labels to collect the code that belongs to a particular version. This feature can be very important for supporting or testing the product.

Even more exciting is the opportunity to view the complete history of a project (right-click the project folder and select Show History from the pop-up menu) and determine many historical facts about the project, such as which changes were performed on it after a particular release:

# NAMING CONVENTIONS

One of the most important things you can do to improve the quality and readability of your code is to use standards to name variables, procedures, and objects in your database. The preceding sentence may sound like an obvious truism or rule of thumb, but as rules of thumb go, this one is more often honored in the breach than in the observance.

## Why Bother?

Unfortunately, many developers dislike and avoid using standards. Their usual explanation is that standards stifle their creativity, or that the constant need to comply with standards distracts them from what they are really being paid to do. While there may be some truth in these claims, compliance with reasonable standards is another one of those habits that differentiates the professional from the amateur (not to mention the prima donna). Often, however, the problem lies not in the presence or content of a standard but in the spirit of its enforcement. Frequently organizations (or the people in them) get carried away. They forget the reasons for enforcing standards, and the standards become an end in themselves.

There are several valid reasons for introducing naming conventions:

▼ The main reason for the existence of naming conventions is to make code readable, understandable, and easy to remember.

■ A standard allows developers to speak a common "language" that will help the team to communicate more efficiently.

■ Team members will be able to understand and learn parts of the code with which they are not familiar.

■ New team members will have to learn only one standard way of coding instead of the distinct habits of individual team members.

▲ Time will be saved and confusion avoided, since it will be easier to give and find unique names for objects and variables.

If you are developing a project on your own, you might go through it without a standard (or without being aware that you actually have a standard). However, in some cases, the introduction of a standard becomes critical. For example, when

▼ More than one developer is working on the project.

■ The code or project will be maintained or reviewed by other developers who are not members of the team.

▲ The application under development is too complex for one person to analyze all aspects at once and requires different components to be designed and implemented separately.

Conventions do not have to be complicated. Let's investigate one simple example. If you name a variable @OrderNum, you will become confused about its contents, because the name does not convey its purpose clearly. Does it contain the total number of orders or the index of a particular order? To resolve this confusion, you could establish a convention that indexes are named with "Id" and totals with "Count" at the end of the name. In this case, the variable becomes @OrderId or @OrderCount.

# Naming Objects and Variables

The naming of objects should take into account the following details:

▼ Entity description

■ Name length

■ Abbreviations

▲ Name formatting

## Entity Description

It is common knowledge that variables, procedures, and objects should be named after the entities or processes that they represent. Therefore just to type a full description is a good start. The advantages of this approach are

▼ Nobody will be confused about its contents.

■ It makes for easy-to-read code, since no cryptic abbreviations are used.

▲ It makes the entity name easy to understand and memorize, since the description closely matches the entity.

Just compare the names in the following table:

| Good | Bad |
|---|---|
| @@CurrentDate | @D |
| @@ActivityCount | @ActNum |
| @@EquipmentType | @ET |
| CalculateOrderTotal | RunCalc |

**NOTE:** Such descriptions are usually just the basis for a name. Standards generally prescribe the use of different prefixes or suffixes to further describe other attributes such as the type of object, the datatype of a variable, and the scope.

A very common mistake is to use computer-oriented instead of business-oriented terminology. For example, "ProcessRecord" is a confusing name for a procedure. It should be replaced with a business description of the process such as "CompleteOrder."

## Name Length

Unfortunately, if you are too literal in naming procedures according to their business descriptions, you end up with names like

▼ PickupReconciliationInventoryIdentifier

■ TotalAmountOfMonthlyPayments

▲ GetParentOrganizationalUnitName

Although SQL Server supports the use of identifiers up to 128 characters long, research has shown that code in which most variable names have a length between 8 and 15 characters is easiest to develop, read, debug, and maintain. This fact does not imply that all of your variables must have lengths in that range, but you can use it as a rule of thumb.

Another rule of thumb is that you should try to limit names to three (3) words. Otherwise, names become too long, and thus too difficult to use and maintain.

You could go to an extreme in the other direction as well. If you are using a variable as a temporary counter in a loop, you could name it "@I." But even in that case, it might be easier to understand your code if you name it "@OrderItem."

## Abbreviations

A simple way to reduce the length of a name is to abbreviate it. If you can find an abbreviation in a thesaurus or dictionary, you should use it. You will avoid potential confusion. If not, you can simply remove vowels (except at the beginning of the word) and duplicate letters from each word, as in these examples:

▼ Current ⇨ Crnt

■ Address ⇨ Adr

■ Error ⇨ Err

▲ Average ⇨ Avg

You could also use the first letters of words or first few letters of a word, but make sure that the names you create will not be confused with other more common abbreviations. For example, you could abbreviate Complete Order Management to COM, but Visual Basic programmers might assume it stands for "component."

If you do not want to confuse readers of your code (such as the fellow programmers trying to maintain it months after you have moved to California to join an Internet start-up), you should *avoid* using phonetic abbreviations like

▼ 4tran (Fortran)

■ xqt (execute)

▲ b4 (before)

Abbreviations are great, but you should be careful not to confuse your colleagues. Try to be consistent. If you start abbreviating one word, you should do the same in all occurrences (variables, procedures, objects). It is potentially confusing to abbreviate the word "Equipment" as "Eq" in one case and leave the full word in another case. You will cause confusion as to which to use and whether they are equivalent.

To avoid confusion, you can write a description (using full words) in comments beside the declaration of a variable, in the definition of an object, or in the header of a procedure, for example

```
declare @ErrCd int   -- Error Code
```

## Name Formatting

I have seen people have endless debates about formatting identifiers. To underscore or not to underscore—that is the question:

▼ LeaseScheduleId

▲ lease_schedule_id

The truth is: it does not matter. You should avoid mixing these two conventions, because developers will never know what they have used for which variable. Unfortunately, you can catch even Microsoft developers mixing them. They are just human beings, after all.

In some rare cases, I believe it is justifiable to mix these two conventions in one identifier. For example, I like to note modification statements at the end of the name of a trigger (insert and update trigger on OrderItem table):

```
trOrderItem_IU
```

I also use an underscore to divide table names joined with a foreign key (such as a foreign key between Order and OrderItem tables):

```
fk_Order_OrderItem
```

## Suggested Convention

In computer science theory, you can find several well-documented formal conventions. The most famous one is the Hungarian convention (**http://msdn.microsoft.com/isapi/msdnlib.idc?theURL=/library/**

techart/hunganotat.htm). I will present a convention that is rather informal and tailored for use in Transact-SQL. You do not have to follow it literally, but you should have a good reason to break any rule.

**TIP:** Rules are made to be broken, but only if the solution is thereby improved.

## Variables

Variable identifiers should consist of two parts:

▼ The *base part*, which describes the content of the variable

▲ The *prefix*, which describes the datatype of the variable

Table 8-1 shows datatype abbreviations that should be used as prefixes:

| Datatype | Prefix | Example |
|---|---|---|
| Char | chr | @chrFirstName |
| Varchar | chv | @chvActivity |
| Nchar | chrn | @chrnLastName |
| Nvarchar | chvn | @chvnLastName |
| Text | txt | @txtNote |
| Ntext | txtn | @txtnComment |
| Datetime | dtm | @dtmTargetDate |
| Smalldatetime | dts | @dtsCompletionDate |
| Tinyint | iny | @inyActivityId |
| Smallint | ins | @insEquipmentTypeId |
| Integer | int | @intAsset |
| Bigint | inb | @inbGTIN |
| Numeric or Decimal | dec | @decProfit |

**Table 8-1.**    Datatype Prefixes

| | | |
|---|---|---|
| Real | rea | @reaVelocity |
| Float | flt | @fltLength |
| Smallmoney | mns | @mnsCost |
| Money | mny | @mnyPrice |
| Binary | bin | @binPath |
| Varbinary | biv | @bivContract |
| Image | img | @imgLogo |
| Bit | bit | @bitOperational |
| Timestamp | tsp | @tspCurrent |
| Uniqueidentifier | guid | @guidOrderId |
| sql_variant | var | @varPrice |
| Cursor | cur | @curInventory |
| Table | tbl | @tblLease |

**Table 8-1.**    Datatype Prefixes *(continued)*

## Database Objects

Names of database objects should consist of two parts:

▼ The *base part*, which describes the content of the object

▲ The *prefix*, which describes the type of database object

Table 8-2 shows database object abbreviations that should be used as prefixes:

| Database object | Prefix | Sample |
|---|---|---|
| table | — | Activities |
| column | — | ActivityId |
| view | v | vActivities |

**Table 8-2.**    Database Object Prefixes

| | | |
|---|---|---|
| stored procedure | pr | prCompleteOrder |
| trigger | tr | trOrder_IU |
| default | df | dfToday |
| rule | rul | rulCheckZIP |
| index | ix | ix_LastName |
| primary key | pk | pk_ContactId |
| foreign key | fk | fk_Order_OrderType |
| user-defined datatype | udt | udtPhone |
| user-defined functions | fn | fnDueDates |

**Table 8-2.**   Database Object Prefixes *(continued)*

**NOTE:**  Tables and columns should not have prefixes describing the object type.

## Triggers

Names of triggers should consist of three parts:

- ▼ The *prefix* (tr), which implies the database object type
- ■ The *base part,* which describes the table to which the trigger is attached
- ▲ The *suffix,* which shows modification statements (Insert, Update, and Delete)

For example:

```
trOrder_IU
```

If more than one trigger per modification statement is attached to the table, the base part should contain the name of the table and a reference to a business rule implemented by a trigger:

- ▼ **trOrderCascadingDelete_D**   Delete trigger on Order table that implements cascading deletes of order items

▲ **trOrderItemTotal_D**   Delete trigger on Order table that maintains a total of order item prices

SQL Server 2000 has an additional type of trigger—*instead-of* triggers. We will review them in detail in Chapter 9. To differentiate them from standard triggers (called *after* triggers in SQL Server 2000 documentation), you should use a different naming convention for them. We will use *itr* as a prefix:

▼ **itr_Order_D**   Instead-of delete trigger on the Order table

## Stored Procedures

The base name of a stored procedure should usually be created from a verb followed by a noun to describe the process the stored procedure performs on an object.

▼ prGetEquipment

▲ prCloseLease

You can also adopt the opposite role—noun followed by verb:

▼ prEquipmentGet

▲ prLeaseClose

If the procedure performs several tasks, all of those tasks should become part of the procedure name. It is okay to make procedure names longer than variable names. You should be able to pack a name into between 20 and 40 characters.

Some developers use the "sp_" prefix in front of the base name of a stored procedure. This prefix should be reserved for system stored procedures that reside in the master database and that are accessible from all databases.

You should also avoid computer-oriented or fuzzy names like:

▼ prProcessData

▲ prDoAction

Names such as these are often a symptom of a poorly designed stored procedure.

# SUMMARY

Source code control is necessary when a team of developers is working concurrently on a project, but experienced developers also use it even when they are working alone. Even the simplest project can grow larger than your memory. Implementing source code control on all projects, regardless of size, is one of those habits that helps to differentiate between the amateur and the professional.

With SQL Server 7.0 and 2000, Microsoft has finally adapted Visual SourceSafe to work with SQL Server. Work with stored procedures is integrated into the Visual Studio environment. Other database objects can also be managed through Visual SourceSafe, but not directly. They have to be saved and managed as script files.

The use of naming conventions makes code readable, understandable, and memorable. It is better to use any standard rather than none at all. Both management and developers must maintain reason in the introduction of standards with a view to preventing rigid and inflexible enforcement and establishing meaningful conventions.

Names should describe the contents of a variable, object, action, or procedure. Although SQL Server supports identifiers of up to 128 characters in length, the practical range is 8 to 15 characters for variables and 20 to 40 characters for stored procedures.

Imprecise names will misdirect the reader, and they are usually a symptom of a poorly designed stored procedure or an unclear purpose for an object or variable.

Although a development team can decide to follow some formal convention such as Hungarian notation, even simple informal conventions will serve the purpose. The introduction of a standard becomes critical when multiple developers are working on a project, when the code will be maintained by developers other than those on the project team, or when the development project is too complex for one person to hold in his or her head in its entirety.

This chapter presents a simple convention designed specifically for use in Transact-SQL statements.

# CHAPTER 9

# Special Types of Procedures

This chapter examines other types of procedures available in the SQL Server environment. Some of these procedures are just special types of stored procedures and others are completely different types of database objects. However, they all share a common attribute: that is, they are used to describe or implement an algorithm for the purpose of achieving some result.

# TYPES OF STORED PROCEDURES

There are six types of stored procedures:

▼ User-defined

■ System

■ Extended

■ Temporary

■ Global temporary

▲ Remote

## User-Defined Stored Procedures

As you may infer from the name, user-defined stored procedures are simply groups of Transact-SQL statements assembled by administrators or developers for later repetitive use. The design of this type of stored procedure is the primary focus of this book.

## System Stored Procedures

Microsoft delivers a vast set of stored procedures as a part of SQL Server. They are designed to cover all aspects of system administration. Before Microsoft SQL Server 6.0, administrators had to use scripts from isql to control the server and their databases. Although administrators

today customarily use Enterprise Manager, stored procedures are still
very important, since Enterprise Manager uses the same system stored
procedures, through SQL-DMO, behind the scenes.

> **NOTE:**   SQL-DMO stands for SQL Distributed Management Objects. It is a
> collection of objects designed to manage the SQL Server environment. You
> can use it to create your own Enterprise Manager or automate repetitive
> tasks. It is interesting that it does not support the return of a recordset to the
> caller. You should use other objects (such as ADO) to achieve this result.

System stored procedures are stored in the system databases (master
and msdb), and they have the prefix sp_. This prefix is more than just a
convention. It signals to the server that the stored procedure is located in
the master database and that it should be accessible from all databases
without the user's needing to insert the database name as a prefix to fully
qualify the name of the procedure:

```
Exec sp_who      -- instead of exec master..sp_who
```

It also signals to the server that the stored procedure should be executed
in the context of the current database. For example, the script shown in
Figure 9-1 will return information about the current database, and not
the master.

> **NOTE:**   There is a small behavioral inconsistency between stored procedures
> in the master database and the msdb database. Stored procedures in the msdb
> database are delivered with SQL Server, but they must be referenced with the
> database name (for example: msdb..sp_update_job), and they do not work in
> the context of the current database. In this respect, you can understand them as
> "system-supplied stored procedures" rather than as "system stored procedures"
> as we have defined them.

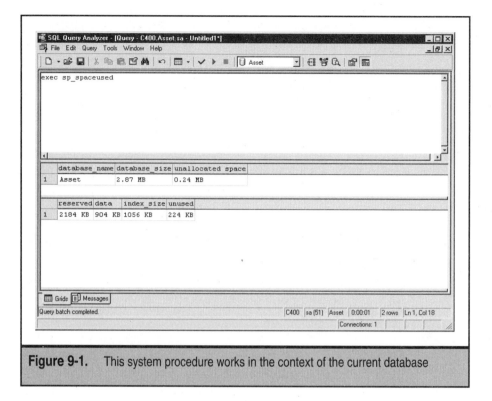

**Figure 9-1.**   This system procedure works in the context of the current database

## Extended Stored Procedures

Certain SQL Server features cannot be implemented through Transact-SQL statements. The designers of SQL Server have developed a way to use the functionality encapsulated in special .dll libraries written in languages such as C or C++. Extended stored procedures are actually these C functions encapsulated in .dll files. They have a wrapper stored in the master database that uses the prefix xp_. Using this wrapper, you can access them just as you would any other stored procedure.

**NOTE:**   Selected extended stored procedures stored in the master database are named with the prefix sp_ to allow users to access them from any database (such as sp_execute, sp_executesql, sp_sdidebug).

In the following example, the extended stored procedure runs an operating system command to list all scripts in the BINN directory. Since it is not declared with the sp_ prefix, you must qualify its name with that of the database in which it is located:

```
Exec master..xp_cmdshell 'dir c:\mssql7\binn\*.sql'
```

## Design of Extended Stored Procedures

It is not possible to create an extended stored procedure from just any .dll file. The file must be prepared in a special way. It is also not possible to create these files from Visual Basic, since it does not create classic .dll files, but just in-process versions of COM objects.

> **NOTE:** Fortunately, it is possible to access code in the form of COM objects from Transact-SQL. Chapter 11 describes the creation and execution of such code in detail.

The development of extended stored procedures is based on the use of ODS API (Open Data Services API). In the past, it was a tedious job and the developer had to perform all tasks manually. Nowadays, the process is automated in the Enterprise Edition of Visual C++ through the Extended Stored Procedure Wizard. We will quickly demonstrate its use.

With the proper initialization code, the Extended Stored Procedure wizard generates Win32 DLL projects that contain an exported function. The developer should change the content of the exported function to perform the job of the future extended stored procedure. The wizard includes the header file (srv.h) and a library (opends60.lib) needed for using ODS in the code.

To create an extended stored procedure:

1. In Visual C++ Enterprise Edition, select New from the File menu. The New dialog box should appear with Projects tab opened. You need to set the name of the project. You could and should also use the name of the extended stored procedure as

the name of the project. Extended stored procedure names commonly begin with the xp_ prefix.

2. Select Extended Stored Proc AppWizard from the list of project types:

3. When you click OK, the program will launch the Extended Stored Proc Wizard. It prompts you to name your extended stored procedure:

4. Click Finish. The wizard generates the following project files:

- **proc.cpp**   The exported Win32 function, which is the extended stored procedure

- **[projname].dsp**   The Visual C++ project file

- **[projname].cpp**   A file that includes DLL initialization code

- **StdAfx.h**   An include file for standard system include files, or project-specific include files that are used frequently

- **StdAfx.cpp**   A source file that includes just the standard includes

5. Open proc.cpp and change the code to implement features of the extended stored procedure. Figure 9-2 shows Visual Studio with the code of the extended stored procedure.

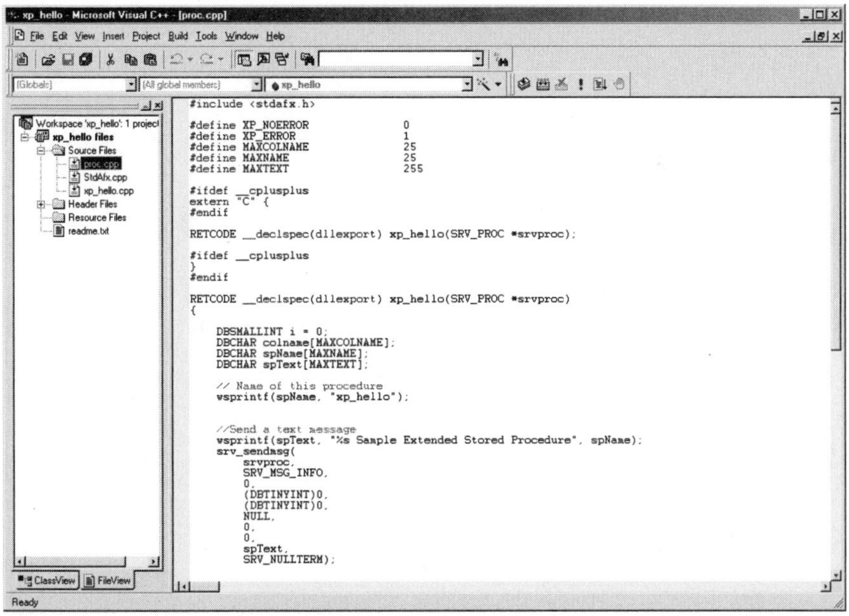

**Figure 9-2.**   Code of the extended stored procedure

6. Compile the generated project to generate a
DLL—**[projname].DLL**.

Let's review the code. The following code listing shows the
contents of proc.cpp. It contains the exported Win32 function
xp_hello. The function was generated by the wizard, and it returns
a simple message and a recordset that contains three records:

```cpp
#include <stdafx.h>
#define XP_NOERROR              0
#define XP_ERROR                1
#define MAXCOLNAME              25
#define MAXNAME                 25
#define MAXTEXT                 255


#ifdef __cplusplus
extern "C" {
#endif


RETCODE __declspec(dllexport) xp_hello(SRV_PROC *srvproc);


#ifdef __cplusplus
}
#endif


RETCODE __declspec(dllexport) xp_hello(SRV_PROC *srvproc)
{

    DBSMALLINT i = 0;
    DBCHAR colname[MAXCOLNAME];
    DBCHAR spName[MAXNAME];
    DBCHAR spText[MAXTEXT];

    // Name of this procedure
    wsprintf(spName, "xp_hello");



    //Send a text message
```

```
wsprintf(spText, "%s Sample Extended Stored Procedure", spName);
srv_sendmsg(
    srvproc,
    SRV_MSG_INFO,
    0,
    (DBTINYINT)0,
    (DBTINYINT)0,
    NULL,
    0,
    0,
    spText,
    SRV_NULLTERM);


//Set up the column names
wsprintf(colname, "ID");
srv_describe(srvproc, 1, colname, SRV_NULLTERM, SRVINT2,
            sizeof(DBSMALLINT), SRVINT2, sizeof(DBSMALLINT), 0);

wsprintf(colname, "spName");
srv_describe(srvproc, 2, colname, SRV_NULLTERM, SRVCHAR, MAXNAME,
            SRVCHAR, 0, NULL);

wsprintf(colname, "Text");
srv_describe(srvproc, 3, colname, SRV_NULLTERM, SRVCHAR, MAXTEXT,
            SRVCHAR, 0, NULL);


// Update field 2 "spName", same value for all rows
srv_setcoldata(srvproc, 2, spName);
srv_setcollen(srvproc, 2, strlen(spName));


// Send multiple rows of data
for (i = 0; i < 3; i++) {

    // Update field 1 "ID"
    srv_setcoldata(srvproc, 1, &i);
```

```
        // Update field 3 "Text"
        wsprintf(spText,
"%d) Sample rowset generated by the %s extended stored procedure", i,
spName);

        srv_setcoldata(srvproc, 3, spText);
        srv_setcollen(srvproc, 3, strlen(spText));

        // Send the entire row
        srv_sendrow(srvproc);
    }


    // Now return the number of rows processed
    srv_senddone(srvproc, SRV_DONE_MORE | SRV_DONE_COUNT,
(DBUSMALLINT)0, (DBINT)i);

    return XP_NOERROR ;
}
```

## Registering the Extended Stored Procedure

Once the DLL is compiled, the extended stored procedure has to be registered on the server before it can be used:

1. Copy the XP_HELLO.dll file to the SQL Server \...\Binn folder.

2. Register the new extended stored procedure using the SQL Server Enterprise Manager, or by executing the following SQL command:

   ```
   sp_addextendedproc 'xp_hello', 'XP_HELLO.DLL'
   ```

Once the extended stored procedure is registered, you can test it using Query Analyzer (see Figure 9-3).

```
SQL Query Analyzer - [Query - C400.Asset.sa - Untitled1*]
File  Edit  Query  Tools  Window  Help

exec master..xp_hello

xp_hello Sample Extended Stored Procedure
ID      spName                  Text
------  ----------------------  -----------------------------------------------------------
0       xp_hello                0) Sample rowset generated by the xp_hello extended stored pr
1       xp_hello                1) Sample rowset generated by the xp_hello extended stored pr
2       xp_hello                2) Sample rowset generated by the xp_hello extended stored pr

(3 row(s) affected)

  Results
Query batch completed.                                    C400  sa (51)  Asset  0:00:00  3 rows  Ln 1, Col 22
                                                                            Connections: 1
```

**Figure 9-3.**    Using the extended stored procedure

You should carefully test the new extended stored procedure. If you find out that it is not working as expected or that you need to make some modification, you will need to unregister (drop) the extended stored procedure by using the following SQL command:

```
sp_dropextendedproc 'xp_hello'
```

When the extended stored procedure is executed in SQL Server, it is loaded into memory. It stays there until SQL Server is shut down or until you issue a command to remove it from memory:

```
DBCC xp_hello(FREE)
```

To register an extended stored procedure from Enterprise Manager, you need to right-click the Extended Stored Procedures node in the master database and select New Extended Stored Procedure. Enterprise Manager prompts you for the name of the extended stored procedure and the location of the .dll file:

It is also simple to remove an extended stored procedure using Enterprise Manager. You merely right-click it and select Delete from the pop-up menu.

*NOTE:*   The trouble with extended stored procedures is that they work in the address space of SQL Server. Therefore, an extended stored procedure that doesn't behave properly could crash SQL Server. Such a problem is not likely to occur, since SQL Server monitors the behavior of extended stored procedures. If an extended stored procedure, attempts to reference memory outside of its address space, for example, SQL Server will terminate it. Common sense programming practices (using error checking, doing exception handling, and thoroughly testing final code) will further reduce the possibility of errors.

*TIP:*   There is another problem. If you are fluent enough in the techniques required to create extended stored procedures, you should not be spending your time creating business applications. You should be working on more fundamental stuff like operating systems or RDBMS, and devoting your time to hacking. Let the rest of us collect the easy money.;)

# Temporary Stored Procedures

Temporary stored procedures are related to stored procedures as temporary tables are to tables. You will use them when you expect to reuse the execution plan of a stored procedure within a limited time frame. Although you can achieve the same functionality with a standard user-defined stored procedure, temporary stored procedures are a better solution, because you do not have to worry about maintenance issues (such as dropping the stored procedure).

Temporary stored procedures reside in the tempdb and must have the prefix '#'. You create them in the same manner as you do user-defined stored procedures. The only change is the use of a '#' as a name prefix. This prefix signals the server to create the procedure as a temporary stored procedure. This kind of stored procedure can only be used from the session in which it was created. When the session is closed, it will be dropped automatically. This behavior indicates why this type of stored procedure is often also referred to as a *private temporary stored procedure*.

```
Create Procedure #GetId
     @Make varchar(50),
     @Model varchar(50)
as
     Select EquipmentId
     from Equipment
     where Make = @Make
     and Model = @Model
```

Sometimes administrators refer to user-defined stored procedures in tempdb as temporary stored procedures. This equation is incorrect, since there are major differences between the two. For example, user-defined stored procedures in tempdb are accessible to all authorized users. These stored procedures stay in tempdb until the server is shut down. At that time, the complete content of tempdb is flushed.

## Global Temporary Stored Procedures

Global temporary stored procedures are related to temporary stored procedures as global temporary tables to private temporary tables. They also reside in tempdb, but they use the prefix '##'. You create them in the same manner as you do temporary stored procedures. The only difference is that they are visible and usable from all sessions. In fact, permissions are not required and the owner cannot even deny other users access to them.

When the session that has created the procedure is closed, no new sessions will be able to execute the stored procedure. After all instances of the stored procedure already running are finished, the procedure is dropped automatically.

```
Create Procedure ##InsertEquipment
    @Make varchar(50),
    @Model varchar(50),
    @EqType varchar(50)
as
    declare @EqTypeId smallint
    select @EqTypeId = EqTypeId    -- This is OK in perfect world,
    from EqType                    -- but it is based on
    Where EqType = @EqType         -- unreasonable assumption.

    Insert Equipment (Make, Model, EqTypeId)
    Values (@Make, @Model, @EqTypeId)
```

## Remote Stored Procedures

This type is actually a user-defined stored procedure that resides on a remote server. The only challenge implicit in this type of stored procedure is that the local server has to be set to allow the remote use of stored procedures. For more information, search SQL Server Books Online using the following string: How to set up a remote server to allow the use of remote stored procedures.

*TIP:* Microsoft, in fact, considers this mechanism as a legacy of older versions of SQL Server. Heterogeneous queries are the recommended way to execute stored procedures or access tables on other servers.

# USER-DEFINED FUNCTIONS

The ability to design Transact-SQL functions is a new feature in SQL Server 2000. In earlier versions, users were only able to use built-in functions.

## Design of User-Defined Functions

*User-defined functions* can be created using the Create Function statement, changed using Alter Function, and deleted using Drop Function. You can use sp_help and sp_stored_procedures to get information about a function, and sp_helptext to obtain its source code. From Enterprise Manager, the administrator can use the same tools used to create and manage stored procedures.

Functions can have zero, one, or more parameters. They must return a single return value. The returned value can be scalar, or it can be a table. Input parameters can be values of any datatype except timestamp, cursor, and table. Return values can be of any datatype except timestamp, cursor, text, ntext, and image.

The Create Function statement has the following syntax:

```
Create Function [owner_name.]function_name
(
     [ {@parameter_name scalar_data_type [= default]} [,...n] ]
)
returns scalar_data_type
        |Table
        |return_variable Table({column_def|table_constraint}[,…n])
[With {Encryption|Schemabinding}[,…n] ]
[As]
{Begin function_body End}
| Return [(] {value|select-stmt} [)]
```

The following example produces a function that will return the quarter for a specified date:

```
Create Function fnQuarterString
-- returns quarter in form of '3Q2000'.
    (
    @dtmDate datetime
    )
Returns char(6) -- quarter like 3Q2000
As
Begin
    Return (DateName(q, @dtmDate) + 'Q' + DateName(yyyy, @dtmDate))
End
```

As we mentioned in Chapter 5, and as you can see in Figure 9-4, to reference a function, a user must specify both the object owner and the object identifier.

The function in the previous example had just one `Return` statement in the body of the function. In fact, a function can be designed with flow control and other Transact-SQL statements. A function can even contain more than one `Return` statement. Under different conditions, they can serve as exit points from the function. The only requirement is that the last statement in the function body be an unconditional `Return` statement. The following function illustrates this principle in returning a date three business days after the specified date:

```
Create Function fnThreeBusDays
-- returns date 3 business day after the specified date
    (@dtmDate datetime)
Returns datetime
As
Begin
Declare @inyDayOfWeek tinyint
Set @inyDayOfWeek = DatePart(dw, @dtmDate)
Set @dtmDate = Convert(datetime, Convert(varchar, @dtmDate, 101))
```

```
If @inyDayOfWeek = 1 -- Sunday
     Return DateAdd(d, 3, @dtmDate )
If @inyDayOfWeek = 7 -- Saturday
     Return DateAdd(d, 4, @dtmDate )
If @inyDayOfWeek = 6 -- Friday
     Return DateAdd(d, 5, @dtmDate )
If @inyDayOfWeek = 5 -- Thursday
     Return DateAdd(d, 5, @dtmDate )
If @inyDayOfWeek = 4 -- Wednesday
     Return DateAdd(d, 5, @dtmDate )


Return DateAdd(d, 3, @dtmDate )
End
```

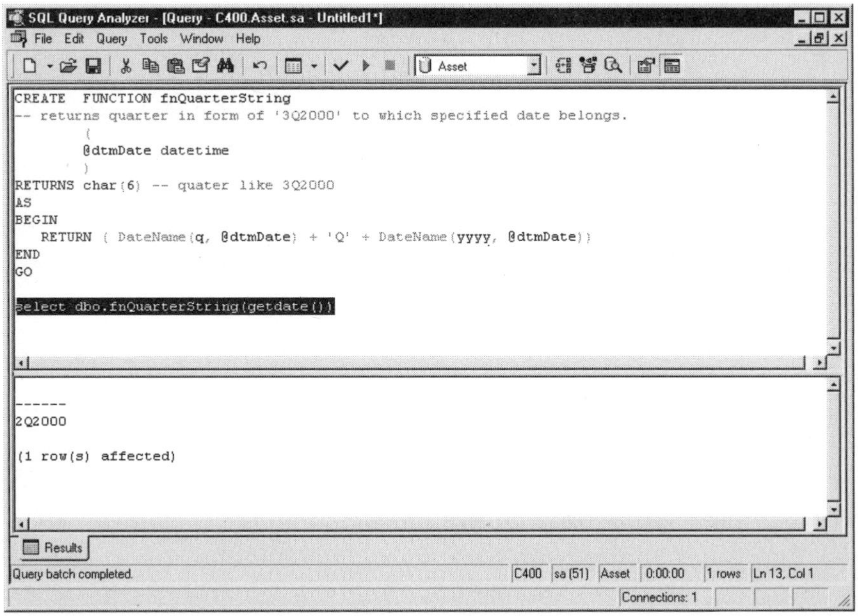

**Figure 9-4.** Using a function by specifying an object owner and an object identifier

## Side Effects

User-defined functions have one serious limitation. They cannot have side effects. A *function side effect* is any permanent change to resources (such as tables) that have a scope outside of the function (such as a non-temporary table that is not declared in the function). Basically, this requirement means that a function should return a value while changing nothing in the database.

*TIP:*  In some development environments like C or Visual Basic, a developer can write a function that can perform some additional activities or changes, but it is a matter of good design and discipline not to abuse that opportunity.

SQL Server forces the user not to create side effects by limiting which Transact-SQL statements can be used inside a function:

▼  Assignment statements (Set or Select) referencing objects local to the function (such as local variables and a return value)

■  Flow control statements

■  Update, Insert, and Delete statements that update local table variables

■  Declare statements that define local variables or cursors

▲  Statements that declare, open, close, fetch, and deallocate local cursors (the only Fetch statements allowed are ones that retrieve information from a cursor into local variables)

## Use of Built-in Functions

User-defined functions cannot call built-in functions that return different data on each call, such as these:

| | |
|---|---|
| @@CONNECTIONS | @@TIMETICKS |
| @@CPU_BUSY | @@TOTAL_ERRORS |

| | |
|---|---|
| @@IDLE | @@TOTAL_READ |
| @@IO_BUSY | @@TOTAL_WRITE |
| @@MAX_CONNECTIONS | GETDATE |
| @@PACK_RECEIVED | NEWID |
| @@PACK_SENT | RAND |
| @@PACKET_ERRORS | TEXTPTR |

Notice that `GetDate()` is also among the forbidden functions. If you try to use it inside a user-defined function, SQL Server will report an error as shown in Figure 9-5.

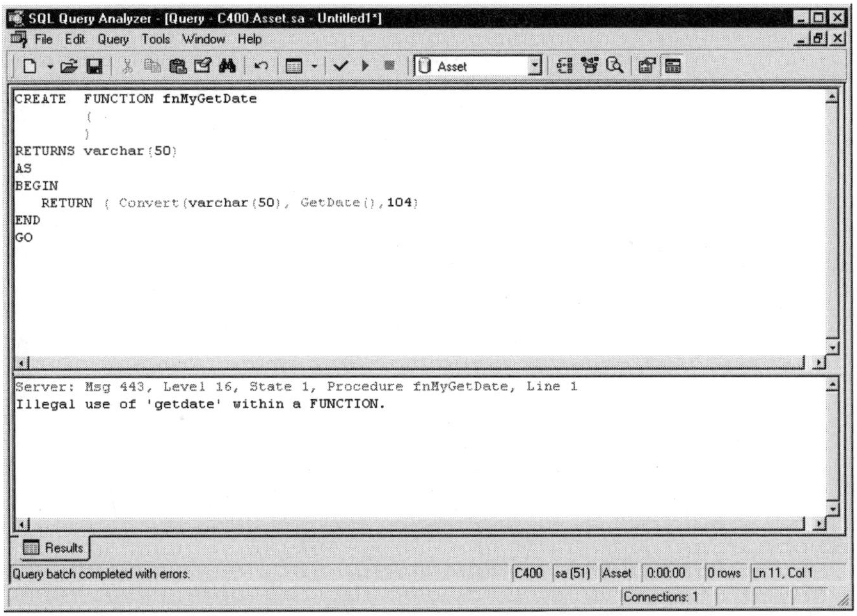

**Figure 9-5.**    A limitation on use of built-in functions in user-defined functions

## Encryption

As is the case with stored procedures, functions can be encrypted so that nobody can see their source code. The developer just needs to create or alter the function using the `With Encryption` option.

## Schema-Binding

A new option, `With Schemabinding`, allows developers to *schema-bind* a user-defined function to database objects (such as tables, views, and other used-defined functions) that it references. Once the function is schema-bound, it is not possible to make schema changes on underlying objects. All attempts to drop the objects and all attempts to `Alter` underlying objects (which would change the object schema) will fail.

A function can be schema-bound only if all of the following criteria are satisfied:

▼ All user-defined functions and views referenced by the function must already be schema-bound.

■ All database objects that the function references must reside in the same database as the function. References to database objects cannot have server or database qualifiers. Only object owner qualifiers and object identifiers are allowed.

▲ The user who executes the `Create` (or `Alter`) `Function` statement has References permissions on all referenced database objects.

# Table-Valued User-Defined Functions

Since SQL Server 2000 has a table datatype, it is possible to design a user-defined function that returns a table. The primary use of table-valued user-defined functions is similar to the use of views. However, these functions are far more flexible and provide additional functionality.

You can use a table-valued user-defined function anywhere you can use a table (or view). In this respect, they implement the functionality of views, but functions can have parameters and

therefore they are dynamic. Views are also limited to a single
`Select` statement. Functions can have one or more Transact-SQL
statements inside and in this way implement more complex
functionality. That is why functions of this type are often referred to
as *multi-statement table-valued user-defined functions*. Stored procedures
can also return a resultset, but the use of such resultsets is somewhat
limited. For example, only a resultset returned by a function can be
referenced in the `From` clause of a `Select` statement.

Let's demonstrate this functionality. The following `Select`
statement references the user-defined function `fnDueDays`, which
returns a list of lease payment due dates. The statement returns a
list of remaining payments and due dates:

```
select DD.TermId, DD.DueDate, Inventory.Lease
from dbo.fnDueDays('1/1/2000','1/1/2004','monthly') DD, Inventory
where InventoryId = 8
and DD.DueDate > GetDate()
```

The result will look like this:

```
TermId       DueDate                        Lease
----------   --------------------------    ------------
3            2000-04-01 00:00:00            87.7500
4            2000-05-01 00:00:00            87.7500
5            2000-06-01 00:00:00            87.7500
6            2000-07-01 00:00:00            87.7500
7            2000-08-01 00:00:00            87.7500
. . .
```

Stored procedure prListTerms has functionality similar to the
functionality of the `DueDates` function. But to perform additional
filtering of the resultset returned by the stored procedure, the developer
would first need to receive the resultset into a temporary table:

```
Create Table #tbl(TermId int, DueDate smalldatetime)

Insert Into #Tbl(TermId, DueDate)
     Exec prListTerms '1/1/2000','1/1/2004','monthly'

Select #tbl.TermId, #tbl.DueDate, Inventory.Lease
```

```
From #tbl, Inventory
Where InventoryId = 8
And #tbl.DueDate > GetDate()

Drop Table #tbl
```

This is much more complicated than using the comparable function. Let's investigate the internals of the fnDueDate function:

```
Create Function fnDueDays
-- return list of due days for the leasing
(
    @dtsStartDate smalldatetime,
    @dtsEndDate smalldatetime,
    @chvLeaseFrequency varchar(20)
)
Returns @tblTerms table
    (
    TermID int,
    DueDate smalldatetime
    )

As
Begin

Declare @insTermsCount smallint -- number of intervals
Declare @insTerms smallint -- number of intervals

-- calculate number of terms
Select @insTermsCount =
  Case @chvLeaseFrequency
    When 'monthly'
            then DateDIFF(month, @dtsStartDate, @dtsEndDate)
    When 'semi-monthly'
            then 2 * DateDIFF(month, @dtsStartDate, @dtsEndDate)
    When 'bi-weekly'
            then DateDIFF(week, @dtsStartDate, @dtsEndDate)/2
    When 'weekly'
            then DateDIFF(week, @dtsStartDate, @dtsEndDate)
```

```
        When 'quarterly'
                then DateDIFF(qq, @dtsStartDate, @dtsEndDate)
        When 'yearly'
                then DateDIFF(y, @dtsStartDate, @dtsEndDate)
    End


-- generate list of due dates
Set @insTerms = 1
While @insTerms <= @insTermsCount
Begin
  Insert @tblTerms (TermID, DueDate)
  Values (@insTerms, Convert(smalldatetime, CASE
        When @chvLeaseFrequency = 'monthly'
            then DateADD(month,@insTerms, @dtsStartDate)
        When @chvLeaseFrequency = 'semi-monthly'
        and @insTerms/2 =  Cast(@insTerms as float)/2
            then DateADD(month, @insTerms/2, @dtsStartDate)
        When @chvLeaseFrequency = 'semi-monthly'
        and @insTerms/2 <> Cast(@insTerms as float)/2
            then DateADD(dd, 15,
                        DateADD(month, @insTerms/2, @dtsStartDate))
        When @chvLeaseFrequency = 'bi-weekly'
            then DateADD(week, @insTerms*2, @dtsStartDate)
        When @chvLeaseFrequency = 'weekly'
            then DateADD(week, @insTerms, @dtsStartDate)
        When @chvLeaseFrequency = 'quarterly'
            then DateADD(qq, @insTerms, @dtsStartDate)
        When @chvLeaseFrequency = 'yearly'
            then DateADD(y, @insTerms, @dtsStartDate)
        End , 105))


    Select @insTerms = @insTerms + 1
End


Return
End
```

Let me point out to you a few differences between these functions and scalar functions. User-defined functions that return a table have a table variable definition in the Returns clause:

```
. . .
Returns @tblTerms table
    (
    TermID int,
    DueDate smalldatetime
    )
. . .
```

In the body of the function, there are statements that fill the contents of the table variable:

```
. . .
    Insert @tblTerms (TermID, DueDate)
    Values (@insTerms, Convert(smalldatetime, CASE
                    When @chvLeaseFrequency = 'monthly'
. . .
```

The Return statement at the end of the function does not specify a value. As soon as it is reached, SQL Server returns the contents of the table variable to the caller:

```
Return
End
```

## In-Line Table-Valued User-Defined Functions

An *in-line table-valued user-defined function* is a special type of table-valued user-defined function. Its purpose is to implement parameterized views.

The syntax of an in-line table-valued user-defined function is a bit different from the syntax of other functions:

```
Create Function [owner_name.]function_name
(
     [ {@parameter_name scalar_data_type [= default]} [,...n] ]
)
Returns Table
        [With {Encryption|Schemabinding}[,...n] ]
[As]
| Return (select-stmt)
```

You do not have to define the format of the return value. It is enough to specify just the `table` keyword. An in-line table-valued function does not have the body of a function. A resultset is created by a single `Select` statement in the `Return` clause. It is best to demonstrate this feature with an example. The following function returns only a segment of a table based on a role the user belongs to. The idea is that a manager or any other employee can see only equipment from his own department:

```
Create Function fn_DepartmentEquipment
     ( @chvUserName sysname )
Returns table
As
Return (
     Select InventoryId, Make + ' ' + model Model, Location
     From Inventory inner join Contact C
     On Inventory.OwnerId = C.ContactId
          Inner Join Contact Manager
          On C.OrgUnitId = Manager.OrgUnitId
               Inner Join Equipment
               On Inventory.EquipmentId = Equipment.EquipmentId
                    Inner Join Location
                    On Inventory.LocationId = Location.LocationId
     Where Manager.UserName = @chvUserName
     )
Go
```

You can use this function in any place where a view or table is allowed, such as in a Select statement:

```
Select *
From fn_DepartmentEquipment ('tomj')
Go
```

Figure 9-6 shows the result of such a statement.

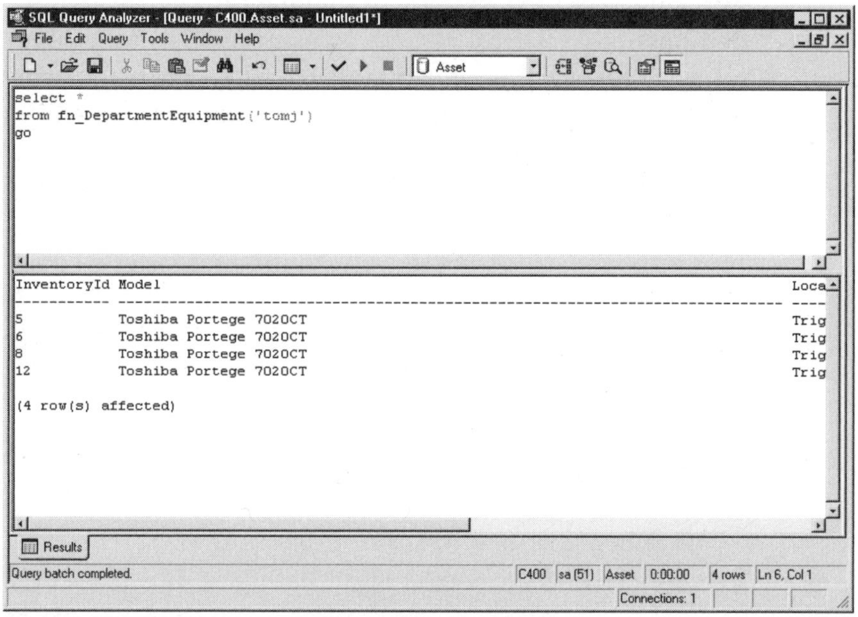

**Figure 9-6.**    Using an in-line table-valued user-defined function

# Managing User-defined Functions in Enterprise Manager

You can access user-defined functions from Enterprise Manager as shown in Figure 9-7.

If you double-click a function, SQL Server displays a modal form for editing its properties (that is, code and permissions). This editor is identical to the editor you use to edit stored procedures (see Figure 9-8).

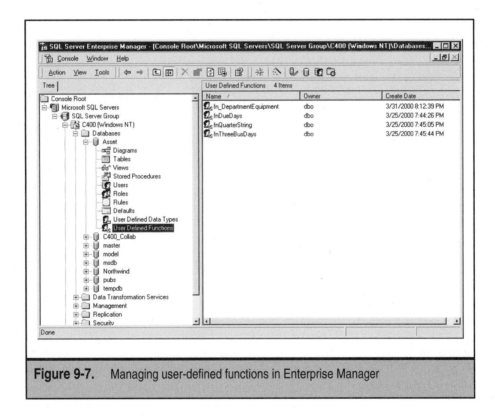

**Figure 9-7.**   Managing user-defined functions in Enterprise Manager

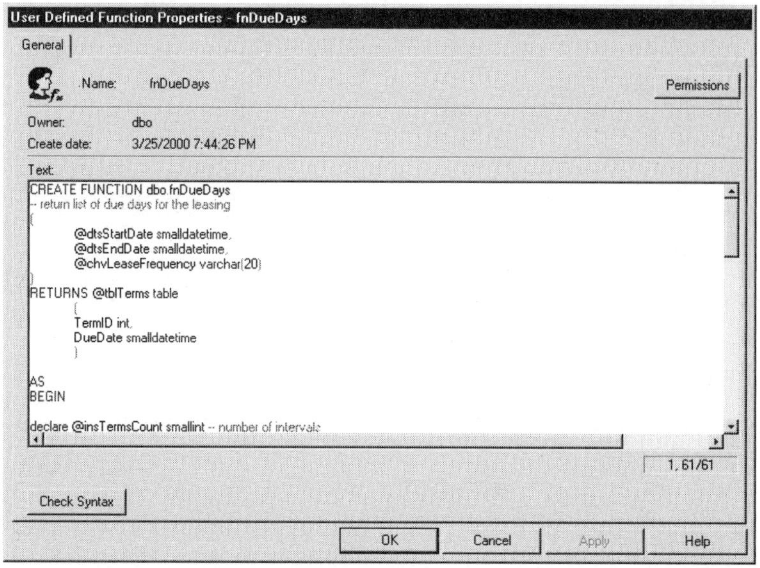

**Figure 9-8.** Editing user-defined functions

If you right-click a function and select New User Defined Function, SQL Server opens a form with a template for creating a new function (see Figure 9-9).

Once you have written or changed the function, you can use the Check Syntax button to verify it, then select OK or Apply to compile and save it. You can also create and save a function template.

# TRIGGERS

*Triggers* are a unique type of procedure. Triggers are very similar to events—a type of procedure in certain programming languages such as Visual Basic. Events in Visual Basic are initiated by the system when certain actions occur (for instance, a form is loaded, a text box receives focus, or a key is pressed).

```
User Defined Function Properties - New User Defined Function

General

     Name:    <New User Defined Function>                              Permissions

Owner:
Create date:
Text:
CREATE FUNCTION [OWNER] [FUNCTION NAME] (PARAMETER LIST)
RETURNS (return_type_spec) AS
BEGIN
(FUNCTION BODY)
END

                                                            4, 5/5

   Check Syntax   Save as Template

                                 OK        Cancel        Help
```

**Figure 9-9.** A function template

Triggers are associated with a table in a database and executed by SQL Server when a specific change occurs in the table. The change could be the result of the following modification statements:

▼  Insert

■  Update

▲  Delete

SQL Server 7.0 and earlier versions recognized only one type of trigger. In SQL Server 2000, this type is called an *after trigger*. SQL Server 2000 introduces a new type—an *instead-of trigger*. In the following sections, we first examine the standard (after) triggers and then we introduce the new instead-of type.

## Physical Design

Let's look at the simplified syntax for implementing the core functionality of triggers:

```
Create Trigger trigger_name
On table
{For { [Delete] [,] [Insert] [,] [Update] }
   As
     sql_statement [...n]
```

As a stored procedure, a trigger logically consists of

▼ A *header*, which is a Transact-SQL statement for creating a trigger. It consists of three components:

■ The name of the trigger

■ The name of the table with which the trigger will be associated

■ A modification statement (that is, an event) that will initiate the trigger

▲ A *body*, which contains Transact-SQL statement(s) to be executed at runtime

In the following example, we first create a new table called MyEquipment. We populate it with Make and Model information from the Equipment table, and finally we create a trigger.

The trigger is named `trMyEquipment_D` and is associated with the MyEquipment table. It is fired after a `Delete` statement is executed against the table. Its function is very simple—it notifies the user regarding actions and the number of records that have been deleted.

```
Create Table MyEquipment
     (Id int identity,
     Description varchar(50))
GO

-- populate table
Insert MyEquipment(Description)
```

```
      Select Make + ' ' + Model from Equipment
GO


Create Trigger trMyEquipment_D
On dbo.MyEquipment
After Delete   -- For Delete
As
      Print 'You have just deleted '
            + Cast(@@rowcount as varchar)
            + ' record(s)!'
Go
```

To execute the trigger, we need to execute the `Delete` statement:

```
Delete MyEquipment
Where Id = 2
```

SQL Server will return the following:

```
You have just deleted 1 record(s)!


(1 row(s) affected)
```

You can also execute the `Delete` statement to delete multiple records:

```
Delete MyEquipment
```

Even in this case, the trigger will *not* be fired once for each record. We will receive just one message:

```
You have just deleted 4 record(s)!


(4 row(s) affected)
```

For this reason, it is important to design your trigger to handle actions against multiple records. You will see more reasons in following paragraphs.

## Inserted and Deleted Virtual Tables

SQL Server maintains two temporary virtual tables during the execution of a trigger. They are called *Deleted* and *Inserted*. These tables contain all the records inserted or deleted during the operation that fired the trigger. You can use this feature to perform additional verification or additional activities on affected records.

You are probably wondering if there is an Updated table. No. Because an Update can be performed as a combination of the Delete and Insert statements, records that were updated will appear in both the Deleted and Inserted tables.

SQL Server will not create both tables in all cases. For example, in a trigger fired during a Delete statement, only Deleted items will be accessible. A reference to an Inserted item will cause an error.

The following table will summarize the presence of virtual tables in the relevant Transact-SQL statements:

| Modification Statement | Deleted | Inserted |
| --- | --- | --- |
| INSERT | N/A | New records |
| UPDATE | Old version of updated records | New version of updated records |
| DELETE | Deleted records | N/A |

Let's modify the trigger from the previous section to display which records are deleted:

```
Alter Trigger trMyEquipment_D
On dbo.MyEquipment
After Delete      -- For Delete
As
     Select 'You have just deleted following '
          + Cast(@@rowcount as varchar)
          + ' record(s)!'

     Select * from deleted
go
```

When you delete all records from the MyEquipment table, SQL Server returns the following:

```
------------------------------------------------------------
You have just deleted following 5 record(s)!
```

```
(1 row(s) affected)


Id          Description
----------- -------------------------------------------------
1           Toshiba Portege 7020CT
2           Sony Trinitron 17XE
3           NEC V90
4           HP LaserJet 4
5           HP LaserJet 4


(5 row(s) affected)
```

You can use values from these tables, but you cannot modify them directly. If you need to perform some operation on records that were inserted, for example, you should not try to change them in the Inserted table. The proper method would be to issue a regular Transact-SQL statement against the original table. In the Where or From clause, you can reference the virtual table (Inserted) and in that way limit the subset of the original table that you are targeting.

In the following example, the trigger calculates a SOUNDEX code for the Make and Model of the Equipment records affected by the Insert or Update statement that has fired the trigger:

```
Alter Trigger trEquipment_IU
On dbo.Equipment
After Insert, Update     -- For Insert, Update
As
    -- precalculate ModelSDX and MakeSDX field
    -- to speed up use of SOUNDEX function
    update Equipment
    Set ModelSDX = SOUNDEX(Model),
        MakeSDX = SOUNDEX(Make)
    where EquipmentId IN (Select EquipmentId from Inserted)
```

## What Triggers a Trigger?

A trigger is executed *once for each modification statement* (Insert, Update, or Delete). An after trigger is fired *after* the modification statement finishes *successfully.* If a statement fails for another reason (for example: foreign key or check constraints), the trigger is not invoked. For example, the Equipment table has the following `Delete` trigger:

```
Alter Trigger Equipment_DeleteTrigger
On dbo.Equipment
After Delete      -- For Delete
As
Print 'One or more rows are deleted in Equipment table!'
```

Attempt to delete all records from the table:

```
delete Equipment
```

SQL Server aborts the execution because there is a foreign key relationship with the Inventory table. The execution is aborted before the trigger is invoked:

```
Server: Msg 547, Level 16, State 1, Line 1
DELETE statement conflicted with COLUMN REFERENCE constraint
'FK_Inventory_Equipment'. The conflict occurred in database
'Asset', table 'Inventory', column 'EquipmentId'.
The statement has been terminated.
```

A trigger and developer might have different definitions of what is a successfully finished modification to a table. The trigger will fire even when a modification statement affected zero records. The following example is based on the assumption that the record with EquipmentId set to 77777 does not exist in the database:

```
Delete Equipment
Where EquipmentId = 77777
```

SQL Server nonchalantly prints from the trigger:

```
One or more rows are deleted in Equipment table!
```

## Full Syntax in SQL Server 7.0

Let's investigate a complete syntax for triggers in SQL Server 7.0. After triggers in SQL Server 2000 have the same syntax except that the keyword `For` could be replaced with `After`.

```
Create Trigger trigger_name
On table
[With Encryption]
{
    {For { [Delete] [,] [Insert] [,] [Update] }
        [With Append]
         [Not For Replication]
        As
            sql_statement [...n]
    }
    |
    {For { [Insert] [,] [Update] }
        [With Append]
        [Not For Replication]
        As
        {    If Update (Column)
            [{And | Or} Update (Column)]
                [...n]
            | If (Columns_Updated()
                            {bitwise_operator}
                            updated_bitmask)
                { comparison_operator} column_bitmask [...n]
        }
            sql_statement [ ...n]
    }
}
```

If a trigger is defined with the With Encryption clause, SQL
Server encrypts it so that its code remains concealed. Keep in mind
that you need to preserve the source code in a script outside SQL
Server if you plan to modify it later.

The Not For Replication clause indicates that SQL Server
should not fire a trigger during replication of the table.

The With Append clause is used only when the compatibility
mode of SQL Server is set to a value less then 70. For more details,
refer to SQL Server Books Online.

It is possible to determine which columns were updated during the
Insert or Update operation. Transact-SQL includes two functions that
you can use within the trigger \UPDATE and COLUMNS_UPDATED.

```
If Update (column)
sql_statement [ ...n]


If (Columns_Updated() {bitwise_operator} updated_bitmask)
                    {comparison_operator} column_bitmask [...n]
     sql_statement [ ...n]
```

We can now modify our previously used trigger to update only the fields that were updated:

```
Alter Trigger trEquipment_IU
On dbo.Equipment
After Insert, Update    -- For Insert, Update
As
     -- precalculate ModelSDX and MakeSDX field
     -- to speed up use of SOUNDEX function
     if Update(Model)
          update Equipment
          Set ModelSDX = SOUNDEX(Model)
          where EquipmentId IN (Select EquipmentId from Inserted)

     if Update(Make)
          update Equipment
          Set MakeSDX = SOUNDEX(Make)
          where EquipmentId IN (Select EquipmentId from Inserted)
     go
```

The Update() function might not perform exactly as you expect. In fact, it returns True for columns that were *referenced* during the Transact-SQL statement, rather than for columns that were actually *changed*. For example, if you issue the following update statement, SQL Server references the Make column of all records and the trigger recalculates the SOUNDEX code in all records:

```
Update Equipment
Set Make = Make
```

This behavior might cause some problems for you if you forget about it. However, in some cases, you can use it to your advantage. For example, to speed up the upload of information to the table, you can temporarily disable triggers (see the "Disabling Triggers" section later in this chapter). Later, when you want to execute the triggers (for example, to verify their validity and/or perform additional activities), you can use this feature to initiate triggers for records that are present in the table.

> **TIP:**    Too often, developers forget that the presence of a `default` constraint in a column causes the `Update()` function to return True for that column during the execution of the `Insert` statement. This will occur even if the `Insert` statement did not reference the column itself.

The `Columns_Updated()` function operates with a bitmap that is related to the positions of columns. You can investigate its contents if you use an integer bitmask. To test whether the third column in a table was updated, you can use:

```
if Columns_Updated() & 3 = 3
      print 'Column 3 was updated!'
```

The ampersand (&) is a *binary and* operator and you can test the value of the flag using it.

Naturally, hard-coding the order of columns does not make much sense. The real value of this function is as a means of looping through all the columns that were updated and performing specified actions.

The following trigger loops through columns and displays which ones were updated:

```
Create Trigger trEquipment_IU_2
-- list all columns that were changed
On dbo.Equipment
after Insert, Update    -- For Insert, Update
As

    Set Nocount Off
    declare @intCountColumn int,
            @intColumn int

    -- count columns in the table
    Select @intCountColumn = Count(Ordinal_position)
```

```
            From Information_Schema.Columns
            Where Table_Name = 'Equipment'

            Select Columns_Updated() "COLUMNS UPDATED"
            Select @intColumn = 1

            -- loop through columns
            while @intColumn <= @intCountColumn
            begin
                if Columns_Updated() & @intColumn = @intColumn
                    Print 'Column ('
                        + Cast(@intColumn as varchar)
                        + ') '
                        + Col_Name('Equipment', @intColumn)
                        + ' has been changed!'
        End
```

Use the following statement to test this trigger:

```
Insert Equipment(Make, Model, EqTypeID)
Values('Acme', '9000', 1)
```

## Handling Changes on Multiple Records

Let's investigate a trigger designed to record the name of the user that changed the status of an order in the ActivityLog table, along with some additional information:

```
Create Trigger trOrderStatus_U_1
On dbo.[Order]
After Update     -- For Update
As
     declare @intOldOrderStatusId int,
             @intNewOrderStatusId int

     If Update (OrderStatusId)
     Begin

         select @intOldOrderStatusId = OrderStatusId from deleted
         select @intNewOrderStatusId = OrderStatusId from inserted
```

```
Insert into ActivityLog( Activity,
                         LogDate,
                         UserName,
                         Note)
    values ( 'Order.OrderStatusId',
             GetDate(),
             User_Name(),
             'Value changed from '
             + Cast( @intOldOrderStatusId as varchar)
             + ' to '
             + Cast((@intNewOrderStatusId) as varchar)
           )
End
```

This method is far from perfect. Can you detect the problem?

It records the user who has changed the status of an order only when the user changes no more than a single order.

```
select @intOldOrderStatusId = OrderStatusId from deleted
```

Let me remind you that if the Select statement returns more than one record, the variable(s) will be filled with values from the last record. This is sometimes all that is required. If the developer has restricted access to the table and the only way to change the status is through a stored procedure (which allows only one record to be modified at a time), then this is sufficient.

Unfortunately, there is always a system administrator who can work around any restriction and possibly issue an Update statement that will change the status of all tables. Let's see the proper solution:

```
Alter Trigger trOrderStatus_U
On dbo.[Order]
After Update -- For Update
As
    If Update (OrderStatusId)
    begin

        Insert into ActivityLog( Activity,
                                 LogDate,
                                 UserName,
                                 Note)
```

```
Select    'Order.OrderStatusId',
          GetDate(),
          User_Name(),
          'Value changed from '
          + Cast( d.OrderStatusId as varchar)
          + ' to '
          + Cast( i.OrderStatusId as varchar)

from deleted d inner join inserted i
on d.OrderId = i.OrderId
end
```

In this case, a set operation is used and one or more records from the deleted and inserted tables will be recorded in the ActivityLog.

## Nested and Recursive Triggers

A trigger can initiate triggers on the same or other tables when it inserts, updates, or deletes records in them. This technique is called *nesting triggers.*

If a trigger changes records in its own table, it can fire another instance of itself. Such an invocation is called *direct invocation of recursive triggers.*

There is another scenario in which recursive invocation of triggers might occur. The trigger on one table might fire a trigger on a second table. The trigger on the second table might change the first table again, and the first trigger will fire again. This scenario is called *indirect invocation of recursive triggers.*

All these scenarios might be ideal for implementing referential integrity and business rules, but they might also be too complicated to design, understand, and manage. If you are not careful, the first trigger might call the second, then the second might call the first, then the first the second, and so on.

Very often, the SQL Server environment is configured to prevent this kind of behavior. To disable nested triggers and recursive triggers, you need to use the stored procedure sp_configure to set the Nested Triggers server option and the Alter Table statement to set the Recursive_Triggers option to 'off' mode. Keep in mind that recursive triggers will be disabled automatically if you disable nested triggers.

# Trigger Restrictions

The trigger must be created as the first statement in a batch.

The name of the trigger is its Transact-SQL identifier, and it therefore must be no more than 128 characters long. The trigger's name must be unique in the database.

A trigger can only be associated with one table, but one table can be associated with many triggers. In the past, only one trigger could be associated with one modification statement on one table. Now, each feature of the system can be implemented in a separate trigger. By implementing these features in separate triggers, you assure that the triggers will be easier to understand and manage.

Triggers cannot be nested more than 32 times, nor can they be invoked recursively more than 32 times. Attempting to do so causes SQL Server to return an error.

A trigger must not contain any of following Transact-SQL statements:

| | |
|---|---|
| Alter Database | Drop Database |
| Alter Procedure | Drop Default |
| Alter Table | Drop Index |
| Alter Trigger | Drop Procedure |
| Alter View | Drop Rule |
| Create Database | Drop Table |
| Create Default | Drop Trigger |
| Create Index | Drop View |
| Create Procedure | Grant |
| Create Rule | Load Database |
| Create Schema | Load Log |
| Create Table | Reconfigure |
| Create Trigger | Restore Database |
| Create View | Restore Log |
| Deny | Revoke |
| Disk Init | Truncate Table |
| Disk Resize | Update Statistics |

These restrictions will not usually cause you any difficulties.

## Triggers in SQL Server 2000

The syntax of triggers in SQL Server 2000 is just a little more complicated than in SQL Server 7.0:

```
Create Trigger trigger_name
On {table | view}
[With Encryption]
{
{{For | After | Instead Of} { [Delete] [,] [Insert] [,] [Update] }
    [With Append]
    [Not For Replication]
    As
    sql_statement [...n]
}
|
{(For | After | Instead Of) { [Insert] [,] [Update] }
    [With Append]
    [Not For Replication]
    As
    { If Update (Column)
    [{And | Or} Update (Column)]
    [...n]
    | If (Columns_Updated() {bitwise_operator} updated_bitmask)
    { comparison_operator} column_bitmask [...n]
    }
    sql_statement [...n]
}
}
```

Basically, there are two important changes:

▼ There is a new type of trigger—the *instead-of trigger*. Note the new keyword (Instead Of). The old type of trigger is now called an *after trigger*. You should use the new keyword (After) when creating them. The old keyword (For) can still be used for compatibility reasons, but it is not recommended.

▲ It is possible to create an instead-of trigger on a view (not just on a table).

## Instead-of Triggers

*Instead-of* triggers are executed instead of the modification statement that has initiated them. The following trigger is executed when anybody attempts to delete records from the MyEquipment table. It will report an error instead of allowing the deletion:

```
Create Trigger itrMyEquipment_D
On dbo.MyEquipment
instead of Delete
As
     -- deletion in this table is not allowed
     raiserrror(60012, 16, 1)
GO
```

Instead-of triggers are executed after changes to base tables occur in Inserted and Deleted virtual tables, but before any change to the base tables is executed. Therefore, the trigger can use information in the Inserted and Deleted tables. In the following example, a trigger tests whether some of the records that would have been deleted are in use in the Equipment table:

```
Create Trigger itrEqType_D
On dbo.EqType
instead of Delete
As
If exists(select *
     from Equipment
     where EqTypeId in (select EqTypeId
                          from deleted)
     )
     raiserror('Some recs in EqType are in use in Equipment table!',
               16, 1)
else
     delete EqType
     where EqTypeId in (select EqTypeId from deleted)
GO
```

Instead-of triggers are initiated before any constraints. This behavior is very different from that of after triggers. Therefore, the code for an instead-of trigger must perform all checking and processing that would normally be performed by constraints.

Usually, an instead-of trigger executes the modification statement (`Insert`, `Update`, or `Delete`) that initiates it. The modification statement does not initiate the trigger again. If there are some after triggers and/or constraints defined on the table or view, they will be executed as though the instead-of trigger does not exist.

A table or a view can have only one instead-of trigger (and more than one after trigger).

## Triggers on Views

Instead-of triggers can be defined on views also. In the following example, a trigger is created on a view that displays fields from two tables:

```
Create View dbo.vEquipment
AS
Select Equipment.EquipmentId,
       Equipment.Make,
       Equipment.Model,
       EqType.EqType
From Equipment Inner Join EqType
On Equipment.EqTypeId = EqType.EqTypeId
Go


Create Trigger itr_vEquipment_I
On dbo.vEquipment
instead of Insert
As


-- If the EQType is new, insert it
If exists(select EqType
          from inserted
          where EqType not in (select EqType
                               from EqType))
    -- we need to insert the new ones
```

```
    insert into EqType(EqType)
        select EqType
        from inserted
        where EqType not in (select EqType
                               from EqType)

-- now you can insert new equipment
Insert into Equipment(Make, Model, EqTypeId)
Select inserted.Make, inserted.Model, EqType.EqTypeId
From inserted Inner Join EqType
On inserted.EqType = EqType.EqType

GO

Insert Into vEquipment(EquipmentId, Make, Model, EqType)
Values (-777, 'Microsoft', 'Natural Keyboard', 'keyboard')
```

The trigger first examines whether the Inserted table contains EqType values that do not exist in EqTable. If they exist, they will be inserted in the EqType table. At the end, values from the Inserted table are added to the Equipment table.

The previous example illustrates one unusual feature in the use of instead-of triggers on views. Since EquipmentId is referenced by the view, it can (and must) be specified by the modification statement (`Insert` statement). The trigger can (and will) ignore the specified value since it is inserted automatically (EquipmentId is an identity field in the base table). The reason for this behavior is that the Inserted and Deleted tables have different structures from the base tables on which the view is based. They have the same structure as the `Select` statement inside the view.

Columns in the view can be nullable or not nullable. The column is nullable if its expression in the select list of the view satisfies one of the following criteria:

▼ The view column references a base table column that is nullable.

▲ The view column expression uses arithmetic operators or functions.

If the column does not allow nulls, an `Insert` statement must provide a value for it. This is the reason we needed to provide a value for EquipmentId column in the previous example. An `Update` statement must provide values for all non-nullable columns referenced by the `Set` clause in a view with an instead-of update trigger.

**NOTE:**   You must specify values even for view columns that are mapped to timestamp, identity, or computed base table columns.

You can use the AllowNull field of the `COLUMN_PROPERTY` function (table function) to examine which fields are nullable from code.

**NOTE:**   The previous example is much more important than you might think. It allows you to insert a whole set of records at one time into the view (actually to the set of base tables behind the view). Before instead-of triggers, we had to do this record by record with a stored procedure. This capability is very useful for loading information into a SQL Server database. For example, you can load information from a denormalized source (such as a flat file) and store it in a set of normalized, linked tables.

Another unusual feature of instead-of triggers is the fact that they support *text, ntext,* and *image* columns in Inserted and Deleted tables. After triggers cannot handle such values. In base tables, text, ntext, and image columns actually contain pointers to the pages holding data. In Inserted and Deleted tables, text, ntext, and image columns are stored as continuous strings within each row. No pointers are stored in these tables, and therefore the use of the `TEXTPTR` and `TEXTVALID` functions and the `Readtext`, `Updatetext`, and `Writetext` statements is not permitted. All other uses, such as references in the `Select` list or `Where` clause, or use of `CHARINDEX`, `PATINDEX`, or `SUBSTRING` functions, are valid.

## Trigger Order of Execution

SQL Server 7.0 introduced the idea that more than one trigger could be created per modification statement. However, the execution order of such triggers could not be controlled. In SQL Server 2000, it possible to define which after trigger to execute first and which to execute last against a table. For example, the following statement will set trInventory_I to be the first trigger to be executed in the case of an Insert modification statement:

```
Exec sp_settriggerorder @triggername = 'trInventory_I',
                        @order = 'first'
```

The @order parameter must have one of these values: 'first', 'last', or 'none'. The value 'none' is used to reset the order of the execution of the trigger after it has been specified.

Since only one instead-of trigger can be associated with a table, and since it is executed before any other trigger (or constraint), it is not possible to set its order.

Alter Trigger statements reset the order of the trigger. After altering the trigger, you must execute the sp_settriggerorder statement to set it again.

Replications generate the first trigger for any table that is a queued or an immediate subscriber. SQL Server reports an error if you try to set your trigger to be the first instead. It will also report an error if you try to make a table with a first trigger queued or an immediate subscriber.

# Managing Triggers

You can manage triggers using GUI tools such as Enterprise Manager, Query Analyzer Object Browser, or Visual Database Tools. Other methods include using Transact-SQL statements within tools like Query Analyzer.

## Managing Triggers in Enterprise Manager

You can access triggers from Enterprise Manager by right-clicking the table with which the trigger is associated. Select All Tasks, then Manage Triggers from the cascading pop-up menus (see Figure 9-10).

SQL Server displays a modal form for editing trigger properties. This editor is very similar to the editor you use to edit stored procedures (see Figure 9-11).

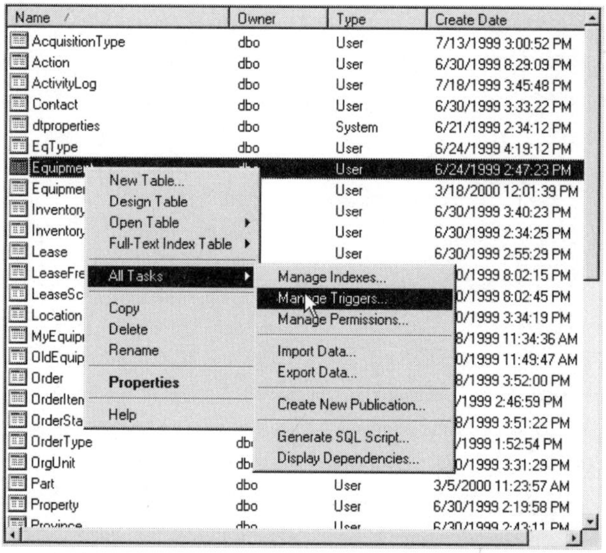

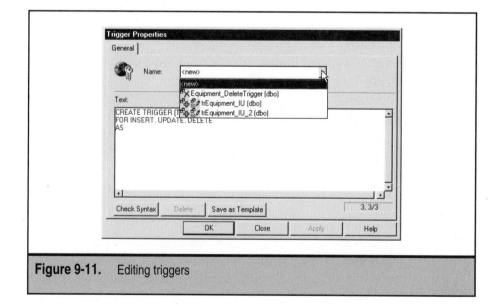

**Figure 9-10.**    Managing triggers in Enterprise Manager

**Figure 9-11.**    Editing triggers

SQL Server initially fills the form with a template for creating a new trigger. If you want to access the trigger that is already attached to the table, use the Name list box to select it.

Once you have written or changed the trigger, you can use the Check Syntax button to verify it, then select OK or Apply to attach it to the table. After you have attached the trigger to the table, you can delete it using the Delete button on the form.

## Managing Triggers in Query Analyzer Object Browser

You can access triggers from Object Browser when you open the tree node under the table with which the trigger is associated. Open the Triggers node, and Query Analyzer will display a list of triggers. You can right-click any trigger and the program will offer you the usual options, for instance, Edit and Delete.

## Managing Triggers Using Transact-SQL Statements

SQL Server has a rich pallet of system stored procedures for managing triggers from Transact-SQL.

**Listing Triggers**   To list triggers associated with a table, use the system stored procedure sp_helptrigger:

```
sp_helptrigger 'Order'
```

The server returns the list of triggers associated with the specified table and displays the type of trigger found in the isupdate, isdelete, and isinsert columns.

| trigger_name | trigger_owner | isupdate | isdelete | isinsert |
| --- | --- | --- | --- | --- |
| trOrderStatus_U | dbo | 1 | 0 | 0 |
| trOrderStatus_U_1 | dbo | 1 | 0 | 0 |

```
(2 row(s) affected)
```

**Viewing Triggers**   You can obtain the code for a trigger using the system stored procedure sp_helptext:

```
sp_helptext 'trOrderStatus_U'
```

The server returns the code for the specified trigger:

```
Text
----------------------------------------------------------------
CREATE Trigger trOrderStatus_U
On dbo.[Order]
After Update      -- For Update
As
     If Update (OrderStatusId)
     Begin

         Insert into ActivityLog( Activity,
                                  LogDate,
                                  UserName,
                                  Note)
         Select        'Order.OrderStatusId',
                       GetDate(),
                       USER_NAME(),
                       'Value changed from '
                       + Cast( d.OrderStatusId as varchar)
                       + ' to '
                       + Cast( i.OrderStatusId as varchar)
         From deleted d inner join inserted i
         On d.OrderId = i.OrderId
     End
```

**Deleting Triggers**    A trigger can be deleted, as can all other database objects, using the appropriate DROP statement:

```
Drop Trigger 'Orders_Trigger1'
```

**Modifying Triggers**    Earlier in this chapter, you saw details of the syntax of a Transact-SQL statement for creating triggers. Triggers can be modified using the Alter Trigger statement. Since the features of the Alter Trigger and Create Trigger statements are identical, we will not explore the syntax a second time.

It is much better to use the Alter Trigger statement to modify a trigger than to drop and then recreate the trigger. During the period between dropping and creating a trigger, a user might make a change to the table and the rules that are usually enforced by the trigger will not be enforced.

> **NOTE:** Keep in mind that the order of execution is lost when the trigger is altered—you must reset it again using sp_setTriggerorder.

**Renaming Triggers** Triggers are often renamed using Transact-SQL statements designed for the creation and modification of triggers. As with all other database objects, a trigger can be forced to change its name using the following system stored procedure:

```
Exec sp_rename 'Orders_Trigger1', 'trOrders_IU'
```

The first parameter is the current name of the database object, and the second parameter is the new name of the object.

**Disabling Triggers** It is possible to temporarily disable and enable triggers without dropping them:

```
Alter Table Order Disable Trigger trOrders_IU
```

After the execution of this statement, the specified trigger will not fire, but it will still be associated with the table. This technique is often used by database administrators to set up initial data in the table without initiating the business logic encapsulated in the trigger.

# Trigger Design Recommendations

Since triggers are relatively complex database objects, it is easy to make design, performance, or maintainability problems inside your database. Therefore, we will spend some time pointing out a proper way to use them.

## Go Out ASAP

Triggers take time to execute. If your server is very busy and/or other users are locking resources in the database, execution might take much more time than expected. On the other hand, locks that you (or rather SQL Server) have placed in the database while the trigger is executing will not be released until the trigger is finished. Thus, your trigger may also increase competition for resources and affect other users and their sessions.

For these reasons, you should always try to exit a trigger as soon as possible. For example, you could start (almost) every trigger with the following test:

```
If @@rowcount = 0
     Return
```

It will abort further execution of the trigger if no records were changed.

Keep in mind that this If clause must occur at the very beginning of the trigger. If you put it after any other statement, @@rowcount will return the number of records affected by that statement. For example, if you put a simple Print statement at the beginning of the trigger and then this test, the remainder of the trigger will not be executed.

```
Alter Trigger trOrderStatus_U
On dbo.[Order]
After Update     -- For Update
As

Print 'Start of trOrderStatus_U'
If @@Rowcount = 0   -- This is always true
                    -- and the rest will NEVER be executed.
     Return

     If Update (OrderStatusId)
     Begin

          Insert into ActivityLog( Activity,
                                   LogDate,
                                   UserName,
                                   Note)
          Select    'Order.OrderStatusId',
                    GetDate(),
                    USER_NAME(),
                    'Value changed from '
                    + Cast( d.OrderStatusId as varchar)
```

```
            + ' to '
            + Cast( i.OrderStatusId as varchar)


        From deleted d inner join inserted i
        On d.OrderId = i.OrderId
    End
```

## Make It Simple

It is true that triggers are suitable for implementing complex business rules, particularly if those business rules are too complex to be handled by simpler database objects such as constraints. However, just because you are using them to handle complex business rules, you do not have to make your code so complex that it is difficult to understand and follow. It is challenging enough to work with triggers: keep them as simple as possible.

## Divide and Conquer

In earlier versions of Microsoft SQL Server, only one trigger per modification statement could be associated with a table. This physical restriction led developers to produce poor code. Features that were not related had to be piled up in a single trigger. However, this restriction no longer applies. There is no reason to couple the code for multiple triggers. Each distinct piece of functionality can be implemented in a separate trigger.

## Do Not Use Select and Print Inside a Trigger

The `Print` and `Select` commands are very useful in triggers during the debugging process. However, they can be very dangerous if left in a trigger after it has been introduced into production. These statements generate additional resultsets, which might cause the client application to fail if it is not able to handle them or does not expect them.

## Do Not Use Triggers At All

If you can implement the required functionality using constraints, do not use triggers!

If you can implement the required functionality using stored procedures, and if you can prevent users from accessing your tables directly, do not use triggers!

Triggers are more difficult to implement, debug, and manage. You will save both time and money for your company or your client if you can find simpler ways to implement the required functionality.

## Transaction Management in Triggers

A trigger is always part of the transaction that initiates it. That transaction can be explicit (when SQL Server has executed BEGIN TRANSACTION). It can also be implicit—basically SQL Server treats each Transact-SQL statement as a separate transaction that will either succeed completely or fail completely.

It is possible to abort the transaction from inside the trigger using ROLLBACK TRANSACTION. This command is valid for both implicit and explicit transactions.

```
Alter Trigger trOrderStatus_U
On dbo.[Order]
After Update     --For Update
As

    If @@Rowcount = 0
        Return

    If Update (OrderStatusId)
    Begin

        Insert into ActivityLog( Activity,
                                 LogDate,
                                 UserName,
                                 Note)
        Select     'Order.OrderStatusId',
                   GetDate(),
                   USER_NAME(),
                   'Value changed from '
                   + Cast( d.OrderStatusId as varchar)
                   + ' to '
```

```
                        + Cast ( i.OrderStatusId as varchar)

        From deleted d inner join inserted i
        On d.OrderId = i.OrderId

        If @@Error <> 0
        Begin
            RAISERROR ("Error in trOrderStatus_U", 16, 1)
            Rollback Transaction
        End
    End
```

In this trigger, SQL Server investigates the presence of the error and rolls back the complete operation if it is unable to log changes to the OrderStatusId field.

The processing of `Rollback Transaction` inside a trigger differs from its processing inside a stored procedure. It also differs in different versions of Microsoft SQL Server.

When a `Rollback` statement is encountered in a stored procedure, changes made since the last `Begin Transaction` are rolled back, but the processing continues.

In Microsoft SQL Server 2000 and SQL Server 7.0, when a `Rollback` statement is executed within a trigger, a complete batch is aborted and all changes are rolled back. SQL Server continues to process from the beginning of the next batch (or stops if the next batch does not exist).

Microsoft SQL Server 4.2 and all versions of Sybase SQL Server behaved in this manner. In version 6.0, execution was continued through the trigger, but the batch was canceled. Version 6.5 went to an opposite extreme. Execution of both the trigger and the batch was continued. It was the responsibility of the developer to detect an error and stop further processing.

# Using Triggers

In SQL Server, triggers may have the following roles:

▼ To enforce data integrity (referential integrity, cascading deletes)

- To enforce complex business rules (complex defaults and checks)

- To log changes and send notification to administrators (e-mail)

▲ To maintain derived information (calculated columns, running totals, aggregates)

Triggers can be implemented to replace all other constraints on a table. A typical example is the use of a trigger to replace the functionality enforced by a foreign key constraint.

It is possible to implement *cascading deletes* using triggers. For example, if we do not have a foreign key between the Inventory and InventoryProperty tables, we might implement a trigger to monitor the deletion of Inventory records and to delete all associated InventoryProperty records.

Check and default constraints are limited in that they can base their decision only on the context of current records in the current tables. You can implement a trigger that will function in a manner similar to check constraints that bases its verification on the contents of multiple records or even on the contents of other tables.

Triggers can be set to create an audit trail of activities performed on a table. For example, we might be interested in obtaining information on who changed the contents or specific columns in the Lease table, and when that user made the changes.

It is possible to create a trigger to notify the administrator when a specific event occurs in the database. For example, in a service database, we might send e-mail to a person responsible for dispatching technical staff informing that person that a request for technical support has been received in the database. In certain inventory systems, we might automatically generate an order if the quantity of a selected type of equipment or spare part falls below a specified level.

Triggers are suitable for computing and storing calculated columns, running totals, and other aggregations in the database. For example, to speed up reporting, you might decide to keep a total of ordered items in an order table.

## Cascading Deletes

Usually, referential integrity between two tables is implemented with a foreign key. In the following illustration, you can see two tables that are linked in such a manner:

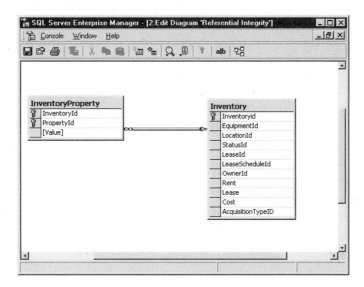

In such cases, a foreign key will prevent the user from deleting records from a referenced table (Inventory) if a record is referenced in a linked table (InventoryProperty). The only way to delete the record would be to use the following code:

```
Delete InventoryProperty
Where InventoryId = 222


Delete Inventory
Where InventoryId = 222
```

In some cases, the system design requirements might call for *cascading deletes,* which automatically delete records from the linked table when the record in the referenced table is deleted. In this case only, one command will be required to delete any trace of an asset with its InventoryId set to 222.

```
Delete Inventory
Where InventoryId = 222
```

SQL Server 2000 introduces cascading referential integrity constraints that can implement such behavior. In SQL Server 7.0 and earlier versions, developers needed to use triggers to implement it. In the following example, we create two new tables (without a foreign key), populate them with a few records, and create a trigger that will implement a cascading delete:

```
Create Table MyInventory
     (
     Inventoryid int Not Null Identity (1, 1),
     EquipmentId int Null,
     LocationId int Null,
     StatusId tinyint Null,
     LeaseId int Null,
     LeaseScheduleId int Null,
     OwnerId int Null,
     Rent smallmoney Null,
     Lease smallmoney Null,
     Cost smallmoney Null,
     AcquisitionTypeID tinyint Null
     )
Go


Alter Table MyInventory Add Constraint
     PK_Inventory Primary Key Nonclustered
     (
     Inventoryid
     )
Go


Create Table MyInventoryProperty
     (
     InventoryId int Not Null,
     PropertyId smallint Not Null,
     Value varchar(50) Null
     )
Go
Alter Table MyInventoryProperty Add Constraint
```

```
       PK_InventoryProperty Primary Key Nonclustered
       (
       InventoryId,
       PropertyId
       )
Go


Create Trigger trMyInventory_CascadingDelete_D
On MyInventory
After Delete      --For delete
As


If @@Rowcount = 0
      Return
Delete MyInventoryProperty
where InventoryId In (Select InventoryID from deleted)
Go


Insert into myInventory(EquipmentId) Values (1)
Insert into myInventory(EquipmentId) Values (2)
Insert into myInventory(EquipmentId) Values (3)
Insert into myInventory(EquipmentId) Values (4)
Insert into myInventory(EquipmentId) Values (5)


Insert into myInventoryProperty(InventoryId, PropertyId, Value)
Values (1, 1, 'ACME')
Insert into myInventoryProperty(InventoryId, PropertyId, Value)
Values (1, 2, 'Turbo')
Insert into myInventoryProperty(InventoryId, PropertyId, Value)
Values (1, 3, '311')
Insert into myInventoryProperty(InventoryId, PropertyId, Value)
Values (2, 1, 'ACME')
Insert into myInventoryProperty(InventoryId, PropertyId, Value)
Values (2, 2, 'TurboPro')
Insert into myInventoryProperty(InventoryId, PropertyId, Value)
Values (2, 3, '312')
Go
```

```
Delete MyInventory
Where InventoryId = 1


Select * from myInventory
Select * from myInventoryProperty
```

## Aggregates

Let's imagine that users of an Asset database are often clogging the Inventory table. One operation that they perform often is the execution of reports that, for example, prepare the sum of all monthly lease payments per lease schedule. If the sum is prepared in advance, the report is available in an instant, the table is less clogged, and the user experiences fewer locking and deadlocking problems.

Next, we could create one or more triggers to maintain the PeriodicTotalAmount field in the LeaseSchedule table. The field should contain the sum of Lease payments for assets in the Inventory table (which are associated with a lease schedule).

It is possible to implement diverse solutions for this task. This solution is based on separate triggers for different modification statements.

The Insert trigger is based on a relatively complex Update statement with a subquery based on the contents of the *inserted* table. Each new record increments the total in the related lease schedule.

The Coalesce statement is used to replace Nulls with zeros in the calculation. The trigger evaluates the number of records affected by the modification statement at the beginning and, if no records are affected, it aborts further execution.

This solution executes properly even when multiple records are inserted with one statement.

```
Create Trigger trInventory_Lease_I
On dbo.Inventory
after Insert       -- For Insert
As


If @@Rowcount = 0
     return
```

```
-- add inserted leases to total amount
Update LeaseSchedule
Set LeaseSchedule.PeriodicTotalAmount =
    LeaseSchedule.PeriodicTotalAmount
    + Coalesce(i.Lease, 0)
from LeaseSchedule inner join inserted i
    on LeaseSchedule.ScheduleId = i.LeaseScheduleId

Go
```

The `Delete` trigger is very similar to the previous trigger. The main difference is that the values from the deleted table are subtracted from the total.

```
Create Trigger trInventory_Lease_D
On dbo.Inventory
After Delete      -- For delete
As


If @@Rowcount = 0
    Return


-- subtract deleted leases from total amount
Update LeaseSchedule
Set LeaseSchedule.PeriodicTotalAmount =
    LeaseSchedule.PeriodicTotalAmount
    - Coalesce(d.Lease, 0)
from LeaseSchedule inner join deleted d
    on LeaseSchedule.ScheduleId = d.LeaseScheduleId
Go
```

The `Update` trigger is the most complicated. The calculation of a total is performed only if the Lease and LeaseScheduleId fields are referenced by the `Update` statement. The trigger then subtracts the Lease amounts from the deleted records and adds the Lease amounts from the inserted records to the related totals.

```
Create Trigger trInventory_Lease_U
On dbo.Inventory
After Update   -- For Update
```

```
As

if @@Rowcount = 0
     return

If Update (Lease) or Update(LeaseScheduleId)
begin
     -- subtract deleted leases from total amount
     Update LeaseSchedule
     Set LeaseSchedule.PeriodicTotalAmount =
             LeaseSchedule.PeriodicTotalAmount
             - Coalesce(d.Lease, 0)
     From LeaseSchedule inner join deleted d
         On LeaseSchedule.ScheduleId = d.LeaseScheduleId

     -- add inserted leases to total amount
     Update LeaseSchedule
     Set LeaseSchedule.PeriodicTotalAmount =
             LeaseSchedule.PeriodicTotalAmount
             + Coalesce(i.Lease, 0)
     From LeaseSchedule inner join inserted i
         On LeaseSchedule.ScheduleId = i.LeaseScheduleId

End
Go
```

# SUMMARY

In this chapter, we set out to examine types of stored procedures other than the user-defined variety that we use throughout the remainder of this book.

In the course of this examination, we learned:

▼  How to use system stored procedures to perform various aspects of system administration

- ■ How SQL Server uses extended stored procedures to capture the functionality of dynamic link library files developed in programming languages such as C and C++

- ■ How temporary stored procedures are useful in situations where the required functionality is not required after the session is over, and how their use can reduce maintenance requirements

- ■ How global temporary stored procedures are useful when you need to access a temporary stored procedure from multiple databases

- ▲ How we can use remote stored procedures to execute stored procedures that reside on a remote server.

The design and use of user-defined functions is a new feature in SQL Server 2000. User-defined functions can return tables using the table datatype—also new to SQL Server 2000.

The power of in-line user-defined functions can be harnessed to implement parameterized views.

Triggers are standard and powerful tools in the utility belt of a database administrator. In this chapter, we have learned how to use triggers to enforce referential integrity and to implement business rules. We have also mastered the use of the virtual tables, *Inserted* and *Deleted,* to access changed records from within a trigger. We have witnessed how valuable it is to be able to obtain information concerning which table columns in a table have been updated. We have examined techniques for designing triggers to handle changes on more than one record, for managing triggers in different GUI environments (Enterprise Manager, Query Analyzer), and using Transact-SQL. Last, we have seen how to roll back a transaction from within the trigger.

Earlier versions of SQL Server had only one type of trigger. SQL Server 2000 has introduced two types of triggers (although one type is equivalent to the only type available in previous versions). The type that was in use in earlier versions is now called an *after trigger.* The new type, known as an *instead-of trigger,* replaces the modification statement that initiates the trigger. The instead-of trigger creates some exciting opportunities for developers. It is possible to create instead-of triggers on views as well as on tables. Such triggers can normalize data and store it in a set of base tables behind the view.

## EXERCISES

1. Create a function that returns the last date of a month containing a specified date.

2. Create a function that returns a table containing the last days of months in a specified number of following years.

3. Create a trigger on the Inventory table that will record in the ActivityLog table the user who is deleting assets from the database. The log should contain the user name of the person deleting records, the date of the deletion, and the IDs of the assets deleted.

4. How can you disable nested and recursive triggers in SQL Server?

5. How can an administrator temporarily disable a trigger to allow the performance of administrative activities on a table?

6. Create a view for displaying denormalized information contained in the Inventory table. Design an instead-of insert trigger on the view to accommodate uploading of Inventory information from an external source.

# CHAPTER 10

## Advanced Stored Procedure Programming

T his chapter introduces some advanced techniques for coding stored procedures, including

▼ Dynamically constructed queries

■ Optimistic locking using timestamps

■ Full-text search and indexes

■ Nested stored procedures

■ Temporary tables

■ Parameterized queries

■ Putting the results of a stored procedure into a table

■ Techniques for generating unique identifiers and potential problems associated with their use

■ The Uniqueidentifier (GUID) datatype

▲ Property management—using extended properties

# DYNAMICALLY CONSTRUCTED QUERIES

In this section, we will examine some ways in which you can construct queries dynamically, including

▼ Executing a string statement

■ Querying by form

▲ Using parameterized queries

## Executing a String

Transact-SQL contains a variation of the Execute statement that you can use to run a batch recorded in the form of a character string:

```
EXEC[UTE] ({@string_variable | [N]'tsql_string'} [+...n])
```

Developers can supply a Transact-SQL batch in the form of a character string, a variable, or an expression.

```
Exec ('select * from Contact')
```

This statement allows you to assemble a batch or a query dynamically. This might look like magic to you:

```
declare @chvTable sysname
set @chvTable = 'Contact'
Exec ('select * from ' + @chvTable)
```

This syntax is required because the following batch, which you might expect to work, will actually result in a syntax error:

```
declare @chvTable sysname
set @chvTable = 'Contact'
select * from @chvTable  -- this will cause an error
```

The error occurs because SQL Server expects a table name rather than a string expression in a From clause.

It is important for you to realize that you are dealing with two separate batches in the first example. You cannot use variables from the batch that initiated the Execute statement in the other batch. For example, the following code will result in a syntax error:

```
declare @chvTable sysname
set @chvTable = 'Contact'
Exec ('select * from @chvTable')
```

You cannot use a database context from the other batch either:

```
Use Asset
exec ('Use Northwind select * from Employees')
select * from Employees    -- Error
```

## Query By Form

One of the simplest way to create a search form in a client application is to list all the fields in a table as text boxes on a form. The user will fill some of them in, and they can be interpreted as search criteria:

The trouble with this kind of solution is that most of the time, most of the text-boxes will be left empty. This does not mean that the user wants to find only those records in which the values of these fields are set to empty strings, but that those fields that the user leaves blank should not be included in the criteria. Stored procedures have a static structure, but something dynamic would be more appropriate to launch this kind of query.

The following stored procedure assembles a character-string query. The contents of the Where clause are based on the criteria that were specified (that is, fields that were not set to null). When all components are merged, the query returns a list of matching contacts:

```
Create Procedure prQbfContact_1
-- Dynamically assemble a query based on specified parameters.
    (
            @chvFirstName      varchar(30)    = NULL,
            @chvLastName       varchar(30)    = NULL,
            @chvPhone          typPhone       = NULL,
            @chvFax            typPhone       = NULL,
            @chvEmail          typEmail       = NULL,
            @insOrgUnitId      smallint       = NULL,
            @chvUserName       varchar(50)    = NULL,
            @debug             int            = 0
    )
```

```
As
set nocount on

Declare @intErrorCode int,
        @intTransactionCountOnEntry int,
        @chvQuery varchar(8000),
        @chvWhere varchar(8000)
Select @intErrorCode = @@Error,
        @chvQuery = 'SET QUOTED_IDENTIFIER OFF SELECT * FROM Contact',
        @chvWhere = ''

If @intErrorCode = 0 and @chvFirstName is not null
Begin
    Set @chvWhere = @chvWhere + ' FirstName = "'
                  + @chvFirstName + '" AND'
    Select @intErrorCode = @@Error
End


If @intErrorCode = 0 and @chvLastName is not null
Begin
    Set @chvWhere = @chvWhere + ' LastName = "'
                  + @chvLastName + '" AND'
    Select @intErrorCode = @@Error
End


If @intErrorCode = 0 and @chvPhone is not null
Begin
    set @chvWhere = @chvWhere + ' Phone = "' + @chvPhone + '" AND'
    Select @intErrorCode = @@Error
End


If @intErrorCode = 0 and @chvFax is not null
Begin
    set @chvWhere = @chvWhere + ' Fax = "' + @chvFax + '" AND'
    Select @intErrorCode = @@Error
End


If @intErrorCode = 0 and @chvEmail is not null
Begin
    set @chvWhere = @chvWhere + ' Email = "' + @chvEmail + '" AND'
    Select @intErrorCode = @@Error
End
```

```
If @intErrorCode = 0 and @insOrgUnitId is not null
Begin
    set @chvWhere = @chvWhere + ' OrgUnitId = '
                    + @insOrgUnitId + ' AND'
    Select @intErrorCode = @@Error
End

If @intErrorCode = 0 and @chvUserName is not null
Begin
    set @chvWhere = @chvWhere + ' UserName = "' + @chvUserName + '"'
    Select @intErrorCode = @@Error
End

if @debug <> 0 select @chvWhere chvWhere

-- remove ' AND' from the end of string
If @intErrorCode = 0 And
    Substring(@chvWhere, Len(@chvWhere) - 3, 4) = ' AND'
Begin
    set @chvWhere = Substring(@chvWhere, 1, Len(@chvWhere) - 3)
    Select @intErrorCode = @@Error
      if @debug <> 0 select @chvWhere chvWhere
End

If @intErrorCode = 0 and Len(@chvWhere) > 0
Begin
    set  @chvQuery = @chvQuery + ' WHERE ' + @chvWhere
    Select @intErrorCode = @@Error
End

if @debug <> 0
    select @chvQuery Query

-- get contacts
If @intErrorCode = 0
Begin
    exec (@chvQuery)
    Select @intErrorCode = @@Error
End

return @intErrorCode
```

To avoid problems with the mixing of single and double quotes, I used the `Set Quoted_Identifier Off` statement at the beginning of the query. Figure 10-1 shows the result of the stored procedure (along with some debugging information).

**TIP:** You are right if you think that this solution can probably be implemented more easily using client application code (for example, in Visual Basic).

## Using the sp_executesql Stored Procedure

In Chapter 3, we saw that an important advantage stored procedures have over ad hoc queries is their capability to reuse an execution plan. SQL Server, and developers working in it, can use two methods to improve the reuse of queries that are not designed as stored procedures. The first of these is autoparameterization, which we

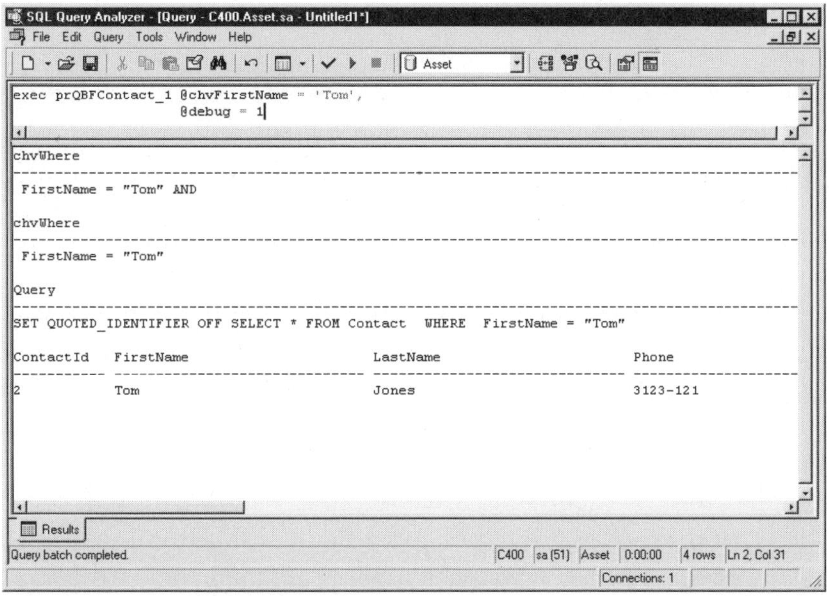

**Figure 10-1.** The results of Query By Form

covered in Chapter 3. Now we will focus on using a stored procedure to enforce parameterization of a query.

If a developer knows that a query will be reexecuted with different parameters and that reuse of its execution plan will not degrade performance, he or she can use sp_executesql to run it. This stored procedure has the following syntax:

```
sp_executesql [@stmt =] stmt
[

    {, [@params =] N'@parameter_name data_type [,...n]' }
    {, [@param1 =] 'value1' [,...n] }


]
```

The first parameter is a string with a batch of Transact-SQL statements. If the batch uses parameters, the developer must also supply their definitions as the second parameter of the procedure. The definition is followed by a list of parameters and their values. The following script executes one batch twice using different parameters:

```
EXECUTE sp_executesql
    @Stmt = N'SELECT * FROM Asset.dbo.Contact WHERE ContactId = @Id',
    @Parms = N'@Id int',
    @Id = 11
EXECUTE sp_executesql
    @Stmt = N'SELECT * FROM Asset.dbo.Contact WHERE ContactId = @Id',
    @Parms = N'@Id int',
    @Id = 313
```

There is one unpleasant requirement to this exercise. If all database objects are not *fully qualified* (that is, hard-coded with the database name and object owner), the SQL Server engine will not reuse the execution plan.

In some cases, you may be able to ensure that all database objects are fully qualified. However, this requirement will become a problem if you are building a database that will be deployed under a different name or even if you use more than one instance of the database in your development environment (for example, one instance for development and one for testing).

The solution is to obtain the name of a current database using the DB_NAME function. You can then incorporate it in a query:

```
Declare @chvQuery nvarchar(200)
Set @chvQuery = N'Select * From ' + DB_NAME()
                + N'.dbo.Contact Where ContactId = @Id'
EXECUTE sp_executesql @stmt = @chvQuery,
                      @Parms = N'@Id int',
                      @Id = 1
EXECUTE sp_executesql @stmt = @chvQuery,
                      @Parms = N'@Id int',
                      @Id = 313
```

Solutions based on this stored procedure are better than solutions based on the execution of a character string. The latter are not reused very often. It might happen that they will be reused only when parameter values also match. Even in a situation where we are changing the structure of a query, there are a finite number of possible combinations of query parameters (and some of them are more probable then others). Therefore, reuse will be much more frequent if you force parameterization using sp_executesql.

When you use Execute, the complete batch has to be assembled in the form of a string each time. This requirement also takes time. If you are using sp_executesql, the batch will be assembled only the first time. All subsequent executions can use the same string and supply an additional set of parameters.

Parameters that are passed to sp_executesql do not have to be converted to characters. That time is wasted when you are using Execute. By using them in their native format in sp_executesql, you may be able to detect errors more easily.

# OPTIMISTIC LOCKING USING TIMESTAMPS

When more than one user is working against a database, we might expect some concurrency problems to appear. Let's describe the most common problem. User A reads a record. User B also reads the record and then changes it. Any changes user A now decides to post to the database will overwrite the changes that user B made to it.

Two standard solutions for this kind of problem are pessimistic locking and optimistic locking. In the *pessimistic locking* scenario, user A puts a lock on the record so that nobody can change it until he or she is finished with it. (We will not go into the details of how locks are implemented. Locks are covered in detail in other SQL Server books. At this time, it is important to know that it is possible to mark a record so that no,body else can change it.) When user A changes the record, he or she also releases the lock and user B can now access the record and change it.

The trouble with this solution is that user A might go out for lunch—or on vacation—and, if he or she didn't close the application calling SQL Server, the lock will not be removed from the record. This scenario is one of the reasons why this kind of solution is not recommended in a client/server environment.

In the *optimistic locking* scenario, user A locks the record only while he or she is actually performing the change. A mechanism in SQL Server notifies a user if somebody has changed the record in the meantime. The user can then decide either to abandon changes or to overwrite the record.

A simple way to find out if somebody has changed the record since user A read it would be to compare all fields. To run this comparison, user A must keep both an "original" and a "changed" record, and he or she needs to send them both to the server. Then a process on the server must compare the "original" record with the record in the table to make sure that it wasn't changed. Only then can the record be updated. This process is obviously slow and it increases network traffic, but there are solutions in the industry that use precisely this method.

## Timestamp

SQL Server has a `timestamp` datatype. It is used for versioning records in a table. When you insert or update a record in a table with a `timestamp` field, SQL Server "timestamps" the change. Figure 10-2 demonstrates such behavior.

The table is created with a `timestamp` field. When a record is inserted, SQL Server automatically sets its value. When the record is updated, SQL Server increases the value of the `timestamp`.

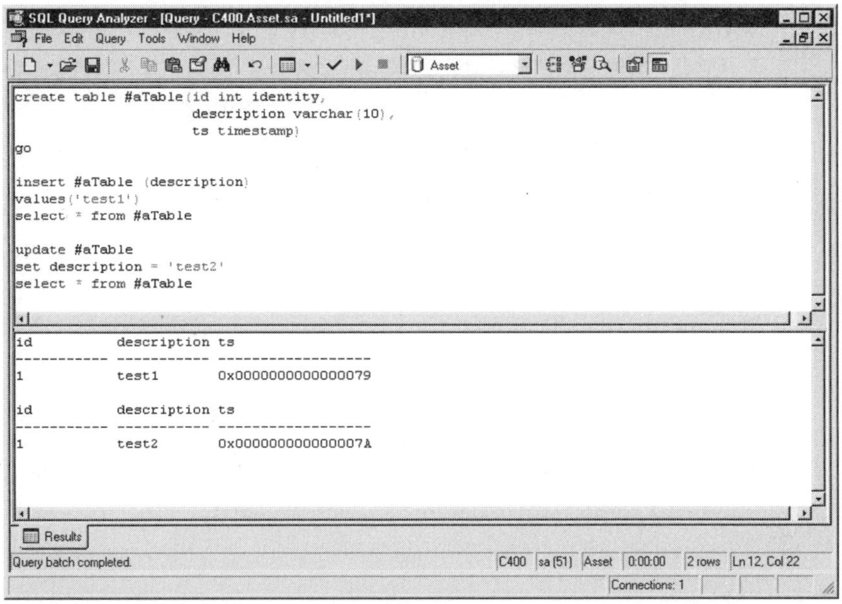

**Figure 10-2.**   Use of the `timestamp` datatype

It is important to realize that `timestamp` values are not actually a kind of timekeeping. They are just binary values that are increased with every change in the database, and therefore they are unique within the database. You should not make any assumptions about their values and growth. Somebody (or some process) might change something in the database concurrently, and even two changes that you executed consecutively might not have consecutive `timestamp` values.

To make sure that nobody has changed a record in the meantime, you might decide to update it like this:

```
update #aTable
set description = 'test3'
where id = 1
and ts = 0x000000000000007A  -- not a perfect solution
```

The record will be updated only if the `timestamp` is unchanged. The trouble with this solution is that you will not know what happens after the statement is executed. Maybe everything is okay and the record has been successfully changed. It is possible that the record was not updated, because the `timestamp` was changed, but it is also possible that the record is not in the table any more.

## TSEQUAL Function

SQL Server has the `TSEqual` function (no longer described in SQL Server Books Online), which compares `timestamp` values in the table and the Transact-SQL statement (see Figure 10-3). If they do not match, this function will raise an error 532 and abort the statement. This function allows a developer to write code that handles errors properly (for example, the user can be prompted for further action). If you executed the previous `Update` statement, the following one should cause SQL Server to force an error:

```
update #aTable
set description = 'test4'
where id = 1
and TSEQUAL(ts, 0x000000000000007A)
```

You can use this function in stored procedures to implement optimistic locking:

```
Create Procedure prUpdateContact_1
-- update conrecord from contact table
-- prevent user from overwriting changed record
    (
        @intContactId int,
        @chvFirstName varchar(30),
        @chvLastName varchar(30),
        @chvPhone typPhone,
        @chvFax typPhone,
        @chvEmail typEmail,
        @insOrgUnitId smallint,
        @chvUserName varchar(50),
        @tsOriginal timestamp
    )
```

```
As
Set nocount on

Update Contact
Set FirstName = @chvFirstName,
    LastName = @chvLastName,
    Phone = @chvPhone,
    Fax = @chvFax,
    Email = @chvEmail,
    OrgUnitId = @insOrgUnitId,
    UserName = @chvUserName
Where ContactId = @intContactId
and TSEQUAL(ts, @tsOriginal)

Return @@Error
```

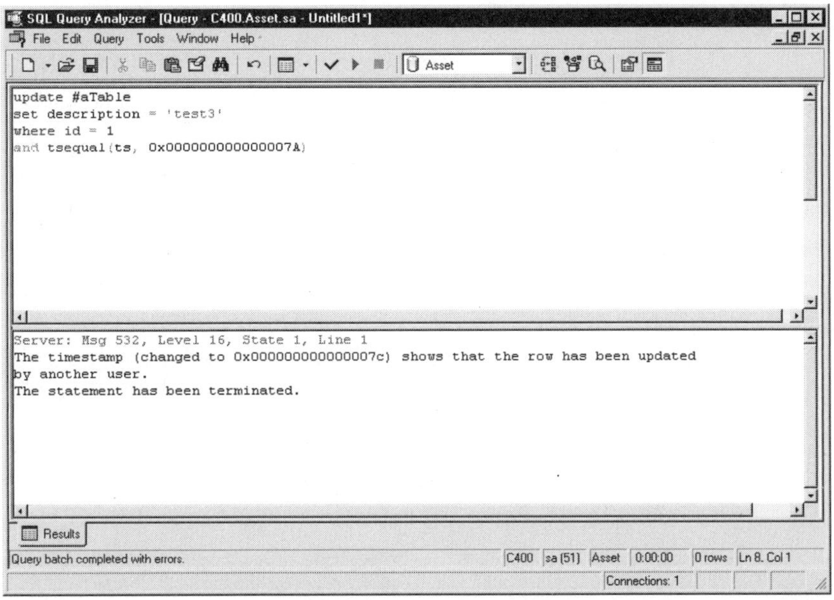

**Figure 10-3.**    Use of the *TSEQUAL* function

You will have no problem in executing this code from Transact-SQL:

```
Declare @intErrorCode int
Exec @intErrorCode = prUpdateContact_1
                1,              'Dejan',      'Sunderic',
                '121-1111', '111-1112', 'dejans@hotmail.com',
                1,              'dejans',     0x00000000000009C3
Select @intErrorCode ErrorCode
```

Unfortunately, some versions of client development tools (for example, Visual Basic) and some data access methods (for example, RDO and ADO) have problems retrieving and using timestamp values.

Before you implement 50 stored procedures in this manner, you should test whether your client development tools support timestamps. If they do not, you must implement a workaround.

## Timestamp Conversion

The first workaround that comes to mind is to pass the timestamp as some other datatype. Binary(8) and varchar are the first options most people try. Unfortunately, client tools usually do not support binary datatypes either. The trouble with varchar is that SQL Server converts the timestamp to an empty string.

One solution that works is based on the conversion of the timestamp to a datetime or money datatype (sounds strange, doesn't it?). Conversion in the opposite direction results in the same timestamp as well. You can test this workaround using the following code:

```
declare @dtmOriginal datetime,
        @tsOriginal timestamp

Set @tsOriginal = 0x00000000000009C3

select @dtmOriginal = Convert(datetime, @tsOriginal)
select @dtmOriginal, Convert (timestamp, @dtmOriginal)
```

> **NOTE:** Both of these datatypes are eight bytes long, as is the
> `timestamp` datatype. Converted `datetime` or `money` values do
> not have any meaning. Although "`timestamp`" sounds as if it contains
> date information, it is, as we have said before, just a sequential number
> that is increased with every database change.

The stored procedure will have to be modified:

```
Create Procedure prUpdateContact
-- update conrecord from contact table
-- prevent user from overwriting changed record
    (
        @intContactId int,
        @chvFirstName varchar(30),
        @chvLastName varchar(30),
        @chvPhone typPhone,
        @chvFax typPhone,
        @chvEmail typEmail,
        @insOrgUnitId smallint,
        @chvUserName varchar(50),
        @dtmOriginalTS datetime
    )
As
set nocount on
declare    @tsOriginalTS timestamp,
           @intErrorCode int

set @intErrorCode = @@Error

if @intErrorCode = 0
begin
    Set @tsOriginalTS = Convert(timestamp, @dtmOriginalTS)
set @intErrorCode = @@Error
end
```

```
if @intErrorCode = 0
begin
    Update Contact
    Set FirstName = @chvFirstName,
        LastName = @chvLastName,
        Phone = @chvPhone,
        Fax = @chvFax,
        Email = @chvEmail,
        OrgUnitId = @insOrgUnitId,
        UserName = @chvUserName
    where ContactId = @intContactId
    and TSEqual(ts, @tsOriginalTS)

    set @intErrorCode = @@Error
end

return @intErrorCode
```

Naturally, you will have to read records using a stored procedure that will convert the `timestamp` to a `datetime` or `money` datatype too:

```
Create Procedure prGetContact
-- get Contact record with timestamp converted to datetime
    (
        @intContactId int
    )
As
    set nocount on

    SELECT ContactId,
        FirstName,
        LastName,
        Phone,
        Fax,
        Email,
        OrgUnitId,
        UserName,
```

```
            Convert(datetime, ts) dtmTimestamp
FROM Contact
    where ContactId = @intContactId


return @@Error
```

# FULL TEXT SEARCH AND INDEXES

The Standard and Enterprise Editions of SQL Server 2000 and SQL Server 7.0 include *Microsoft Search Service,* a search engine that allows *full-text indexing and querying* like the search engines we use to query the Web. You can search for combinations of words and phrases. It allows linguistic searches where the engine will also match modifications of the original word (singular, plural, tenses, and so on). The result could be a simple list or a table that ranks how well the results match the search criteria. Part of the criteria could be the proximity of words and phrases.

These capabilities are different from those of standard database search engines where you can

▼ Search for an exact match of a word or phrase

■ Use wild card characters and the LIKE operator to search for character patterns

▲ Use indexes only if a pattern matches the beginning of the field

Microsoft Search Service was first introduced as a component of Internet Information Server. At that time, it was called Index Server.

We will not go into details of Microsoft Search Service architecture and administration, except to note that

▼ Indexes are not stored in databases but in files (usually in c:\Program Files\Microsoft SQL Server\MSSQL\FTDATA).

■ You have to set full-index search capability and indexes on tables and columns explicitly.

■ After indexed tables are updated, you have to start the update of the full-text index explicitly. Microsoft SQL Server will not update them in the background as it does with the table indexes.

▲ A table must have a unique index based on a single field to be indexed in this manner.

We will focus on full-text search capabilities. The two most important predicates are Contains and Freetext. They are designed to be used in the Where clause of a Select statement.

The Contains predicate returns true or false for records that contain specified keywords. Variations of this predicate accommodate linguistic searches for variations of words and for words that are in proximity to other words. For more details, see SQL Server Books Online.

Freetext orders the search engine to evaluate specified text and extract "important" words and phrases. It then constructs Create queries in the background to be executed against the table.

The following stored procedure implements different forms of full-text search on the ActivityLog.Note field:

```
Alter Procedure prFTSearchActivityLog
-- full-text search of ActivityLog.Note
-- this will only work if you enable full-text search
    (
        @chvKeywords varchar(255),
        @inySearchType tinyint
    )
As
set nocount on
--------- Constants -----------
declare     @c_Contains int,
            @c_FreeText int,
            @c_FormsOf int

Set         @c_Contains = 0
Set         @c_FreeText = 1
Set         @c_FormsOf = 2
--------- Constants -----------
```

```
if @inySearchType = @c_Contains
    exec ('select * from Activity Where Contains(Note, '
        + @chvKeywords + ')')
else if @inySearchType = @c_FreeText
    exec ('select * from Activity Where FreeText(Note, '
        + @chvKeywords + ')')
else if @inySearchType = @c_FormsOf
    exec ('select * from Activity '
        + 'Where FreeText(Note, FORMSOF(INFLECTIONAL,'
        + @chvKeywords + ')')

Return
```

# NESTED STORED PROCEDURES

As an example of nested stored procedures, I have prepared a set of procedures designed to convert monetary amounts into their text equivalents:

```
Create Procedure prCnvDigit
-- convert digit to word
-- 8 -> eight
    @chrDigit char,
    @chvWord varchar(15) OUTPUT,
    @debug int = 0
As
set nocount on

Select @chvWord = Case @chrDigit
                    when '1' Then 'one'
                    when '2' Then 'two'
                    when '3' Then 'three'
                    when '4' Then 'four'
                    when '5' Then 'five'
                    when '6' Then 'six'
                    when '7' Then 'seven'
                    when '8' Then 'eight'
                    when '9' Then 'nine'
                    else ''
                end
```

```
return
go

Alter Procedure prCnvDecade
-- convert 20, 30, 40...
    @chrDecade varchar(2),
    @chvWord varchar(500) OUTPUT
As
set nocount on

Select @chvWord = Case @chrDecade
                        when '2' Then 'twenty'
                        when '3' Then 'thirty'
                        when '4' Then 'forty'
                        when '5' Then 'fifty '
                        when '6' Then 'sixty'
                        when '7' Then 'seventy'
                        when '8' Then 'eighty'
                        when '9' Then 'ninety'
            end

return
go

Alter Procedure prCnvTeen
-- convert numbers between 10 and 19 to word
    @chvNumber varchar(2),
    @chvWord varchar(15) OUTPUT
As
set nocount on

Select @chvWord = Case @chvNumber
                        when '10' Then 'ten'
                        when '11' Then 'eleven'
                        when '12' Then 'twelve'
                        when '13' Then 'thirteen'
                        when '14' Then 'fourteen'
                        when '15' Then 'fifteen '
                        when '16' Then 'sixteen'
                        when '17' Then 'seventeen'
                        when '18' Then 'eighteen'
                        when '19' Then 'nineteen'
            end
```

```
return
go

Alter Procedure prCnvTwoDigitNumber
-- convert 2-digit numbers to words
    @inyNumber tinyint,
    @chvResult varchar(500) OUTPUT,
    @debug int = 0
As
set nocount on

declare @chvNumber varchar(2),
        @chrLastDigit char,
        @chrFirstDigit char,
        @chvWord varchar(500)

set @chvNumber = Convert(varchar(2), @inyNumber)

if @inyNumber = 0
begin
    Set @chvResult = ''
    return
end
else if @inyNumber < 10
begin
    exec prCnvDigit @chvNumber, @chvResult OUTPUT
    return
end
else if @inyNumber < 20
begin
    exec prCnvTeen @chvNumber, @chvResult OUTPUT
    return
end

Set @chrLastDigit = Substring(@chvNumber, 2, 1)
if @debug <> 0
    Select @chrLastDigit LastDigit

Set @chrFirstDigit = Substring(@chvNumber, 1, 1)
if @debug <> 0
    Select @chrFirstDigit FirstDigit
```

```
exec prCnvDecade @chrFirstDigit, @chvWord output
set @chvResult = @chvWord

exec prCnvDigit @chrLastDigit, @chvWord output
set @chvResult = @chvResult + ' ' + @chvWord

return
go

Alter Procedure prCnvThreeDigitNumber
-- convert numbers between 0 and 999
    @chvNumber varchar(3),
    @chvResult varchar(500) OUTPUT,
    @debug int = 0
As
set nocount on
declare @intNumber int,
        @chvLastTwoDigits varchar(2),
        @chvWord varchar(500),
        @chrDigit char

-- get numeric representation
Set @intNumber = Convert(int, @chvNumber)

If @intNumber > 99
begin
    -- get first digit
    Set @chrDigit = SubString(@chvNumber, 1,1)
    -- convert first digit to text
    execute prCnvDigit @chrDigit, @chvResult output, @debug
    -- add 'hundred'
    set @chvResult = @chvResult + ' hundred'

    set @chvLastTwoDigits = Substring(@chvNumber, 2, 2)
end
else
begin
    set @chvLastTwoDigits = @chvNumber
    set @chvResult = ''
end
exec prCnvTwoDigitNumber @chvLastTwoDigits, @chvWord output, @debug
```

```
if @chvResult <> ''
     set @chvResult = @chvResult + ' ' + @chvWord
else
     set @chvResult = @chvWord


return
go


Alter Procedure prCnvNumber
-- convert monetary number to text
     @mnyNumber money,
     @chvResult varchar(500) OUTPUT,
     @debug int = 0
As
set nocount on
declare @chvNumber varchar(50),      -- 000,000,000,000.00
        @chvWord varchar(500),
        @chvDollars varchar(25),     -- 000,000,000,000
        @chvCents varchar(2),        -- 00
        @intLenDollars int,          -- 12
        @intCountTriplets int,       -- 4
        @chrTriplet char(3),         -- 000
        @intCount int


-- get character representation
Set @chvNumber = Str(@mnyNumber, 22, 2)


-- get dollars
Set @chvDollars = LTrim(Str(@mnyNumber, 22, 0))
-- get cents
Set @chvCents = Substring(@chvNumber, Len(@chvNumber) - 1, 2)


if @debug <> 0
     select @chvNumber, @chvDollars, @chvCents


Set @intLenDollars = Len(@chvDollars)


-- get number of triplets
Set @intCountTriplets = @intLenDollars/3
-- loop through triplets
if @debug <> 0
     Select @intCountTriplets CountTriplets, @chvDollars chvDollars
```

```
if @intLenDollars = @intCountTriplets * 3
    Set @chrTriplet = Left(@chvDollars, 3)
else
    Set @chrTriplet = Left(@chvDollars,
                              @intLenDollars - @intCountTriplets * 3)

Set @intCount = @intCountTriplets
Set @chvResult = ''

While @intCount > 0
Begin
    If @debug <> 0
        Select @intCount intCount, @chrTriplet Triplet
    Exec prCnvThreeDigitNumber @chrTriplet, @chvWord output, @debug

    Set @chvResult = @chvResult + ' '
                    + @chvWord + ' ' +  Case @intCount
                                        When 1 Then 'dollars'
                                        When 2 Then 'thousand'
                                        When 3 Then 'million'
                                        When 4 Then 'billion'
                                        When 5 Then 'trillion'
                                        End
    Set @intCount = @intCount - 1

    Set @chrTriplet = Convert(varchar, Convert(int,
Substring(@chvDollars, @intLenDollars - @intCount * 3 + 1, 3
    )))
end

exec prCnvTwoDigitNumber @chvCents, @chvWord output, @debug
Set @chvWord = Ltrim(Rtrim(@chvWord))
if  @chvWord <> ''
    Set @chvResult = @chvResult + ' and ' + @chvWord  + ' cents'
return
go
```

To test this code, you can use the batch shown in the Figure 10-4.

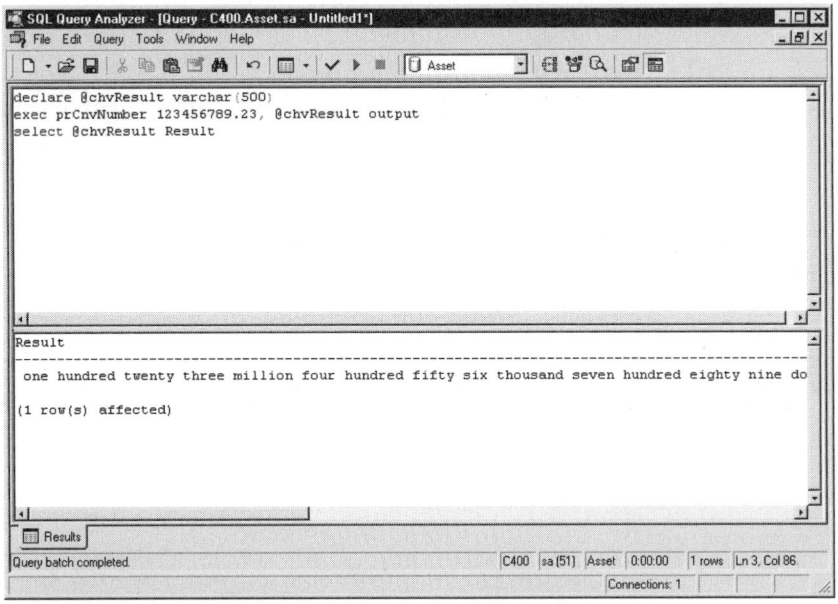

**Figure 10-4.**   Digit conversion

## Using Temporary Tables to Pass a Recordset to a Nested Stored Procedure

Some programming languages (such as Visual Basic and Pascal) use the concept of global and module variables. Those types of variables are very useful for passing complex parameters (like arrays or record sets) to a procedure when its parameter list supports only basic datatypes.

The same problem exists with stored procedures. You cannot pass a recordset through a parameter list to a stored procedure from the current batch or stored procedure, and neither recordsets nor local variables from the outer stored procedure (or batch) are visible to the inner stored procedure.

Unfortunately, SQL Server does not support user-defined global variables. Modules, and therefore module variables, do not even exist in Transact-SQL.

One way to pass a recordset is to create and fill a temporary table. Inner stored procedures will be able to see and access its content. The following example consists of two stored procedures. The first is business-oriented and collects a list of properties associated with an inventory asset. The list is implemented as a temporary table:

```
Alter Procedure prGetInventoryProperties_TempTbl_Outer
/*
Return comma-delimited list of properties
that are describing asset.
i.e.: Property = Value unit;Property = Value unit;Property =
Value unit; Property = Value unit; Property = Value unit; Property =
Value unit;
*/
     @intInventoryId int
As
set nocount on

declare      @chvProperties varchar(8000)

Create table #List(Id int identity(1,1),
                   Item varchar(255))

-- identify Properties associated with asset
insert into #List (Item)
    select Property + '=' + Value + ' ' +  Coalesce(Unit, '') + '; '
    from InventoryProperty inner join Property
    on InventoryProperty.PropertyId = Property.PropertyId
    where InventoryProperty.InventoryId = @intInventoryId

-- call sp that converts records to a single varchar
exec prConvertTempTbl @chvProperties OUTPUT

-- display result
select @chvProperties Properties

drop table #List

return 0
go
```

The nested stored procedure is not business-oriented. It loops through records in the temporary table (which was created in calling the batch or stored procedure) and assembles them into a single varchar variable:

```
Alter Procedure prConvertTempTbl
-- Convert information from Temporary table to a single varchar
    @chvResult varchar(8000) output
As
set nocount on

declare @intCountItems int,
        @intCounter int,
        @chvItem varchar(255),
        @insLenItem smallint,
        @insLenResult smallint

-- set loop
select @intCountItems = Count(*),
       @intCounter = 1,
       @chvResult = ''
from #List

-- loop through list of items
while @intCounter <= @intCountItems
begin
    -- get one property
    select @chvItem = Item
    from #List
    where Id = @intCounter

    -- check will new string fit
    select @insLenItem = DATALENGTH(@chvItem),
           @insLenResult = DATALENGTH(@chvResult)

    if @insLenResult + @insLenItem > 8000
    begin
        print 'List is too long (over 8000 characters)!'
        return 1
    end

    -- assemble list
    set @chvResult = @chvResult + @chvItem
```

```
        -- let's go another round and get another item
        set @intCounter = @intCounter + 1
end

return 0
go
```

You can execute this example from Query Analyzer, as shown in Figure 10-5.

You may ask when is this kind of solution justified and are these stored procedures coupled? It is true that neither of these stored procedures can function without the other. If we have other stored procedures that also use prConvertTempTbl, I would consider this solution justified.

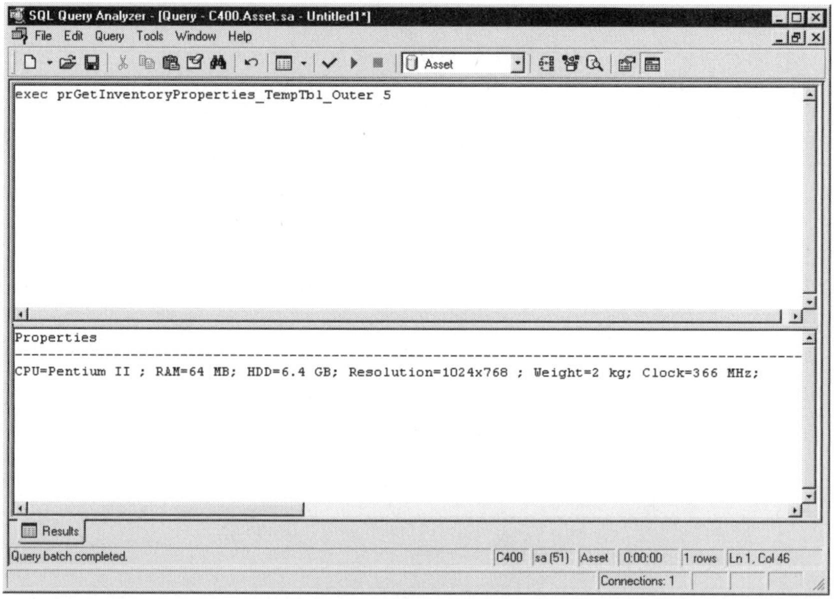

**Figure 10-5.** Using temporary tables to pass a recordset to a nested stored procedure

# Using a Cursor to Pass a Recordset to a Nested Stored Procedure

Similar solutions can be implemented using cursors. Cursors are also visible and accessible from nested stored procedures.

The following example also consists of two stored procedures. The first is business-oriented and creates a cursor with properties associated with specified inventory.

```
create Procedure prGetInventoryProperties_Cursor_Nested
/*
Return comma-delimited list of properties
that are describing asset.
i.e.: Property = Value unit;Property = Value unit;Property =
Value unit; Property = Value unit; Property = Value unit; Property =
Value unit;
*/

    (
        @intInventoryId int,
        @chvProperties varchar(8000) OUTPUT,
        @debug int = 0
    )

As

Select @chvProperties = ''

Declare curItems Cursor For
    Select Property + '=' + [Value] + ' '
        + Coalesce([Unit], '') + '; ' Item
    From InventoryProperty Inner Join Property
    On InventoryProperty.PropertyId = Property.PropertyId
    Where InventoryProperty.InventoryId = @intInventoryId

Open curItems

Exec prProcess_Cursor_Nested @chvProperties OUTPUT, @debug
```

```
Close curItems
Deallocate curItems

Return 0
Go
```

The second stored procedure is generic and converts information from cursors into a single variable:

```
Create Procedure prProcess_Cursor_Nested
-- Process information from cursor initiated in calling sp.
-- Convert records into a single varchar.
    (
        @chvResult varchar(8000) OUTPUT,
        @debug int = 0
    )

As

Declare   @intCountProperties int,
          @intCounter int,
          @chvItem varchar(255),
          @insLenItem smallint,
          @insLenResult smallint

Fetch Next From curItems
Into @chvItem

While (@@FETCH_STATUS = 0)
Begin

    If @debug <> 0
        Select @chvItem Item

    -- check will new string fit
    Select @insLenItem   = DATALENGTH(@chvItem),
           @insLenResult = DATALENGTH(@chvResult)

    If @insLenResult + @insLenItem > 8000
    Begin
        Select 'List is too long (over 8000 characters)!'
        Return 1
    End
```

```
-- assemble list
If @insLenItem > 0
     Set @chvResult = @chvResult + @chvItem

If @debug <> 0
     Select @chvResult chvResult

Fetch Next From curItems
Into @chvItem


End


Return 0
Go
```

You can execute this code from Query Analyzer, as shown in
Figure 10-6.

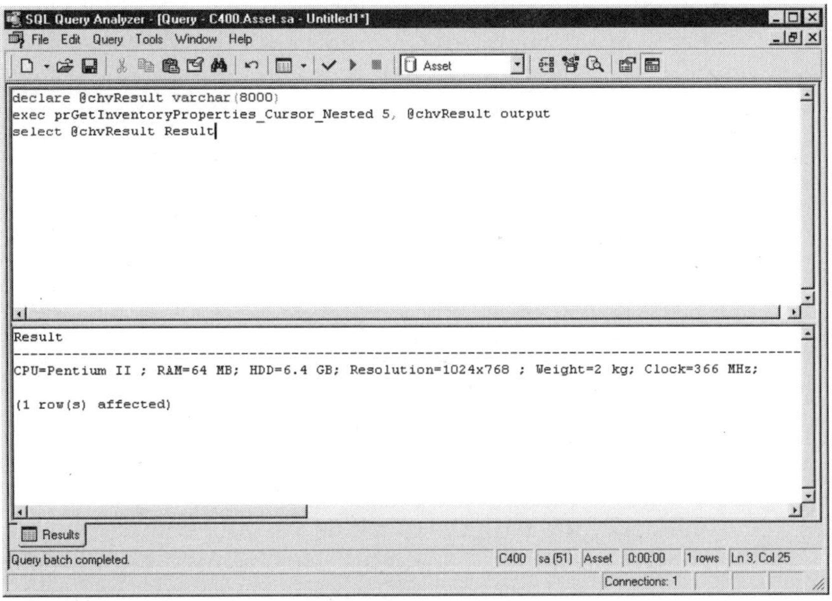

**Figure 10-6.**   Using a cursor to pass a recordset to a nested stored procedure

# HOW TO PROCESS THE RESULTSET OF A STORED PROCEDURE

From time to time, you will encounter stored procedures that return resultsets you need to process. This is not as simple as it sounds.

One option is to receive the resultset in a client application or middleware component and to process it further from there. Sometimes this option is not acceptable for a variety of reasons. For example, the resultset might be too big and network traffic could be considerably increased in this way. Since the resultset needs to be transferred to the middleware server before it is processed, the performance of the system could be degraded. There might be security implications—for example, if a user should have access only to a segment of a resultset and not to the complete resultset.

Another option is to copy the source code of the stored procedure into your stored procedure. This could be illegal. It will also reduce the maintainability of your code since you have two copies to maintain. If the other stored procedure is a system stored procedure, Microsoft can change its internals with the release of each new version of SQL Server. Your stored procedure will then need to be changed.

It is possible to collect the resultset of a stored procedure in Transact-SQL code. You need to create a (temporary) table, the structure of which matches the structure of the resultset exactly, and then redirect (insert) the resultset into it. Then you can do whatever you want with it.

The following stored procedure uses the sp_dboption system stored procedure to obtain a list of all database options and to obtain a list of database options that are set on the Asset database. Records that have a structure identical to that of the resultset as returned by the stored procedure are collected in temporary tables. The Insert statement can then store the resultset in the temporary table. The contents of the temporary tables are later compared and a list of database options not currently set is returned to the caller.

```
Create Procedure prNonSelectedDBOption
-- return list of non-selected database options

    @chvDBName sysname
```

```
As

Set Nocount On

Create Table #setable
    (
        name nvarchar(35)
    )
Create Table #current
    (
        name nvarchar(35)
    )


-- collect all options
Insert Into #setable
    Exec sp_dboption

-- collect current options
Insert Into #current
    Exec sp_dboption @dbname = @chvDBName

-- return non-selected
Select name non_selected
From #setable
Where name not in ( Select name
                    From #current
                  )

Drop Table #setable
Drop Table #current

Return 0
```

The only trouble with this method is that you need to know the structure of the resultset of the stored procedure in advance in order to create a table with the same structure. This is not a problem for user-defined stored procedures. It used to be a problem for system stored procedures, but SQL Server Books Online now provides that information.

> **NOTE:** Unfortunately, it is not possible to collect information if a stored procedure returns more than one resultset, as is the case with sp_spaceused.

This technique also works with the Exec statement. For example, if you try to collect a resultset from the DBCC command this way, SQL Server will return an error. But you can encapsulate the DBCC statement in a string and execute it from Exec.

The following stored procedure returns the percentage of log space used in a specified database:

```
Create Procedure prLogSpacePercentUsed
-- return percent of space used in transaction log for
-- specified database
    (
        @chvDbName sysname,
        @fltPercentUsed float OUTPUT
    )

As
Set Nocount On

Declare @intErrorCode int

Set @intErrorCode = @@Error

If @intErrorCode = 0
Begin
    Create Table #DBLogSpace
        (    dbname sysname,
            LogSizeInMB float,
            LogPercentUsed float,
            Status int
        )
    Set @intErrorCode = @@Error
End
```

```
-- get log space info. for all databases
If @intErrorCode = 0
Begin
     Insert Into #DBLogSpace
          Exec ('DBCC SQLPERF (LogSpace)')
     set @intErrorCode = @@Error
end

-- get percent for specified database
if @intErrorCode = 0
begin
     select @fltPercentUsed = LogPercentUsed
     from #DBLogSpace
     where dbname = @chvDbName

     set @intErrorCode = @@Error
end

drop table #DBLogSpace

return @intErrorCode
```

You can test this stored procedure from Query Analyzer, as shown on Figure 10-7.

These techniques were extremely important before SQL Server 2000. It is now possible to use the `table` datatype as a return value for user-defined functions. We showed how can you use table-valued user-defined functions in Chapter 9. Unfortunately, it is (still) not possible to use a `table` variable as the output parameter of a stored procedure.

You have another option when you want to pass a resultset (or multiple resultsets) to a calling stored procedure. You can use the `cursor` datatype as the output parameter of a stored procedure. In the following example, prGetInventoryProperties_CursorGet creates

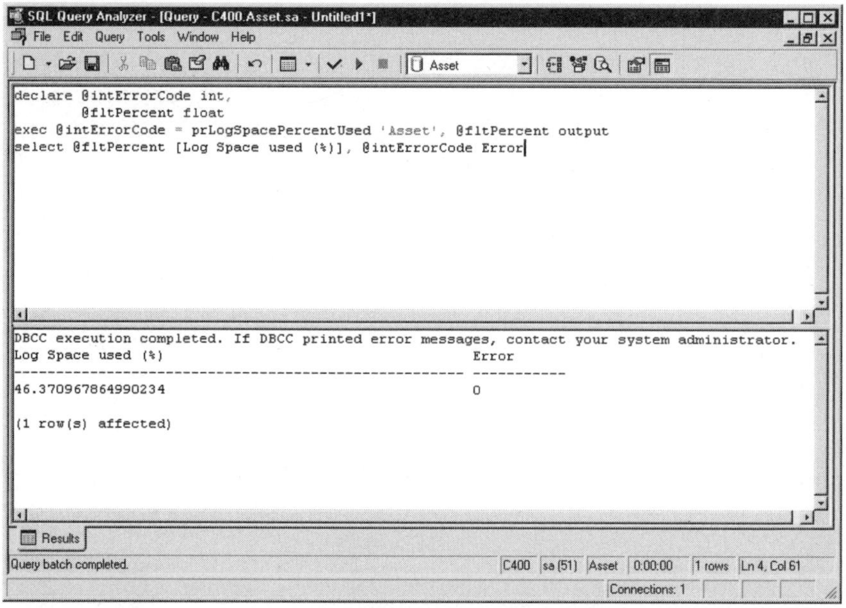

**Figure 10-7.** Percentage of log space used in a specified database

and opens a cursor. It is then returned as a cursor output parameter to the calling procedure:

```
Create Procedure prGetInventoryProperties_CursorGet
-- Return Cursor that contains properties
-- that are describing selected asset.

    (
        @intInventoryId int,
        @curProperties Cursor Varying Output
    )

As

Set @curProperties = Cursor Forward_Only Static For
    Select Property, Value, Unit
```

```
    From InventoryProperty inner join Property
    On InventoryProperty.PropertyId = Property.PropertyId
    Where InventoryProperty.InventoryId = @intInventoryId


Open @curProperties


Return 0
```

The nested stored procedure will be called from following stored procedure:

```
Create Procedure prGetInventoryProperties_UseNestedCursor
-- return comma-delimited list of properties
-- that are describing asset.
-- i.e.: Property = Value unit;Property = Value unit;
-- Property = Value unit;Property = Value unit;...

    (
        @intInventoryId int,
        @chvProperties varchar(8000) OUTPUT,
        @debug int = 0
    )


As


Declare @intCountProperties int,
        @intCounter int,
        @chvProperty varchar(50),
        @chvValue varchar(50),
        @chvUnit varchar(50),
        @insLenProperty smallint,
        @insLenValue smallint,
        @insLenUnit smallint,
        @insLenProperties smallint


Set @chvProperties = ''


Declare @CrsrVar Cursor
```

```
Exec prGetInventoryProperties_CursorGet @intInventoryId,
                                        @CrsrVar Output

Fetch Next From @CrsrVar
Into @chvProperty, @chvValue, @chvUnit

While (@@FETCH_STATUS = 0)
Begin

    Set @chvUnit = Coalesce(@chvUnit, '')

    If @debug <> 0
        Select @chvProperty Property,
               @chvValue [Value],
               @chvUnit [Unit]

    -- check will new string fit
    Select @insLenProperty = DATALENGTH(@chvProperty),
           @insLenValue = DATALENGTH(@chvValue),
           @insLenUnit = DATALENGTH(@chvUnit),
           @insLenProperties = DATALENGTH(@chvProperties)

    If @insLenProperties + 2
       + @insLenProperty + 1
       + @insLenValue + 1 + @insLenUnit > 8000
    Begin
        Select 'List of properties is too long (over 8000
chrs)!'
        Return 1
    End

    -- assemble list
    Set @chvProperties = @chvProperties
                       + @chvProperty + '='
                       + @chvValue + ' '
                       + @chvUnit + '; '
```

```
If @debug <> 0
   Select @chvProperties chvProperties

Fetch Next From @CrsrVar
Into @chvProperty, @chvValue, @chvUnit

End

Close @CrsrVar
Deallocate @CrsrVar

Return 0
```

It is the responsibility of the caller to properly close and deallocate the cursor at the end.

**TIP:**   You should not use a cursor as an output parameter of a stored procedure unless you have to. Such a solution is inferior because procedures are coupled and prone to errors. If you are working with SQL Server 2000, you should use table-valued user-defined functions instead.

# USING IDENTITY VALUES

In previous chapters, we introduced the function of identity values in a table. They are used to generate surrogate keys—unique identifiers often based on sequential numbers.

## A Standard Problem and Solution

Identity values are similar to the Autocount datatype in Access tables. But there is one difference that generates many questions in Usenet newsgroups among developers who are used to Access/DAO behavior. When a developer uses a resultset to insert a record into a table, the value of the AutoNumber field is immediately available in Access. Unfortunately, due to the nature of the client/server environment, this is not the case with recordsets in SQL Server.

The best way to insert a record into a SQL Server table and obtain an identity key is to use a stored procedure. The following stored procedure prInsertInventory is such a solution. A new record is first inserted into a table and then the key is read using the `@@identity` function/global variable.

```
Create Procedure prInsertInventory
-- insert inventory record and return Id
    @intEquipmentId int,
    @intLocationId int,
    @inyStatusId tinyint,
    @intLeaseId int,
    @intLeaseScheduleId int,
    @intOwnerId int,
    @mnsRent smallmoney,
    @mnsLease smallmoney,
    @mnsCost smallmoney,
    @inyAcquisitionTypeID int,
    @intInventoryId int output

As
Set Nocount On

Declare @intErrorCode int
Select @intErrorCode = @@Error

If @intErrorCode = 0
Begin
    Insert into Inventory (EquipmentId, LocationId, StatusId,
                    LeaseId, LeaseScheduleId, OwnerId,
                    Rent, Lease, Cost,
                    AcquisitionTypeID)
    Values (        @intEquipmentId, @intLocationId, @inyStatusId,
                    @intLeaseId, @intLeaseScheduleId, @intOwnerId,
                    @mnsRent, @mnsLease, @mnsCost,
                    @inyAcquisitionTypeID)

    Select @intErrorCode = @@Error,
            @intInventoryId = @@identity
End

Return @intErrorCode
```

## Identity Values and Triggers

Unfortunately, the previous solution does not always work. SQL Server has a bug/feature that can change a value stored in the @@identity global variable. If the table in which the record was inserted (in this case, Inventory) has a trigger that inserts a record into some other table with an identity key, the value of that key will be recorded in @@identity.

You can reproduce this behavior using the following script. It must be executed against the tempdb database.

```
Create Table a (a_id int identity(1,1),
                a_desc varchar(20),
                b_desc varchar(20))
Go


Create Table b (b_id int identity(1,1),
                b_desc varchar(20))
Go


Create Trigger tr_a_I
On dbo.a
After Insert      -- For Insert
As

If @@Rowcount = 0
     Return

Insert Into b (b_desc)
     Select b_desc from inserted
Go
```

Now execute this batch:

```
Insert into b (b_desc)
Values ('1')

Insert into a (a_desc, b_desc)
```

```
Values ('aaa', 'bbb')

Select @@identity [IdentityValue]
```

Query Analyzer returns the following result:

```
(1 row(s) affected)


(1 row(s) affected)



IdentityValue
----------------------------------------
2

(1 row(s) affected)
```

The first `Insert` statement adds the first record to table b. The second `Insert` statement adds the first record in a table. Because there is a trigger on the table, another record (the second one) will be inserted into table b, and the value of `@@identity` will be set to 2. If there was no trigger, the `Select` statement would return a value of 1.

## Sequence Number Table

Unfortunately, it is not easy to solve this problem. One solution is to create a table (for example, SequenceNumbers) that contains the highest sequence numbers for each table. So, each time that you want to insert a record into a table, you need to obtain a value from the sequence numbers table and increment that number by one. This value will then be used as a unique identifier (`id`) for the record that you want to insert.

**SequenceNumbers \***

| Column Name | Condensed Type | Nullable |
| --- | --- | --- |
| TableName | nvarchar(128) | NOT NULL |
| SequenceNumber | int | NULL |

**a table \***

| Column Name | Condensed Type | Nullable |
| --- | --- | --- |
| id | int | NOT NULL |
| Description | varchar(30) | NOT NULL |

This technique was a standard way to implement surrogate keys in earlier versions of SQL Server before identity values were introduced. Unfortunately, this technique is prone to concurrency contention problems, because there might be more processes competing to read, lock, and update a sequence key value. In earlier versions of SQL Server, it was not possible to lock a record, but only a page. A page could contain more than one record. Therefore, the process could lock a record even if the intent was to update some other record.

This problem used to be solved by mechanically increasing the size of the record so that only one record could fit on a page. Dummy fields used to be added so that the size of the record became larger than half of the page (2K / 2 = 1K). This trick is called *padding*.

**SequenceNumbers ***

| | Column Name | Condensed Type | Nullable | |
|---|---|---|---|---|
| 🔑 | TableName | nvarchar(128) | NOT NULL | |
| | SequenceNumber | int | NULL | |
| | Dummy1 | char(255) | NULL | |
| | Dummy2 | char(255) | NULL | |
| | Dummy3 | char(255) | NULL | |
| | Dummy4 | char(255) | NULL | |

**a table ***

| | Column Name | Condensed Type | Nullable | |
|---|---|---|---|---|
| 🔑 | id | int | NOT NULL | |
| | Description | varchar(30) | NOT NULL | |

In SQL Server 2000 and SQL Server 7.0, there is no need for this because these versions automatically lock a record. However, processes can still compete to read, lock, and update a sequence key value in the same record. This can lead to a *deadlock*.

The following stored procedure might be used to obtain an identifier from a table with sequence numbers:

```
Create Procedure prGetSequenceNumber
-- return next Id for selected table
-- and increment the value in SequenceNumbers table
    @chvTableName sysname,
    @intId int Output

As


-- read next Id
Select @intId = SequenceNumber
```

```
From SequenceNumbers
Where Tablename = 'a table'

-- increment SequenceNumber
Update SequenceNumbers
Set SequenceNumber = @intId + 1
Where Tablename = 'a table'

Return
```

For example, it could happen that we have two processes on a server that need to insert a record into table a. One process might read a record from the SequenceNumbers table. Let's assume that the second process is just a little behind and that it manages to read a record before the first process can do anything else. Each of them places a *shared lock* on the record. Such a lock allows other processes to read the record but prevents them from updating it until the originating process finishes. Unfortunately, the first process cannot update this record any more because of the lock placed on it by the second process, and the second process cannot update the record because of the lock by the first process. Each will wait for the other process to give up. This situation is called a deadlock. SQL Server has a mechanism that will eventually kill one of the processes so that the other one can continue. The trouble is that the client application needs to execute everything again, and that valuable time has been lost.

The standard way to avoid such deadlock is to place a *hint* in the From clause of the Select statement that will force SQL Server to put an *update lock* instead of a shared lock on a record. An update lock will prevent other processes from reading and putting locks on a record until the originating process is complete. Thus, the second process will wait until the first process is finished. Processes are thus *serialized*.

```
Create Procedure prGetSequenceNumber
-- return next Id for selected table
-- and increment the value in SequenceNumbers table
    @chvTableName sysname,
    @intId int OUTPUT
```

```
As


-- read next Id
Select @intId = SequenceNumber
From SequenceNumbers (updlock)
Where Tablename = 'a table'


-- increment SequenceNumber
Update SequenceNumbers
Set SequenceNumber = @intId + 1
Where Tablename = 'a table'


Return
```

**NOTE:**   Unfortunately, although very interesting, a detailed discussion of locks, deadlocks, concurrency, and other such issues is beyond the scope of this book.

## Preserving an Identity Value in a Temporary Table

I hope you haven't forgotten the original problem we set out to solve. The problem is how to preserve an identity value if a table has a trigger that inserts another record in some other table with the same identity key.

The key word is *preserve*. You can create a private temporary table and preserve the value of the identity key in it. Private tables are not visible to other processes, and you should not have concurrency issues with this solution. In this case, a temporary table needs to be created from the stored procedure that is inserting a record into the table.

You should then use a trigger (you can use the same one that is causing the problem) to pick an identity value and preserve it in the temporary table. When the triggers are finished, the stored procedure will be able to read an identity value from a temporary table.

We will demonstrate this solution by changing an earlier example.
You should execute the following against the tempdb database:

```
Drop Trigger tr_a_I
Drop Table a
Drop Table b


Create Table a (a_id int identity(1,1),
a_desc varchar(20),
b_desc varchar(20))
Go



Create Table b (b_id int identity(1,1),
b_desc varchar(20))
Go



Create Trigger tr_a_I
On dbo.a
After Insert    --For Insert
As

If @@Rowcount = 0
    Return

-- preserve identity value
Insert Into #ids (TableName, id)
Values ('a', @@identity)

-- add inserted leases to total
Insert Into b (b_desc)
Select b_desc From inserted
Go
```

As you can see, the trigger preserves the identity value in temporary table #ids. This table has to be created from the outer stored procedure or batch that will insert a record.

```
Create Table #ids(
        TableName sysname,
        id int)

Insert Into b (b_desc)
Values ('1')
Insert Into a (a_desc, b_desc)
Values ('aaa', 'bbb')

-- right identity value
Select id [IdentityValue]
From #ids
Where TableName = 'a'

Drop Table #ids
```

This time, the result is correct:

```
IdentityValue
-------------
1
```

**TIP:**  I do not like either of these solutions. The sequence table is an archaic approach. It requires many manual steps, and the performance of the database will suffer because of concurrency problems.

I find the second solution even more distasteful. The trigger is coupled with the code that is calling it. It depends on the existence of a temporary table. The developer might forget to create the trigger, or the user might try to insert records with some other tool. Too many things can go wrong.

Let's keep this problem in mind and solve it by avoiding such triggers!

# GUIDS

Distributed environments have different requirements for the generation of unique keys. A typical example is a database of sales representatives who are carrying notebook computers with local databases installed on them. These users do not have to be connected to a central database. They do the majority of their work locally and then replicate the information in their local database to the central database once in awhile. The use of identity fields in this case will lead to repetition, unless the key is composite and consists of an identity field and another field that is unique to the user. Another solution could be to divide key ranges between users (for example by setting an identity seed differently in each database). Each of these solutions has different limitations.

One way to generate unique keys is to use GUID (Global Unique Identification) fields. We discussed the `uniqueidentifier` datatype in Chapter 4. When a column in a table is assigned this datatype, it does not mean that its (unique) value will be generated automatically. Some other database object needs to generate a unique value using the `NewID()` function.

Typically a GUID value is generated as a default value of a table:

```
Create Table Location(
 LocationId uniqueidentifier NOT NULL DEFAULT newid(),
 Location varchar(50) not null,
 CompanyId int NOT NULL,
 PrimaryContactName varchar(60) NOT NULL,
 Address varchar(30) NOT NULL,
 City varchar(30) NOT NULL,
 ProvinceId varchar(3) NULL,
 PostalCode varchar(10) NOT NULL,
 Country varchar(20) NOT NULL,
 Phone varchar(15) NOT NULL,
 Fax varchar(15) NULL
 )
Go
```

You can also generate it in a stored procedure:

```
Create Procedure prInsertLocation
 @Location varchar(50),
 @CompanyId int,
 @PrimaryContactName varchar(60),
 @Address varchar(30) ,
 @City varchar(30) ,
 @ProvinceId varchar(3) ,
 @PostalCode varchar(10),
 @Country varchar(20) ,
 @Phone varchar(15),
 @Fax varchar(15),
 @LocationGUID uniqueidentifier OUTPUT

AS
Set @LocationGUID  = NewId()

Insert Into Location (Location_id, Location, CompanyId,
                      PrimaryContactName, Address, City,
                      ProvinceId, PostalCode, Country,
                      Phone, Fax)
values (@LocationGUID, @Location, @CompanyId,
        @PrimaryContactName, @Address, @City,
        @ProvinceId, @PostalCode, @Country,
        @Phone, @Fax)
Return @@ERROR
```

The stored procedure will also return a GUID to the caller.

# A WHILE LOOP WITH MIN OR MAX FUNCTIONS

It is possible to iterate through a table or recordset using a While statement with the aggregate function, which returns extreme values: MIN and MAX. Take a look at the following batch:

```
-- get first value
Select @Value = MIN(Value)
From aTable
```

```
-- loop
While @Value is not null
Begin
     -- do something instead of just displaying a value
     Select @Value value

     -- get next value
     Select @Value = MIN(Value)
     From aTable
     Where Value > @Value
End
```

The first `Select` statement with the `Min()` function obtains a first value from the set (table):

```
Select @Value = MIN(Value)
From aTable
```

The next value is obtained in a loop as a minimal value bigger then the previous one:

```
Select @Value = MIN(Value)
From aTable
Where Value > @Value
```

If no records qualify as members of the set, an `aggregate` function will return NULL. We can then use NULL as a criterion to exit a loop:

```
While @Value is not null
```

To demonstrate this method, let's rewrite prSpaceUsedByTables, which displays the space used by each user-defined table in the current database:

```
Create Procedure prSpaceUsedByTables_4
-- loop through table names in current database
     -- display info about amount of space used by each table

-- demonstration of while loop
```

```
As
Set nocount on
Declare @TableName sysname

-- get first table name
Select @TableName = Min(name)
From sysobjects
Where xtype = 'U'

While @TableName is not null
Begin

    -- display space used
    Exec sp_spaceused  @TableName

    -- get next table
    Select @TableName = Min(name)
    From sysobjects
    Where xtype = 'U'
    And name > @TableName
End

Return 0
```

This was just an academic example. Naturally, the proper solution will include a temporary table to collect all results and display them at the end in one recordset. Note that I am not talking about a temporary table like we have used for looping using a While statement in Chapter 4.

You can step backward through the recordset if you use the MAX function and if you compare the old record and the remainder of the set using the '<' operator.

**TIP:** This method can be a quick solution for problems that require iteration. However, solutions based on set operations usually provide superior performance.

# PROPERTY MANAGEMENT

One of the features that I have always wanted to see in SQL Server is the capability to add descriptions to database objects. Microsoft Access already has that feature. Naturally, you could be even more ambitious. It would be perfect on some projects to be able to store additional attributes such as field formats, input masks, captions, and the location and size of screen fields in the database as well. The more things you manage centrally, the fewer maintenance and deployment issues you will have later in production.

SQL Server 2000 introduces *extended properties.* Users can define extended properties, store them in the database, and associate them with database objects. Each database object can have any number of extended properties. An extended property can store a sql_variant value up to 7,500 bytes long.

SQL Server 2000 introduces three stored procedures and one function for managing extended properties. sp_addextendedproperty, sp_updateextendedproperty, and sp_dropextendedproperty are used to create, change, or delete extended properties. They all have very unusual syntax. We will examine this syntax in sp_addextendedproperty:

```
sp_addextendedproperty
    [@name =]{'property_name'}
    [, [@value =]{'extended_property_value'}
        [, [@level0type =]{'level0_object_type'}
        , [@level0name =]{'level0_object_name'}
            [, [@level1type =]{'level1_object_type'}
            , [@level1name =]{'level1_object_name'}
                [, [@level2type =]{'level2_object_type'}
                , [@level2name =]{'level2_object_name'}
                ]
            ]
        ]
    ]
```

Here, @name and @value are the name and value of the extended property. Other parameters define the name and type of the object with which the extended property will be associated. For this reason, database objects are divided into three levels:

1. User, user-defined type

2. Table, view, stored procedure, function, rule, default

3. Column, index, constraint, trigger, parameter

If you want to assign an extended property to an object of the second level, you must also specify an object of the first level. If you want to assign an extended property to an object of the third level, you must also specify an object of the second level. For example, to specify an extended property 'Format' to associate with the column 'Phone' in the table 'Contact', you must specify the owner of the table:

```
Exec sp_addextendedproperty 'Format', '(999)999-9999',
                'user', dbo,
                        'table', Contact,
                                'column', Phone
```

The FN_LISTEXTENDEDPROPERTY function is designed to list the extended properties of an object. It requires that you specify objects in the same manner as the stored procedures do. You can see the resultset returned by the function in Figure 10-8.

# SUMMARY

In this chapter, we have demonstrated techniques for the dynamic construction of queries. We have compared different techniques to see how SQL Server reuses execution plans and what effect such reuse has on performance.

We have demonstrated the use of timestamp fields to implement optimistic locking in SQL Server and solutions for loading timestamp values into client applications.

Microsoft Search Service is a search engine that allows full-text indexing and querying much like the services we use to query the Web. The engine is not relational, but it is possible to use it from stored procedures and Transact-SQL. It gives a new dimension to documents stored in SQL Server databases.

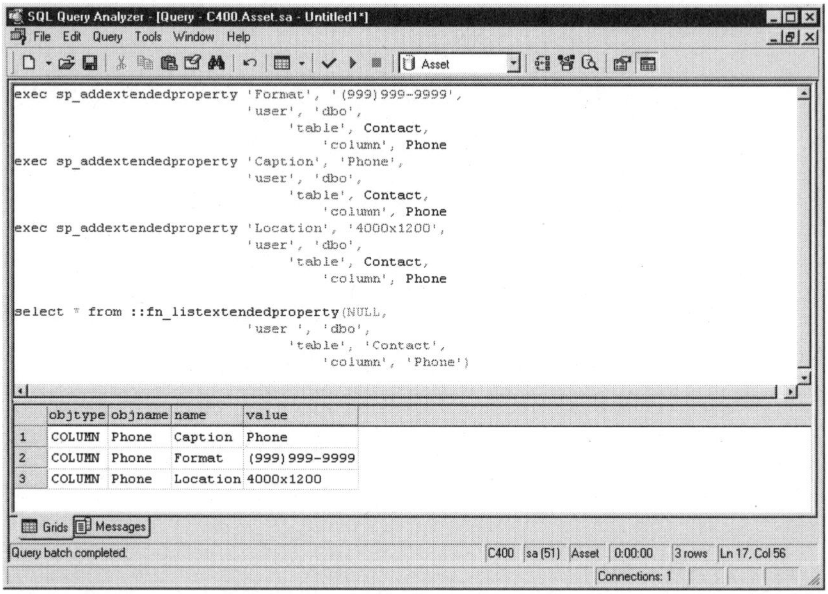

**Figure 10-8.** Extended properties of an object

Special attention was paid to the issue of nested stored procedures and the use of cursors and temporary tables to transfer information from outer to inner stored procedures and back.

Some implementations require additional work to generate and use unique identifiers for records in tables. Several problems, solutions, and techniques were discussed.

Pay special attention to the implementation of looping using Min() and Max() functions. This solution is superior to the use of cursors (better performance, better maintainability, and reduced chance of errors).

An interesting new feature is the capability to associate additional attributes called extended properties with database objects. This new feature provides some interesting opportunities. For example, it is possible to manage some application behaviors using data from a single source within the database.

# EXERCISES

1. Create a pair of stored procedures that use optimistic locking to obtain and update a record in the Inventory table. Assume that the client application cannot handle the `timestamp` datatype and that you have to use the `money` datatype instead.

2. Take a stored procedure from exercises 7 and 12 in Chapter 4 and exercise 6 in Chapter 7 and return the results in a single resultset.

3. Create a new version of the prGetInventoryProperties stored procedure that uses a `While` statement with a `Min()` function.

# CHAPTER 11

## Interaction with the SQL Server Environment

This chapter focuses on the ways you can use system and extended stored procedures to interact with the SQL Server environment. It also discusses the ways user-defined stored procedures can help you leverage the existing functionality of various elements within the SQL Server environment.

By the end of this chapter you will be able to

▼   Use OLE Automation in Transact-SQL

■   Run programs and operating system commands from the command shell

■   Manage jobs in Job Scheduler

■   Read and write Registry entries

■   Install a database on another server

■   Use the e-mail capabilities of SQL Server to notify users of events on the server

■   Use the e-mail capabilities of SQL Server to send queries, process them, and receive resultsets

■   Publish the contents of the database on the Web

■   Perform some administration tasks with stored procedures

▲   Manage application security

# EXECUTION OF OLE AUTOMATION OBJECTS

Microsoft has developed technology that enables developers to encapsulate executable code/objects into code components. They can be used from programs developed in the same or any other programming language that supports these kinds of objects. Through the years, this technology has been known by different names: *OLE, OLE Automation, COM, DCOM, Automation, ActiveX, COM+...* (and the saga continues).

SQL Server can initiate code components and access properties and methods encapsulated in them. There is a set of system stored procedures (with the prefix 'sp_OA') designed to accomplish such tasks.

**NOTE:** When Microsoft first unveiled this feature in SQL Server, code components were known as "OLE Automation objects." For this reason, Microsoft attached the 'OA' prefix to these stored procedure names, and I continue this usage in this section's heading.

We will demonstrate the use of Automation on a trivial Visual Basic function:

1. Create the `DjnToolkit` ActiveX DLL project in Visual Basic and then create a `DjnTools` class.

2. To start with, let's create a trivial method called `SpellNumber`, which ignores the input value (currency amount) and returns a constant string (see Figure 11-1).

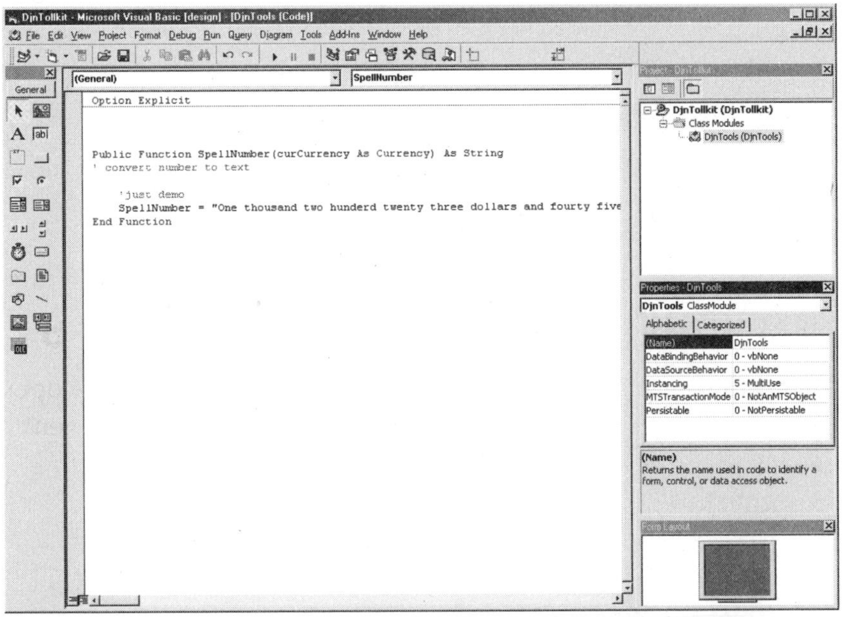

![Screenshot of Microsoft Visual Basic design environment showing the DjnToolkit project with the DjnTools class code. The code reads: Option Explicit; Public Function SpellNumber(curCurrency As Currency) As String; ' convert number to text; 'just demo; SpellNumber = "One thousand two hunderd twenty three dollars and fourty five; End Function]

**Figure 11-1.** A COM object created in Visual Basic

**NOTE:** Even if you run the object from the Visual Basic IDE (instead of compiling and installing it), you will still be able to access it from Transact-SQL code. This is an important feature for debugging the object.

The following stored procedure first initiates the COM object using the sp_OACreate system stored procedure. It obtains a token @intObject, which is used from that point to access the class.

The sp_OAMethod stored procedure is used to execute class methods. The return value and input parameter of the method are placed at the end of the stored procedure's parameter list.

Before the stored procedure is complete, the COM object must be destroyed using sp_OADestroy.

If an automation error occurs at any point, sp_OAGetErrorInfo can be used to obtain the source and description of the most recent error.

```
Alter Procedure prSpellNumber
-- demo of use of Automation objects
    @mnsAmount money,
    @chvAmount varchar(500) output,
    @debug int = 0

As
set nocount on

Declare @intErrorCode int,
        @intObject int,  -- hold object token
        @bitObjectCreated bit,
        @chvSource varchar(255),
        @chvDesc varchar(255)

Select @intErrorCode = @@Error

If @intErrorCode = 0
    exec @intErrorCode = sp_OACreate 'DjnToolkit.DjnTools',
                                        @intObject OUTPUT
```

```
If @intErrorCode = 0
     Set @bitObjectCreated = 1
else
     Set @bitObjectCreated = 0


If @intErrorCode = 0
     exec @intErrorCode = sp_OAMethod @intObject,
                                     'SpellNumber',
                                     @chvAmount OUTPUT,
                                     @mnsAmount


If @intErrorCode <> 0
begin
     Raiserror ('Unable to obtain spelling of number', 16, 1)
     exec sp_OAGetErrorInfo @intObject,
                           @chvSource OUTPUT,
                           @chvDesc OUTPUT
Set @chvDesc = 'Error ('
                    + Convert(varchar, @intErrorCode)
                    + ', ' + @chvSource  + ') : ' + @chvDesc
     Raiserror (@chvDesc, 16, 1)
end


if @bitObjectCreated = 1
     exec  sp_OADestroy @intObject


return @intErrorCode
```

Once you are sure that the communications between Transact-SQL and Visual Basic code are working, you can use Visual Basic to write code that converts numbers to text. Since this is not a book about Visual Basic, we will not go into detail on that subject. Instead, we will examine system stored procedures that use OLE Automation in more detail.

## sp_OACreate

Before any code component can be accessed, it has to be initialized. This stored procedure creates an instance of a code component and returns a reference to it (that is, an *objecttoken*):

```
sp_OACreate progid, | clsid, objecttoken OUTPUT[, context]
```

You can specify the code component using either a programmatic identifier (*progid*) or a class identifier (*clsid*).

A *programmatic identifier (progid)* is a string that serves as a name for the code component. It always appears in the form *Component.Object*. For example, Excel can be referenced as *Excel.Application*.

A *class identifier* is a unique identifier (GUID) for a class. It appears as a string in the following form:

```
{nnnnnnnn-nnnn-nnnn-nnnn-nnnnnnnnnnnn}
```

Thus, Excel can also be referenced as

```
{00024500-0000-0000-C000-000000000046}
```

An *objecttoken* is a reference to an instance of an object that is created. It appears in the form of an int datatype. All other OLE Automation stored procedures need this token to reference the object.

The *context* of the object determines whether the code component runs as an in-process component or an out-process component. If you do not specify a mode, both modes are supported.

Parameters must be passed by position, rather than by name.

## sp_OAMethod

You can use this stored procedure to execute a *method* of the object specified by *objecttoken*:

```
sp_OAMethod objecttoken,
            method
            [, returnvalue OUTPUT]
            [, [@parametername =] parameter [OUTPUT] [...n]]
```

If the method is a function, the stored procedure can access a *return value*.

At the end of the stored procedure's parameter list, you should list the parameters of the code components. The direction of the parameters is controlled by the Output keyword in the usual Transact-SQL manner.

Parameters can be passed both by position and by name. If passed by name, the *parametername* (when the '@' sign is removed) must match the name of the parameter in the code component.

During execution, sp_OAMethod converts Transact-SQL datatypes to OLE Automation (that is, Visual Basic) datatypes. You can find more details on this process later in this chapter.

# sp_OASetProperty

This stored procedure sets the property of the object specified by *objecttoken* to the new value:

```
sp_OASetProperty   objecttoken,
                   propertyname,
                   newvalue
                   [, index...]
```

# sp_OAGetProperty

This stored procedure reads the property of the object specified by *objecttoken*.

```
sp_OAGetProperty   objecttoken,
                   propertyname
                   [, @propertyvalue OUTPUT]
                   [, index...]
```

If you specify the *@propertyvalue*, it must be a local variable of the appropriate type.

If you do not specify the *@propertyvalue*, the stored procedure returns it in the form of a single-column, single-row resultset.

## sp_OADestroy

When the OLE Automation object is no longer needed, you should use this stored procedure to destroy the instance of it:

```
exec sp_OADestroy objecttoken
```

## sp_OAGetErrorInfo

Each OLE Automation stored procedure returns a value that signals its success status. If it returns '0', the stored procedure was completed successfully. Any other number returned is actually an error code. You can pass that error code value to the sp_OAGetErrorInfo stored procedure to find the source and description of the error as well as the name and context ID of the help file that describes the error:

```
sp_OAGetErrorInfo [objecttoken ]
                  [, source OUTPUT]
                  [, description OUTPUT]
                  [, helpfile OUTPUT]
                  [, helpid OUTPUT]
```

You should be meticulous in performing error handling when you use OLE Automation. So many things can go wrong that an up-front investment in error handling will pay huge dividends later on in the development cycle.

# Datatype Conversion

Keep in mind that code components and Transact-SQL code use different datatypes. You have to set compatible datatypes on both sides to allow the OLE Automation system stored procedures to automatically convert data between them. You can identify most of the compatible datatypes using common sense (for example,

varchar, char, text -> String, int -> Long). However, some
deserve special attention.

When values are converted from Transact-SQL to Visual Basic,
binary, varbinary, and image are converted to a one-dimensional
Byte array. Any Transact-SQL value set to Null is converted to a
Variant set to Null. Decimal and numeric are converted to
string (not currency).

When values are converted from Visual Basic to Transact-SQL,
Long, Integer, Byte, Boolean, and Object are converted to the
int datatype. Both Double and Single datatypes are converted
to float. Strings shorter than 255 characters are converted to
varchar, and strings longer then 255 characters are converted
to the text datatype. One-dimensional Byte() arrays shorter
then 255 become varbinary values, and those longer than 255
become image values.

> **TIP:** If you have some spare time, you can try something that I've always
> wanted to do. Create a COM object that will display a message over the
> entire screen and play a sound file. You can use this object on a SQL Server
> machine to draw your attention to it. This technique can be useful if you
> have a "farm" of SQL Servers to administer.

# RUNNING PROGRAMS

Before Microsoft included support for OLE Automation and/or
COM in SQL Server, administrators ran command prompt programs
and commands using the xp_cmdshell extended stored procedure:

```
xp_cmdshell {'command'} [, no_output]
```

When xp_cmdshell is executed, a *command* string is passed to the
command shell of the operating system to be executed. Any rows of
text that are normally displayed by the command shell are returned

by the extended stored procedure as a resultset. There is also an option to ignore the output.

The status of the execution is set as a return parameter of the extended stored procedure. Its value is set to '0', if successful, and '1', if failed. In Windows 95 and Windows 98, its value will always be set to '0'.

Figure 11-2 shows the use of the command prompt instruction to list files in the Backup folder. This output can be received in a temporary table and further processed in Transact-SQL code.

The following batch copies files from the Backup folder to another drive.

```
exec master..xp_cmdshell 'copy e:\w2kPro~1\Mocros~1\'
                    + 'MSSQL\BACKUP\*.* m:', no_output
```

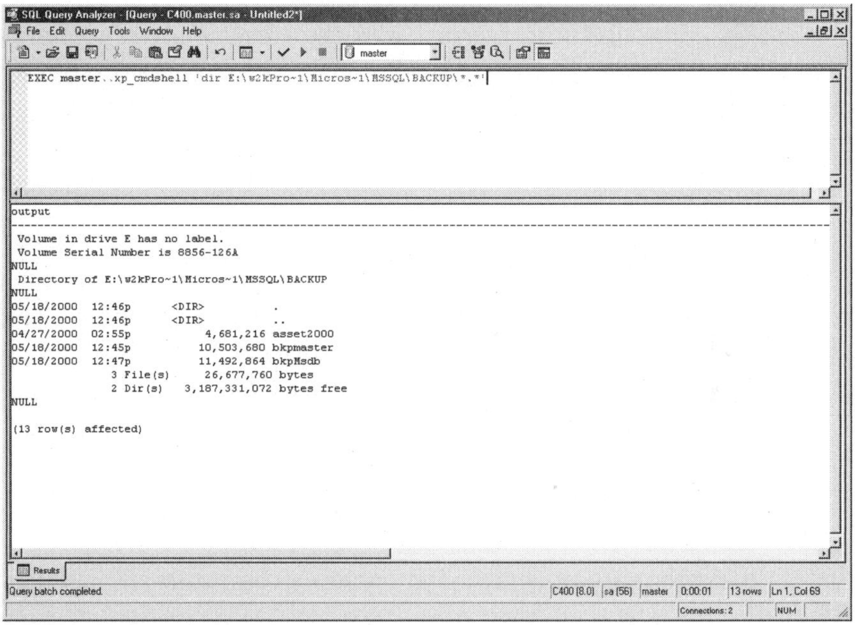

**Figure 11-2.** Using xp_cmdshell to run commands and programs

# RUNNING WINDOWS SCRIPT FILES

The Windows Script Host enables users to write and execute scripts in VBScript, JavaScript, and other languages compatible with the Windows environment. It was initially developed as an additional component, but it is now integrated into the Windows 98, ME, and 2000 platforms.

Script files usually have .vbs and .js extensions. They are executed from the Windows environment using Wscript.exe or from the command prompt using Csript.exe.

Execution of script files can also be initiated from Transact-SQL code. The following statement runs a demo script that starts Excel and populates a worksheet with information:

```
exec xp_cmdshell 'c:\windows\command\cscript.exe '
    + 'c:\windows\samples\wsh\Excel.vbs', NO_OUTPUT
```

# INTERACTING WITH THE NT REGISTRY

Developers of client applications in a Win32 environment often use the Registry as a repository for application configuration data and defaults. The Registry is a database (but not an RDBMS) that stores configuration information centrally. It is a hierarchical database that consists of

▼ Subtrees

■ Hives

■ Keys (and sometimes subkeys)

▲ Value entries

## Registry Subtrees

The largest division within the Registry hierarchy is the subtree, which is a folder within the Registry database that stores information of a particular type. These subtrees reside directly under the root of the Registry. Each subtree has an HKEY prefix to indicate to developers that it is a handle that can be used by a program. (A *handle* is a value that uniquely identifies a resource and allows programs to access that resource.) The Registry subtrees are

▼ *HKEY_LOCAL_MACHINE*, which contains information about the local computer system, including hardware and operating system data, such as bus type, system memory, device drivers, and startup control data.

■ *HKEY_CLASSES_ROOT*, which contains object linking and embedding (OLE) and file-class association data.

■ *HKEY_CURRENT_USER*, which contains the user profile for the user who is currently logged on, including environment variables, desktop settings, network connections, printers, and application preferences.

■ *HKEY_USERS*, which contains all actively loaded user profiles, including HKEY_CURRENT_USER, which always refers to a child of HKEY_USERS, and the default profile. Users accessing a server remotely do not have profiles under this key on the server; their profiles are loaded into the Registry on their own (local) computers.

▲ *HKEY_CURRENT_CONFIG*, which contains information about the hardware profile used by the local computer system at startup. This information is used to configure settings such as the device drivers to load and the display resolution to use.

## Keys and Subkeys

*Keys* are the building blocks that compose the Registry hierarchy. Each key can contain data items (called *value entries*), as well as additional subkeys. Structurally, keys are analogous to directories, and value entries are analogous to files.

A *value entry* is the value for a specific entry under a key or subkey in the Registry. Value entries appear as a string consisting of three components: the name of the value, the data type of the value, and the value itself, which can be data of any length.

The Registry Editor is the main tool for viewing and editing contents of the Registry.

**NOTE:** Since the Registry contains system configuration information, Microsoft recommends caution when managing its contents.

# THE REGISTRY AND SQL SERVER

Although the majority of server and database settings are stored in databases, SQL Server has some information stored in the Registry as well. However, most of this information consists of configuration settings for client tools and user information. These user-specific settings reside in HKEY_CURRENT_USER, and settings that are common for all users reside in the HKEY_LOCAL_MACHINE subtree. Figure 11-3 shows the MSSQLServer branch of the HKEY_LOCAL_MACHINE subtree.

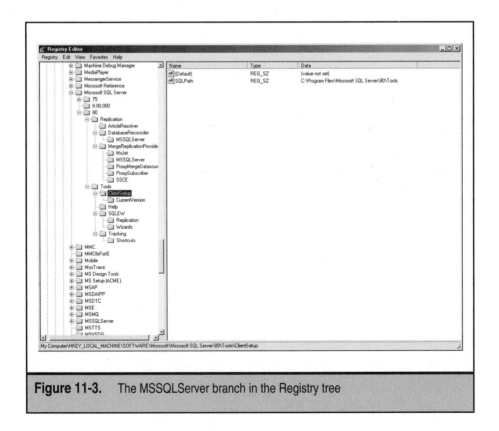

**Figure 11-3.** The MSSQLServer branch in the Registry tree

Since version 6.5, SQL Server has included extended stored procedures for manipulating the Registry. Unfortunately, these stored procedures are never described in Microsoft's documentation. There could be several reasons for this omission:

▼ Manipulation of the Registry requires skill and great care. The system can crash if critical parts of the Registry are deleted or changed.

■ Although the Registry can be defined theoretically as a "hierarchical database," it is not really a database in the sense that we are using the term. It can sustain neither the quantity of information nor the frequency of transactions that are normal for a database system such as Microsoft SQL Server. Reading data from the Registry is much more expensive (in terms of resource use) than reading from a relational database.

■ Microsoft reserves the right to change the interface for these extended stored procedures.

▲ Server and database settings are (mostly) stored in the master database and system tables of user databases.

SQL Server exposes the following extended stored procedures for manipulating the Registry:

| Extended Stored Procedure | Purpose |
| --- | --- |
| xp_regread | Reads a Registry value |
| xp_regwrite | Writes to the Registry |
| xp_regdeletekey | Deletes a key |
| xp_regdeletevalue | Deletes a key's value |
| xp_regenumvalues | Lists names of value entries |
| xp_regaddmultistring | Adds a multi string (zero-delimited string) |
| xp_regremovemultistring | Removes a multi string (zero-delimited string) |

# xp_regread

This stored procedure enables you to read the value of the Registry key located on the specified path of the specified subtree:

```
xp_regread subtree,
          path,
          key,
          @value    OUTPUT
```

In the following example, this extended stored procedure reads the root directory of the SQL Server installation:

```
declare @chvSQLPath varchar(255)
exec master..xp_regread
     'HKEY_LOCAL_MACHINE'
    ,'SOFTWARE\Microsoft\MSSQLServer\Setup'
    ,'SQLPath',@chvSQLPath    OUTPUT
select   @chvSQLPath SQLPath
go
```

# xp_regwrite

This stored procedure enables you to write a new value to the Registry key located on the specified path of the specified subtree:

```
xp_regwrite subtree,
           path,
           key,
           datatype,
           newvalue
```

In the following example, this extended stored procedure adds one value to the Setup key:

```
exec master..xp_regwrite
     'HKEY_LOCAL_MACHINE'
    ,'SOFTWARE\Microsoft\MSSQLServer\Setup'
```

```
                            ,'Test'
                            ,'REG_SZ'
                            ,'Test'
        go
```

## xp_regdeletevalue

This stored procedure enables you to delete the value in the Registry key located on the specified path of the specified subtree:

```
xp_regdeletevalue subtree,
                  path,
                  key
```

In the following example, this extended stored procedure deletes the key that we added in the previous section:

```
exec master..xp_regdeletekey
    'HKEY_LOCAL_MACHINE'
    ,'SOFTWARE\Microsoft\MSSQLServer\Setup'
    ,'Test'
go
```

> **TIP:**  I have to admit that I do not use these extended stored procedures, which is probably the reason I do not have better examples of writing to and deleting from the Registry.
>     You should be very careful when writing and deleting Registry keys using Transact-SQL. It is often a better idea (performance-wise) to store most of your configuration parameters in a special table in the application database.

# JOBS

One valuable administrative feature of Microsoft SQL Server is the capability to launch the execution of custom jobs at specified times. Each job has properties such as name, description, schedule, and a list of operators to be notified in case of failure, as well as a list of steps that need to be performed as part of the job. These steps can

be defined as Transact-SQL code, Active Script code, or operating
system commands.

# Administration of Jobs

We will take a look at the basics of job creation from Enterprise
Manager to show the potential of this feature, but we will not go into
too much detail. The following exercise creates a job that performs
a backup of the transaction log if it is more then 95 percent full. It is
based on the prBackupIfLogAlmostFull stored procedure.

You can create a job using a wizard or directly from the Enterprise
Manager tree:

1.  Open Enterprise Manager and expand the local server in the
    tree pane.

2.  Expand Management, then SQL Server Agent. Make sure that
    it is running.

3.  Click Jobs; SQL Server displays a list of existing jobs.

4.  Right-click Jobs and choose New Job. Enterprise Manager
    displays a New Job Properties form.

5.  Fill in the General tab with the information shown in the
    following illustration:

6.  Click the Steps tab.

7. Click New to start creating the first step. The application displays the New Job Step form.

8. In the Step Name field, type **do backup**.

9. Select Transact-SQL Script in the Type list.

10. Specify Asset as the working database.

11. The Command text box can be populated with script from the file (using the Open button), or as in this case, you can enter code manually for the execution of a stored procedure. Type:

```
exec prBackupIfLogAlmostFull 'Asset', 95
```

The dialog box should eventually look like this:

12. Click the Advanced tab to see other options. You can specify behavior in the case of an error and of successful completion, the log file to record the output of the script, and other such options. For this exercise, accept the default values and close the form. SQL Server returns us to the Steps tab of the New Job Properties form.

13. We will create only one step for this job, so now we can click the Schedules tab to set a schedule.

14. Click the New Schedule button to display the New Schedule dialog.

15. Name the schedule **Every 5 min**.
    The Schedule Type is set to Recurring, but the default frequency is not what we want. Click the Change button.
    The Edit Recurring Job Schedule dialog appears.

16. Select Daily in the Occurs group.

17. Set Daily Frequency to Occurs Every 5 Minute(s), as shown in the following illustration:

18. Click OK to close the form; the application displays a message describing the schedule. Close the message box; the application returns you to the New Job Properties form.

19. Click the Notification tab to set activities that will occur when the job completes. It is possible to page or send e-mail to

operators, write status to the Windows NT application event log, or automatically delete the job:

20. Accept the default values and click OK to close the form.

Keep in mind that SQL Server will execute this job every five minutes from now on. If you want to disable it, you can edit the job or just right-click the job in Enterprise Manager and select Disable Job from the pop-up menu.

All of the functionality in this job is actually provided by the prBackupIfLogAlmostFull stored procedure. The only requirement that such a stored procedure must comply with is that it needs to return a success status ('0' in the case of success; any other number represents an error code). SQL Server Agent uses this value to determine the success of the completed job and potentially execute some other step. Returning a success status is a highly recommended practice whether the stored procedure works inside the job or not.

The prBackupIfLogAlmostFull stored procedure calls the prLogSpacePercentUsed stored procedure to obtain the amount of log space available in the database. If the limit is reached, it creates a backup device using the sp_addumpdevice system stored procedure and performs a backup of the transaction log.

```
CREATE Procedure prBackupIfLogAlmostFull
-- Do backup of transaction log
-- if percent of space used is bigger then @fltPercentLimit
    (
        @chvDbName sysname,
        @fltPercentLimit float,
        @debug int = 0
    )
As
set nocount on

declare    @intErrorCode int,
           @fltPercentUsed float,
           @chvDeviceName sysname,
           @chvFileName sysname

set @intErrorCode = @@Error

-- how much of log space is used at the moment
if @intErrorCode = 0
    exec @intErrorCode = prLogSpacePercentUsed @chvDbName,
                                        @fltPercentUsed OUTPUT

-- if limit is not reached, just go out
if @intErrorCode = 0 and @fltPercentUsed < @fltPercentLimit
    return 0

if @intErrorCode = 0
begin
    Select @chvDeviceName = @chvDbName
                            + Convert(Varchar, GetDate(), 112),
           @chvFileName    = 'C:\PROGRAM FILES\MICROSOFT.SQL SERVER'
                            + '\MSSQL\BACKUP\bkp'
                            + @chvDeviceName
                            + '.dat'
    set @intErrorCode = @@Error
end
```

```
if @debug <> 0
     select @chvDeviceName chvDeviceName,
            @chvFileName chvFileName


if @intErrorCode = 0
begin
     EXEC sp_addumpdevice 'disk', @chvDeviceName, @chvFileName
     set @intErrorCode = @@Error
end


-- 15061 it is OK if dump device already exists
if @intErrorCode = 0 or @intErrorCode = 15061
begin
     BACKUP LOG @chvDbName TO @chvDeviceName
     set @intErrorCode = @@Error
end


return @intErrorCode
```

*TIP:*   Some might argue that such a stored procedure and job are not needed in Microsoft SQL Server 2000 and 7.0, since it can increase the size of a transaction log automatically if it approaches its specified limit. This is true but only valid if you can afford unlimited storage. If your disk resources Ware limited, it is a much better solution to clear the log.

## Alternative to Job Scheduler

Microsoft has significantly improved Job Scheduler (formerly known as Task Scheduler in SQL Server 6.*x*) in SQL Server 7.0 and 2000.

▼ Steps are included as components of jobs to allow better control.

■ The user can continue or even stop execution from different points, depending on the success or failure of each step.

■ Operators can be notified according to predefined criteria.

▲ Each step can be coded in a different language (including Transact-SQL, ActiveX Script, operating system commands, or commands to replication and maintenance services and utilities).

In the past, the only way to create a complex job was to code everything in Transact-SQL. Now, simpler jobs can be implemented using steps. If you really need a sophisticated solution, you still need the power of Transact-SQL or ActiveX Script.

SQL Server includes a set of stored procedures and extended stored procedures inside Enterprise Manager that can achieve everything that you can do within Job Scheduler. They reside in the msdb database. (This database is used by SQL Server Agent to hold information about jobs, schedules, and operators.)

In the following paragraphs, we will quickly review some of these numerous stored procedures.

## Stored Procedures for Maintaining Jobs

The sp_help_job stored procedure returns information about jobs. If no parameters are specified, the stored procedure returns a resultset with a list of jobs and their attributes. If the job name (or ID) is specified, the stored procedure returns an additional resultset that describes the job's steps, schedules, and target servers.

The sp_add_job, sp_delete_job, and sp_update_job stored procedures are used to create, delete, and change existing jobs.

The sp_add_jobstep and sp_add_jobschedule are designed to associate a schedule and steps with an existing job. Naturally, there are also stored procedures that allow you to delete or update schedules and steps and obtain information about them.

The following example creates a single-step job to perform a backup of the transaction log and assigns a nightly schedule to it:

```
USE msdb
EXEC sp_add_job @job_name = 'Asset Backup Log',
    @enabled = 1,
    @description = 'Backup transaction Log of Asset database',
    @owner_login_name = 'sa',
    @notify_level_email = 2,
```

```
    @notify_email_operator_name = 'dejan'

EXEC sp_add_jobstep @job_name = 'Asset Backup Log',
    @step_name = 'Backup Log',
    @subsystem = 'TSQL',
    @command = ' BACKUP LOG Asset TO bkpAssetLog'
    @retry_attempts = 5,
    @retry_interval = 5

EXEC sp_add_jobschedule @job_name = ' Asset Backup Log ',
    @name = 'Nightly Backup',
    @freq_type = 4,    -- daily
    @freq_interval = 1,
    @active_start_time = '23:00:00'
```

I do not think that you will use this technique very often. It is much easier to create jobs, schedules, and steps from Enterprise Manager. It is more likely that you will use sp_start_job to instruct SQL Server Agent to run the job immediately, as in the following example:

```
USE msdb
EXEC sp_start_job @job_name = 'Asset Backup Log'
```

There is also an orthogonal stored procedure sp_stop_job that is designed to stop execution of a job that is in progress.

Once a job is completed, SQL Server agent will record its success in history. You can view the history of a job using sp_help_jobhistory, or you can delete old records from history using sp_purge_jobhistory.

## Operators and Alerts

SQL Server Agent also maintains a list of operators and a list of alerts.

*Operators* are administrators who should be notified if something unusual happens in SQL Server. The system keeps track of the operator's network, e-mail, and pager addresses, as well as a timetable indicating when the operator wears the pager during the week.

*Alerts* are events that can occur in SQL Server, such as specific errors, errors of a certain severity, and conditions that can occur in a database, as well as the actions that need to be taken to handle the event (such as sending a message to the operator or executing a job).

There is also a third type of object that serves as a link between alerts and operators. *Notifications* are used to assign and send a message to operator(s) to handle alerts.

Naturally, there are stored procedures to manage these lists of operators and alerts:

▼ sp_help_operator, sp_add_operator, sp_delete_operator, sp_update_operator

■ sp_help_alert, sp_add_alert, sp_delete_alert, sp_update_alert

▲ sp_help_notification, sp_add_notification, sp_delete_notification, sp_update_notification

## SQL SERVER AND THE WEB

SQL Server is not designed as a tool for publishing content to the Web, but support for the basic tasks is built into it. Users can

▼ Publish the contents of the database on the Web

■ Create a Web page based on the result of a query

■ Use HTML templates to format resultsets

■ Update a Web page periodically or on demand to incorporate changes to the database

▲ Set a database to update a Web page whenever underlying tables are changed

Many tools and technologies are available that are suitable for creating Web applications, but Visual InterDev is one that you should investigate before others because of the seamless integration between it and SQL Server.

*TIP:* Unfortunately, Web publishing from SQL Server is available only from the Standard and Enterprise Editions of SQL Server 2000 and SQL Server 7.0.

## Web Assistant

The easiest way to generate Web pages is to use the Web Assistant Wizard:

1. From Enterprise Manager, select Tools | Wizards. The Select Wizard tree appears.

2. Expand the Management subtree, select the Web Assistant Wizard, then click OK.

3. Click Next to open the second page; the wizard prompts you for the database to be used as a source of information.

4. The next page prompts you for the name of the Web page you want to generate. You will also have to specify the type of query you want to use to get a resultset from the database. The query can be a stored procedure, an ad hoc query, or a selection of table columns to be assembled into a query by the wizard.

5. Select the first option (Data From The Tables And Columns That I Select), click Next, and the wizard prompts you to select a table and the columns that should appear in the resultset.

6. Select the table and columns you want and click Next.

7. The application prompts you to filter a recordset of your database. You can type a `Where` clause or use list boxes to specify column, operators, and the values of criteria. When you have finished specifying criteria, click Next.

8. The next page prompts you to schedule the job to create a Web page. You can also specify that the Web page needs to be generated at scheduled intervals or when data changes. SQL Server will schedule a recurring job or create triggers that will fire when the table changes. The trouble with using a recurring job is that changes will not be published immediately to the Web; the trouble with the trigger approach is that the generation of the Web page will become part of (that is, overhead for) the transaction. Click Next to continue.

9. Specify the location of the Web page to be generated. Click Next to continue.

10. The Web Assistant Wizard then asks you to format the Web page. It prompts you to specify a predefined template that you want to use, or it helps you to format all elements of the

page. We will talk about templates later. In this case, just let SQL Server help you to format the page. Click Next to continue.

11. The next page lets you specify titles for the page and the table, and specify font sizes for those titles. Click Next to continue.

12. The next page lets you specify the formatting of the table containing the resultset. You can change the font style, decide whether you want to display columns, and choose whether you want borders around the table. Click Next to continue.

13. The next page prompts you to add one or an entire list of hyperlinks to the page. If you specify a list, it should be the result of a query that returns labels and links as columns of the resultset. Click Next to continue.

14. The next page provides options that are helpful if the table is very long. You can limit the number of rows that you want to display on the page or decide to create a set of linked pages with a specified number of rows on each. Click Next to continue.

15. The final page allows you to save and execute the command for creating the Web task that you have defined. Click the Write Transact SQL To File button to save the script created by the wizard, or click Finish to execute the script immediately.

## Web Task Stored Procedures

Everything that the Web Assistant does can be accomplished using a set of three stored procedures:

▼ sp_makewebtask

■ sp_runwebtask

▲ sp_dropwebtask

These stored procedures are designed to manage *Web tasks*, which are just regular jobs. You can see them in the SQL Server Agent's list of jobs.

**NOTE:** The reason these stored procedures use "webtask" in their names is that they were introduced in SQL Server 6.5. At that time, "jobs" were called "tasks."

# sp_makewebtask

This stored procedure creates a job that produces an HTML document containing the resultset of a query (or a stored procedure).

The syntax of the command looks terrifying:

```
sp_makewebtask [@outputfile =] 'outputfile', [@query =] 'query'
    [, [@fixedfont =] fixedfont]
    [, [@bold =] bold]
    [, [@italic =] italic]
    [, [@colheaders =] colheaders]
    [, [@lastupdated =] lastupdated]
    [, [@HTMLHeader =] HTMLHeader]
    [, [@username =] username]
    [, [@dbname =] dbname]
    [, [@templatefile =] 'templatefile']
    [, [@webpagetitle =] 'webpagetitle']
    [, [@resultstitle =] 'resultstitle']
    [
        [, [@URL =] 'URL', [@reftext =] 'reftext']
        | [, [@table_urls =] table_urls, [@url_query =] 'url_query']
    ]
    [, [@whentype =] whentype]
    [, [@targetdate =] targetdate]
    [, [@targettime =] targettime]
    [, [@dayflags =] dayflags]
    [, [@numunits =] numunits]
    [, [@unittype =] unittype]
    [, [@procname =] procname ]
    [, [@maketask =] maketask]
    [, [@rowcnt =] rowcnt]
    [, [@tabborder =] tabborder]
    [, [@singlerow =] singlerow]
    [, [@blobfmt =] blobfmt]
    [, [@nrowsperpage =] n]
    [, [@datachg =] table_column_list]
    [, [@charset =] characterset]
    [, [@codepage =] codepage]
```

Fortunately, there is usually no need for you to start populating all these parameters by hand. Use Web Assistant to specify everything and save the command during the final step of the wizard. You can later modify it using Query Analyzer.

The @whentype parameter specifies when the Web task should be executed. The default value is 1, meaning that a Web task should be created and executed immediately. A job will actually be created, executed, and then deleted. However, most of the other settings will leave the job for SQL Server Agent to launch.

When sp_makewebtask is executed, several database objects may be created. A new record is added to the list of jobs in the msdb database. A new stored procedure is created in the database specified by the @dbname parameter. The new stored procedure has the same name as the job. It encapsulates the query that returns the recordset to be published (@query). If the Web task is designed to update a Web page whenever underlying data changes, the wizard also creates a trigger to run the job.

For discussion of other parameters, consult SQL Server Books Online.

## sp_runwebtask

This is a stored procedure for managing Web tasks that you use more often than others. It is designed to run an existing Web task:

```
sp_runwebtask [[@procname =] 'procedurename']
    [, [@outputfile =] 'outputfile'
```

The result of the Web task is an HTML file (outputfile) that can be specified by either the sp_runwebtask or the sp_makewebtask stored procedure.

## sp_dropwebtask

This stored procedure is designed to delete Web tasks. It deletes all objects that belong to the Web task (for example: job, stored procedure with query, triggers):

```
sp_dropwebtask [[@procname =] 'procedurename']
               [,[@outputfile =] 'outputfile'
```

# Web Page Templates

The best way to format your Web page is to use a *template file,* which is an ordinary HTML file with placeholders for incorporating a resultset.

There are two types of placeholders:

▼ <%insert_data_here%>

▲ <%begindetail%>, <%enddetail%>

### <%insert_data_here%>

This placeholder is used to mark the spot where SQL Server is to place a complete resultset. The placeholder is formatted as a regular HTML table.

The following code is extracted from such a template file:

```
<html>

<head>
<title>Price List</title>
</head>

<body>
<H1>Price List<H1>

<%insert_data_here%>
</body>

</html>
```

Naturally, you can enrich your template with logos, links, additional text, and other elements. A simple trick is to design your page first in an HTML editor such as FrontPage and add the table placeholder later.

### <%begindetail%>, <%enddetail%>

If you want more control over the look of your table, you can use these placeholders. They mark the beginning and end of the HTML code that will be replicated for each row in the resultset. Between them you should use the `<%insert_data_here%>` placeholder to mark the position where each field should be inserted.

The following code was generated in FrontPage. It is a simple page that uses a table with two rows and three columns. We have inserted column heading in the first row and then marked a block around the next record with the `<%begindetail%>` and `<%enddetail%>` tags. Inside each table cell in the row, we have inserted a placeholder for the fields.

```html
<html>

<head>
<title>Price List</title>
</head>

<body>

<table border="1" width="336">
  <tr>
    <td>Action ID</td>
    <td>Action</td>
    <td>List Price</td>
  </tr>
<%begindetail%>
  <tr>
    <td><%insert_data_here%></td>
    <td><%insert_data_here%></td>
    <td><%insert_data_here%></td>
  </tr>
<%enddetail%>
</table>

</body>

</html>
```

Of course, the point of this whole exercise is to create a more complex layout. You can also include code for implementing links or more complex formatting options.

# STRING TEMPLATES

SQL Server has two extended stored procedures designed after their C counterparts to compose strings and extract sections of a string:

▼  xp_sprintf

▲  xp_sscanf

C is hardly the paradigm for a language with good string manipulation tools, but if you are used to C's approach, you might find these stored procedures useful.

## xp_sprintf

The xp_sprintf extended stored procedure assembles a *result_string* by filling placeholders in a *template* with *parameters* from the list:

```
xp_sprintf {result_string OUTPUT, template}
    [, parameter [,...n]]
```

In SQL Server, only the %s (character string) type of format parameter is supported.

The following batch assembles a Transact-SQL statement with the datename() function and then executes it:

```
declare @command varchar(8000)
exec master..xp_sprintf @command OUTPUT,
                        'select date%s(%s, GetDate())',
                        'name',
                        'month'
select @command
exec (@command)
```

## xp_sscanf

The xp_sscanf extended stored procedure extracts parameters from a *string* using a *template:*

```
xp_sscanf {string, template}
    [, parameter OUTPUT [,...n]]
```

In SQL Server, only the %s (character string) type of format parameter is supported.

The following batch extracts an error number and description from the Note field in the ActivityLog table:

```
declare @Note varchar(2000),
        @chvErrorCode varchar(20),
        @ErrorDesc varchar(8000)


Select @Note = Note from ActivityLog where LogId = 3721
exec master..xp_sscanf @Note,
                        'Error(%s): %s',
                        @chvErrorCode output,
                        @ErrorDesc output


Select @chvErrorCode, @ErrorDesc
```

# MAIL

SQL Server has the capability to interact with administrators and users via e-mail. Usually, administrators are notified by SQL Server when something unusual happens. You can use the Alert and Operator mechanisms to implement such behavior.

This feature is an alternative to standard methods of processing errors such as recording critical errors in the Error Log. If SQL Server is in critical need of attention, and your operators do not possess pagers, SQL Server can send them e-mail. This approach is also practical for notifying administrators of successfully completed jobs.

Another common use for SQL Mail is for processing mail that contains database queries. Remote users can send queries to the SQL Server and have it return resultsets to them.

SQL Server can also send messages that include resultsets in the form of a report to one or more users. Although these resultsets are rather crude (just ASCII text), it is possible to envision and create an application that uses this capability to notify management when some change occurs in the database.

SQL Server 2000 and 7.0 contain two services that handle mail. The *MSSQLServer* service contains a component called *SQL Mail* that processes all extended stored procedures that use mail. SQL Server Agent contains a separate mail capability in a component often called *SQLAgentMail*.

We will not go into detail on the implementation and configuration of these services. Refer to SQL Server Books Online and the Microsoft Support Web site for more details.

# Extended Stored Procedures for Work with E-Mail

To implement custom behavior and features, developers need to use extended stored procedures and build their own code in the form of stored procedures. These stored procedures can be executed from a client application or in Job Scheduler. See Table 11-1 for a list of extended stored procedures for e-mail.

## xp_sendmail

This stored procedure can send a text message and/or query result to the list of recipients.

The following statement will notify an administrator that the transaction log is almost full:

```
EXEC xp_sendmail
    @recipients = 'SQLAdmin',
    @Message = 'The transaction log of Asset database is over 95% full.'
```

| Extended Stored Procedure | Use |
|---|---|
| xp_sendmail | Sends mail |
| xp_readmail | Returns a message in the form specified by output parameters |
| xp_findnextmsg | Finds a pointer to the next mail message |
| sp_processmail* | Reads incoming mail messages with queries in them. Returns the resultsets to the message senders |
| xp_deletemail | Deletes a message from the inbox |
| xp_startmail | Runs an administrative procedure that starts SQL Mail |
| xp_stopamail | Runs an administrative procedure that stops SQL Mail |

*Actually, sp_processmail is a Transact-SQL system stored procedure, not an extended stored procedure.

**Table 11-1.** Extended Stored Procedures for Work with E-Mail

**NOTE:** You cannot use e-mail addresses in the `@recipients` parameter. The stored procedure expects the name of a contact that is defined in the address book of an e-mail client application.

The next example sends the resultset of the query to the receiver. It could be a job that periodically lists all databases and their log usage and sends this information to the database administrator:

```
Exec xp_sendmail
    @recipients = 'SQLAdmin',
    @query = 'DBCC SQLPERF (LogSpace)'
```

A query can be returned in the form of an attached file:

```
Exec xp_sendmail
     @recipients = 'SQLAdmin; NetAdmin',
     @query = 'DBCC SQLPERF (LogSpace)',
     @subject = 'Transaction Log usage',
     @attach_results = 'TRUE'
```

Attachment files are also used to overcome the message size limit of 8,000 characters:

```
create table #Message(msg text)

Insert into #Message
values ('You can put more then 8000 chrs in a text field.')

Exec xp_sendmail
     @recipients = 'SQLAdmin; NetAdmin',
     @query = 'select * from #Message',
     @attach_results = 'TRUE'

drop #Message
```

## xp_readmail

This extended stored procedure can be used to

▼ Read a single message

▲ Return a list of e-mail messages and their contents

When the stored procedure is executed without a specified @messageid parameter, SQL Server will return an elaborate recordset with an elaborate list of messages. The resultset will contain fields to identify:

▼ Message ID

■ Subject

■ Body of message

■ Sender

- cc list
- bcc lists
- Attachments
- Date received
- Read status
- ▲ Message type

To read a single message, you have to specify the @messageid parameter. You get it either from the previous list or by using the xp_findnextmsg extended stored procedure.

```
EXEC @status = xp_readmail
    @msg_id = @intMessageId,
    @originator = @chvOriginator OUTPUT,
    @cc_list = @chvCC OUTPUT,
    @bcc_list = @chvBCC OUTPUT,
    @subject = @chvSubject OUTPUT,
    @message = @query OUTPUT
```

Unfortunately, this extended stored procedure can read messages only in segments that are not longer than 255 characters. Two parameters control where to start reading and the length of the message. Using them, you can implement a loop that will read the whole message. See SQL Server Books Online for an example of such a procedure.

## sp_processmail

This system stored procedure reads e-mail messages from the inbox, executes the queries specified in them, and returns a resultset to the sender and all recipients specified on the cc list. It is usually used internally within a job that is periodically executed on the SQL Server.

The following statement can be placed in the Job Scheduler and executed periodically to process mail that contains the string 'Asset' in the subject against the Asset database. A resultset is returned in the form of a comma-separated value (CSV) attachment file:

```
exec sp_processmail @Subject = 'Asset',
                     @filetype = 'CSV',
                     @separator = ',',
                     @dbuse =   'Asset'
```

This stored procedure uses xp_readmail, xp_deletemail, xp_findnextmsgl, and xp_sendmail to process messages.

*TIP:* Open this stored procedure and study its code. It is a good example of Transact-SQL code.

# DATABASE DEPLOYMENT

The problem that you will face relatively often is that, while you develop your database (and application) in a development environment, you must deploy the database somewhere else. When you work with a file-database system like Access, this is not a big issue. You usually create a setup program for your client application, and your .mdb file is just one more file installed on the client computer.

When you are working in a client/server environment, you might decide that you will not use an automated procedure to install the database server. Traditionally, RDBMS installation is perceived as complicated, and your customer will understand that you need to send an administrator (or a couple of them) to set up the environment. Unfortunately, this has not always been the case.

## A Long Time Ago, in an Environment Not So Far Away...

Whether administrators used a manual or automatic procedure in earlier versions of SQL Server (before 7.0), they had to use many tricks to transfer a database from one server to another. Sometimes it was easy and all that was needed was to use Enterprise Manager to transfer objects (one or more times). Unfortunately, previous versions of SQL Server required that dependent objects be present on the server when a new object was created. The transfer of objects often failed because of that requirement.

Some database developers collected and maintained sets of scripts that could be reused to create database objects in the right order.

Another solution was based on creating a backup of the database on a development server and then restoring the database on a production server. Unfortunately, this solution needed some administrator intervention to recreate links between server logins and database users.

## Now

SQL Server (after version 7.0) has changed all that. Anybody can perform an installation of SQL Server, and usually there are no problems. SQL Server 7.0 and 2000 even administer themselves pretty well, and there is seldom a need for DBA intervention.

In fact, Microsoft SQL Server Personal Edition and Desktop Engine (MSDE) are designed to be deployed on client computers—for example, in a distributed environment. This means that you need to create a setup program to allow easy deployment on a large number of client computers. Such a program has to cover installation of both SQL Server and your database. A couple of new features are designed to overcome problems in this area.

The installation of both SQL Server and MSDE can be performed unattended. You can even include MSDE setup files in your setup programs.

Deferred Name Resolution is a new feature of SQL Server that allows a database object (such as a stored procedure) to be created even if dependent objects (such as tables or other stored procedures) are not yet in the database. This feature helps if you want to create a Transact-SQL script to recreate all database objects or when you use DTS to transfer a complete database between connected servers.

You can even copy database files from a development server to a production server. Naturally, it is not quite as simple as that. Before you can copy database files, you should detach the database from the server, and when a file is copied to the production server, you should attach it to the server. To detach the Asset database, you can use the following script:

```
EXEC sp_detach_db 'Asset'
```

SQL Server checks the integrity of the database, flushes everything that is in memory to disk, and stops further changes to the database.

You can then copy the database files (in this case, Asset.mdf and Asset_log.ldf) from the \mssql\data folder to a data folder on the target server. To attach the Asset database, you can use

```
EXEC sp_attach_db @dbname = 'Asset',
                  @filename1 = 'c:\Program Files\Microsoft SQL',
                            + 'Server\mssql\data\Asset.mdf'
                  @filename2 = 'c:\Program Files\Microsoft SQL'
                            + 'Server\mssql\data\Asset_log.ldf'
```

If your database consists of more files, simply add them to the list of parameters. But if your database contains just one data file, you can use an alternative command:

```
EXEC sp_attach_single_file_db @dbname = 'Asset',
                              @physname = 'c:\mssql7\data\Asset.mdf'
```

You can execute these Transact-SQL statements manually in one of the administrative tools or from the setup program. The setup program can use the command prompt utility isql.exe to run a script file or use ADO to execute the script.

Unfortunately, this technique will corrupt links between server logins and database users. Server logins are stored in the master database; on different servers, different logins will have different IDs. Database users are stored in the user database. One of its parameters is the ID of the login to which they are attached. However, that ID refers to a different login on the production server. The simplest ways to handle this problem are either to create all users again using Enterprise Manager or a script that you have prepared in advance, or to use roles instead of users as the foundation of your security solution. See the discussion about security in the following section for more information. SQL Server offers another solution to this problem— see "Synchronization of Login and User Names" later in this chapter.

A new feature found in SQL Server 2000 is the Database Copy Wizard. You can use it to copy (or move) a database on a known (production, testing, or some other) server. Behind the scenes, the wizard uses stored procedures for detaching and attaching the database. It also contains features for copying logins, error messages, jobs, and system stored procedures.

# SECURITY

Implementing security on SQL Server is not difficult, but the developer or administrator has to have a good understanding of its security architecture before he or she selects and implements a security solution.

## Security Architecture

A user (a person or program) has to go through four levels of security before performing an action on a database object:

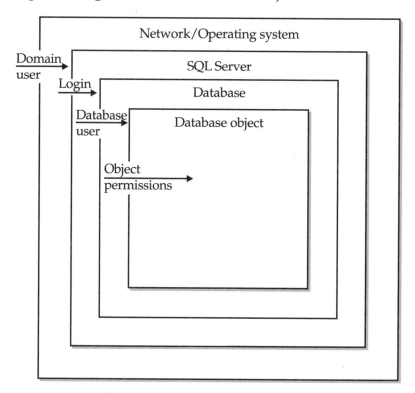

## Network/OS access

A user needs access to the client computer, operating system, and network on which the server is located. Usually, this access is the responsibility of technical support specialists or network administrators. However, in smaller environments, this responsibility may fall to a DBA or developer instead.

## Server Access

The first level of security that pertains strictly to SQL Server allows a client to access a server. This security is always the responsibility of database administrators.

SQL Server supports three security models:

▼ SQL Server Authentication

■ Windows NT/2000 Authentication

▲ Mixed mode—SQL Server and Windows NT/2000 Authentication

The *SQL Server Authentication* model requires a *login* and password from each user. These may be different from his or her network login and password and they may be different from one SQL Server to another. This model was the first to be developed; it was implemented by Sybase. Before SQL Server 7.0, it was called *standard security*. In fact, in SQL Server 7.0 and SQL Server 2000, it is not possible to configure a server to work in this mode only. If SQL Server Authentication is needed, the DBA should configure the server to use Mixed model security.

*Windows NT/2000 Authentication* was introduced by Microsoft. It allows SQL Server logins and passwords to be based on Windows NT network logins and passwords. This practice is easier for both the user (who has to remember only one login and password combination) and the administrator (who can manage all passwords centrally). Before SQL Server 7.0, it was called *integrated security*.

*Mixed model—SQL Server and Windows NT/2000 Authentication* is a combination of the previous two models. It allows some users to log in with their network accounts while other users use their SQL Server logins.

## Database Access

Access to the server does not provide the user with access to the database. An administrator has to assign a database to a login in one of the following manners:

▼ The administrator creates a *database user* that corresponds to the login in each database to which the user needs access.

■ The administrator configures a database to treat a login/database user as a member of a *database role*. Such a user inherits all permissions from the role.

▲ The administrator sets a login to use one of the *default user accounts: guest* or *database owner (dbo)*.

Once access to a database has been granted, the user can see all database objects, because the object definitions are stored in system tables to which every user has read access.

## Permissions

Permissions are the final level of SQL Server security. In order to have access to user-defined database objects, a user has to have *permissions* to perform actions on them. There are three types of permissions in SQL Server:

▼ *Object permissions* allow a user to read and change data and execute stored procedures.

■ *Statement permissions* allow a user to create and manage database objects.

▲ *Implied permissions* allow members of fixed roles and owners of database objects to perform activities that are not part of the object or statement Permissions.

**Roles**    Users can be granted permissions individually or as members of a *database role*. Roles, introduced in Microsoft SQL Server 7.0, are equivalent to groups in Windows NT or roles in Microsoft Transaction Server.

In earlier versions, a user could belong to only one SQL Server group. This restriction led to some pretty unrefined security solutions.

A user can now be a member of many database roles. Therefore, roles can be created to provide sophisticated access to needed functionality and information.

**Object Permissions**   The following table indicates which object permissions are applicable to which database objects:

| | Table | View | Stored Procedure | User-Defined Function | Column |
|---|---|---|---|---|---|
| Select | ✓ | ✓ | | | ✓ |
| Update | ✓ | ✓ | | | ✓ |
| Insert | ✓ | ✓ | | | |
| Delete | ✓ | ✓ | | | |
| Reference | ✓ | | | | ✓ |
| Execute | | | ✓ | ✓ | |

Database users can be given *Select, Update, Insert,* and *Delete* permissions to tables and views. This access level means that the user can read, write, delete, or change data in the respective tables or views. *Reference* permission allows a user to use a foreign key constraint to validate an entry to a column or table. Permissions to select, update, and reference can also be handled at the column level.

To access a stored procedure or a user-defined function, a user has to have *Execute* permission on it.

**Statement Permissions**   Database users can be granted the following permissions to create and manage other databases or database objects:

▼ Create Database

■ Create Table

■ Create View

■ Create Default

■ Create Rule

■ Backup Database

▲ Backup Log

## Implementing Security

You can implement a security solution using Enterprise Manager or system and extended stored procedures. Security stored procedures can also be used to manage security or implement some additional security features from a client application.

### Selection of Security Model

You select a security model in the SQL Server Properties dialog box:

To open this dialog, select Tools | SQL Server Configuration Properties.

## Managing Logins

To create a login, expand the Security branch of the SQL Server in Enterprise Manager, then right-click Logins and select New Login from the pop-up menu. To manage an existing login, right-click the login in the list pane and select Properties from the pop-up menu. The application opens the SQL Server Login Properties dialog box to enable you to manage login properties. You can select a name and type of login, password, default database and language, and membership in Server Roles:

The Database Access tab controls the databases the user can access and the user's membership in roles:

You can also grant logins using stored procedures. You can use sp_grantlogin to create a login on SQL Server. To give a Windows user access to a SQL Server, only the name of the user is required as a parameter:

```
exec sp_grantlogin 'Accounting\TomB'
```

However, when you create a login for SQL Server, you usually specify an authentication password and a default database as well:

```
exec sp_grantlogin 'TomB', 'password', 'Asset'
```

## Granting Database Access

As we have shown, database access can be granted to a login during the login's creation. There is also a way to grant access to additional databases after the login has been created. Database users can be managed from the Users node of a database in Enterprise Manager. You can both manage existing users and create new users.

Login names have to be selected from the list box. The User Name is set by default to the name of the login. This default is not required, but it simplifies user management. In the Database Role Membership section, you check all databases to which you want to grant the user membership:

You can perform the same operation from Transact-SQL. To grant access to the database, use sp_grantdbaccess:

```
exec sp_grantdbaccess 'TomB', 'TomB'
```

You can review access using sp_helpusers and revoked using sp_revokedbaccess.

To assign a user to a user-defined database role, you issue a command such as

```
exec sp_addrolemember 'TomB', 'Management'
```

You can review membership using sp_helprolemember and revoke it using sp_droprolemember. You can create roles using sp_addrole:

```
exec sp_addrole 'Management'
```

You can remove roles using sp_droprole. To view a list of roles, use sp_helpfixeddbroles and sp_helproles.

## Assigning Permissions

The system of permissions controls user and role access to database objects and statements. Permissions can exist in one of following three states:

▼   Granted

■   Denied

▲   Revoked

*Granted* means that a user has permission to use an object or statement. *Denied* means that a user is not allowed to use a statement or object, even if the user has previously inherited permission (that is, he is member of a role that has permission granted). Physically, a record is stored in the sysprotects table for each user (or role) and object (or statement) for which permission has been granted or denied.

When a permission is *Revoked*, records that were stored for that security account (that is, the records granting or revoking permissions) are removed from the sysprotects table.

Because of their physical implementation, permissions are cumulative. For example, a user can receive some permissions from one role and missing permissions from some other role. Or, the user can lose some permissions that have been granted to all other members of a role.

You can control statement permissions from the Permissions tab of a database's Properties dialog. You can set object permissions using the Permissions button in a database object's Properties dialog. In both cases, you see a list of users and roles:

An administrator can grant (☑), deny (☐), or revoke (☒) permissions.

**Grant Statement** To grant statement permission, an administrator can issue a `Grant` statement with the following syntax:

```
Grant {ALL | statement_name_1
[, statement_name_2, … statement_name_n]
     }
To account_1[, account_2, … account_n]
```

To grant object permission, an administrator can issue a `Grant` statement with the following syntax:

```
Grant {All [Privileges]| permission_1[,permission_2, … permission_n]}
{
    [column_1, column_2, … column_n] ON {table | view }
    | On {table | view } [column_1, column_2, … column_n]
    | On {stored_procedure }
}
To account_1[, account_2, … account_n]
[With Grant Option]
As {group | role}
```

The following statement allows JohnS (SQL Server login) and TomB from the Accounting domain (Windows domain user) to create a table in the current database:

```
Grant Create Table
To JohnS, [Accounting\TomB]
```

The following statement allows members of the AssetOwners role to view, store, delete, and change records in the Inventory table:

```
Grant Select, Insert, Update, Delete
On Inventory
To AssetOwners
```

**Deny Statement**   The Deny statement is used to negate permissions. Its syntax is basically the same as the syntax of the Grant statement (except that the keyword Deny is used).

The following statement prevents TomB from the Accounting domain from creating a database:

```
Deny Create Database
To [Accounting\TomB]
```

The following statement prevents JohnS from deleting and changing records from the Inventory table, even though he has inherited rights to view, store, delete, and change records as a member of the AssetOwners role:

```
Deny Update, Delete
On Inventory
To JohnS
```

**Revoke Statement**   The Revoke statement is used to deactivate statements that have granted or denied permissions. It has the same syntax as the Grant and Deny statements (except that the keyword Revoke is used).

It is easy to understand that permission can be removed using this statement. It is a little more challenging to understand how a permission can be granted by revoking it. Let's review an example in which a user JohnS is a member of the AssetOwners role, which has permission to insert, update, select, and delete records from the Inventory table.

```
exec sp_addrolemember 'JohnS', 'AssetOwners'
```

The Administrator then decides to deny JohnS permission to delete and update records from Inventory:

```
Deny Update, Delete
On Inventory
To JohnS
```

After a while the administrator issues the following statement:

```
Revoke Update, Delete
On Inventory
To JohnS
```

In effect, this command has granted Update and Delete permission on the Inventory table to JohnS.

Since the `Revoke` statement removes records from the sysprotects table in the current database, the effect of the `Revoke` statement is to return permissions to their original state. Naturally, this means that the user will not have access to the object (or statement). In that respect, its effect is similar to the `Deny` statement. However, there is a major difference between revoked and denied permissions: the `Revoke` statement does not prevent permissions from being granted in the *future*.

## Synchronization of Login and User Names

In the section earlier in this chapter called "Database Deployment," I mentioned the common problem of mismatches between users and logins when databases are copied from one server to another. The problem is a product of the fact that records in the sysusers table of the copied database point to the records in the syslogins table with matching `loginid` field. One solution is to create and manage a script that recreates logins and users on the new server after a database is copied.

SQL Server also offers the sp_change_users_login procedure. You can use it to display mapping between user and login:

```
exec sp_change_users_login @Action = 'Report',
                           @UserNamePattern = 'B%'
```

You can set a login manually for a single user:

```
exec sp_change_users_login @Action = 'Update_one',
                           @UserNamePattern = 'TomB',
                           @LoginName = 'TomB'
```

SQL Server can also match database users to logins with the same name:

```
exec sp_change_users_login @Action = 'Auto_Fix',
                           @UserNamePattern = '%'
```

For each user, SQL Server tries to find a login with the same name and to set the login ID.

**TIP:** sp_change_users_login with `Auto_Fix` does a decent job, but the careful DBA should inspect the results of this operation.

## Managing Application Security Using Stored Procedures, User-Defined Functions, and Views

When a permission is granted on a complex object like a stored procedure, a user-defined function, or a view, a user does not need to have permissions on the objects or statements inside it.

We can illustrate this characteristic in the following example:

```
Create Database Test
Go


sp_addlogin @loginame = 'AnnS',
            @passwd = 'password',
            @defdb = 'test'
GO
```

```
Use Test

Exec sp_grantdbaccess @loginame = 'AnnS',
                       @name_in_db = 'AnnS'
Go

Create Table aTable(
     Id int identity(1,1),
     Description Varchar(20)
     )
Go

Create Procedure ListATable
as
     Select * from aTable
go

Create Procedure InsertATable
     @Desc varchar(20)
as
     Insert Into aTable (Description)
     Values (@Desc)
Go

Deny Select, Insert, Update, Delete
On Atable
To Public

Grant Execute
On InsertATable
To Public

Grant Execute
On ListATable
To Public
Go
```

A table is created along with two stored procedures for viewing and inserting records into it. All database users are prevented from using the table directly but granted permission to use the stored procedures.

**NOTE:** All database users are automatically members of the Public role. Whatever is granted or denied to the Public role is automatically granted or denied to all database users.

After this script is executed, you can log in as AnnS in Query Analyzer and try to access the table directly and through stored procedures. Figure 11-4 illustrates such attempts.

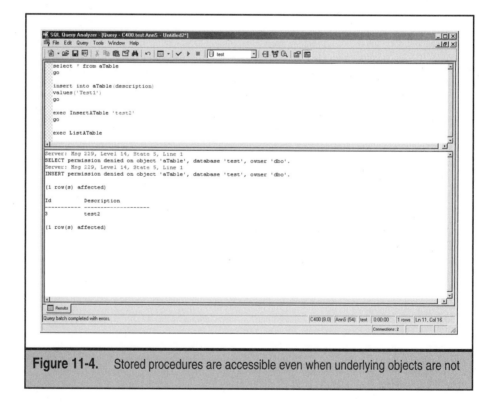

**Figure 11-4.** Stored procedures are accessible even when underlying objects are not

Stored procedures, user-defined functions, and views are important tools for implementing sophisticated security solutions in a database. Each user should have permissions to perform activities tied to the business functions for which he or she is responsible and to view only related information. It is also easier to manage security in a database on a functional level than on the data level. Therefore, client applications should not be able to issue ad hoc queries against tables in a database. Instead, they should execute stored procedures.

Users should be grouped in roles by the functionality they require, and roles should be granted execute permissions to related stored procedures. Since roles are stored only in the current database, using them helps you avoid problems that occur during the transfer of the database from the development to the production environment (see "Database Deployment" earlier in the chapter).

**NOTE:** There is one exception to the rule we have just described. If the owner of the stored procedure is not the owner of the database objects by the stored procedure, SQL Server will check the object's permissions on each underlying database object. Usually, this is not an issue because all objects are owned by dbo.

# Managing Application Security Using a Proxy User

Security does not have to be implemented on SQL Server. If the application is developed using three-tier architecture, objects can use roles, users, and other security features of Microsoft Transaction Server (on Windows NT) or Component Services (in Windows 2000) to implement security. Security is sometimes also implemented inside the client application.

In both cases, database access is often accomplished through a single database login and user. Such a user is often called a *proxy user*.

**NOTE:** The worst such solution occurs when the client application developer completely ignores SQL Server security and achieves database access using the *sa* login. I have seen two variants on this solution.

One occurs when the developer hard-codes the sa password inside an application. The administrator is then prevented from changing the password and the security of the entire SQL Server is exposed.

The other occurs when a developer stores login information in a file or Registry so that it can be changed later. Unfortunately, it can also be read by unauthorized persons, and again, SQL Server security is compromised.

## Managing Application Security Using Application Roles

*Application roles* are a new feature that can be used in SQL Server 7.0 and SQL Server 2000. These are designed to implement security for particular applications. They are different from standard database roles in that

▼ Application roles require passwords to be activated.

■ They do not have members. Users access a database via an application. The application contains the name of the role and its password.

▲ SQL Server ignores all other user permissions when the application role is activated.

To create an application role, administrators should use sp_addapprole:

```
Exec sp_addapprole @rolename = 'Accounting', @password = 'password'
```

Permissions are managed using Grant, Deny, and Revoke statements in the usual manner.

A client application (or a middle-tier object) should first log into SQL Server in the usual manner and then activate the application role using sp_setapprole:

```
Exec sp_setapprole @rolename = 'Accounting', @password = 'password'
```

> **NOTE:**   Solutions based on application roles are good replacements for solutions based on proxy users. However, my recommendation is to use the solution described in "Managing Application Security Using Stored Procedures, User-Defined Functions, and Views" earlier in the chapter.

# SUMMARY

The primary function of SQL Server is to serve clients with answers to their queries. However, it has become the norm in development environments to access programs and procedures implemented in other languages and installed in other environments.

Earlier versions of SQL Server were able to run operating system commands and programs from the command shell and to return output in the form of a resultset. Extended stored procedures gave developers the opportunity to write and use code written in C to implement things that were not possible in Transact-SQL statements.

One of the interesting new features in SQL Server is the ability to execute methods and use the properties of COM (OLE Automation) objects. This feature opens a whole new world to Transact-SQL code. It is possible to run complicated numeric calculations, notify administrators using graphics and/or sound, and initiate processes on other machines, to name but a few applications. We have also demonstrated in this chapter how to create such COM objects in Visual Basic.

The standard ways that SQL Server uses to notify administrators of events that have occurred on a SQL Server is by pager and by e-mail. SQL Server can also receive and answer queries by e-mail. It is possible to set and use these features from Enterprise Manager, but in cases where more control is needed, developers can use system stored procedures and extended stored procedures.

An important channel for communications with users and administrators today is the Web. SQL Server can create Web pages based on the contents of database tables or generated resultsets. SQL Server includes a wizard to generate common Web pages, but it also includes a set of stored procedures for creating and executing Web tasks. The result of the wizard and system stored procedures are pages that are far from perfect but that can be used to get and display results quickly.

System and user-defined stored procedures can be used to perform all administrative activities in SQL Server. Everything you can do through Enterprise Manager can also be done using stored procedures. It is also possible to create and execute scheduled jobs that consist of steps written in Transact-SQL, operating system commands, or ActiveX Script.

One of the final activities in the database development cycle is the deployment of a database (developed in a test environment) into a production environment. In the past, developers and administrators had to use various tricks to accomplish this migration, but SQL Server 2000 and SQL Server 7.0 treat database files like any other files. It is possible to detach them, copy them, and then attach them to another server.

Stored procedures are an important tool for managing application, database, and SQL Server security. On the system level, you can use system or custom stored procedures to manage logins, users, roles, and their permissions. On the application level, security is easiest to design and manage when functionality is implemented as stored procedures, user-defined functions, and views, and when groups of users are granted access to the appropriate functionality through database roles.

## EXERCISES

1.  Create a trigger on the ActivityLog table that will send e-mail to the administrator when any record that contains the word "Critical" as the first word of a Note is inserted.

2.  Create a Transact-SQL batch that will compress files in the backup folder and transfer them to a drive on another machine.

3.  Create a Transact-SQL batch that will create a scheduled job for compressing backup files. The job should be scheduled to run once a day.

# CHAPTER 12

# XML Support in SQL Server 2000

Microsoft SQL Server has become a giant among the select group of enterprise-ready Relational Database Management Systems, but as with those other RDBMSs, its roots are in pre-Internet solutions.

The Internet revolution has highlighted a set of old tactical and strategic challenges for the Microsoft SQL Server development team. These challenges include

▼ Storing the large amounts of textual information that Web-based, user-friendly database applications require

■ Delivering that textual (and other) stored information to the Web

▲ Sharing information with other departments and organizations that do not use the same RDBMS system

In earlier editions of SQL Server, Microsoft has addressed these issues with such features as Full Text Search, the Web Publishing Wizard, DTS, ADO, and OLE DB. SQL Server 2000 introduces XML compatibility—the new holy grail of the computing industry and the latest attempt to tackle the same old problems.

# XML (R)EVOLUTION

To communicate with customers in today's rich-content world, you need to provide them with information. Until very recently, such information was inevitably encapsulated in proprietary, document-based formats that are not shared easily. For example, word processor documents are optimized for delivery on paper, and relational databases are often structured and normalized in formats unsuitable to end users.

The first step in the right direction was *Standard Generalized Markup Language (SGML)*. Although it was designed by Charles Goldfarb in the late 1960s, it became the international standard for defining markup languages in 1986 after the creation of the ISO standard. In the late 1980s, companies and government agencies started to adopt this tag-based language. It allowed them to create and manage paper documentation in a way that was easy to share with others.

Then in the 1990s, the Web appeared on the scene and our collective focus shifted from isolated islands of personal computers and local networks to a global network of shared information. SGML's tagged structure would seem to make it a perfect candidate to lead the Internet revolution, but the complexity of SGML makes it difficult to work with and unsuited to Web application design.

Instead of SGML, the developers of the Internet adopted the *Hypertext Markup Language* (*HTML*), a simple markup language used to create hypertext documents that are portable from one platform to another. HTML is a simplified subset of SGML. It was defined in 1991 by Tim Berners-Lee as a way to organize, view, and transfer scientific documents across different platforms. It uses the *Hypertext Transfer Protocol* (*HTTP*) to transfer information over the Internet. This new markup language was an exciting development and soon found nonscientific applications. Eventually, companies and users started to use it as a platform for e-commerce—the processing of business transactions without the exchange of paper-based business documents.

Unfortunately, HTML has some disadvantages. One of the biggest is a result of its main purpose. HTML is designed to describe only how information should appear—that is, its format. It was not designed to define the syntax (logical structure) or semantics (meaning) of a document. It could make a document readable to a user, but it required that user to interact with the document and interpret it. The computer itself could not parse the document because the necessary "meta-information" (literally, information about the information) was not included with the document.

Another problem with HTML is that it is not extensible. It is not possible to create new tags. HTML is also a "standard" that exists in multiple versions—and multiple proprietary implementations. Web developers know that they have to test even their static HTML pages in all of the most popular browsers (and often in several versions of each), because each browser (and each version of each browser) implements this "standard" somewhat differently. Different development toolsets support different versions of this standard (and often different features within a single standard).

In 1996, a group working under the auspices of the World Wide Web Consortium (W3C) created a new standard tagged language called *eXtensible Markup Language* (*XML*). It was designed to address some of the problems of HTML and SGML. XML is a standardized document formatting language, a subset of SGML, that enables a publisher to create a single document source that can be viewed, displayed, or printed in a variety of ways. As is the case with HTML, XML is primarily designed for use on the Internet. HTML, however, is designed primarily to address document formatting issues, while XML addresses issues relating to data and object structure. XML provides a standard mechanism for any document builder to define new XML tags within any XML document. Its features lower the barriers for creation of integrated, multiplatform, application-to-application protocols.

# INTRODUCTION TO XML

In today's world, words such as "tag," "markup," "element," "attributes," and "schema" are buzzwords that you can hear anywhere (well, at least in the IT industry), but what do these terms mean in the context of markup languages?

## Introduction to Markup Languages

In a broader sense, a *markup* is anything that you place within a document that provides additional meaning or additional information. For example, in this book we use italic font to emphasize each new phrase or concept that we define or introduce. I have a habit of using a highlighter when I am reading books. Each time I use my highlighter, I change the format of the text as a means of helping me find important segments later.

Markups usually define

▼ Formatting

■ Structure

▲ Meaning

A reader has to have an implicit set of rules for placing markups in a document—otherwise those markups are meaningless to him. A *markup language* is a set of rules that defines

▼ What constitutes a markup

▲ What a markup means

## Building Blocks of Markup Languages

The syntax of markup languages such as SGML, HTML, and XML is based on tags, elements, and attributes.

A *tag* is a markup language building block that consists of delimiters (angled brackets) and the text between them:

```
<TITLE>
```

An *element* is a markup language building block that consists of a pair of tags and the content between them:

```
<TITLE>SQL Server 2000 Stored Procedure Programming</TITLE>
```

Each element has an *opening tag* and a *closing tag*. The text between these tags is called the *content* of the element.

An *attribute* is a building block in the form of a name/value pair that delimits a tag:

```
<font size="2">
```

Okay, let's say that you have created a document and that you have marked up some parts of it. Now what? You can share it with others. They will use something called a *user agent* to review the document. In a broader context, a user agent could be a travel agent that helps a customer buy tickets for a trip. However, in the IT industry, a user agent is a program that understands the markup language and presents information to an end user. An example of such a program is a Web browser designed to present documents created using HTML.

# XML

Let's take a look at a simple example of an XML document:

```
<Inventory>
  <Asset Inventoryid="5">
    <Equipment>Toshiba Portege 7020CT</Equipment>
    <EquipmentType>Notebook</EquipmentType>
    <LocationId>2</LocationId>
    <StatusId>1</StatusId>
    <LeaseId>1234</LeaseId>
    <LeaseScheduleId>1414</LeaseScheduleId>
    <OwnerId>83749271</OwnerId>
    <Cost>6295.00</Cost>
    <AcquisitionType>Lease</AcquisitionType>
  </Asset>
</Inventory>
```

## Elements

An XML document must contain one or more elements. One of them is not part of any other element and therefore it is called the document's *root element*. It must be uniquely named. In the preceding example, the root element is named `Inventory`.

Each element can contain one or more other elements. In the preceding example, the `Inventory` element contains one `Asset` element. The `Asset` element also contains other elements. The `Equipment` element contains just its content—the text string "Toshiba Portege 7020CT".

Unlike HTML, XML is *case sensitive*. Therefore, `<Asset>`, `<asset>`, and `<ASSET>` are different tag names.

It is possible to define an *empty element*. Such elements can be displayed using standard opening and closing tags:

```
<Inventory></Inventory>
```

or using special notation:

```
<Inventory/>
```

If an element contains attributes but no content, an empty element is an efficient way to write it.

```
<Asset Inventoryid="5"/>
```

An element can have more than one attribute. The following example shows an empty element that contains nine attributes:

```
<Asset Inventoryid="12" EquipmentId="1" LocationId="2" StatusId="1"
LeaseId="1" LeaseScheduleId="1" OwnerId="1" Lease="100.0000"
AcquisitionTypeID="2"/>
```

You are not allowed to repeat an attribute in the same tag. The following example shows a syntactically incorrect element:

```
<Inventory Inventoryid="12" Inventoryid="13"/>
```

## Processing Instructions

An XML document often starts with a tag that is called a *processing instruction*. For example, the following processing instruction notifies the reader that the document it belongs to is written in XML that complies with version 1.0.

```
<?xml version="1.0"?>
```

A processing instruction has the following format:

```
<?name data?>
```

The *name* portion identifies the processing instruction to the application that is processing the XML document. Names must start with XML. The *data* portion that follows is optional. It could be used by the application.

**TIP:**  It is not required but is recommended that you start an XML document with a processing instruction that explicitly identifies that document as an XML document defined using a specified version of the standard.

## Document Type Definition and Document Type Declaration

We mentioned earlier that markups are meaningless if it is not possible to define rules for

▼ What constitutes a markup

▲ What a markup means

A *Document Type Definition (DTD)* is a type of document that is often used to define such rules for XML documents. The DTD contains descriptions and constraints (naturally, not Transact-SQL constraints) for each element (such as the order of element attributes and membership). User agents can use the DTD file to verify that an XML document complies with its rules.

The DTD can be an external file that is referenced by an XML document:

```
<!DOCTYPE Inventory SYSTEM "Inventory.dtd">
```

or it can be part of the XML document itself:

```
<?xml version="1.0"?>
<!DOCTYPE Inventory [
<!ELEMENT Inventory (Asset+)>
<!ELEMENT Asset (EquipmentId, LocationId, StatusId, LeaseId,
                 LeaseScheduleId, OwnerId, Cost, AcquisitionTypeID)>
<!ATTLIST Asset Inventoryid CDATA #IMPLIED>
<!ELEMENT EquipmentId (#PCDATA)>
<!ELEMENT LocationId (#PCDATA)>
<!ELEMENT StatusId (#PCDATA)>
<!ELEMENT LeaseId (#PCDATA)>
<!ELEMENT LeaseScheduleId (#PCDATA)>
<!ELEMENT OwnerId (#PCDATA)>
<!ELEMENT Cost (#PCDATA)>
<!ELEMENT AcquisitionTypeID (#PCDATA)>
]>
<Inventory>
  <Asset Inventoryid="5">
    <EquipmentId>1</EquipmentId>
    <LocationId>2</LocationId>
```

```
    <StatusId>1</StatusId>
    <LeaseId>1</LeaseId>
    <LeaseScheduleId>1</LeaseScheduleId>
    <OwnerId>1</OwnerId>
    <Cost>1295.00</Cost>
    <AcquisitionTypeID>1</AcquisitionTypeID>
  </Asset>
</Inventory>
```

The DTD document does not have to be stored locally. A reference can include a URL or URI that provides access to the document:

```
<!DOCTYPE Inventory SYSTEM "http://www.trigonblue.com/dtds/Inventory.dtd">
```

A *universal resource identifier (URI)* identifies a persistent resource on the Internet. It is a number or name that is globally unique. A special type of URI is a *universal resource locator (URL)* that defines a location of a resource on the Internet. A URI is more general because it should find the closest copy of a resource or because it would eliminate problems in finding a resource that was moved from one server to another.

## XML Comments and CDATA sections

It is possible to write comments within an XML document. The basic syntax of the comment is

```
<!--commented text-->
```

Commented text can be any character string that does not contain two consecutive hyphens "--" and that does not end with a hyphen "-". Comments can stretch over more than one line:

```
<!-- This is a comment. -->
<!--
This is another comment.
-->
```

Comments cannot be part of any other tag:

```
<Order <!-- This is an illegal comment. --> OrderId = "123">
...
</Order>
```

You can use CDATA sections in XML documents to insulate blocks of text from XML parsers. For example, if you are writing an article about XML and you want also to store it in the form of an XML document, you can use CDATA sections to force XML parsers to ignore markups with sample XML code.

The basic syntax of a CDATA section is

```
<![CDATA[string]]>
```

The *string* can be any character string that does not contain "]]>" in sequence. CDATA sections can occur anywhere in an XML document where character data is allowed.

```
<Example>
    <Text>
        <![CDATA[<Inventory Inventoryid="12"/>]]>
    </Text>
</Example>
```

## Character and Entity References

Like HTML and SGML, XML also includes a simple way to reference characters that do not belong to the ASCII character set. The syntax of a *character reference* is

```
&#NNNNN;
&#xXXXX;
```

The decimal (*NNNNN*) or hexadecimal (*XXXX*) code of the character must be preceded by "&#" or "&#x", respectively, and followed by a semicolon ";".

Entity references are used in XML to insert characters that would cause problems for the XML parser if they were inserted directly into the document. This type of reference is basically a mnemonic alternative to a character reference. There are five basic *entity references*:

| Entity | Meaning |
|--------|---------|
| &amp;  | &       |
| &apos; | '       |
| &lt;   | <       |
| &gt;   | >       |
| &quot; | "       |

Entity references are often used to represent characters with special meaning in XML. In the following example, entity references are used to prevent the XML parser from parsing the content of the <Text> tag:

```
<Example>
    <Text>
        &lt;Inventory Inventoryid="12"/&gt;
    </Text>
</Example>
```

## Structure of XML Documents

XML Documents consists of the three parts that you can see in the following illustration:

The first part of the document is called the *prolog* or *document type declaration* (not Document Type Definition). It is not required. It can contain processing instructions, a DTD, and comments. The *body* of the document contains the document's elements. The data in these elements is organized into a hierarchy of elements, their attributes, and their content. Sometimes an XML document contains an *epilog*, an optional part that can hold final comments, or processing instructions, or just white space.

## XML Document Quality

There are two levels of document quality in XML:

▼ Well-formed documents

▲ Valid documents

An XML document is said to be a *well-formed document* when

▼ There is one and only one root element.

■ All elements that are not empty are marked with start and end tags.

■ The order of the elements is hierarchical; that is, an element A that starts within an element B also ends within element B.

■ Attributes do not occur twice in one element.

▲ All entities used have been declared.

An XML document is said to be a *valid document* when

▼ The XML document is well-formed.

▲ The XML document complies with a specified DTD document.

The concept of a valid document has been imported to XML from SGML. In SGML all documents must be valid. XML is not so strict. It is possible to use an XML document even without a DTD document. If the user agent knows how to use the XML document without the DTD, then the DTD need not even be sent over the Net. It just increases traffic and ties up bandwidth.

## XML Schema

DTD is not the only type of document that can store rules for an XML document. Several companies (including Microsoft) have submitted a proposal to W3C for an alternative type of metadata document called an *XML schema*. In fact, there are other proposed standards for the same use, which are all referred to as XML schemas. These are the major differences between a DTD and an XML schema:

▼ XML schemas support datatypes and range constraints.

■ The language in which XML schemas are written is XML. Developers do not have to read an additional language as they do with DTDs.

▲ XML schemas support namespaces (XML entities for defining context).

## XML–Data Reduced (XDR)

At the time of this writing, the W3C had not yet adopted the XML schema as a standard. Microsoft has implemented a variation of XML schema syntax called *XML–Data Reduced (XDR)* in the MSXML parser that is delivered as a part of Internet Explorer 5.

Microsoft has promised complete support for the XML schema when the W3C awards it Recommended status, but for the time being, more and more tools and organizations are using XML–Data Reduced. It is also important to note that Microsoft uses XDR in BizTalk, one of the most important initiatives in the Web application market. It is an initiative intended to create e-commerce vocabularies for different vertical markets. SQL Server 2000 also uses XDR for its XML schema.

Let's review an example of an XML schema document:

```
<Schema name="Schema"
  xmlns="urn:schemas-microsoft-com:xml-data"
  xmlns:dt="urn:schemas-microsoft-com:datatypes">
<ElementType name="Inventory" content="empty" model="closed">
    <AttributeType name="Inventoryid" dt:type="i4"/>
```

```
        <AttributeType name="EquipmentId" dt:type="i4"/>
        <AttributeType name="LocationId" dt:type="i4"/>
        <AttributeType name="StatusId" dt:type="ui1"/>
        <AttributeType name="LeaseId" dt:type="i4"/>
        <AttributeType name="LeaseScheduleId" dt:type="i4"/>
        <AttributeType name="OwnerId" dt:type="i4"/>
        <AttributeType name="Rent" dt:type="fixed.14.4"/>
        <AttributeType name="Lease" dt:type="fixed.14.4"/>
        <AttributeType name="Cost" dt:type="fixed.14.4"/>
        <AttributeType name="AcquisitionTypeID" dt:type="ui1"/>
        <attribute type="Inventoryid"/>
        <attribute type="EquipmentId"/>
        <attribute type="LocationId"/>
        <attribute type="StatusId"/>
        <attribute type="LeaseId"/>
        <attribute type="LeaseScheduleId"/>
        <attribute type="OwnerId"/>
        <attribute type="Rent"/>
        <attribute type="Lease"/>
        <attribute type="Cost"/>
        <attribute type="AcquisitionTypeID"/>
    </ElementType>
</Schema>
```

This schema describes the structure of an XML document that contains Inventory information. The schema describes just one element. It is defined in the `<ElementType>` tag. The definition also specifies its *name* (`"Inventory"`), *content* (the tag is `"empty"` because all information will be carried in attributes), and content *model* (`"closed"`—it is not possible to add elements that are not specified in the schema).

The element contains multiple attributes. Each attribute is first *defined* in an `<AttributeType>` tag and then *instantiated* in an `<attribute>` tag:

```
    <AttributeType name="Cost" dt:type="fixed.14.4"/>
...
    <attribute type="Cost"/>
```

For each attribute, the schema defines a name and a datatype. You can see a list of acceptable datatypes in Appendix A.

The following listing shows an XML document that complies with the previous schema:

```
<Inventory xmlns="x-schema:Schema.xml"
           Inventoryid="5"
           EquipmentId="1"
           LocationId="2"
           StatusId="1"
           LeaseId="1"
           LeaseScheduleId="1"
           OwnerId="1"
           Cost="1295.0000"
           AcquisitionTypeID="1"/>
```

## Schema Constraints

Let's review schema attributes that can be used to declare elements and attributes. These can be classified as

▼ Element constraints

■ Attribute constraints

■ XML datatypes

▲ Group constraints

**Element Constraints**    Elements in a schema can be constrained using attributes of the `<ElementType>` tag:

▼ name

■ content

■ model

■ order

■ group

■ minOccurs

▲ maxOccurs

The *name* attribute defines the name of the subelement.
Possible values for the *content* attribute are listed in the Table 12-1.

| Content | Meaning |
|---|---|
| "textOnly" | Only text is allowed as content |
| "eltOnly" | Only other elements are allowed as content |
| "empty" | No content |
| "mixed" | Both text and elements are allowed |

**Table 12-1.**   Content Attribute Values

An important innovation in XML schemas (that was not available in DTDs) is the capability to add nondeclared elements and attributes to an XML document. By default, every element of every XML document has its *model* attribute set to "open". To prevent the addition of nondeclared elements and attributes, the *model* attribute has to be "closed".

It is also possible to define how many times a subelement can appear in its parent element using the *maxOccurs* and *minOccurs* attributes. Positive integer values and "*" (unlimited number) are allowed in the *maxOccurs* attribute, and "0" and positive integer values are allowed in the *minOccurs* attribute. The default value for minOccurs is "0". The default value for *maxOccurs* is "1", except that when the *content* attribute is "mixed", *maxOccurs* must be "*".

An *order* attribute specifies the order and quantity of subelements (see Table 12-2).

The default value for order is "seq" when the content attribute is set to "eltOnly" and "many" when the content attribute is set to "mixed".

**Attribute Constraints**   By their nature, attributes are more constrained than elements. For example, attributes do not have subelements (or subattributes), and it is not possible to have more than one instance of an attribute within the element.

| Order | Meaning |
|---|---|
| "seq" | Subelements must appear in the order listed in the schema. |
| "one" | Only one of the subelements listed in the schema can appear in the XML document. |
| "many" | Any number of subelements can appear in any order. |

**Table 12-2.**    Order Attribute Values of ElementType

The *required* attribute (constraint) in a schema specifies that the attribute is mandatory in XML documents that follow the schema. The *default* attribute (constraint) in a schema specifies the default value of the attribute in an XML document (the parser will use that value if an attribute is not present).

The schema can be set so that an attribute value is constrained to a set of predefined values:

```
<AttributeType name="status"
               dt:type="enumeration"
               dt:values="open in-process completed" />
```

**XML Datatypes**    The schema can also enforce the datatype of the attribute or element. Table A-2 in Appendix A lists datatypes and their meanings, and Table A-3 in Appendix A maps XML datatypes to SQL Server datatypes.

**Group Constraints**    The *group* element allows an author to apply certain constraints to a group of subelements. In the following example, only one price (rent, lease, or cost) can be specified for the Inventory element:

```
<Schema name="Schema" xmlns="urn:schemas-microsoft-com:xml-data"
 xmlns:dt="urn:schemas-microsoft-com:datatypes">
<ElementType name="Inventory" content="eltOnly"
```

```
            model="closed" order="many">
    <element type="Inventoryid"/>
    <element type="EquipmentId"/>
    <element type="LocationId"/>
    <element type="StatusId"/>
    <element type="LeaseId"/>
    <element type="LeaseScheduleId"/>
    <element type="OwnerId"/>
    <group order = "one">
       <element type="Rent"/>
       <element type="Lease"/>
       <element type="Cost"/>
    </group>
    <element type="AcquisitionTypeID"/>
</ElementType>
</Schema>
```

The *group* constraint accepts *order*, *minOccurs*, and *maxOccurs* attributes.

## XML Namespaces

Some entities from different areas of a document can have the same name. For example, you could receive a purchase order document that contains a <name> tag for the customer and a <name> tag for the reseller company. People reading this document would be able to distinguish them by their context. However, an application would need additional information to correctly interpret the data.

An answer to this problem is to create *XML namespaces* to provide the XML document with a vocabulary (that is, a context). After that, customer and company names can be referenced using a context prefix:

```
<contact:name>Tom Jones</contact:name>
<Company:name>Trigon Blue</Company:name>
```

Naturally, before these prefixes can be used, they have to be defined. The root element of the following document contains three attributes. Each of them specifies a namespace and a prefix used to reference it:

```
<PurchaseOrders
   xmlns:contact="http://www.trigonblue.com/schemas/Contact.xml"
   xmlns:Company="http://www.trigonblue.com/schemas/Company.xml"
   xmlns:dsig="http://dsig.org">
<PurchaseOrder>
   <Customer>
     <contact:name>Tom Jones</contact:name>
</Customer>
<PurchaseDate>2000-09-11</PurchaseDate>
<SalesOrganization>
     <Company:name>Trigon Blue</Company:name>
     <Company:DUNS>817282919</Company:DUNS>
     <Company:ID>1212</Company:ID>
   </SalesOrganization>
   <dsig:digital-signature>78901314</dsig:digital-signature>
  </PurchaseOrder>
</PurchaseOrders>
```

# XML Parsers and DOM

Applications (or user agents) that use XML documents can use proprietary procedures to access the data in them. Usually, such applications use special components called XML parsers. An *XML parser* is a program or component that loads the XML document into an internal hierarchical structure of nodes (see Figure 12-1) and provides access to the information stored in these nodes to other components or programs.

The XML *Document Object Model (DOM)* is a set of standard objects, methods, events, and properties used to access elements of an XML document. DOM is a standard that has received Recommended status from W3C. Different software vendors have created their own implementations of DOM so that you can use it from (almost) any programming language on (almost) any platform.

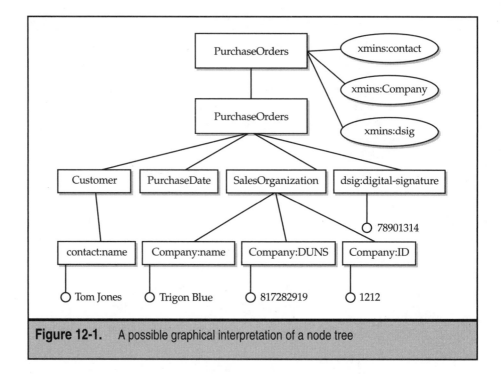

**Figure 12-1.** A possible graphical interpretation of a node tree

Microsoft has implemented DOM as a COM component called Microsoft.XMLDOM in msxml.dll. It is delivered, for example, with Internet Explorer 5, or you can download it separately from Microsoft's Web site. Developers can use it from any programming language that can access COM components or ActiveX objects such as Visual Basic, VBScript, Visual J++, Jscript, and Visual C++.

Nevertheless, it is unlikely that you will use it from Transact-SQL. Microsoft has built special tools for development in Transact-SQL. We will review them later in this chapter.

## Linking and Querying in XML

XML today represents more than a simple language for encoding documents. W3C is working on a whole other set of specifications for using information in XML documents. Specifications such as XLink, XPointer, XPath, and XQL allow querying, linking, and access to specific parts of an XML document.

This is a vast topic, and we will briefly review only XPointer and XPath, since they are used in SQL Server 2000.

## XPointer

The XPointer reference works in a fashion very similar to the HTML hyperlink. You can point to a segment of an XML document by appending an *XML fragment identifier* to the URI of the XML document. A fragment identifier is often enclosed in `xpointer()`. For example, the following pointer directs the parser to an element with the ID attribute set to "`Toshiba`" in the document at a specified location:

```
http://www.trigonblue.com/xml/Equipment.xml#xpointer(Toshiba)
```

The character "#" is a *fragment specifier*. It serves as a delimiter between the URI and the fragment identifier, and it specifies the way that the XML parser will render the target. In the preceding case, the parser renders the whole document to access only a specified fragment. To force the parser to parse only the specified fragment, you should use "|" as a fragment specifier:

```
http://www.trigonblue.com/xml/Equipment.xml|xpointer(Toshiba)
```

Use of the "|" fragment specifier is recommended, as it leads to reduced memory usage.

`xpointer()` is not always required. If a document has a schema that specifies the ID attribute of an element, you can omit the `xpointer()` and point to a fragment of the document using only the ID attribute value:

```
http://www.trigonblue.com/xml/Equipment.xml#Toshiba
```

*Child sequence fragment identifiers* use numbers to specify a fragment:

```
http://www.trigonblue.com/xml/Equipment.xml#/2/1/3
```

The preceding example should be interpreted as follows: "/"— start from the top element of the document; "2"—then go to the second child element of the top element; "1"—then go to the first subelement of that element; "3"—then go to the third subelement of that element.

Child sequence fragment identifiers do not have to start from the top element:

```
http://www.trigonblue.com/xml/Equipment.xml#Toshiba/1/3
```

In the preceding example, fragment identification starts from the element with its ID set to "Toshiba". The parser then finds its first subelement and points to its third subelement.

## XPath

The full XPointer syntax is built on the W3C XPath recommendation. XPath was originally built to be used by XPointer and XSLT (a language for transforming XML documents into other XML documents), but it has found application in other standards and technologies. We will see later how it is used by OpenXML in SQL Server 2000, but first let's examine its syntax.

*Location steps* are constructs used to select nodes in an XML document. They have the following syntax:

```
axis::node_test[predicate]
```

The location step points to the location of other nodes from the position of the *current node*. If a current node is not specified in any way, the location step is based on the root element.

*Axes* break up the XML document in relation to the current node. You can think of them as a first filter that you apply to an XML document to point to target nodes. Possible axes are listed in Table 12-3.

| Axes | Description |
| --- | --- |
| parent | The parent of the current node. |
| ancestor | All ancestors (parent, grandparent, and so on) to the root of the current node. |
| child | All children of the current node (first generation). |
| descendant | All descendants (children, grandchildren, and so forth) of the current node. |
| self | The current node only. |
| descendant-or-self | All descendant nodes and the current node. |
| ancestor-or-self | All ancestor nodes and the current node. |
| attribute | All attributes of the current node. |
| namespace | All namespace nodes of the current node. |
| following | All nodes after the current node in the XML document. The set does not include attribute nodes, namespace nodes, or ancestors of the context node. |
| preceding | All nodes before the current node in the XML document. The set does not include attribute nodes, namespace nodes, or ancestors of the current node. |

**Table 12-3.**    Axes in XPath

| Axes | Description |
|---|---|
| following-sibling | All siblings (children of the same parent) after the current node in the XML document. |
| preceding-sibling | All siblings (children of the same parent) before the current node in the XML document. |

**Table 12-3.** Axes in XPath *(continued)*

The *node test* is a second filter that you can apply on nodes specified by axes. Table 12-4 list all node tests that can be applied.

| Node test | Description |
|---|---|
| *element name* | Selects just node(s) with specified name in the set specified by axes. |
| * or node() | All nodes in the set specified by axes. |
| comment() | All comment elements in the set specified by axes. |
| text() | All text elements in the set specified by axes. |
| processing-instruction() | All processing instructions elements in the set specified by axes (if the name is specified in brackets, the parser will match only processing instructions with the specified name). |

**Table 12-4.** Node Tests in XPath

A *predicate* is a filter in the form of a Boolean expression that evaluates each node in the set obtained after applying axes and node test filters. Developers have a rich set of functions (string, node set, Boolean, and number), comparative operators (=, ! =, <=, >= <, >), Boolean operators (and, or), and operators (+, –, *, div, mod). The list is very long (especially the list of functions), and we will not go into detail here. We will just mention the most common function, `position()`. It returns the position of the node.

Let's now review how all segments of the location step function together.

```
child::Equipment[position()<=10]
```

This location set first points to child nodes of the current node (root if none is selected). Of all child nodes, only elements named `Equipment` are left in the set. Finally, each of those nodes is evaluated by position and only the first 10 are specified.

Very often, you will try to navigate from node to node through the XML document. You can attach location sets using the forward slash (/). The same character is often used at the beginning of the expression to establish the current node.

In the following example, the parser is pointed to the Inventory.xml file, then to its root element, and then to the first child called `Equipment`, and finally to the first `Model` node among its children:

```
Inventory.xml#/child::Equipment[position() = 1]/child::
Model[position() = 1]
```

It all works in a very similar fashion to the notation of files and folders, and naturally you can write them all together:

```
http://www.trigonblue.com/xml/Inventory.xml#/child::
Equipment[position() = 1]/child::Model[position() = 1]
```

XPath constructs are very flexible, but also very complex and laborious to write. To reduce the effort, a number of abbreviations are defined. `position() = X` can be replaced by *X* (it is enough to type just the number). Thus, an earlier example can be written as

```
Inventory.xml#/child::Equipment[1]/child::Model[1]
```

If an axis is not defined, the parser assumes that the `child` axis was specified. Thus the preceding example could be written as

```
Inventory.xml#/Equipment[1]/Model[1]
```

The `attribute::` axis can be abbreviated as "@". Therefore, the following two expressions are equivalent:

```
Inventory.xml#/child::Equipment[1]/attribute::EquipmentId
Inventory.xml#/child::Equipment[1]/@EquipmentId
```

The current node can be specified using either `self::node()` or period (`.`). The following two expressions are equivalent:

```
Order.xml#/self::node()/OrderDate
Order.xml#/./OrderDate
```

A parent node can be specified either by `parent::node()` or "`..`". The following two expressions are equivalent:

```
parent::node()/Order
../Order
```

`/descendant-or-self::node()` selects the current node and all descendant nodes. It can be abbreviated with "`//`". The following two examples select all `EquipmentId` attributes in the document:

```
Inventory.xml#/descendant-or-self::node()/@EquipmentId
Inventory.xml#//@EquipmentId
```

## Transforming XML

In many cases in business, information that is already in the form of an XML document needs to be converted to another XML structure. For example, a client of mine is participating in RossetaNet, an e-commerce consortium of IT supply chain organizations that defines standard messages to be sent between partners. Although messages are standardized, each pair of partners can agree to modify their messages slightly to better serve their needs. Such changes are mostly structural—new nodes (fields) can be defined, standard ones can be dropped, a node can change its type from element to attribute, and so on. Instead of generating completely different messages each time (and developing two separate procedures for performing similar tasks), it is preferable to create a simple procedure that will transform a standard XML message into another form.

Another typical situation occurs when an application uses a browser to display an XML document. Although modern browsers such as the latest versions of Internet Explorer are able to display the content of an XML document in the form of a hierarchical tree, this format is not user-friendly. More often, the XML document is transformed into an HTML document and information is organized visually into tables and frames. Such HTML applications usually allow the end user to modify the displayed information interactively (for example, to sort the content of the tables, to display different information in linked tables, or to present data in different formats). Each of these tasks could be performed by modifying the original XML document.

A typical problem with HTML browsers from different vendors is that they are not compatible. Naturally (well, actually, it seems quite unnatural), even different versions of the same browser behave differently. Each of them uses a different variation of the HTML standard. However, these differences are not major, and instead of generating a separate XML document for each of them, a Web developer can create a procedure to transform the XML document so that it fits the requirements of the browser currently in use.

You can think of XML as just one type of rendering language. Some systems use other types of rendering languages and appropriate browsers. For example, more and more PDAs and wireless devices such as cellular phones are offering Internet access. They often use a special protocol (Wireless Application Protocol—WAP) that has its own markup language (Wireless Markup Language—WML) based on XML. A Web server offering information should be able to transform the XML document to fulfill the needs of different viewers.

## XSL

The *eXtensible Stylesheet Language (XSL)* addresses the need to transform XML documents from one XML form to another and to transform XML documents to other formats such as HTML and WML. It is based on *Cascading Style Sheets* (*CSS*), a language for styling HTML documents. Over time, XSL has been transformed into three other languages:

▼ *XSLT* for transforming XML documents

■ *XSLF* for rendering

▲ *XPath* for accessing a specific part of an XML document

## XSLT

XSLT is a (new) language for transforming XML documents. W3C gave it Recommended status in November 1999. XSLT style sheet files are also well-formed XML documents. These files are processed by *XSLT processors*. Such a processor can be a separate tool or part of an XML parser (as in the case of MSXML).

At this point we will not go into detail about XSL and XSLT syntax. Such topics are really beyond the scope of this book. You will have to refer to **http://www.w3.org/Style/XSL/** and **http://www.w3.org/TR/xslt** for more information on this topic. However, we will cover the use of XSLT in SQL Server 2000 later in the chapter.

# WHY XML?

We have described XML, which is all well and fine, but of course the questions arise: why do we need XML and what can we do with it? Two major areas of application are

▼ Exchange of information between organizations

▲ Information publishing

# Exchange of Information Between Organizations

XML provides platform-independent data transport for a variety of types of information from simple messages (commands, information requests) to the most complex business documents. Its extensible nature—the ease with which you can add new nodes or branches, create multiple instances of the same element, and use open schemas to add elements as necessary (provided they comply with schema rules)—makes XML an ideal development language for the rapidly evolving "dotcom" economy. You can use XML to implement solutions that can grow and evolve with an organization and be relatively certain that your solution will not end up on next year's scrap heap and that the organization will not have to replace it at an enormous cost as the needs of the organization grow and change.

It is no wonder that Microsoft has incorporated support for XML in its new releases of applications such as SQL Server, Exchange, Visual Studio, and Internet Explorer. This support allows Microsoft to remain the major player in operating systems and network solutions even as businesses organize themselves into trading communities and industry associations defined by their ability to exchange information seamlessly and securely via the Internet.

## EDI: a Cautionary Tale

XML is finding extensive application within the "B2B" (business-to-business) and "B2C" (business-to-consumer) arenas, to name but two of this young century's most ubiquitous buzzwords. XML's success in this emerging marketplace is largely due to its platform independence, which translates directly to the bottom line in terms of low implementation costs. Trading partners require only Internet access and a Web browser to conduct secure business transactions over the Internet.

One of the buzzwords of the early 1990s was *Electronic Data Interchange (EDI)*. EDI is still around, but it has never fulfilled its promise to make the exchange of paper documents between businesses obsolete. It was the cost of implementation that prevented

EDI from fulfilling this promise. The problem that EDI encountered is a variation on the "Tower of Babel" theme: the proliferation of languages and protocols ensured that each implementation would be unique, and therefore costly.

Classic EDI follows a hub-and-spoke model: a large company (the "hub") that must manage business relationships with a large number of suppliers (the "spokes") decrees that the spoke organizations must implement EDI or lose their trading partner status. The spoke organizations have to bear the considerable cost of implementation or lose a considerable portion of their business income.

A company that is forced to implement EDI by virtue of a trading relationship with a hub company receives an "implementation guide" that describes the EDI standard with which it must comply. One EDI veteran described the difference between classic EDI and XML-based e-commerce succinctly: with EDI, your postal carrier delivers an implementation guide printed on paper; with XML-based e-commerce, the implementation guide is attached to the electronic business document/transaction in the form of a DTD or XML schema.

This comparison is a gross oversimplification of the relationship between these two technologies, but it does highlight one reason that XML-based e-commerce has succeeded with small- to medium-sized businesses where EDI could not, and that is its relatively low cost of implementation.

The other reason for this success is that XML-based e-commerce leverages Internet-based communications. The dial-up *Value Added Networks* (*VANs*) of the EDI world are more or less glorified (and generally expensive) electronic mailboxes to which you post business documents and from which you download business documents from your trading partners. The XML revolution has spawned Internet-based, third-party *Application Service Providers* (*ASPs*) and "Infomediaries" to take the place of the VANs and use XML to conduct business transactions between diverse trading partners.

Of course, these ASPs and Infomediaries are in the business of developing data-based applications for the Web, so we can begin to see why it is so important that SQL Server be XML-ready. The new XML features in SQL Server 2000, along with SQL Server's ease of use, make it a leader in this emerging market.

## Information Publishing

Just as trading partners can use XML to exchange business documents, organizations and individuals can use XML to develop data-based applications that publish information. The only real difference between business document exchange and information publishing is that the information itself becomes the commodity.

Using XML to publish information located in a SQL Server database combines the easy access of the Internet with the power and data integrity of a mature RDBMS. Browser-based applications allow users to retrieve data dynamically from diverse databases.

# XML SUPPORT IN SQL SERVER

Microsoft has developed XML support in SQL Server in the following major areas:

▼ Transact-SQL language extensions

■ OpenXML—the DOM alternative for accessing the content of an XML document

▲ SQL XML support in IIS—a new ISAPI driver and new IIS extensions

## Transact-SQL Language Extensions

SQL Server can now return data stored in a database in the form of an XML document. The foundation of all new features related to publishing database information in XML format is the extended syntax of the `Select` statement.

## For XML Clause

The `Select` statement has a new `For XML` clause:

```
[ For { XML { Auto | Raw | Explicit }
            [ , XMLData ]
            [ , Elements ]
            [ , Binary base64 ]
    }
]
```

This clause allows a caller to request an XML document instead of a recordset that matches the query. The structure of the XML document depends on the XML mode that the caller has selected:

▼ Auto

■ Raw

▲ Explicit

## Auto Mode

Let's use Auto mode against the Inventory table in the Asset database:

```
Select *
From Inventory
For XML Auto
```

**TIP:**  Before you issue such a query against the database yourself, go to Tools | Options in Query Analyzer and open the Results tab. Change the Maximum Characters per Column value to **8192** (the maximum allowed value). The default value is too short. If you do not change it, you will wonder why the resulting XML document is shortened.

Figure 12-2 shows how Query Analyzer displays results. To analyze the result, I either copy and paste it into some other editor or insert line breaks and tabs to emphasize the structure of the document:

```
<Inventory Inventoryid="5"
           EquipmentId="1"
           LocationId="2"
           StatusId="1"
           LeaseId="1"
           LeaseScheduleId="1"
           OwnerId="1"
           Cost="1295.0000"
           AcquisitionTypeID="1"/>
<Inventory Inventoryid="6"
           EquipmentId="6"
           LocationId="2"
           StatusId="2"
           LeaseId="1"
...
```

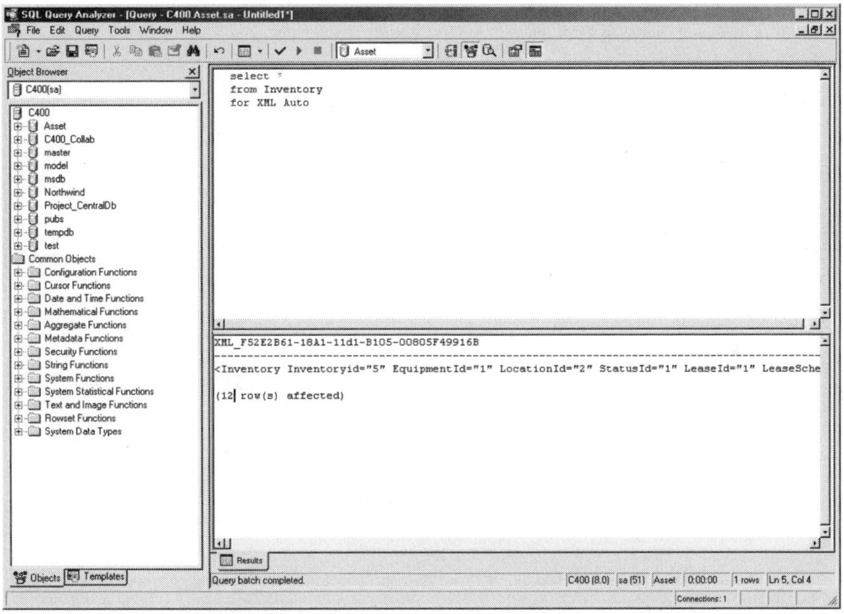

**Figure 12-2.** An XML document as a result of a query

Each record in the Inventory table is represented by an element. The tag is named after the table, `<Inventory>`. All columns are represented as attributes of the tag. Since there is no other content aside from these attributes, each tag is coded as an empty tag: `<Inventory/>`.

**NOTE:** There is one problem with this XML document. Strictly speaking, it is not an XML document (it is not valid). There is no root element. The first element, `<Inventory/>`, does not qualify because it is not unique within the document (we have one instance for each record). We will show you later how to handle this problem.

Let's see what happens when we add another table to the query:

```
select *
from Inventory inner join Equipment
on Inventory.EquipmentId = Equipment.Equipmentid
for XML Auto
```

I will execute this query and then add some line breaks so that you can more easily spot the characteristics of the XML document:

```
XML_F52E2B61-18A1-11d1-B105-00805F49916B
-------------------------------------------------------------
<Inventory Inventoryid="5" EquipmentId="1" LocationId="2"
           StatusId="1" LeaseId="1" LeaseScheduleId="1"
           OwnerId="1" Cost="1295.0000" AcquisitionTypeID="1">
   <Equipment EquipmentId="1" Make="Toshiba"
           Model="Portege 7020CT" EqTypeId="1" ModelSDX="P632"/>
</Inventory>
<Inventory Inventoryid="6" EquipmentId="6" LocationId="2"
           StatusId="2" LeaseId="1" LeaseScheduleId="1"
           OwnerId="1" Rent="200.0000" Lease="0.0000"
           AcquisitionTypeID="3">
   <Equipment EquipmentId="6" Make="NEC" Model="V90"
           EqTypeId="1" ModelSDX="V000"/>
</Inventory>
<Inventory Inventoryid="8" EquipmentId="5" LocationId="2"
           StatusId="1" OwnerId="1" Lease="87.7500"
           AcquisitionTypeID="2">
```

```
      <Equipment EquipmentId="5" Make="HP" Model="LaserJet 4"
             EqTypeId="7" ModelSDX="L262"/>
</Inventory>
<Inventory Inventoryid="12" EquipmentId="1" LocationId="2"
          StatusId="1" LeaseId="1" LeaseScheduleId="1"
          OwnerId="1" Lease="100.0000" AcquisitionTypeID="2">
   <Equipment EquipmentId="1" Make="Toshiba"
             Model="Portege 7020CT" EqTypeId="1" ModelSDX="P632"/>
</Inventory>
...
```

You can also see the result in Figure 12-3.

This time, the result is a simple nested XML tree. The structure of the XML document is based on the content of the From clause. The leftmost table is mapped to the top element; the second leftmost table is mapped as a subelement of the top element; the third leftmost table (if it exists) is

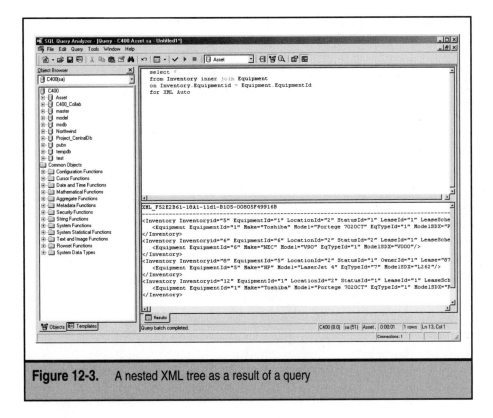

**Figure 12-3.**    A nested XML tree as a result of a query

mapped as a subelement of the second-level element, and so on. Again, table columns are mapped to the attributes of the element.

If we now create a query that joins Inventory with all other lookup tables, we get a nested tree with a number of levels (see Figure 12-4).

In the preceding case, each <Inventory> element contains one <Equipment/> element, which could be very useful for client applications. Each record from the main table is followed by the associated lookup (foreign key) records.

Let's reverse the order of tables in the From clause and use Left Join:

```
Select *
From Equipment Left Outer Join Inventory
On Inventory.EquipmentId = Equipment.Equipmentid
For XML Auto
```

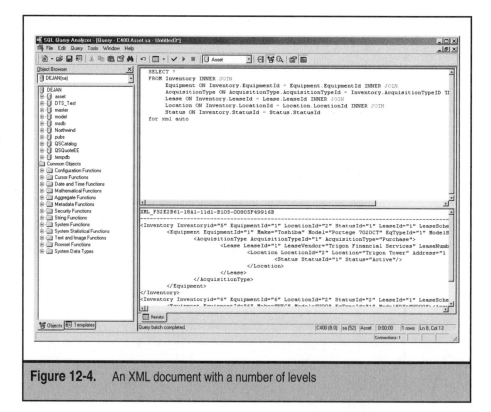

**Figure 12-4.**    An XML document with a number of levels

Now each record in the Equipment table is followed by a variable number of records from the Inventory table. There are Equipment records that are not associated with anything and Equipment records that are associated with more than one Inventory record:

```
XML_F52E2B61-18A1-11d1-B105-00805F49916B
----------------------------------------------------------------
<Equipment EquipmentId="1" Make="Toshiba" Model="Portege 7020CT"
          EqTypeId="1" ModelSDX="P632">
   <Inventory Inventoryid="5" EquipmentId="1" LocationId="2"
             StatusId="1" LeaseId="1" LeaseScheduleId="1"
             OwnerId="1" Cost="1295.0000" AcquisitionTypeID="1"/>
   <Inventory Inventoryid="12" EquipmentId="1" LocationId="2"
             StatusId="1" LeaseId="1" LeaseScheduleId="1"
             OwnerId="1" Lease="100.0000"
             AcquisitionTypeID="2"/>
</Equipment>
<Equipment EquipmentId="2" Make="Sony" Model="Trinitron 17XE"
          EqTypeId="3" ModelSDX="T653">
   <Inventory/>
</Equipment>
<Equipment EquipmentId="6" Make="NEC" Model="V90" EqTypeId="1"
 ModelSDX="V000">
   <Inventory Inventoryid="6" EquipmentId="6" LocationId="2"
             StatusId="2" LeaseId="1" LeaseScheduleId="1"
             OwnerId="1" Rent="200.0000" Lease="0.0000"
             AcquisitionTypeID="3"/>
</Equipment>
<Equipment EquipmentId="4" Make="HP" Model="LaserJet 4"
          EqTypeId="6" ModelSDX="L262">
   <Inventory/>
</Equipment>
<Equipment EquipmentId="5" Make="HP" Model="LaserJet 4"
          EqTypeId="7" ModelSDX="L262">
   <Inventory Inventoryid="8" EquipmentId="5" LocationId="2"
             StatusId="1" OwnerId="1" Lease="87.7500"
             AcquisitionTypeID="2"/>
</Equipment>
(6 row(s) affected)
```

You can see result of the execution in Figure 12-5.

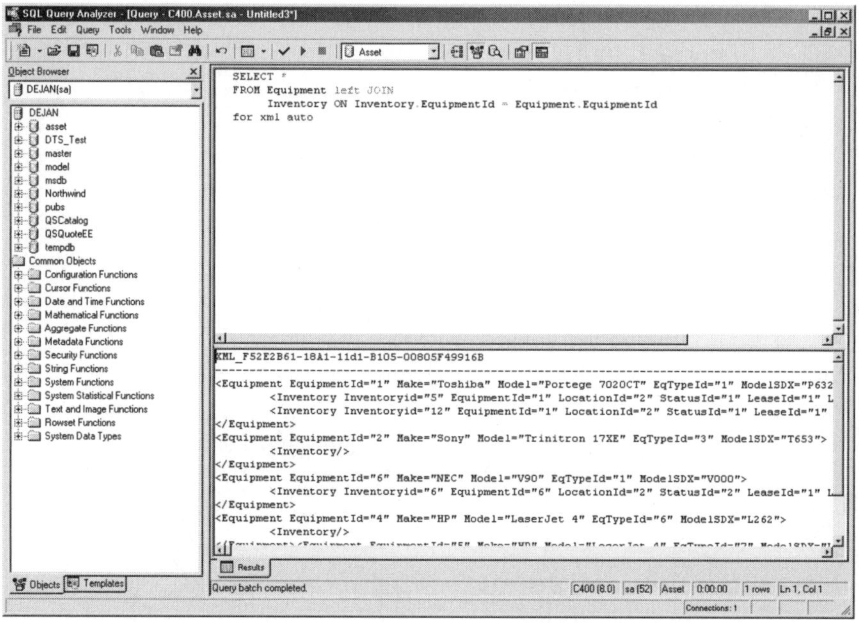

**Figure 12-5.** An XML document with a variable number of matched records

**TIP:** You do not have to use column names as tag names. You can assign aliases to columns and these aliases will be mapped to attributes.

## Aggregate Functions

Aggregate functions and the Group By clause are not supported in Auto mode. However, it is possible to use a simple workaround based on nested subqueries to pool such values into an XML document.

```
Select Inv.InventoryId, Inv.SumCost
From (Select InventoryId, Sum(Cost) SumCost
                    From Inventory
                    Group By InventoryId) Inv
For XML Auto
```

In the preceding example, the inner `Select` table produces all required information and the outer `Select` functions as a wrapper with a `For XML Auto` clause. It is also possible to join the inner `Select` statement with other tables to provide additional information.

If the column list of the `Select` statement references a column that cannot be associated with any table (such as computed columns), SQL Server will map it to the attribute (or subelement) at the deepest nesting level that is present when the column is encountered in the list. For example, if a column is referenced as first in the column list, it is added as an attribute (or a subelement) of the top element; if a computed column is referenced after the columns of two other tables are referenced, the columns are mapped at the second level.

## The Elements Option

Table columns do not have to be encoded as attributes. If you add the `Elements` option to the `For XML` clause, all columns will be coded as subelements. You can see the resultset of the following query in Figure 12-6. Nested tables are also encoded as subelements.

```
Select *
From Inventory Inner Join Equipment
On Inventory.EquipmentId = Equipment.Equipmentid
For XML Auto, Elements
```

*NOTE:*   The `Elements` option is supported only in `Auto` mode.

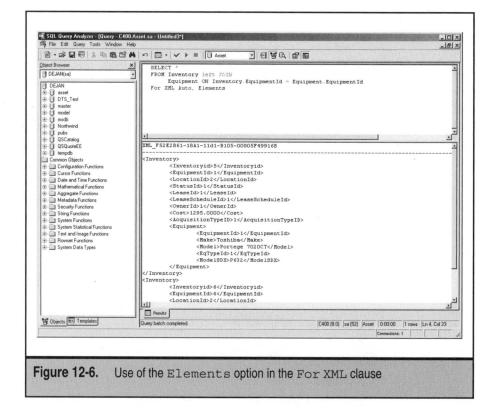

**Figure 12-6.** Use of the `Elements` option in the `For XML` clause

## The XMLData Option

If the `XMLData` option is specified in the `For XML` clause, the XML document also contains an XML-Data schema:

```
select *
from Equipment
for XML Auto, XMLData
```

The schema is added at the beginning of the document as an inline schema:

```
<Schema name="Schema"
    xmlns="urn:schemas-microsoft-com:xml-data"
```

```
          xmlns:dt="urn:schemas-microsoft-com:datatypes">
<ElementType name="Equipment" content="empty" model="closed">
  <AttributeType name="EquipmentId" dt:type="i4"/>
  <AttributeType name="Make" dt:type="string"/>
  <AttributeType name="Model" dt:type="string"/>
  <AttributeType name="EqTypeId" dt:type="i2"/>
  <AttributeType name="ModelSDX" dt:type="string"/>
  <AttributeType name="MakeSDX" dt:type="string"/>
  <attribute type="EquipmentId"/>
  <attribute type="Make"/>
  <attribute type="Model"/>
  <attribute type="EqTypeId"/>
  <attribute type="ModelSDX"/>
  <attribute type="MakeSDX"/>
</ElementType>
</Schema>
<Equipment xmlns="x-schema:#Schema" EquipmentId="1" Make="Toshiba"
          Model="Portege 7020CT" EqTypeId="1" ModelSDX="P632"/>
  <Equipment xmlns="x-schema:#Schema" EquipmentId="2" Make="Sony"
          Model="Trinitron 17XE" EqTypeId="3" ModelSDX="T653"/>
<Equipment xmlns="x-schema:#Schema" EquipmentId="6" Make="NEC"
          Model="V90" EqTypeId="1" ModelSDX="V000"/>
<Equipment xmlns="x-schema:#Schema" EquipmentId="4" Make="HP"
          Model="LaserJet 4" EqTypeId="6" ModelSDX="L262"/>
<Equipment xmlns="x-schema:#Schema" EquipmentId="5" Make="HP"
          Model="LaserJet 4" EqTypeId="7" ModelSDX="L262"/>
```

Data elements will also get an attribute with a reference to a schema:

```
xmlns="x-schema:#Schema"
```

**TIP:**   You have to be very careful when generating a schema this way. The schema could be incorrect if, for example, your query specifies a recordset that contains fields (and/or aliases) with the same name (for example, when fields have the same name in both main and lookup tables). SQL Server will not resolve name or datatype collisions.

## The BINARY Base64 Option

The BINARY Base64 option is designed for encoding binary data such as images, video, and sounds via XML. It is not required in Auto mode, but it must be specified in Explicit and Row modes of the For XML clause. Figure 12-7 shows an encoded photo of an employee from the Northwind database.

```
SELECT Photo
FROM Northwind..Employees
WHERE EmployeeID=2
FOR XML RAW, XMLData, BINARY Base64
```

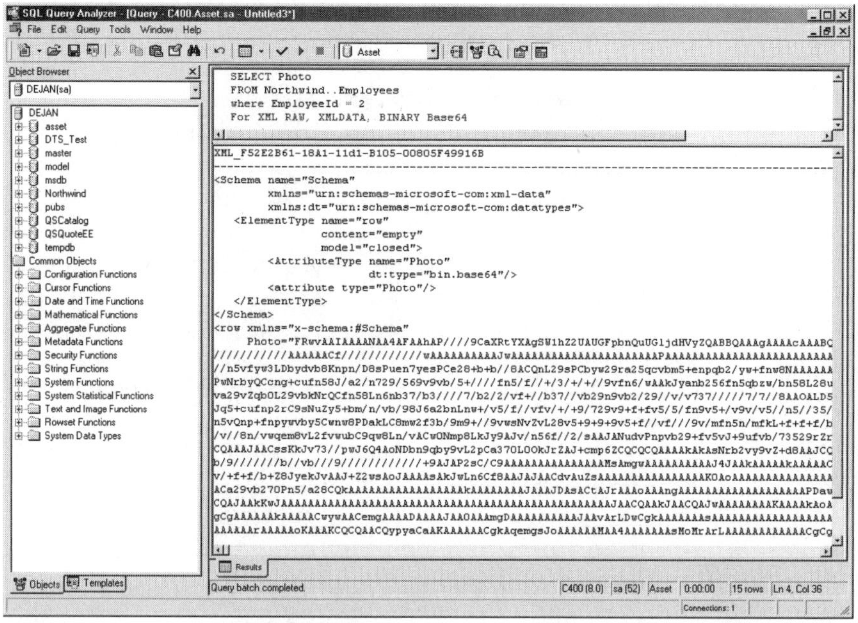

**Figure 12-7.** Encoding of binary data in XML

## The Raw Mode

The Raw mode of the For XML clause returns every row of the resultset as an individual XML element named *row*.

```
Select Equipment.Make, Equipment.Model,
       Inventory.InventoryID, Inventory.Cost
From Inventory Inner Join Equipment
On Inventory.EquipmentId = Equipment.Equipmentid
For XML Raw
```

Note that elements in the resultset are called row and that the mode is called Raw:

```
<row Make="Toshiba" Model="Portege 7020CT"
     InventoryID="5" Cost=
"1295.0000"/>
<row Make="NEC" Model="V90" InventoryID="6"/>
<row Make="HP" Model="LaserJet 4" InventoryID="8"/>
<row Make="Toshiba" Model="Portege 7020CT" InventoryID="12"/>
<row Make="Toshiba" Model="Portege 7020CT" InventoryID="5"Cost="1295.0000"/>
<row Make="NEC" Model="V90" InventoryID="6"/>
<row Make="HP" Model="LaserJet 4" InventoryID="8"/>
<row Make="Toshiba" Model="Portege 7020CT" InventoryID="12"/>
```

Columns that have a Null value are skipped in the list of attributes. Columns are always encoded as attributes because it is not possible to specify the Elements option in this mode. Again, it is important to avoid name collisions.

## The Explicit Mode

The Explicit mode is much more flexible than Auto or Raw mode. It allows a developer to specify all details of an XML document (shape and data). The developer is therefore responsible for ensuring that the XML document is well formed and valid.

The process of creating such a document involves writing a query that defines a *universal table*. The table contains all the information needed to create the XML document (both meta data and data). Table 12-5 shows such a universal table.

| Tag | Parent | Equipment!1!<br>EquipmentID | Equipment!1!<br>Make | Equipment!1!<br>Model | Inventory!2!<br>InventoryID | Inventory!2!<br>StatusID |
|-----|--------|------------------------------|----------------------|------------------------|------------------------------|---------------------------|
| 1 | NULL | 1 | Toshiba | Portege 7020CT | NULL | NULL |
| 2 | 1 | 1 | Toshiba | Portege 7020CT | 5 | 1 |
| 2 | 1 | 1 | Toshiba | Portege 7020CT | 12 | 1 |
| 1 | NULL | 2 | Sony | Trinitron 17XE | NULL | NULL |
| 1 | NULL | 4 | HP | LaserJet 4 | NULL | NULL |
| 1 | NULL | 5 | HP | LaserJet 4 | NULL | NULL |
| 2 | 1 | 5 | HP | LaserJet 4 | 8 | 1 |
| 1 | NULL | 6 | NEC | V90 | NULL | NULL |
| 2 | 1 | 6 | NEC | V90 | 6 | 2 |

**Table 12-5.**   A Universal Table

When the query that generates such a table is executed with the `For XML Explicit` option, SQL Server returns an XML document such as the following:

```
<Equipment EquipmentID="1" Make="Toshiba" Model="Portege 7020CT">
    <Inventory InventoryID="5" StatusID="1"/>
    <Inventory InventoryID="12" StatusID="1"/>
</Equipment>
<Equipment EquipmentID="2" Make="Sony" Model="Trinitron 17XE"/>
<Equipment EquipmentID="4" Make="HP" Model="LaserJet 4"/>
<Equipment EquipmentID="5" Make="HP" Model="LaserJet 4">
    <Inventory InventoryID="8" StatusID="1"/>
</Equipment>
<Equipment EquipmentID="6" Make="NEC" Model="V90">
    <Inventory InventoryID="6" StatusID="2"/>
</Equipment>
...
```

The first two columns of the table (`Tag` and `Parent`) control the shape (that is, the nesting) of the XML document. The `Tag` column contains an identifier for the element. The `Parent` column contains a tag for the parent record. SQL Server uses these to create a hierarchy. The top element will have 0 (zero) or `Null` in the `Parent` column.

Other columns provide elements and attribute names and data. Column names have to be specified using the following template:

```
GI!TagNumber!AttributeName!Directive
```

Table 12-6 explains the meaning of components of the template:

| Component | Meaning |
|---|---|
| GI | Generic identifier of the element. |
| TagNumber | The tag number of the element. |
| AttributeName | The name of the attribute if the Directive is not specified. In the case in which the Directive is specified (as `xml`, `cdata`, or `element`), the AttributeName becomes the name of the contained element. If the Directive is specified, the AttributeName can be empty. |
| Directive | The optional component. If neither the AttributeName nor the Directive are specified, SQL Server defaults to ELEMENT. |

**Table 12-6.**   Components of Column Names

The following example illustrates how the `Tag` and `Parent` columns are used to form the hierarchy of the XML document and how the AttributeName component of the column name is used to name attributes (we have already shown the corresponding global table and the resulting XML document):

```
SELECT    1 as Tag,
          NULL as Parent,
          Equipment.EquipmentID as [Equipment!1!EquipmentID],
          Equipment.Make as [Equipment!1!Make],
          Equipment.Model as [Equipment!1!Model],
          NULL as [Inventory!2!InventoryID],
          NULL as [Inventory!2!StatusID]
FROM      Equipment

UNION ALL
SELECT    2,
          1,
          Equipment.EquipmentID,
          Equipment.Make,
          Equipment.Model,
          Inventory.InventoryID,
          Inventory.StatusID
FROM      Equipment, Inventory
WHERE     Equipment.EquipmentID = Inventory.EquipmentID
ORDER BY  [Equipment!1!EquipmentID], [Inventory!2!InventoryID]
FOR XML EXPLICIT
```

The *Directive* has two purposes. When `hide`, `element`, `xml`, `xmltext`, or `cdata` are used, the Directive controls how the data in the column is mapped into the XML document. `id`, `idref`, and `idrefs` are used to allow the XMLData schema to enable intradocument links.

**The hide Directive**   The content of the column with the `hide` directive will not be displayed in the resulting document. This feature is useful when a developer wants to sort information by invisible columns.

**The element Directive**   The `element` directive will be used most often. It forces SQL Server to generate an element instead of an attribute. If the column contains data that could confuse an XML parser, SQL Server replaces it with entity references (for example, the ampersand character "&" is replaced with "&amp;" or "<" will be replaced with "&lt;").

The following example illustrates the use of the hide and element directives:

```
SELECT    1 as Tag,
          NULL as Parent,
          Equipment.EquipmentID as [Equipment!1!EquipmentID!hide],
          Equipment.Make as [Equipment!1!Make!element],
          Equipment.Model as [Equipment!1!Model!element],
          NULL as [Inventory!2!InventoryID],
          NULL as [Inventory!2!StatusID!element]
FROM      Equipment

UNION ALL
SELECT    2,
          1,
          Equipment.EquipmentID,
          Equipment.Make,
          Equipment.Model,
          Inventory.InventoryID,
          Inventory.StatusID
FROM      Equipment, Inventory
WHERE     Equipment.EquipmentID = Inventory.EquipmentID
ORDER BY [Equipment!1!EquipmentID!hide], [Inventory!2!InventoryID]
FOR XML EXPLICIT
```

A partial result of the query is displayed in the following listing. Make, Model, and StatusId information are displayed as elements. The ampersand character has been replaced with "&amp;" in the Make element:

```
<Equipment>
   <Make>Toshiba</Make>
   <Model>Portege 7020CT</Model>
   <Inventory InventoryID="5">
      <StatusID>1</StatusID>
   </Inventory>
   <Inventory InventoryID="12">
      <StatusID>1</StatusID>
```

```
    </Inventory>
</Equipment>
<Equipment>
    <Make>Bang &amp; Olafson</Make>
    <Model>V3000</Model>
...
```

### The xml and cdata Directives    The xml and cdata directives are similar to the element directive. They just treat special characters differently. If the xml directive is specified, SQL Server does not perform entity encoding but leaves the content intact. If the cdata directive is specified, SQL Server encapsulates the content of the column in the cdata comment. In the following example, the Equipment.Make column is displayed three times and is treated each time with a different directive:

```
SELECT    1 as Tag,
          NULL as Parent,
          Equipment.EquipmentID as [Equipment!1!EquipmentID!hide],
          Equipment.Make as [Equipment!1!Make!element],
          Equipment.Make as [Equipment!1!Make!xml],
          Equipment.Make as [Equipment!1!!cdata],
Equipment.Model as [Equipment!1!Model!element],
          NULL as [Inventory!2!InventoryID],
          NULL as [Inventory!2!StatusID!element]
FROM      Equipment

UNION ALL
SELECT    2,
          1,
          Equipment.EquipmentID,
          Equipment.Make,
          Equipment.Make,
          Equipment.Make,
          Equipment.Model,
          Inventory.InventoryID,
          Inventory.StatusID
FROM      Equipment, Inventory
WHERE     Equipment.EquipmentID = Inventory.EquipmentID
ORDER BY [Equipment!1!EquipmentID!hide], [Inventory!2!InventoryID]
FOR XML EXPLICIT
```

A partial result of the query is displayed in the following listing. Make information is treated differently each time:

```
...
<Equipment>
    <Make>Bang &amp; Olafson</Make>
    <Make>Bang & Olafson</Make>
    <![CDATA[Bang & Olafson]]>
<Model>V3000</Model>
...
```

**The xmltext Directive**    The xmltext directive is used to incorporate an XML document (or section of the document) stored in a column of the record into the resulting document.

Imagine a scenario in which you have created a database table, but the nature of the business is such that new information (and new columns) will often be added. In the past, I have used a solution that you can see in the Asset database in the InventoryProperty table:

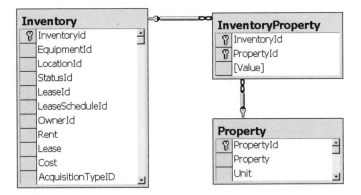

Instead of adding a new field for a property of equipment, I have created a new table in which the properties of one asset are stored in a separate record. Instead of storing information in a mostly empty table

| InventoryId | Make | Model | CPU | Capacity | HDD | Clock | RAM | Resolution |
|---|---|---|---|---|---|---|---|---|
| 1 | HP | LaserJet 4 | null | null | null | null | 4MB | 600dpi |
| 5 | Toshiba | Portege 7020 CT | Pentium II | null | 6.4GB | 366MHz | 64MB | 1024x768 |

information is stored "vertically":

| InventoryId | Property | Value | Unit |
|---|---|---|---|
| 1 | RAM | 4 | MB |
| 1 | Resolution | 600 | dpi |
| 5 | CPU | Pentium II | NULL |
| 5 | RAM | 64 | MB |
| 5 | HDD | 6.4 | GB |
| 5 | Resolution | 1024x768 | NULL |
| 5 | Weight | 2 | kg |
| 5 | Clock | 366 | MHz |

An XML alternative to this solution is to create a special column to store the "overflow" information. In the following statement, the Inventory table is created with a Properties column to store additional information in XML format:

```
CREATE TABLE [InventoryXML] (
    [Inventoryid] [int] IDENTITY (1, 1) NOT NULL ,
    [EquipmentId] [int] NOT NULL ,
    [LocationId] [int] NOT NULL ,
    [StatusId] [tinyint] NOT NULL ,
    [LeaseId] [int] NULL ,
    [LeaseScheduleId] [int] NULL ,
    [OwnerId] [int] NOT NULL ,
    [Rent] [smallmoney] NULL ,
    [Lease] [smallmoney] NULL ,
    [Cost] [smallmoney] NULL ,
    [AcquisitionTypeID] [tinyint] NULL ,
    [Properties] [text] NULL,
) ON [PRIMARY]
```

You can then insert information in the form of an XML document or its subset into the Properties column:

```
<Inventory CPU = "Pentium II"
           RAM = "64 MB"
           HDD = "6.4 GB"
           Resolution = "1024x768"
```

```
                 Weight = "2 kg"
                 Clock="366 MHz"/>
```

To integrate this information into the resulting XML document, you should use the `xmltext` directive:

```
SELECT     1 as Tag,
           NULL as Parent,
           InventoryXML.InventoryID as [Inventory!1!InventoryID],
           InventoryXML.StatusID as [Inventory!1!StatusID],
           InventoryXML.Properties as [Inventory!1!Properties!xmltext]
FROM       InventoryXML
ORDER BY [Inventory!1!InventoryID]
FOR XML EXPLICIT
```

The following listing contains a partial result:

```
<Inventory InventoryID="1" StatusID="1">
   <Properties
       CPU="Pentium II"
       RAM="64 MB"
       HDD="6.4 GB"
       Resolution="1024x768"
       Weight="2 kg"
       Clock="366 MHz"/>
</Inventory>
<Inventory InventoryID="2" StatusID="2"/>
. . .
```

If AttributeName is specified (as in the preceding example), SQL Server uses AttributeName instead of the tag name specified in the column (in the preceding example they were the same).

If AttributeName is omitted, SQL Server appends attributes to the list of attributes in the enclosing element:

```
SELECT     1 as Tag,
           NULL as Parent,
           InventoryXML.InventoryID as [Inventory!1!InventoryID],
           InventoryXML.StatusID as [Inventory!1!StatusID],
           InventoryXML.Properties as [Inventory!1!!xmltext]
FROM       InventoryXML
ORDER BY [Inventory!1!InventoryID]
FOR XML EXPLICIT
```

The following listing displays a partial result:

```
<Inventory
    InventoryID="1"
    StatusID="1"
    CPU="Pentium II"
    RAM="64 MB"
    HDD="6.4 GB"
    Resolution="1024x768"
    Weight="2 kg"
    Clock="366 MHz">
</Inventory>
<Inventory
    InventoryID="2"
    StatusID="2"
...
```

The author of a query using the xmltext Directive assumes a huge responsibility for the validity of the content of the column. If the column does not contain well-formed XML, the results may be unpredictable.

The xmltext directive is permitted (and meaningful) only with columns of character datatypes (varchar, nvarchar, char, nchar, text, ntext).

**The id, idref, and idrefs Directives**    The id, idref, and idrefs directives are used to modify schemas when the XMLDATA option of the For XML clause is specified. When the id directive is specified, elements receive an id attribute. Attributes specified using the idref directive can be used to reference elements with an id attribute. This kind of relationship is the XML equivalent of the foreign key relationship that you are used to in relational databases.

In the following example, we link Equipment.EquipmentId to Inventory.EquipmentId. These two columns are also linked by a foreign key relationship in the database:

```
SELECT    1 as Tag,
          NULL as Parent,
          Equipment.EquipmentID as [Equipment!1!EquipmentID!id],
          Equipment.Make as [Equipment!1!Make],
          Equipment.Model as [Equipment!1!Model],
```

```
              NULL as [Inventory!2!InventoryID],
              NULL as [Inventory!2!StatusID],
              NULL as [Inventory!2!EquipmentID!idref]
FROM          Equipment

UNION ALL
SELECT   2,
         1,
         Equipment.EquipmentID,
         Equipment.Make,
         Equipment.Model,
         Inventory.InventoryID,
         Inventory.StatusID,
         Inventory.EquipmentId
FROM          Equipment, Inventory
WHERE         Equipment.EquipmentID = Inventory.EquipmentID
ORDER BY [Equipment!1!EquipmentID!id], [Inventory!2!InventoryID]
FOR XML EXPLICIT, XMLDATA
```

A partial result is shown in the following XML document. Note that the datatype of the EquipmentId attribute of the Equipment element is set to "id" (it must be unique) and that the EquipmentId attribute of the Inventory element is set to "idref":

```
<Schema name="Schema" xmlns="urn:schemas-microsoft-com:xml-data"
                      xmlns:dt="urn:schemas-microsoft-com:datatypes">
<ElementType name="Equipment" content="mixed" model="open">
   <AttributeType name="EquipmentID" dt:type="id"/>
   <AttributeType name="Make" dt:type="string"/>
   <AttributeType name="Model" dt:type="string"/>
   <attribute type="EquipmentID"/>
   <attribute type="Make"/>
   <attribute type="Model"/>
</ElementType>
<ElementType name="Inventory" content="mixed" model="open">
   <AttributeType name="InventoryID" dt:type="i4"/>
   <AttributeType name="StatusID" dt:type="ui1"/>
   <AttributeType name="EquipmentID" dt:type="idref"/>
   <attribute type="InventoryID"/>
   <attribute type="StatusID"/>
   <attribute type="EquipmentID"/>
</ElementType>
```

```
</Schema>
<Equipment xmlns="x-schema:#Schema"
    EquipmentID="1" Make="Toshiba" Model="Portege 7020CT">
    <Inventory InventoryID="5" StatusID="1" EquipmentID="1"/>
    <Inventory InventoryID="12" StatusID="1" EquipmentID="1"/>
</Equipment>
<Equipment xmlns="x-schema:#Schema"
    EquipmentID="2" Make="Sony" Model="Trinitron 17XE"/>
...
```

# OPENXML

Openxml is a new keyword in Transact-SQL. It provides access to an in-memory rowset similar to a view or a table. Since it is a rowset provider, Openxml can be used in Transact-SQL statements in any place where a table, view, or rowset provider such as OpenRowset can appear. It is a replacement for DOM that Transact-SQL developers can use to parse, access, and return the content of an XML document.

## Document Preparation

Before an XML document can be accessed using Openxml, the document must be loaded into memory using sp_xml_preparedocument. This stored procedure has the following syntax:

```
exec sp_xml_preparedocument hdoc OUTPUT
                        [, xmltext]
                        [, xpath_namespaces]
```

The stored procedure reads the XML document provided in xmltext, parses the document using the MSXML parser, and places a document into an in-memory structure that is ready for use with the OpenXML statement. This structure is a tree that contains assorted nodes such as elements, attributes, comments, and text. The stored procedure returns a handle for the XML document hdoc that OpenXML can use to access the information, and that sp_xml_removedocument uses to remove the document from memory.

The xmltext parameter expects any type of character information (char, varchar, nchar, nvarchar, text, or ntext).

xpath_namespaces is an optional parameter that can provide a namespace declaration for row and column expressions in OpenXML. The default value is '<root xmlns:mp="urn: schemas-microsoft-com:xml-metaprop">'.

The stored procedure returns a value that is different from zero when SQL Server is not able to prepare the document. You should use this information to perform error handling in the usual manner.

```
DECLARE @intDoc int
DECLARE @chvXMLDoc varchar(8000)
-- sample XML document
SET @chvXMLDoc ='
<root>
  <Equipment EquipmentID="1" Make="Toshiba" Model="Portege 7020CT">
    <Inventory InventoryID="5" StatusID="1" EquipmentID="1"/>
    <Inventory InventoryID="12" StatusID="1" EquipmentID="1"/>
  </Equipment>
</root>'
--Load the XML document into memory.
EXEC sp_xml_preparedocument @intDoc OUTPUT, @chvXMLDoc
```

## Closing the Document

After processing, the document should be removed from memory using sp_xml_removedocument. This stored procedure uses very simple syntax:

```
exec sp_xml_removedocument hdoc
```

The hdoc parameter is a handle for a loaded XML document.

```
-- remove the XML document from memory
EXEC sp_xml_removedocument @intDoc
```

## Retrieving the XML Information

OpenXML is a rowset provider that gives access to the internal tree memory structure that contains information from an XML document. It has the following syntax:

```
OpenXML(hdoc, rowpattern, flags)
[With (SchemaDeclaration | TableVariable)]
```

*hdoc* is a handle that points to the tree containing XML data. *rowpattern* is the XPath string used to identify nodes that need to be processed. *flags* is an optional parameter that controls the way that data from the XML document is mapped to the rowset and how data is to be copied to the overflow metaproperty (we will explain this a little later).

*SchemaDeclaration* is a declaration of the structure in which data will be returned. Alternatively, it is possible to use the name of a table variable (*TableVariable*) instead. The rowset will be formed using the structure of the table variable. The *SchemaDeclaration* can be composed using the following syntax:

```
ColName ColType [ColPattern | MetaProperty]
[, ColName ColType [ColPattern | MetaProperty]...]
```

*ColName* is the name and *ColType* is the datatype of the column. This structure is very similar to the table structure of the `Create Table` statement. *ColPattern* is an optional parameter that defines how a column is to be mapped to the XML node. A *MetaProperty* is specified to extract metadata such as datatypes, node types, and namespace information.

Let's finally take a look at an example that uses all these constructs:

```
DECLARE @intDoc int
DECLARE @chvXMLDoc varchar(8000)
-- sample XML document
SET @chvXMLDoc =
'<root>
  <Equipment EquipmentID="1" Make="Toshiba" Model="Portege 7020CT">
    <Inventory InventoryID="5" StatusID="1" EquipmentID="1"/>
    <Inventory InventoryID="12" StatusID="1" EquipmentID="1"/>
  </Equipment>
  <Equipment EquipmentID="2" Make="Sony" Model="Trinitron 17XE"/>
  <Equipment EquipmentID="4" Make="HP" Model="LaserJet 4"/>
  <Equipment EquipmentID="5" Make="Bang &amp; Olafson" Model="V4000">
    <Inventory InventoryID="8" StatusID="1" EquipmentID="5"/>
  </Equipment>
  <Equipment EquipmentID="6" Make="NEC" Model="V90">
    <Inventory InventoryID="6" StatusID="2" EquipmentID="6"/>
```

```
  </Equipment>
</root>'
--Load the XML document into memory.
EXEC sp_xml_preparedocument @intDoc OUTPUT, @chvXMLDoc

-- SELECT statement using OPENXML rowset provider
SELECT    *
FROM      OPENXML (@intDoc, '/root/Equipment/Inventory', 8)
          WITH    (InventoryID int '@InventoryID',
          StatusID int '@StatusID',
          Make varchar(25) '../@Make',
          Model varchar(25) '../@Model',
          comment ntext '@mp:xmltext')
-- remove the XML document from memory
EXEC sp_xml_removedocument @intDoc
```

The result is shown on Figure 12-8.

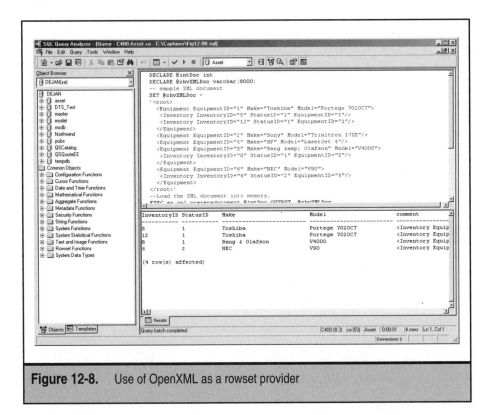

**Figure 12-8.**    Use of OpenXML as a rowset provider

In the preceding example, the `OpenXML` rowset provider is used in a `Select` statement:

```
SELECT    *
From Openxml (@intDoc, '/root/Equipment/Inventory', 8)
     WITH      (InventoryID int '@InventoryID',
                StatusID int '@StatusID',
                Make varchar(25) '../@Make',
                Model varchar(25) '../@Model',
                comment ntext '@mp:xmltext')
```

The *Rowpattern* parameter specifies that information will be extracted (mostly) from Inventory nodes (`'/root/Equipment/Inventory'`).

The third parameter of the `OpenXML` clause sets the way in which the overflow metaproperty is to be filled. In the preceding example, the last column (comment) was filled with metadata provided by the XML parser (since the column is associated with the `@mp:xmltext` attribute). Because the third parameter of `OpenXML` is set to 8 (the `XML_NOCOPY` constant), the overflow attribute does not contain nodes that are extracted into the rowset. Only nodes that are not used are recorded.

Other columns in the rowset are filled from data that exists in attributes. If you remember XPath (and XPattern), introduced earlier in the chapter, the "@" character is used as an abbreviation that points to attribute nodes.

The Make and Model columns are not in the same group of nodes as `InventoryID` and `StatusId`. Since they are attributes of the Equipment node, *ColPattern* has to refer to the parent node (`'../@Model'`) first.

Table 12-7 shows a list of possible values of the *flags* parameter.

`XML_NOCOPY` could be combined (logical OR) with `XML_ATTRIBUTES` (1+8 = 9) or `XML_ELEMENTS` (2 + 8 = 10). This flag can be used to generate either a string with the overflow information or a string with a complete branch of the XML document. The following example extracts the branch of the XML document/tree that describes a node with `Equipment ID` set to 1:

```
Select *
From Openxml (@intDoc, '/root/Equipment', 2)
```

```
    With      (EquipmentID int '@EquipmentID',
                 Branch ntext '@mp:xmltext')
Where EquipmentId = 1
```

## SQL Server 2000 returns the following:

```
EquipmentID Branch
----------- ------------------------------------------------------------
1              <Equipment EquipmentID="1" Make="Toshiba"
Model="Portege 7020CT">
   <Inventory InventoryID="5" StatusID="1" EquipmentID="1"/>
   <Inventory InventoryID="12" StatusID="1" EquipmentID="1"/>
</Equipment>
(1 row(s) affected)
```

XML_ATTRIBUTES and XML_ELEMENTS can also be combined. Attribute-centric mapping is applied on the first level of (selected) nodes. Others are treated with element-centric mapping.

| Mnemonic | Value | Description |
|---|---|---|
| XML_ATTRIBUTES | 1 | Attribute-centric mapping |
| XML_ELEMENTS | 2 | Element-centric mapping |
| XML_DEFAULT | 0 | Default—equivalent to XML_ATTRIBUTES (1) |
| XML_NOCOPY | 8 | Overflow metaproperty of the document (@mp:xmltext) should contain only nodes that were not extracted using the OpenXML rowset provider. |

**Table 12-7.**   Values of the Flags Parameter of OpenXML

## Metaproperties in OpenXML

After the parser loads the XML document into memory, SQL Server allows the `OpenXML` rowset to access a set of properties that describe attributes of the information. These properties are defined in a special namespace (`urn:schemas-microsoft-com:xml-metaprop`). Table 12-8 shows the list of possible values and their meanings:

| Metaproperty | Description |
|---|---|
| `@mp:id` | System-generated identifier. It could be used as a unique identifier on the level of the document (until the document is re-parsed). |
| `@mp:localnamed` | Name of the current node |
| `@mp:namespaceuri` | Namespace URI for the current element |
| `@mp:Prefix` | Prefix of the namespace for the current element |
| `@mp:xmltext` | String containing the XML branch of the current element, its attributes, and subelements. It could be set not to contain nodes that have already been read by other columns of the `OpenXML` provider. |
| `@mp:prev` | ID of the previous sibling of the node |
| `@mp:parented` (equivalent of `../@mp:parentid`) | ID of the parent node |

**Table 12-8.** Metaproperties in OpenXML

| @mp:parentlocalname | Name of the parent node (equivalent of ../@mp:localname) |
| @mp:parentnamespaceuri | Namespace of the parent node (equivalent of ../@mp:namespaceuri) |
| @mp:parentprefix | Prefix of the namespace of the parent node (equivalent of ../@mp:prefix) |

**Table 12-8.**    Metaproperties in OpenXML *(continued)*

The following example and Figure 12-9 demonstrate the use of metaproperties:

```
DECLARE @intDoc int
DECLARE @chvXMLDoc varchar(8000)
-- sample XML document
SET @chvXMLDoc ='
<root>
  <Equipment EquipmentID="1" Make="Toshiba" Model="Portege 7020CT">
   <Inventory InventoryID="5" StatusID="1" EquipmentID="1"/>
   <Inventory InventoryID="12" StatusID="1" EquipmentID="1"/>
  </Equipment>
  <Equipment EquipmentID="2" Make="Sony" Model="Trinitron 17XE"/>
  <Equipment EquipmentID="4" Make="HP" Model="LaserJet 4"/>
  <Equipment EquipmentID="5" Make="Bang &amp; Olafson" Model="V4000">
   <Inventory InventoryID="8" StatusID="1" EquipmentID="5"/>
  </Equipment>
  <Equipment EquipmentID="6" Make="NEC" Model="V90">
   <Inventory InventoryID="6" StatusID="2" EquipmentID="6"/>
  </Equipment>
</root>
'

--Load the XML document into memory.
```

```
EXEC sp_xml_preparedocument @intDoc OUTPUT, @chvXMLDoc

-- SELECT statement using OPENXML rowset provider
SELECT top 4 *
FROM      OPENXML (@intDoc, '/root/Equipment/Inventory')
          WITH     (InventoryID int '@InventoryID',
                   [mp:ID] int '@mp:id',
                   localname varchar(20) '@mp:localname',
                   namespaceuri varchar(40) '@mp:namespaceuri',
                   Prefix varchar(40) '@mp:Prefix',
                   prev varchar(40) '@mp:prev',
                   comment ntext '@mp:xmltext')



-- remove the XML document from memory
EXEC sp_xml_removedocument @intDoc
```

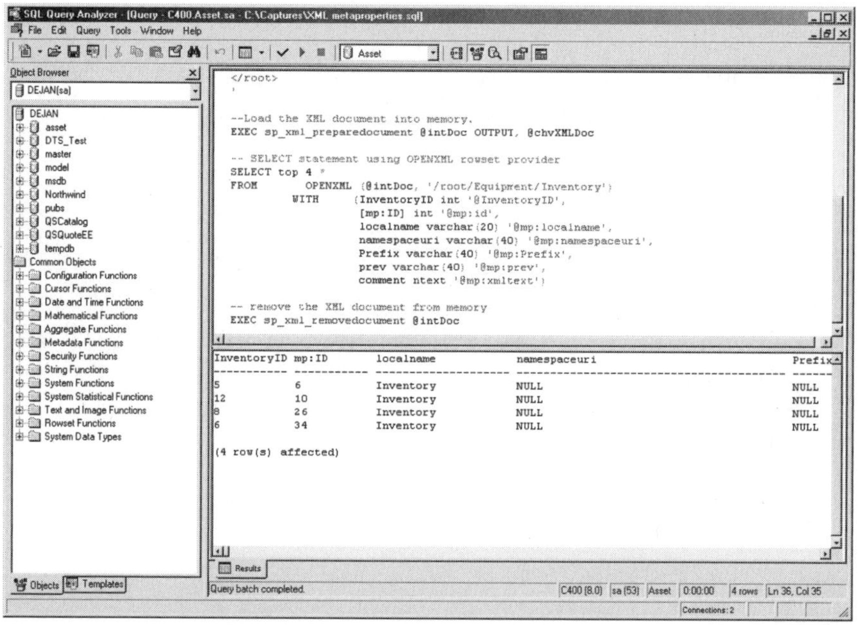

**Figure 12-9.**    Use of metaproperties in OpenXML

## What If an XML Document Is Longer Than 8,000 Characters?

You have probably noticed that we used long `varchar` strings (8,000 characters) in the preceding examples to store XML documents. Naturally, XML documents could be longer than this arbitrary figure. The trouble is that you cannot define local variables of the `text` datatype (and `varchar` is limited to only 8,000 characters).

Fortunately, sp_xml_preparedocument and `OpenXML` can handle `text` parameters. Instead of using a local variable of the `text` datatype, we can use an input parameter of a custom stored procedure as a parameter for sp_xml_preparedocument. The following stored procedure uses this method:

```
Alter  Procedure prTestXML
-- Extract Inventory info. from long XML document.
-- Demonstration of usage of text input parameters
-- to parse long XML document.
    @chvXMLDoc text

As
set nocount on

Declare @intErrorCode int,
        @intTransactionCountOnEntry int
        @intDoc int

Select @intErrorCode = @@Error



--Create an internal representation of the XML document.
EXEC sp_xml_preparedocument @intDoc OUTPUT, @chvXMLDoc


-- SELECT statement using OPENXML rowset provider
SELECT    *
FROM      OPENXML (@intDoc, '/root/Equipment/Inventory', 8)
          WITH    (InventoryID int '@InventoryID',
                   StatusID int '@StatusID',
                   Make varchar(25) '../@Make',
```

```
                            Model varchar(25) '../@Model',
                            comment ntext '@mp:xmltext')
EXEC sp_xml_removedocument @intDoc
return @intErrorCode
```

Figure 12-10 demonstrates the use of the stored procedure. A long XML document was created by copying and pasting the same set of nodes into the string (XML document) over and over.

## Publishing Database Information Using XML

SQL Server 2000 has an external set of components that allow users to access database information in the form of an XML document

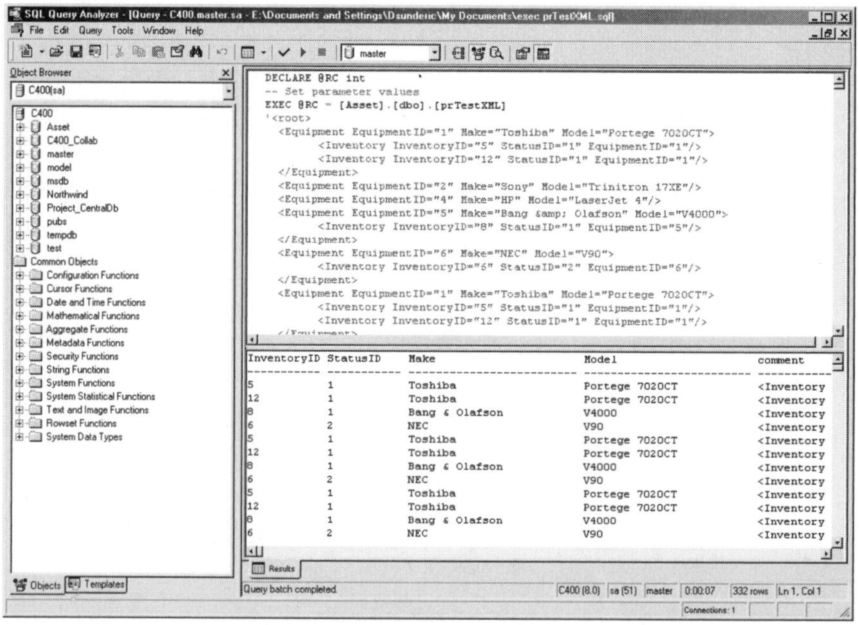

**Figure 12-10.** Use of a text input parameter

through the HTTP protocol. It is important to understand that these components are external. The most important of these is the ISAPI filter that works within IIS (Internet Information Server—a Web server), rather than within SQL Server (see Figure 12-11). It retrieves database information through a SQL Server 2000 OLE DB provider (SQLOLEDB). The OLE DB provider itself has been modified to use a new SQLXML.dll component and to support retuning of the result in the form of a stream. Figure 12-11 illustrates the transfer of information from a client computer to the server and back.

## Configuring Database Access Through HTTP

One new component delivered with SQL Server 2000 is an MMC snap-in called *IIS Virtual Directory Management for SQL Server*. This snap-in provides a graphical user interface for configuring database access through HTTP. Behind the scenes, it operates using the *IIS Virtual Directory Management for SQL Server Object Model*.

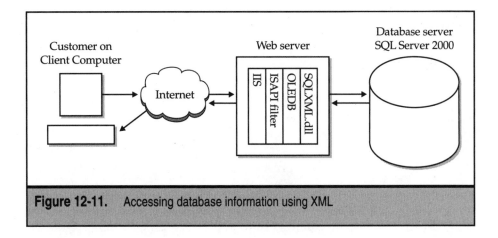

**Figure 12-11.**    Accessing database information using XML

This tool can operate on any edition of Windows NT or Windows 2000. Computers with Windows NT must also have IIS 4.0 or higher (or Peer Web Services 4.0 or higher on Windows NT Workstation) and MMC 1.2 or higher.

The configuration of database access requires only one operation—the administrator needs to create a *virtual directory*. Apart from the usual information (such as name and path), this virtual directory must contain information for accessing the database (login, password, database, server name, database name, and the type of access allowed through the URL and virtual names). Before we explain what a virtual name is, let's first say that there are three types of access that end users can accomplish through IIS:

▼ **dbobject**   Users can issue a `Select` statement as a part of an HTTP request and access a database object (such as a table or a view).

■ **template**   Users can specify a template that is a valid XML document and contains one or more Transact-SQL statements. SQL Server will execute, and the information will be included in the result.

▲ **schema**   The URL can be specified to execute an XPath query against the annotated mapping schema file.

A *virtual name* is a part of a URL that specifies and executes a dbobject, a template, or a schema.

Let's now demonstrate how you can configure IIS to provide access to SQL Server:

1. Launch IIS Virtual Directory Management for SQL Server: Start | Programs | Microsoft SQL Server | Configure SQL XML Support in IIS.

2. When the application appears on the screen, expand the server to display the Default Web Site. Select it and then select Action | New | Virtual Directory. The application displays the New Virtual Directory Properties dialog box.

3. Set the name and the physical path of the virtual directory (see Figure 12-12).

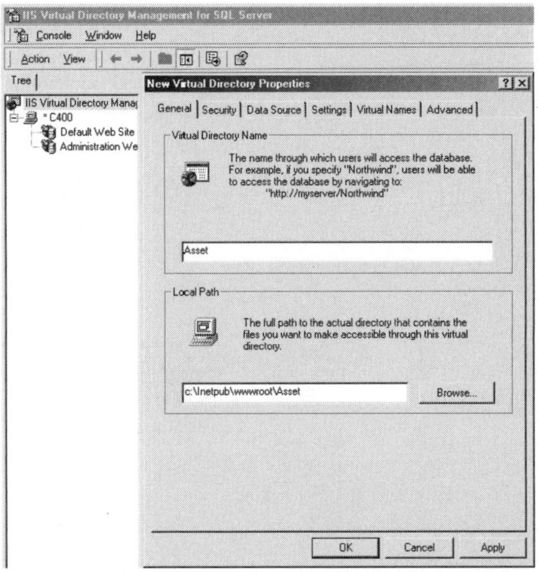

**Figure 12-12.**   Configuring a new virtual directory

4. Select the Security tab and define the authentication method that the user will use to connect to the database:

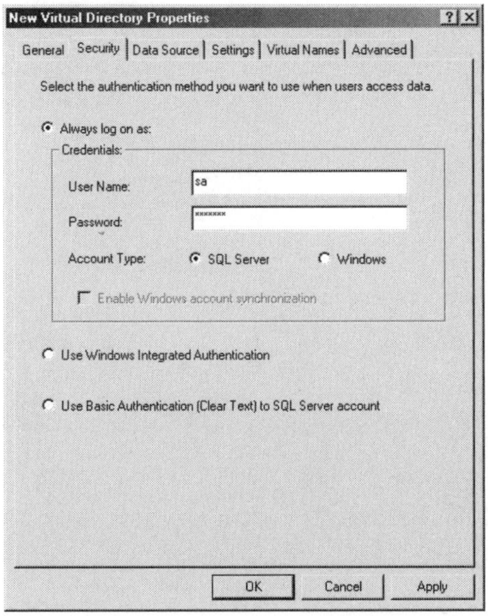

5. Select the Data Source tab to define the server and the database containing the source information:

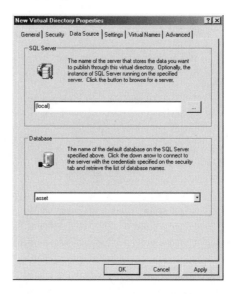

6. Select the Settings tab to specify the type of access to allow through the virtual directory. For training purposes, let's allow them all (although on a production server you will probably allow only templates or XPath).

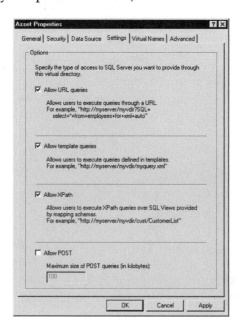

7. Select the Virtual Names tab to associate a specific type of access and optional directory to a virtual name:

8. Click the New button. The application displays the Virtual Name Configuration dialog box. Type a new name, specify a type, select an existing path that will store files, and then click Save:

9. Repeat step 8 to create virtual names for other types, and then click OK in the New Virtual Directory Properties dialog box. The application creates a virtual directory (see Figure 12-13).

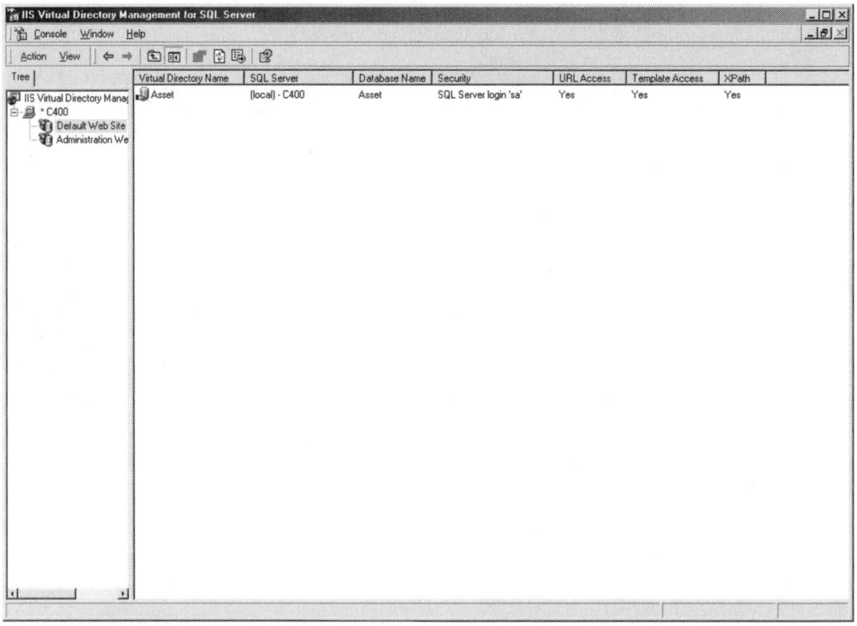

**Figure 12-13.** A new virtual directory

## Accessing Database Information Using a URL

After the virtual directory is created, an end user can use a browser such as Internet Explorer 5.0 to query the database using HTTP GET and POST methods. The simplest syntax for making such queries would be:

```
http://server/virtual_directory/virtual_name?sql=tsql_statement
```

Unfortunately, characters such as " " (space), "?", "/", "%", "#", and "&" have special meanings in URL syntax. Therefore, they must be encoded using their hexadecimal value in the form "%xx". For example, the space character can be replaced using "%20" or "+". Therefore, to query the Inventory table, a user can issue the following statement:

```
http://MyServer/Asset?sql=select%20top%201%20*%20
from%20Inventory%20for%20xml%20auto
```

The query returns an XML document that contains just one node (see Figure 12-14).

If you leave the clause `top 1` out of the query,

```
http://MyServer/Asset?sql=select%20*%20
from%20Inventory%20for%20xml%20auto
```

the parser will not be able to process the result. The Inventory element in the result string is repeated for each record and there is, therefore, no unique top element (see Figure 12-15).

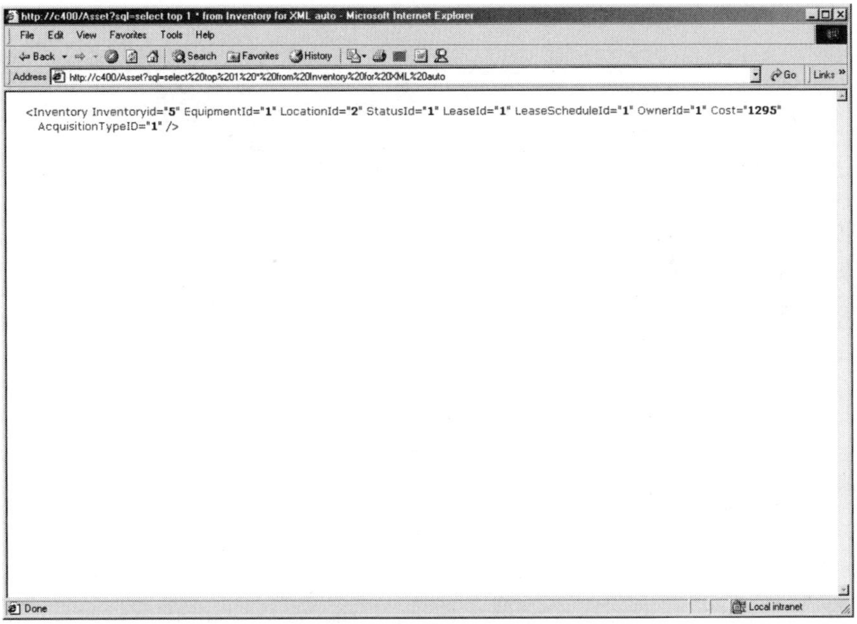

**Figure 12-14.** An XML document as a result of the database query

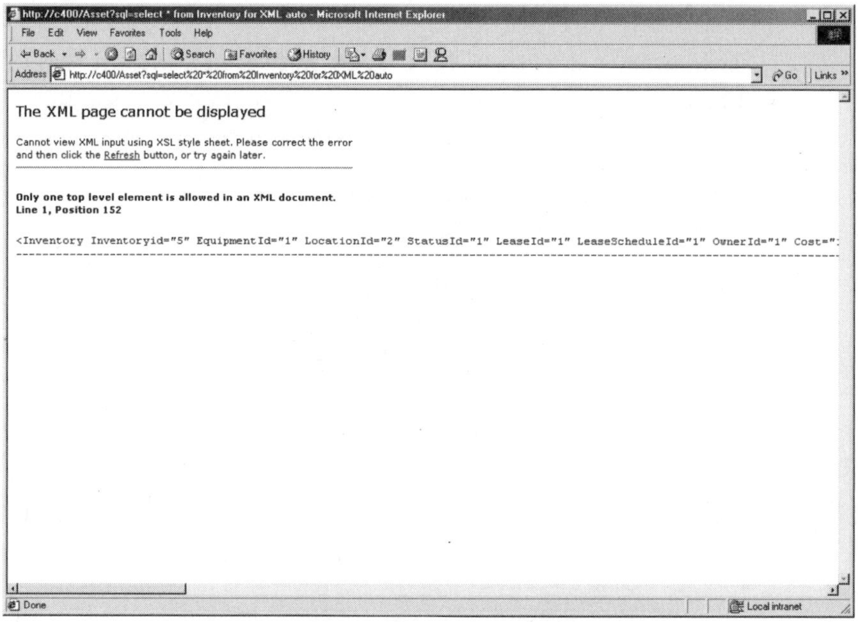

**Figure 12-15.** The problem with no unique top element

There are two solutions to this problem. You can add a *root* parameter to the HTTP GET method, and the server will add a root node to the result:

```
&root=root_node
```

In this case, the previous query would be

```
http://dejan/asset?sql=select%20*%20
from%20Inventory%20for%20xml%20auto&root=ROOT
```

The other alternative is to write the Transact-SQL statement so that it returns a missing root element. In the following example, two additional Select statements were added:

```
http://dejan/Asset?sql=SELECT%20'<Root>';
%20SELECT%20*%20FROM%20Inventory%20FOR%20XML%20AUTO;
%20select%20'</Root>'
```

The results of both methods are identical (see Figure 12-16).

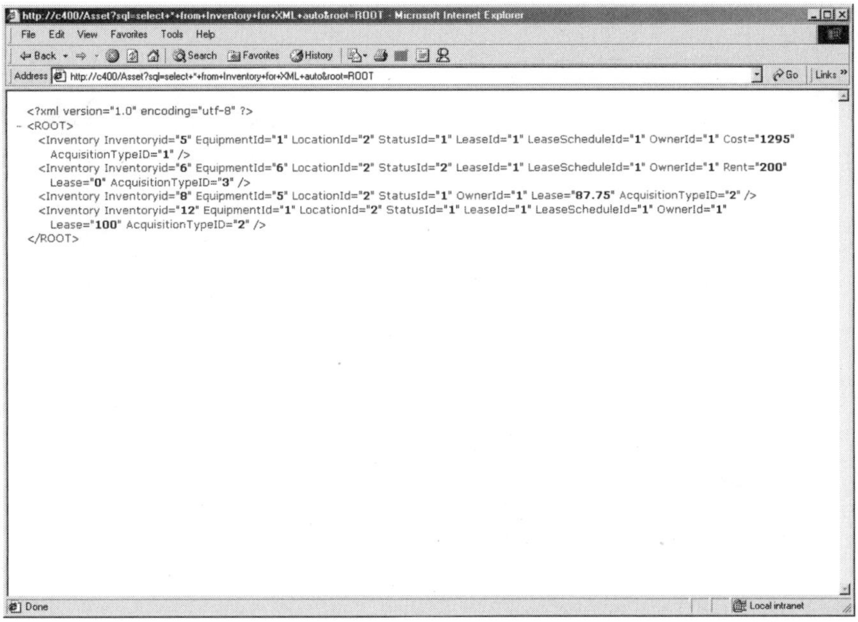

**Figure 12-16.**    The result as an XML document with root element

Unfortunately, many things can go wrong when you connect all these components and try to make them work together. Internet Explorer and the XML parser are not ideal debugging tools, which is understandable considering the number of layers created and the transformations that occurred.

## Using a Stored Procedure Through HTTP

SQL Server 2000 and the ISAPI driver do not force you to use only the Select statement to get information via HTTP. Naturally, you can also use stored procedures. The following stored procedure contains a simple Select statement with a For XML clause:

```
CREATE PROCEDURE prListEquipment_xml
AS
select *
```

```
from Equipment
for xml auto
```

The stored procedure can be called through HTTP:

```
http://dejan/asset?sql=execute%20prListEquipment_xml&root=ROOT
```

In the following example, we demonstrate two things. First, a list of parameters can be included as a part of the Transact-SQL statement that executes the stored procedure. Second, the root element can be created in the stored procedure as well:

```
CREATE PROCEDURE prGetEquipment_xml
    @EquipmentId int
AS

Select '<Root>'
Select * from Equipment
Where EquipmentID= @EquipmentId
For XML AUTO, elements
Select '</Root>'
```

This stored procedure can be called using the following URL:

```
http://dejan/asset?sql=execute%20prGetEquipment_xml%20@EquipmentId=5
```

Naturally, you are not required to use named parameters. The following URL is also legal, but a little bit confusing to read:

```
http://dejan/asset?sql=execute%20prGetEquipment_xml%205
```

## Accessing Database Information Using Templates

In the preceding section, we showed how you can incorporate a Transact-SQL statement as a part of the URL to access information via HTTP. Naturally, you cannot use this technique on a production system, because

▼ It is too complicated for end users.

■ It is prone to errors.

- The security of the system could be compromised easily.

- Browsers support only a limited URL length (2K).

▲ It is unrealistic to expect users to have adequate technical knowledge and understanding of the details of the technical implementation of the system.

Fortunately, there is an alternative—templates.

**Syntax**    A *template* file is an XML document that contains all the technical information such as For XML and XPath queries, parameters, and XSL transformation files required to access and process database information. Template files have the following syntax:

```
<ROOT xmlns:sql="urn:schemas-microsoft-com:xml-sql"
      sql:xsl='XSL_FileName' >
  <sql:header>
    <sql:param name=parameter_name>default_value</sql:param>
  <sql:header>
  <sql:query>
    tsql_statements
</sql:query>
  <sql:XPath-query mapping-schema="Schema_FileName">
    XPath_query
  </sql:XPath-query>
</ROOT>
```

The root element of the template file has one mandatory and one optional parameter. All other elements and attributes of the template file are declared in the urn:schemas-microsoft-com:xml-sql namespace. Therefore, all template files must have an xmlns:sql= "urn:schemas-microsoft-com:xml-sql" attribute. The xsl attribute is optional. It is used to specify the name of the XSL transformation file.

**Using Query**  The `<sql:query>` element is used to specify one or more Transact-SQL statements. The following template file queries the Equipment table:

```
<root xmlns:sql='urn:schemas-microsoft-com:xml-sql'>
   <sql:query>
      select * from Equipment for XML auto, elements
   </sql:query>
</root>
```

If the template file is saved in ListEqupment.xml in the template folder, it can be executed using the following URL:

```
http://dejan/asset/template/ListEquipment.xml
```

You can see the result in Figure 12-17.

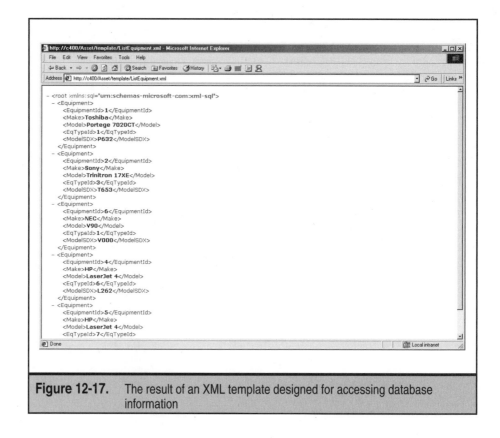

**Figure 12-17.**   The result of an XML template designed for accessing database information

▼ **NOTE:** The template file can contain more than one `<sql:query>` (and `<sql:XPath-query>`). It is important to know that all queries contained within separate elements are treated as separate transactions. Even if some of these transactions fail, others will be executed independently.

**Using Parameters**    If the Transact-SQL statements contain parameters, they are defined in the `<sql:header>` element. The parameter's definition contains the name of the parameter and the default value to be assigned to the parameter if a value is not specified:

```
<sql:param name=parameter_name>default_value</sql:param>
```

The following example contains a simple template file with two parameters:

```
<root xmlns:sql='urn:schemas-microsoft-com:xml-sql'>

  <sql:header>
     <sql:param name='Make' >Toshiba</sql:param>
     <sql:param name='Model'>Portege 7020CT</sql:param>
  </sql:header>

   <sql:query>
      exec prGetEquipment2_xml @Make, @Model
</sql:query>
 </root>
```

Let's assume that the template is stored in the GetEquipment.xml file in the template folder. As usual, the *parameter list* in the URL starts with a "?" character. If multiple parameters are listed, they should be delimited with an "&" character. Parameters such as *strings* (that are delimited with quotes in Transact-SQL) must be delimited without quotes, as shown in the following URL:

```
http://dejan/asset/template/GetEquipment2.xml?Make=Toshiba&Model
=Portege%207020CT
```

You can see the result in Figure 12-18.

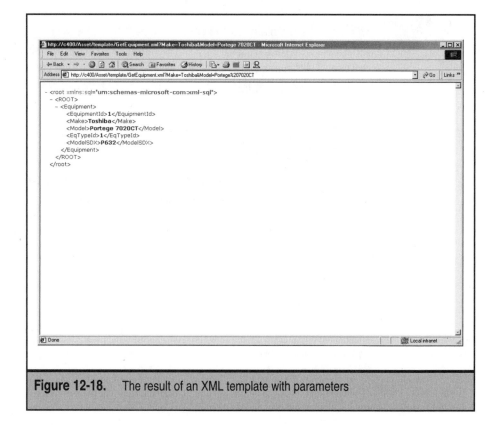

**Figure 12-18.** The result of an XML template with parameters

**Using XSL** It is possible to use XSL files to change the way information is presented in a Web browser. The following template references a query (stored procedure) that provides an XML result and an XSL file that converts it to HTML (Equipment.xsl):

```
<?xml version ='1.0' encoding='UTF-8'?>
 <root xmlns:sql='urn:schemas-microsoft-com:xml-sql'
      sql:xsl='/Equipment.xsl'>
<sql:query>
      exec prListEquipment2_xml
</sql:query>
 </root>
```

If you execute just the stored procedure (for example, from Query Analyzer), you can see the simple XML document it produces:

```
<Equipment
    EquipmentId="1"
    Make="Toshiba"
    Model="Portege 7020CT">
    <EqType EqType="Desktop"/>
</Equipment>
<Equipment
    EquipmentId="2"
    Make="Sony"
    Model="Trinitron 17XE">
    <EqType EqType="Monitor"/>
</Equipment>
<Equipment
    EquipmentId="6"
    Make="NEC"
    Model="V90">
    <EqType EqType="Desktop"/>
</Equipment>
...
```

The XSL file shown in the following code snippet describes how the XML file is converted:

```
<?xml version='1.0' encoding='UTF-8'?>
 <xsl:stylesheet xmlns:xsl='http://www.w3.org/TR/WD-xsl' >
    <xsl:template match = '*'>
        <xsl:apply-templates />
    </xsl:template>
    <xsl:template match = 'Equipment'>
       <TR>
          <TD><xsl:value-of select = '@EquipmentId' /></TD>
          <TD><xsl:value-of select = '@Make' /></TD>
          <TD><xsl:value-of select = '@Model' /></TD>
          <TD><xsl:value-of select = './EqType/@EqType' /></TD>
       </TR>
    </xsl:template>

<xsl:template match = '/'>
<HTML>
<HEAD>
<title>Equipment</title>
```

```
        </HEAD>
        <BODY>
        <TABLE border = "1" width="100%">
        <TR><TH colspan="4" bgcolor="#000000">
            <p align="left"><font color="#FFFFFF" face="Arial">
                              <b>Equipment</b>
                        </font>
            </p>
          </TH></TR>
        <TR>
            <TH align="left" bgcolor="#C0C0C0">
                <b><font face="Arial" size="2">
                    Equipment ID
                </font></b>
            </TH>
            <TH align="left" bgcolor="#C0C0C0">
                 <b><font face="Arial" size="2">
                    Make
                </font></b>
            </TH>
            <TH align="left" bgcolor="#C0C0C0">
                 <b><font face="Arial" size="2">
                    Model
                </font></b>
            </TH>
            <TH align="left" bgcolor="#C0C0C0">
                 <b><font face="Arial" size="2">
                    Equipment Type
                </font></b>
            </TH>
        </TR>
        <xsl:apply-templates select = 'root' />
                </TABLE>
                </BODY>
            </HTML>
        </xsl:template>
</xsl:stylesheet>
```

You can distinguish two segments within the XSL file. The last
`<xsl:template match = '/'>` element defines the static part of the
HTML page. It consists of the `<HEAD>` and `<BODY>` tags of the HTML
page and the definition of the table (the `<TABLE>` tag). Because of the
`match = '/'` attribute, the described transformation is performed on
the root node of the XML document.

The second `<xsl:template match = 'Equipment'>` element
is applied on each element node called `'Equipment'`. Each node is
converted to a row within an HTML table (using row `<TR>` and
column `<TD>` tags):

```
<xsl:template match = 'Equipment'>
    </TR>
        <TD><xsl:value-of select = '@EquipmentId' /></TD>
        <TD><xsl:value-of select = '@Make' /></TD>
        <TD><xsl:value-of select = '@Model' /></TD>
        <TD><xsl:value-of select = 'EqType/@EqType' /></TD>
    </TR>
</xsl:template>
```

The `<xsl:value-of>` elements define the source from which the
parser obtains the values of the table cells. Recall that in the XPath
section earlier in this chapter, `'@EquipmentId'` referred to an
attribute called `EquipmentId` (not a Transact-SQL local variable).
The last node reference (`'EqType/@EqType'`) is most interesting. It
first points to a child node named `EqType` and then to its attribute
named `EqType`.

To execute the template file, you can specify the following URL:

```
http://c400/asset/template/ListEquipmentWithXSL.xml
```

Unfortunately, Internet Explorer displays HTML code as shown in
Figure 12-19.

To see how everything works together, you must prompt Internet
Explorer to treat the content received from the Web server as an

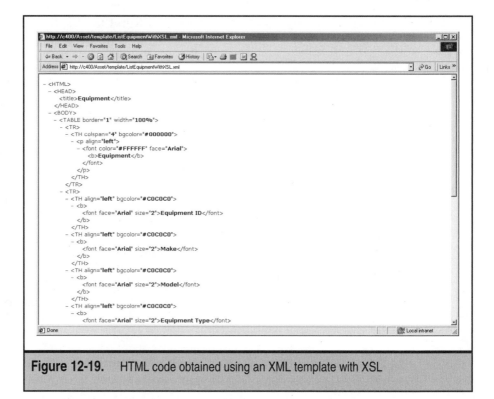

**Figure 12-19.** HTML code obtained using an XML template with XSL

HTML file rather than an XML file. You must specify an additional parameter (`contenttype=text/html`) when you specify the URL:

```
http://c400/asset/template/ListEquipmentWithXSL.xml?contenttype=text/html
```

You can see the result in Figure 12-20.

**Using XPath**    The `<sql:XPath-query>` element of the template is used to specify XPath query expressions and mapping schema against which the XPath query expression is executed. We will not describe mapping schemas until the next section, so we will demonstrate XPath queries in this section on the simplest possible schema.

If you execute a simple `Select` statement with a `For XML` clause that contains an `XMLData` option against the Equipment table,

```
Select EquipmentId, Make, Model from Equipment For XML auto, XMLData
```

you get a simple inline XDR schema at the beginning of the XML
document:

```
<Schema name="Schema" xmlns="urn:schemas-microsoft-com:xml-data"
                      xmlns:dt="urn:schemas-microsoft-com:datatypes">
<ElementType name="Equipment" content="empty" model="closed">
<AttributeType name="EquipmentId" dt:type="i4"/>
<AttributeType name="Make" dt:type="string"/>
<AttributeType name="Model" dt:type="string"/>
<attribute type="EquipmentId"/>
<attribute type="Make"/>
<attribute type="Model"/>
</ElementType>
</Schema>
<Equipment xmlns="x-schema:#Schema" EquipmentId="1" Make="Toshiba"
Model="Portege 7020CT"/>
...
```

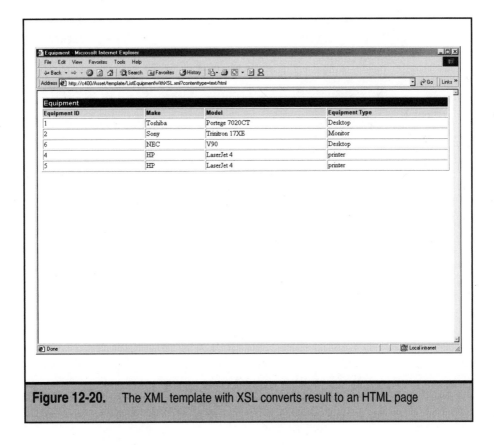

**Figure 12-20.**    The XML template with XSL converts result to an HTML page

To get a proper mapping schema in this case, you need to extract the schema into a separate file and to add another namespace to it (`xmlns:sql="urn:schemas-microsoft-com:xml-sql"`):

```
<Schema name="Schema" xmlns="urn:schemas-microsoft-com:xml-data"
                       xmlns:dt="urn:schemas-microsoft-com:datatypes"
                       xmlns:sql="urn:schemas-microsoft-com:xml-sql">
<ElementType name="Equipment" content="empty" model="closed">
<AttributeType name="EquipmentId" dt:type="i4"/>
<AttributeType name="Make" dt:type="string"/>
<AttributeType name="Model" dt:type="string"/>
<attribute type="EquipmentId"/>
<attribute type="Make"/>
<attribute type="Model"/>
</ElementType>
</Schema>
```

**NOTE:** This is not the only operation needed to create a mapping schema. It is successful in this case only because the target XML document is so simple. We will explore the details of mapping a schema in the following section.

Now it is possible to create a template file to use the XPath query to get information using this schema:

```
<ROOT xmlns:sql="urn:schemas-microsoft-com:xml-sql">
    <sql:xpath-query mapping-schema="EqSchema.xml">
        Equipment
    </sql:xpath-query>
</ROOT>
```

The schema is referenced in a mapping-schema attribute, and the XPath query is specified as the content of the `<sql:xpath>` element. The XPath query in the template references only Equipment nodes. If the template and the schema are stored in EqTemplate.xml and EqSchema.xml in the template virtual directory, they can be executed using:

```
http://c400/asset/template/EqTemplate.xml
```

Figure 12-21 shows the result.

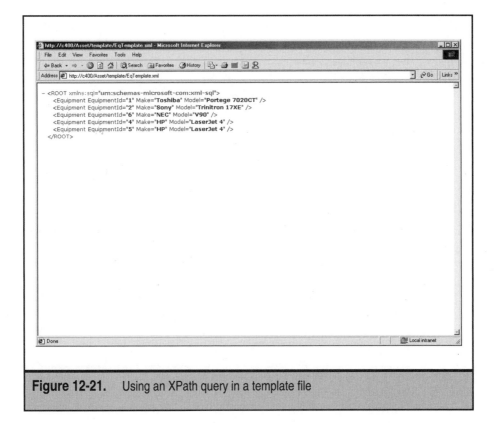

**Figure 12-21.**   Using an XPath query in a template file

We can use more complicated XPath queries in a template:

```
<ROOT xmlns:sql="urn:schemas-microsoft-com:xml-sql">
    <sql:xpath-query mapping-schema="EqSchema.xml">
        Equipment[@EquipmentId=1]
</sql:xpath-query>
</ROOT>
```

This query filters Element nodes that have an EquipmentId attribute with a value set to 1. Figure 12-22 shows the result.

## XML Views Based on Annotations of XDR Schemas

In the preceding section, we demonstrated how XDR schemas and XPath queries can be used to retrieve data from a database. We will now examine the use of XDR schemas for mapping in greater detail.

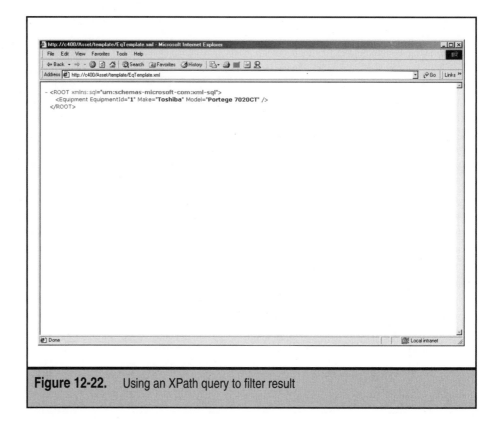

**Figure 12-22.** Using an XPath query to filter result

The main purpose of an XDR schema is to define the structure of the XML document. SQL Server 2000 extends the XDR schema language with *annotations* designed to *map XML nodes* (elements and attributes) and *database objects* (tables, views, and columns). Other annotations allow features such as the definition of *hierarchical relationships* between XML nodes, change of a target namespace, and the retrieval of XML-encoded data from a database. Such XDR schemas produce XML documents that behave in a fashion similar to database views and, therefore, are sometimes called *XML views*.

**Mapping Tables, Views, and Columns** The schema used in the preceding section was based on default mapping between tables and elements, and between columns and attributes. Since SQL Server was able to find a table that corresponded to the specified element and attributes that corresponded to the table's columns, the result was an XML document containing information from the database table.

In the case where an element is named differently than a table (or a view), you must add a `sql:relation` annotation (an attribute of the `<ElementType>` tag) to the schema. In the case where attributes of the element are named differently from the columns of the table (or the view), you must add a `sql:field` annotation (an attribute of the `<attribute>` tag) to the schema. In the following example, the Equipment table is mapped to the element `<Part>` and columns EquipmentId and Make are mapped to attributes PartNum and Manufacturer:

```
<Schema name="Schema"
        xmlns="urn:schemas-microsoft-com:xml-data"
        xmlns:dt="urn:schemas-microsoft-com:datatypes"
        xmlns:sql="urn:schemas-microsoft-com:xml-sql">
<ElementType name="Part" sql:relation="Equipment"
              content="empty" model="closed">
<AttributeType name="PartNum" dt:type="i4" />
<AttributeType name="Manufacturer" dt:type="string" />
<AttributeType name="Model" dt:type="string"/>
<attribute type="PartNum" sql:field="EquipmentId"/>
<attribute type="Manufacturer" sql:field="Make"/>
<attribute type="Model"/>
</ElementType>
</Schema>
```

This schema can be used by the following template:

```
<ROOT xmlns:sql="urn:schemas-microsoft-com:xml-sql">
    <sql:xpath-query mapping-schema="PartSchema.xml">
        Part
</sql:xpath-query>
</ROOT>
```

The result is shown in Figure 12-23.

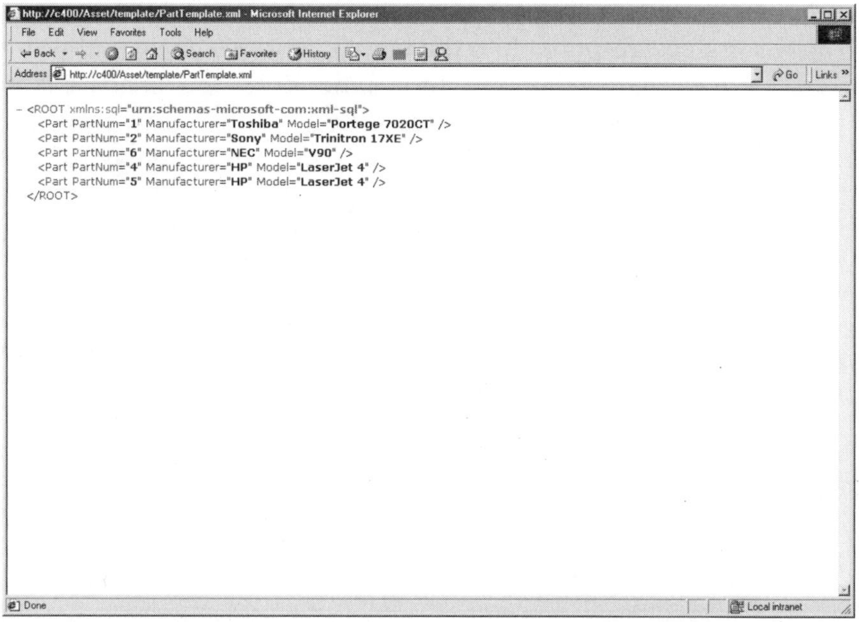

**Figure 12-23.** The result of the annotated schema

`sql:field` annotations can be applied to elements as well. The following schema is not attribute-based, but element-based:

```
<Schema name="Schema"
        xmlns="urn:schemas-microsoft-com:xml-data"
        xmlns:dt="urn:schemas-microsoft-com:datatypes"
        xmlns:sql="urn:schemas-microsoft-com:xml-sql">
    <ElementType name="Part" sql:relation="Equipment"
                content="eltOnly" model="closed" order="many">
    <element type="PartNo" sql:field="EquipmentId"/>
    <element type="Manufacturer" sql:field="Make"/>
    <element type="Model"/>
</ElementType>
<ElementType name="PartNo" content="textOnly"
                model="closed" dt:type="i4"/>
```

```
   <ElementType name="Manufacturer" content="textOnly"
                model="closed" dt:type="string"/>
   <ElementType name="Model" content="textOnly"
                model="closed" dt:type="string"/>
</Schema>
```

You can use this schema through the following template:

```
<ROOT xmlns:sql="urn:schemas-microsoft-com:xml-sql">
   <sql:xpath-query mapping-schema="PartElementSchema.xml">
       Part
   </sql:xpath-query>
</ROOT>
```

The result is shown in Figure 12-24.

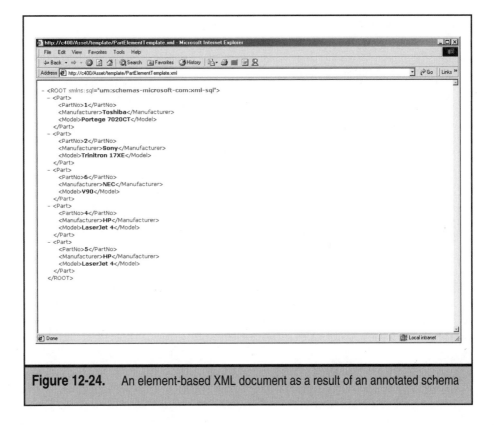

**Figure 12-24.**    An element-based XML document as a result of an annotated schema

**Mapping Relationships**  So far, we have demonstrated only schemas based on a single table (or view). When the XML document has to map to more than one table, that relationship has to be annotated using the `<sql:relationship>` tag. This process is similar to the creation of foreign keys in relational databases. The following attributes of the `<sql:relationship>` tag need to be defined:

| Attribute | Description |
|---|---|
| *key-relation* | Name of the primary relation |
| *key* | Node (field) in a primary relation (table) that serves as primary key |
| *foreign-relation* | Name of the foreign relation (table) |
| *foreign-key* | Node (field) in a foreign relation (table) that serves as foreign key |

The following schema contains such a relationship:

```
<Schema name="Schema"
        xmlns="urn:schemas-microsoft-com:xml-data"
        xmlns:dt="urn:schemas-microsoft-com:datatypes"
        xmlns:sql="urn:schemas-microsoft-com:xml-sql">

<ElementType name="Contact" content="eltOnly"
             model="closed" order="many">
<element type="Inventory" maxOccurs="*">


        <sql:relationship
        key-relation="Contact"
        key="ContactId"
        foreign-key="OwnerId"
        foreign-relation="Inventory" />


</element>
<AttributeType name="ContactId" dt:type="i4"/>
<AttributeType name="FirstName" dt:type="string"/>
<AttributeType name="LastName" dt:type="string"/>
<AttributeType name="Phone" dt:type="string"/>
<AttributeType name="Fax" dt:type="string"/>
```

```
<AttributeType name="Email" dt:type="string"/>
<AttributeType name="OrgUnitId" dt:type="i2"/>
<AttributeType name="UserName" dt:type="string"/>
<AttributeType name="ts" dt:type="i8"/>
<attribute type="ContactId"/>
<attribute type="FirstName"/>
<attribute type="LastName"/>
<attribute type="Phone"/>
<attribute type="Fax"/>
<attribute type="Email"/>
<attribute type="OrgUnitId"/>
<attribute type="UserName"/>
<attribute type="ts"/>
</ElementType>

<ElementType name="Inventory" content="empty" model="closed">
<AttributeType name="Inventoryid" dt:type="i4"/>
<AttributeType name="EquipmentId" dt:type="i4"/>
<AttributeType name="LocationId" dt:type="i4"/>
<AttributeType name="StatusId" dt:type="ui1"/>
<AttributeType name="LeaseId" dt:type="i4"/>
<AttributeType name="LeaseScheduleId" dt:type="i4"/>
<AttributeType name="OwnerId" dt:type="i4"/>
<AttributeType name="Rent" dt:type="fixed.14.4"/>
<AttributeType name="Lease" dt:type="fixed.14.4"/>
<AttributeType name="Cost" dt:type="fixed.14.4"/>
<AttributeType name="AcquisitionTypeID" dt:type="ui1"/>
<attribute type="Inventoryid"/>
<attribute type="EquipmentId"/>
<attribute type="LocationId"/>
<attribute type="StatusId"/>
<attribute type="LeaseId"/>
<attribute type="LeaseScheduleId"/>
<attribute type="OwnerId"/>
<attribute type="Rent"/>
<attribute type="Lease"/>
<attribute type="Cost"/>
<attribute type="AcquisitionTypeID"/>
</ElementType>
</Schema>
```

It can be used through the following template:

```
<ROOT xmlns:sql="urn:schemas-microsoft-com:xml-sql">
    <sql:xpath-query mapping-schema="OwnerSchema.xml">
        Contact
    </sql:xpath-query>
</ROOT>
```

The result is shown in Figure 12-25.

Naturally, you can join more than one table.

**Other Annotations**    There are other annotations that you can also use in mapping schemas: `sql:is-constant="1"` annotations are used on static nodes such as the root node; `id`, `idref`, and `idrefs` attributes can be used to create intradocument links in XML

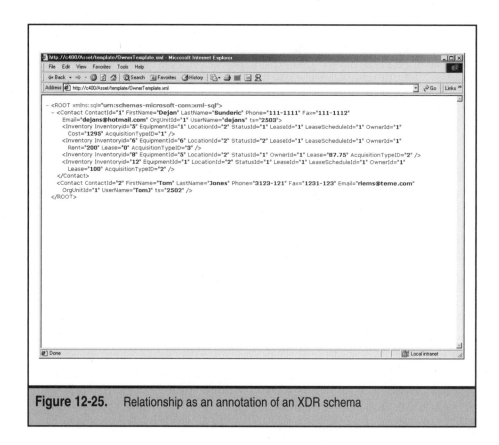

**Figure 12-25.**    Relationship as an annotation of an XDR schema

documents; `sql:id-prefix` annotations can be used to make ID attributes unique; `sql:use-cdate` annotations can be used to specify a CDATA section in the XML document; `sql:overflow-field` attributes are used to retrieve data from fields that contain XML tags; `sql:map-field` attributes are used to prevent nodes from being mapped in the schema; and so on.

**Retrieving Data Using XDR Schemas**    There are three ways to retrieve database information using XDR annotated schemas:

▼   Templates that contain XPath queries

■   Templates with inline mapping schemas

▲   A URL that refers to the mapping schema and specifies an XPath query

So far, all examples have used the first method—a template that contains XPath queries. We will now explore the other two.

**Templates with Inline Mapping Schemas**    It is very simple to create this type of template. In the following example, we have merged template and schema files used earlier into one file:

```
<ROOT xmlns="urn:schemas-microsoft-com:xml-data"
      xmlns:dt="urn:schemas-microsoft-com:datatypes"
      xmlns:sql="urn:schemas-microsoft-com:xml-sql">
<Schema name="Schema"
   sql:id="InlineSchema"
   sql:is-mapping-schema="1">
<ElementType name="Part" sql:relation="Equipment"
             content="empty" model="closed">
    <AttributeType name="PartNum" dt:type="i4" />
    <AttributeType name="Manufacturer" dt:type="string" />
    <AttributeType name="Model" dt:type="string"/>
    <attribute type="PartNum" sql:field="EquipmentId"/>
    <attribute type="Manufacturer" sql:field="Make"/>
    <attribute type="Model"/>
  </ElementType>
</Schema>
    <sql:xpath-query mapping-schema="#InlineSchema">
```

```
        Part
    </sql:xpath-query>
</ROOT>
```

The schema is identified using the `sql:id` attribute and described using the `sql:is-mapping-schema` attribute of the `<Schema>` element. The identifier is used later in the `mapping-schema` attribute of the `<sql:xpath-query>` element. The template can be used with a simple URL reference to the file as shown in Figure 12-26.

**A *URL with a Reference to a Mapping Schema and an XPath Query***    To refer to an XDR-annotated schema in a URL, you must first create a virtual name for the schema of the type described in "Configuring Database Access Through HTTP" earlier in this chapter. Such a URL has the following structure:

```
http://server/virtual_directory/virtual_name/schema_file/XPath_query
```

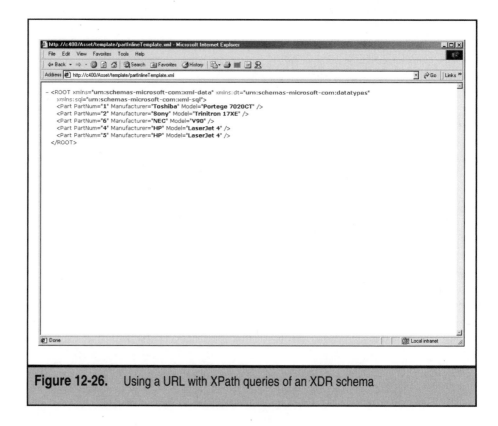

**Figure 12-26.**    Using a URL with XPath queries of an XDR schema

The following schema joins three tables (Inventory, Equipment, and EqType). They are connected in the usual manner using the `<sql:relationship>` tag.

```
<Schema name="Schema"
        xmlns="urn:schemas-microsoft-com:xml-data"
        xmlns:dt="urn:schemas-microsoft-com:datatypes"
        xmlns:sql="urn:schemas-microsoft-com:xml-sql">

<ElementType name="Inventory" content="eltOnly"
             model="closed" order="many">
<element type="Equipment" maxOccurs="*">

        <sql:relationship
            key-relation="Inventory"
            key="EquipmentId"
            foreign-key="EquipmentId"
            foreign-relation="Equipment" />

</element>
<AttributeType name="Inventoryid" dt:type="i4"/>
<AttributeType name="EquipmentId" dt:type="i4"/>
<AttributeType name="LocationId" dt:type="i4"/>
<AttributeType name="StatusId" dt:type="ui1"/>
<AttributeType name="LeaseId" dt:type="i4"/>
<AttributeType name="LeaseScheduleId" dt:type="i4"/>
<AttributeType name="OwnerId" dt:type="i4"/>
<AttributeType name="Rent" dt:type="fixed.14.4"/>
<AttributeType name="Lease" dt:type="fixed.14.4"/>
<AttributeType name="Cost" dt:type="fixed.14.4"/>
<AttributeType name="AcquisitionTypeID" dt:type="ui1"/>
<attribute type="Inventoryid"/>
<attribute type="EquipmentId"/>
<attribute type="LocationId"/>
<attribute type="StatusId"/>
<attribute type="LeaseId"/>
<attribute type="LeaseScheduleId"/>
<attribute type="OwnerId"/>
<attribute type="Rent"/>
<attribute type="Lease"/>
<attribute type="Cost"/>
<attribute type="AcquisitionTypeID"/>
</ElementType>
```

```
<ElementType name="Equipment" content="eltOnly"
            model="closed" order="many">
<element type="EqType" maxOccurs="*">

    <sql:relationship
        key-relation="Equipment"
        key="EqTypeId"
        foreign-key="EqTypeId"
        foreign-relation="EqType" />

</element>
<AttributeType name="EquipmentId" dt:type="i4"/>
<AttributeType name="Make" dt:type="string"/>
<AttributeType name="Model" dt:type="string"/>
<AttributeType name="EqTypeId" dt:type="i2"/>
<AttributeType name="ModelSDX" dt:type="string"/>
<AttributeType name="MakeSDX" dt:type="string"/>
<attribute type="EquipmentId"/>
<attribute type="Make"/>
<attribute type="Model"/>
<attribute type="EqTypeId"/>
<attribute type="ModelSDX"/>
<attribute type="MakeSDX"/>
</ElementType>

<ElementType name="EqType" content="empty" model="closed">
<AttributeType name="EqTypeId" dt:type="i2"/>
<AttributeType name="EqType" dt:type="string"/>
<attribute type="EqTypeId"/>
<attribute type="EqType"/>
</ElementType>

<ElementType name="ROOT" sql:is-constant="1">
    <element type="Inventory"/>
</ElementType>

</Schema>
```

In the preceding examples with template files, it was not necessary to define a unique root element in the schema. The template took care of that requirement. In this case, you have to define the root element explicitly in the XML schema:

```
<ElementType name="ROOT" sql:is-constant="1">
    <element type="Inventory"/>
</ElementType>
```

You can see the complete tree of the XML document if you issue the following URL:

```
http://c400/asset/Schema/InvSchema.xml/ROOT
```

The XPath query refers to the `<ROOT>` node and all nodes that it contains. The result is shown in Figure 12-27.

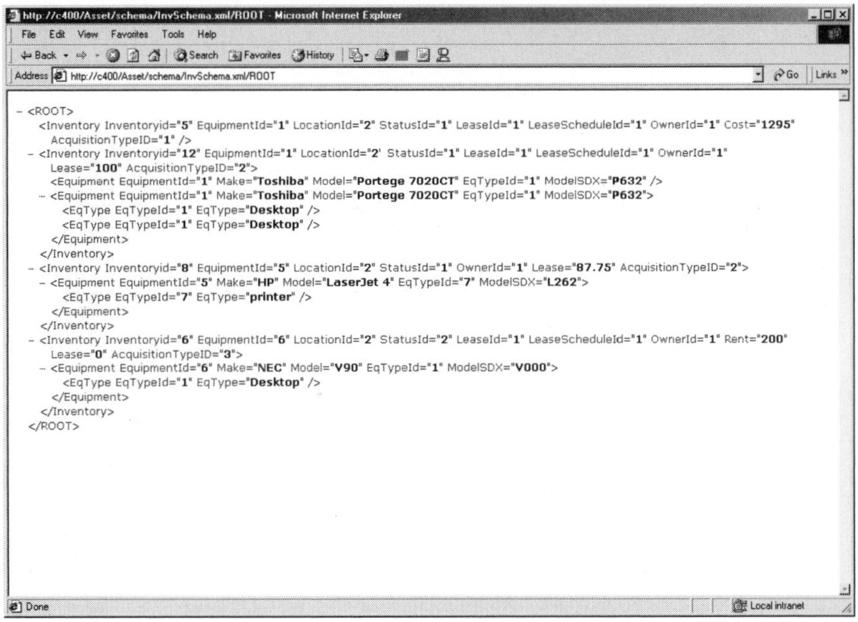

**Figure 12-27.**   Using a template with inline mapping schema

You could use XPath to further filter the result. The following URL retrieves only Inventory nodes that have a `StatusId` attribute set to 2:

```
http://c400/asset/Schema/InvSchema.xml/ROOT/Inventory[@StatusId=2]
```

The result is shown in Figure 12-28.

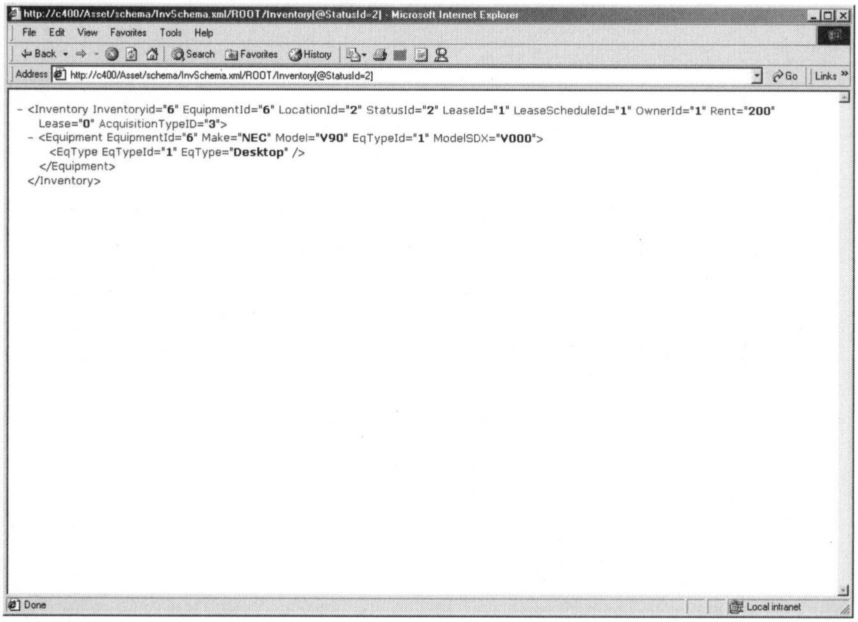

**Figure 12-28.**    Filtering XML documents using an XPath query

## POSTing Queries to the Server

In previous sections, we demonstrated how you can access database information over HTTP using the GET method. This method is simpler to use for testing purposes—you supply parameters in the URL after the "?"-sign in the form of an ampersand (&)–separated list. Unfortunately, this database access method has two problems:

▼ You cannot expect even the most skilled users to be able to type proper queries in the form of a URL address.

▲ The size of the URL is limited to 2K, thus limiting the number and complexity of parameters.

HTTP's POST method does not set limitations on the size of a query, but it is even more difficult to use. You need a custom application (or component) to pass parameters to the Web server.

The simplest version of such an application is an HTML form that uses the POST method to pass the content of its controls to the server. In this case, instead of passing it to an ASP page or some other component on the server, you need to pass it to the virtual directory that processes XML requests. We can demonstrate this technique using the following stored procedure with two parameters:

```
CREATE PROCEDURE prListEquipment3_xml
    @Make varchar(50),
    @Model varchar(50)
AS
select EquipmentId, Make, Model, EqType
from Equipment inner join EqType
on Equipment.EqTypeId = EqType.EqTypeId
where Make like @Make
and Model like @Model
for xml auto
GO
```

Next, we create a Web page with an HTML form. The form contains two visible controls that allow a user to specify the parameters of the query. There are also two hidden controls that will not be visible to the user, but that specify an XML template to be passed to the server and the content type in which the result is expected:

```
<head>
<TITLE>Query Equipment</TITLE>
</head>
<body>
<H3>Query Equipment (use % as wild card).</H3>
<form action="http://C400/Asset" method="POST">
Make:
<input type=text name=Make value='Tosh%'><BR>
Model:
<input type=text name=Model value='Por%'>
<input type=hidden name=contenttype value=text/xml>
<input type=hidden name=template value='
<ROOT xmlns:sql="urn:schemas-microsoft-com:xml-sql" >
<sql:header>
    <sql:param name="Make">%</sql:param>
    <sql:param name="Model">%</sql:param>
</sql:header>
<sql:query>
      exec prListEquipment3_xml @Make, @Model
</sql:query>
</ROOT>
'>

<p><input type="submit">
</form>
</body>
```

When a user opens this form, he or she is prompted to supply parameters (see Figure 12-29).

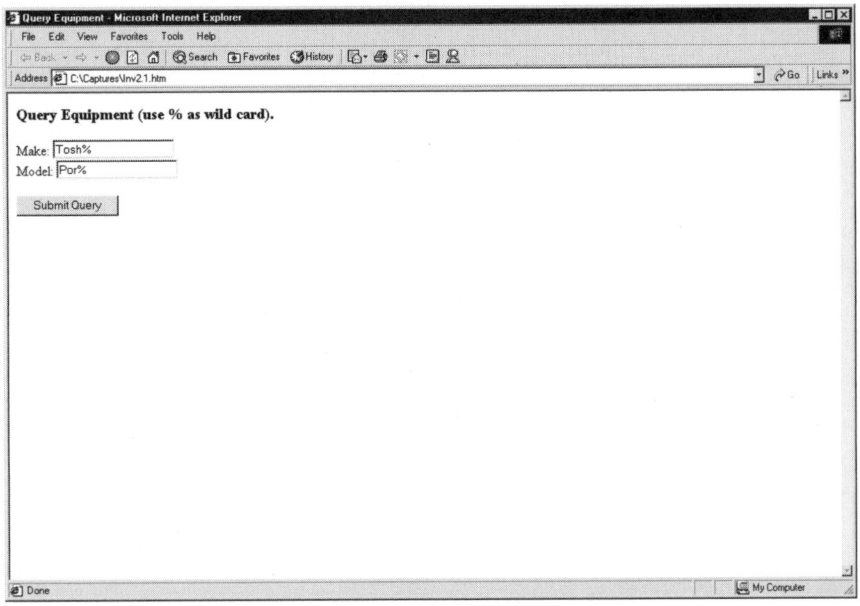

**Figure 12-29.**    HTML form for querying the database

After the form and query are submitted, Internet Explorer displays the result (see Figure 12-30).

You can polish this form if you add an XSL file that will convert the XML result into an HTML form:

```
<head>
<TITLE>Query Equipment</TITLE>
</head>
<body>
<H3>Query Equipment (use % as wild card). </H3>
<form action="http://C400/Asset" method="POST">
Make:
<input type=text name=Make value='Tosh%'><BR>
Model:
<input type=text name=Model value='Por%'>
```

```
<input type=hidden name=contenttype value=text/xml>
<input type=hidden name=xsl value="template\Equipment.xsl">
<input type=hidden name=template value='
<ROOT xmlns:sql="urn:schemas-microsoft-com:xml-sql" >
<sql:header>
    <sql:param name="Make">%</sql:param>
    <sql:param name="Model">%</sql:param>
</sql:header>
<sql:query>
   exec prListEquipment3_xml @Make, @Model
</sql:query>
</ROOT>
'>

<p><input type="submit">
</form>
</body>
```

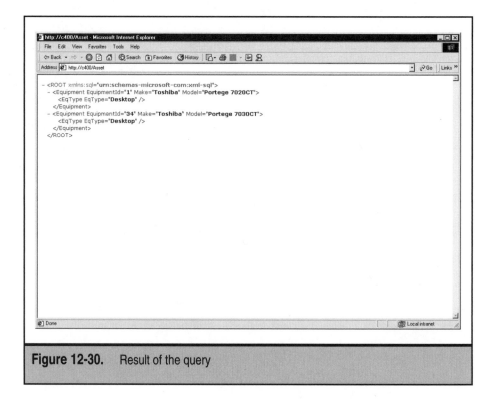

**Figure 12-30.** Result of the query

Now, you can assemble a more complex application by adding more forms, security, links between pages, and other elements, but this type of solution is really more suitable for simple search pages than for such complex applications.

# SUMMARY

XML support is one of the hottest new features of SQL Server 2000. Two major areas for the use of XML are the publishing of database information and B2B exchange of information.

SQL Server 2000 contains tools that are ideal for quick development of XML applications. The `For XML` clause of the `Select` statement can be used to accelerate development and reduce the development costs of XML applications. The flexibility of SQL Server's `Explicit` mode allows development of very complex XML documents. The power of the `OpenXML` statement allows Transact-SQL developers to access information stored in XML documents.

When the hype around XML settles down, Transact-SQL developers like you will be faced with real world problems associated with XML support in SQL Server 2000. At the time of this writing, the performance of XML document generation and parsing is unknown. It is also debatable whether it is better (that is, faster) to perform conversions to XML documents in SQL Server (which does not scale-out as well as middleware servers with COM components) or to use DOM or SAX in the middle layer to achieve the same effect.

Transact-SQL developers will be faced with a steep learning curve in order to utilize this new technology. XML documents are generated in components that are simply black boxes without much information that can be used to verify their integrity, and therefore design and debugging of XML documents and applications is not that simple.

Later releases of SQL Server will target features for updating information in the database through HTTP (UpdateGrams), massive import and export of XML documents (Bulk XML), and SOAP support (Simple Object Access Protocol—a lightweight protocol for exchanging messages and remote procedure calls).

# EXERCISES

1. Create a stored procedure to return an element-centric XML document and schema with information about a specified Order. Associated tables are shown in the following diagram:

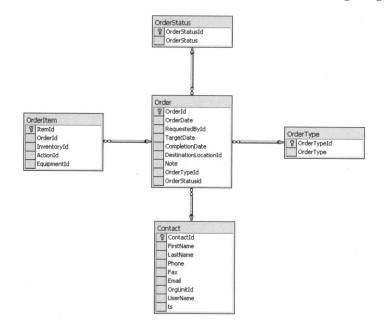

2. Create a stored procedure to return an XML document based on the content of the Order, OrderItem, and Equipment tables with the following structure:

```
<Order oid="1" OrderDate="1999-01-10T00:00:00">
  <OrderItem id="2" InventoryId="5">
    <Equipment EquipmentId="1" Make="Toshiba"
             Model="Portege 7020CT"/>
  </OrderItem>
  <OrderItem id="5" InventoryId="8">
    <Equipment EquipmentId="5" Make="Bang &amp; Olafson"
             Model="V4000"/>
  </OrderItem>
</Order>
<Order oid="6" OrderDate="2000-02-02T00:00:00">
```

```
<OrderItem id="10" InventoryId="6">
  <Equipment EquipmentId="6" Make="NEC" Model="V90"/>
</OrderItem>
<OrderItem id="11" InventoryId="25">
  <Equipment EquipmentId="1" Make="Toshiba"
          Model="Portege 7020CT"/>
</OrderItem>
<OrderItem id="12" InventoryId="29">
  <Equipment EquipmentId="35" Make="NEC"
          Model="Multisync III"/>
</OrderItem>
<OrderItem id="13" InventoryId="27">
  <Equipment EquipmentId="34" Make="Toshiba"
          Model="Portege 7030CT"/>
</OrderItem>
</Order>
<Order oid="7" OrderDate="2000-03-03T00:00:00"/>
...
```

3. Create a stored procedure that receives Order information in
   the form of an XML message, parses it, and stores it in tables.

# APPENDIX A

## T-SQL and XML Datatypes in SQL Server 2000

In this appendix, you will find three tables that provide an overview of the datatypes in use in SQL Server 2000. Table A-1 lists all Transact-SQL datatypes, their synonyms, their most important attributes (range and size), as well as sample constants. Table A-2 lists XML datatypes, and Table A-3 provides a mapping between Transact-SQL and XML datatypes.

| Datatypes and Synonyms | Description | Range | Size | Sample Constant |
|---|---|---|---|---|
| **Character Strings** | | | | |
| char (character) | Character string | 1 to 8,000 | 1 to 8,000 | 'D12-D13A36' |
| varchar (character varying) | Variable-length character string | 1 to 8,000 | 1 to 8,000 | 'Toronto' |
| text | Long variable-length character string | 1 to $2^{31} - 1$ | 16B + 0 to 2GB | 'SQL Server' |
| **Unicode Character Strings** | | | | |
| Nchar (national character) (national char) | Unicode character string | 1 to 4,000 | 2 to 8,000 | N'Никола' |
| Nvarchar (national character varying) (national char varying) | Variable-length Unicode character string | 1 to 4,000 | 2 to 8,000 | N'Никола' |
| Ntext (national text) | Long variable-length Unicode large character | 1 to $2^{30} - 1$ | 16B + 0 to 1GB | N'SQL Server' |
| **Date and Time** | | | | |
| datetime | Date and time | 1-Jan-1753 to 31-Dec-9999; precision: 3ms | 8 | '6/27/1998 10:20:17.31' |
| smalldatetime | Small date and time | 1-Jan-1900 to 6-Jun-2079; precision: 1min | 4 | 'Oct 30, 1993 14:30' |

**Table A-1.**   Transact-SQL Datatypes

| Datatypes and Synonyms | Description | Range | Size | Sample Constant |
|---|---|---|---|---|
| **Integer Numbers** | | | | |
| tinyint | Tiny integer | 0 to 255 | 1 | 17 |
| smallint | Small integer | −32,768 (−32K) to 32768 (32K) | 2 | 23017 |
| int | Integer | −2,147,483,648 to 2,147,483,647 (±2G) | 4 | 343013 |
| bigint | Big integer | ±9,223,372,036,854,775,807 (±2$^{63}$) | 8 | 322121343013 |
| bit | Logical | 0 or 1 | 1 (up to 8 bits per byte) | 1 |
| **Exact Numbers** | | | | |
| numeric (decimal) (dec) | Numeric or decimal | ±10$^{38}$ (depends on precision and scale) | 5 to 17 | −352.4512 |
| **Approximate Numbers** | | | | |
| real | Real (single-precision) number | −3.40 10$^{38}$ to 3.40 10$^{38}$ | 4 | −232.212E6 |
| float | Float (double-precision) number | −1.79 10$^{308}$ to 1.79 10$^{308}$ | 8 | 34.2131343E-64 |
| **Monetary** | | | | |
| smallmoney | Small monetary datatype | ±214,768.3648 | 4 | $120.34 |
| money | Monetary datatype | ±922,33720368547.5807 | 8 | $120000000 |

**Table A-1.** Transact-SQL Datatypes *(continued)*

| Datatypes and Synonyms | Description | Range | Size | Sample Constant |
|---|---|---|---|---|
| **Binary** | | | | |
| binary | Fixed-length binary string | 1 to 8,000 bytes | 1 to 8,000 | 0xa5d1 |
| varbinary | Variable-length binary string | 1 to 8,000 bytes | 1 to 8,000 | 0xa5c2 |
| image | Long variable-length binary string | 1 to $2^{31} - 1$ bytes | | n/a |
| timestamp | Database-wide unique number | n/a | 8 | n/a |
| uniqueidentifier | Global Unique Identifier (GUID) | n/a | 16 | 6F9619FF-8B86-D011-B42D-00C04FC964FF |
| **Special** | | | | |
| cursor | Cursor reference | n/a | | n/a |
| sql_variant | Variant | n/a | | n/a |
| table | Table | n/a | | n/a |

**Table A-1.**   Transact-SQL Datatypes (*continued*)

| XML Datatype | Description |
|---|---|
| `bin.base64` | Binary BLOB MIME-style Base64 encoded |
| `bin.hex` | Hexadecimal digits |
| `Boolean` | 0 ("false") or 1("true") |
| `char` | One character–long string |
| `date` | Date in a subset of ISO 8601 format (no time data). For example: "2000-12-25" |
| `dateTime` | Date in a subset of ISO 8601 format, with optional time. Time zone is not allowed. Time can be specified to the level of nanoseconds. Data and time segments are delimited with "T". For example: "2001-02-12T13:29:19" |
| `dateTime.tz` | Date in a subset of ISO 8601 format, with optional time and time zone (specified as time difference from GTM). Precise as nanoseconds. For example: "2001-02-12T13:29:19-06:00" |
| `fixed.14.4` | Decimal number with up to 14 digits left and up to 4 digits right of decimal point. Optional leading sign |
| `float` | Real number; no limit on digits; optional leading sign, fractional digits, and an exponent. Value range: 1.7976931348623157E+308 to 2.2250738585072014E-308 |
| `int` | Integer number |
| `number` | Real number, with no limit on digits; optional leading sign, fractional digits, and an exponent. Value range: 1.7976931348623157E+308 to 2.2250738585072014E–308 |
| `time` | Time in a subset of ISO 8601 format. No date and no time zone. For example: "04:12:17" |
| `time.tz` | Time in a subset ISO 8601 format, with no date but optional time zone. For example: "14:18:1237-03:00" |
| `i1` | Signed integer represented in one byte |
| `i2` | Signed integer represented in two bytes |
| `i4` | Signed integer represented in four bytes |
| `r4` | Real number; 7-digit precision; optional leading sign, fractional digits, and exponent. Values range: 3.40282347E+38F to 1.17549435E–38F |
| `r8` | Real number; 15-digit precision; optional leading sign, fractional digits, and exponent. Values range: 1.7976931348623157E+308 to 2.2250738585072014E-308 |
| `ui1` | Unsigned integer represented in one byte |
| `ui2` | Unsigned integer represented in two bytes |
| `ui4` | Unsigned integer represented in four bytes |

**Table A-2.** XML Datatypes

| XML Datatype | Description |
| --- | --- |
| uri | Universal Resource Identifier (URI). For example: "urn:schemas-microsoft-com:datatype" |
| uuid | Hexadecimal digits representing octets, optional embedded hyphens that are ignored. For example: "331B7AB4-630B-11F4-AD03-0720B7052C81" |

**Table A-2.**    XML Datatypes *(continued)*

| SQL Server Datatype | XML Datatype |
| --- | --- |
| bigint | i8 |
| binary | bin.base64 |
| bit | Boolean |
| char | char |
| datetime | datetime |
| decimal | r8 |
| float | r8 |
| image | bin.base64 |
| int | int |
| money | r8 |
| nchar | string |
| ntext | string |
| nvarchar | string |
| numeric | r8 |
| real | r4 |
| smalldatetime | datetime |
| smallint | i2 |
| smallmoney | fixed.14.4 |
| sysname | string |
| text | string |

**Table A-3.**    Mapping Between Transact-SQL and XML Datatypes

| SQL Server Datatype | XML Datatype |
| --- | --- |
| timestamp | ui8 |
| tinyint | ui1 |
| varbinary | bin.base64 |
| varchar | string |
| uniqueidentifier | uuid |

**Table A-4.**    Mapping Between Transact-SQL and XML Datatypes *(continued)*

# APPENDIX B

# Solutions to the Exercises

T his appendix presents the solutions to the exercises found at the end of the chapter.

# CHAPTER 2. RELATIONAL DATABASE CONCEPTS AND THE SQL SERVER ENVIRONMENT

## Exercise 2.1

Open SQL Server Books Online and find documentation about the sp_spaceused system stored procedure. Execute it to find out the amount of space used by the Asset database.

### Exercise 2.1 Solution

1. Open SQL Server Books Online.

2. Switch to the Index tab.

3. Type **sp_spaceused** as a keyword. The stored procedure appears selected in the list.

4. Double-click the stored procedure in the list, or click the Display button. Books Online displays a list of topics associated with the stored procedure. Double-click a topic, or select it and then click the Display button. The selected topic appears in the Details Pane (see Figure B-1).

5. Launch Query Analyzer, and switch to the Asset database.

6. In the Query pane, type **exec sp-spaceused**. From the menu that appears, select Query | Execute.

## Exercise 2.2

Create a stored procedure prListEquipment to return a list of equipment defined in the Equipment table of the Asset database.

### Exercise 2.2 Solution

1. Open Enterprise Manager.

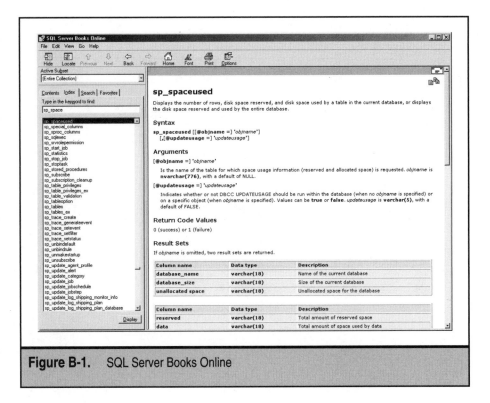

**Figure B-1.** SQL Server Books Online

2. Drill down to Stored Procedures in the Asset database.

3. Right-click any stored procedure and select New Stored Procedure from the pop-up menu. Enterprise Manager displays the Stored Procedure Properties dialog.

4. Type the following code for the stored procedure:

```
CREATE PROCEDURE prListEquipment
AS

select *
from Equipment
```

5. Click Check Syntax to verify that the code is correct.

6. Click OK to store and compile the stored procedure.

# Exercise 2.3

Change the stored procedure prListEquipment so that its resultset includes equipment type in the form of text. See the following diagram:

| EqType | | | |
|---|---|---|---|
| Column Name | Condensed Type | Nullable | |
| EqTypeId | smallint | NOT NULL | |
| EqType | varchar(30) | NOT NULL | |

| Equipment | | | |
|---|---|---|---|
| Column Name | Condensed Type | Nullable | |
| EquipmentId | int | NOT NULL | |
| Make | varchar(50) | NULL | |
| Model | varchar(50) | NULL | |
| EqTypeId | smallint | NULL | |
| ModelSDX | char(4) | NULL | |
| MakeSDX | char(4) | NULL | |

## Exercise 2.3 Solution

1.  Double-click prListEquipment in Enterprise Manager.

2.  Change its code to the following

```
ALTER PROCEDURE prListEquipment
AS

select Equipment.*, EqType.EqType
from Equipment inner join EqType
     on Equipment.EqTypeId = EqType.EqTypeId
```

3.  Click OK to save the stored procedure.

# Exercise 2.4

Execute the stored procedure prListEquipment.

## Exercise 2.4 Solution

1. Open Query Analyzer.

2. Make sure that the current database is Asset. (If it is not, select the Asset database from the DB drop-down list of databases.)

3. Type the following code in the Query Pane:

```
exec prListEquipment
```

4. Optionally, select Query | Results in Grid to set the format of the result.

5. Execute the stored procedure (Query | Execute) and Query Analyzer returns a list of equipment (see Figure B-2).

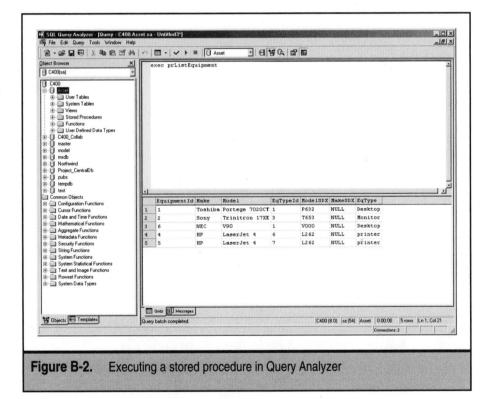

**Figure B-2.**   Executing a stored procedure in Query Analyzer

# CHAPTER 3. STORED PROCEDURE DESIGN CONCEPTS

## Exercise 3.1

Create a stored procedure called prUpdateStatus to update the status field of a specified record in the Inventory table.

### Exercise 3.1 Solution

prUpdateStatus is a simple stored procedure with two input parameters and an Update statement:

```
CREATE PROCEDURE prUpdateStatus
    @InventoryId int,
    @StatusId int
AS

Update Inventory
Set StatusId = @StatusId
where InventoryId  = @InventoryId
```

You can execute the stored procedure from Query Analyzer using the following code:

```
execute prUpdateStatus 121, 2
```

## Exercise 3.2

Create a stored procedure called prListProperties to return a list of properties and their values for a specified Inventory item.

### Exercise 3.2 Solution

prListProperties is a simple stored procedure with one input parameter and a Select statement; it joins two tables:

```
CREATE PROCEDURE prListProperties
    @InventoryId int
```

```
AS

SELECT  Property.Property,
        InventoryProperty.Value,
        Property.Unit
FROM    InventoryProperty INNER JOIN Property
        ON InventoryProperty.PropertyId = Property.PropertyId
WHERE InventoryProperty.InventoryId = @InventoryId
```

You can execute the stored procedure from Query Analyzer using the following code:

```
Execute prListProperties 121
```

# Exercise 3.3

Create a stored procedure to return a LeaseScheduleId for a specified asset.

## Exercise 3.3 Solution

The prGetLeaseScheduleId stored procedure requires one input parameter and one output parameter.

```
Create Procedure prGetLeaseScheduleId
    @InventoryId int,
    @LeaseScheduleId int OUTPUT
AS

Select @LeaseScheduleId = LeaseScheduleId
Where InventoryId = @InventoryIds
```

You can execute the stored procedure from Query Analyzer using the following code:

```
Declare @Result int
Execute prGetLeaseScheduleId
  @LeaseScheduleId = @Result OUTPUT,
  @InventoryId = 121
Select  @Result Result
```

# Exercise 3.4

Create a stored procedure prTest_QA with a simple `Select` statement inside. Using just Query Analyzer, verify that it exists in the current database.

## Exercise 3.4 Solution

Create the stored procedure and then use sp_stored_procedures to list all procedures in the database:

```
CREATE PROCEDURE prTest_QA
AS

SELECT *
from Inventory
go

exec sp_stored_procedures
go
```

# Exercise 3.5

Using just Query Analyzer, obtain the code of prTest_QA.

## Exercise 3.5 Solution

Use sp_helptext to list the code for the stored procedure:

```
exec sp_helptext prTest_QA
```

# Exercise 3.6

Using just Query Analyzer, view dependencies of prTest_QA.

### Exercise 3.6 Solution

Use sp_depends to list dependent and depending objects for the stored procedure:

```
exec sp_depends prTest_QA
```

## Exercise 3.7

Using just Query Analyzer, rename prTest_QA to up_Test_QA.

### Exercise 3.7 Solution

Use sp_rename to rename the stored procedure:

```
exec sp_rename prTest_QA, up_Test_QA
```

## Exercise 3.8

Using just Query Analyzer, delete up_Test_QA.

### Exercise 3.8 Solution

Use DROP PROCEDURE to delete the stored procedure:

```
DROP PROCEDURE up_Test_QA
```

# CHAPTER 4. BASIC TRANSACT-SQL PROGRAMMING CONSTRUCTS

## Exercise 4.1

Which datatypes can store strings and what are the differences among them?

### Exercise 4.1 Solution

Strings are usually stored in variables or columns of char, varchar, or text datatypes. In SQL Server 2000, as with SQL Server 7.0, it is possible to store strings with Unicode characters in Nchar, Nvarchar, and Ntext.

Char and Nchar are designed to store strings of fixed length. When a shorter string is assigned to them, SQL Server pads it with trailing spaces. Varchar and Nvarchar are designed for storing strings of variable sizes. The maximum length of Char and Varchar is 8,000 characters, and the maximum length of Nchar and Nvarchar is 4,000 characters (8,000 bytes). Text and Ntext can contain two billion and one billion characters respectively.

A new feature of SQL Server 2000 is the sql_variant datatype. Objects of the sql_variant datatype can contain information internally using the structures of char, varchar, Nchar, or Nvarchar datatypes.

## Exercise 4.2

Is it better to use decimal or real variables to store monetary values?

### Exercise 4.2 Solution

Decimal variables and columns are better suited for storing monetary values because they do not require conversion from the decimal to the binary system.

## Exercise 4.3

When variables are assigned with a Select statement that returns a recordset instead of a single record, which values will be assigned to the variables?

### Exercise 4.3 Solution

Values from the last record are assigned to the variables. The order of the records depends on the index that SQL Server uses to query the database.

# Exercise 4.4

What values will be assigned to the variable when a `Select` statement returns an empty recordset?

## Exercise 4.4 Solution

The values of variables are not changed in such a case.

# Exercise 4.5

Create two stored procedures prStoreOrder, which will insert an order and return an Order number, and prStoreOrderItem, which will insert the order item.

## Exercise 4.5 Solution

The following stored procedures are designed to store Orders and Order Items:

```
CREATE PROCEDURE prStoreOrder_1
    @OrderDate smalldatetime,
    @RequestedById int,
    @TargetDate smalldatetime,
    @DestinationLocationId int,
    @Note varchar(1000),
    @OrderTypeId int,
    @OrderStatusid int,
    @BillingOrgUnitId int,
    @VendorOrgUnitId int,
    @OrderId int OUTPUT
AS

insert into [Order] (OrderDate, RequestedById, TargetDate,
                    DestinationLocationId, Note, OrderTypeId,
                    OrderStatusid, BillingOrgUnitId,VendorOrgUnitId)
values ( @OrderDate, @RequestedById, @TargetDate,
        @DestinationLocationId, @Note, @OrderTypeId,
        @OrderStatusid, @BillingOrgUnitId, @VendorOrgUnitId)
Select @OrderId = @@identity
go
```

```
CREATE PROCEDURE prStoreOrderItem_1
    @OrderId int,
    @InventoryId int,
    @EquipmentId int,
    @Note varchar(1000)
AS

insert into OrderItem (OrderId, InventoryId, EquipmentId, Note)
values (@OrderId, @InventoryId, @EquipmentId, @Note)
```

You can use the following batch to execute these stored procedures:

```
declare @intOrderId int
exec prStoreOrder_1 @OrderDate = '11/11/1999',
                    @RequestedById = 1,
                    @TargetDate = '11/13/1999',
                    @DestinationLocationId = 1,
                    @Note = 'Handle with care!',
                    @OrderTypeId = 2,
                    @OrderStatusid = 1,
                    @BillingOrgUnitId = 1,
                    @VendorOrgUnitId = 2,
                    @OrderId = @intOrderId OUTPUT

exec prStoreOrderItem_1 @intOrderId, 12, Null, 'Not functional!'
exec prStoreOrderItem_1 @intOrderId, 11, null, 'Not functional!'
```

# Exercise 4.6

Create a stored procedure that creates a temporary table with just one integer field. The stored procedure should then insert numbers from 1 to 100 into the table and at the end return those numbers as a resultset to the caller.

## Exercise 4.6 Solution

This kind of task or stored procedure might look to you like a complete waste of time, but on several occasions I have had to use a solution based on the existence of a table with nothing but sequential integer numbers:

```
CREATE PROCEDURE prInsert100
AS
set nocount on
create table #Numbers(i int)

declare @i int
set @i = 1

-- loop to insert numbers
while @i <= 100
begin
    insert into #Numbers(i)
    values(@i)
    set @i = @i + 1
end

-- display numbers
select * from #Numbers

drop table #Numbers
```

# Exercise 4.7

Stored procedure sp_spaceused can return information about the space used by a database object. Collect the names of all tables in the Asset database using:

```
select name from sysobjects where xtype = 'U'
```

and then loop through them to display space information to users.

## Exercise 4.7 Solution

Use the following code:

```
Create Procedure prSpaceUsedByTables_1
-- loop through table names in current database
    -- display info about amount of space used by each table
As
Set nocount on
```

```
declare @MaxCounter int,
        @Counter int,
        @TableName sysname

Create table #Tables (
     Id int identity(1,1),
     TableName sysname)

-- collect table names
insert into #Tables(TableName)
     select name
     from sysobjects
     where xtype = 'U'

-- prepare loop
Select @MaxCounter = Max(Id),
       @Counter = 1
from #Tables


while @Counter <= @MaxCounter
begin
     -- get table name
     select @TableName = TableName
     from #Tables
     where Id = @Counter

     -- display space used
     exec sp_spaceused  @TableName
     set @Counter = @Counter + 1
end

drop table #Tables
```

This solution is not perfect. The result is not a single resultset but one resultset per table. You can find a better solution in Exercise 10.2.

# Exercise 4.8

Create a stored procedure that lists orders scheduled for today with a status set to 1.

## Exercise 4.8 Solution

Use the following code:

```
Create Procedure prListOrdersScheduledForToday
-- List Orders with status = 1 scheduled for today
As
set nocount on

SELECT     [Order].OrderId,
           [Order].OrderDate,
           Contact.FirstName + ' ' + Contact.LastName [Ordered By],
           Location.Location,
           [Order].Note,
           OrderType.OrderType,
           OrgUnit.OrgUnit,
           Contact1.FirstName + ' '
           + Contact1.LastName AS [Assigned To]
FROM [Order] INNER JOIN Contact
     ON [Order].RequestedById = Contact.ContactId
        INNER JOIN OrderType
        ON [Order].OrderTypeId = OrderType.OrderTypeId
           INNER JOIN Location
           ON [Order].DestinationLocationId = Location.LocationId
              INNER JOIN OrgUnit
              ON [Order].VendorOrgUnitId = OrgUnit.OrgUnitId
              AND Contact.OrgUnitId = OrgUnit.OrgUnitId
                 INNER JOIN Contact Contact1
                 ON [Order].AssignedToId = Contact1.ContactId
WHERE [Order].TargetDate Between Convert(varchar, GETDATE(), 101)
AND Convert(varchar, DateAdd(d, 1, GETDATE()), 101)
AND ([Order].OrderStatusid = 1)

return
```

## Exercise 4.9

Create a stored procedure that lists orders and displays three-character abbreviations of order status and type; that is, Ordered ⇨ Ord, Canceled ⇨ Cnl, Deferred ⇨ Dfr, and so on.

### Exercise 4.9 Solution

Use the following code:

```
Create Procedure prListOrders_CASE
-- list Orders
-- OrderStatus and OrderType are implemented
-- using case statement not tables.
As


set nocount on


SELECT      [Order].OrderId,
            [Order].OrderDate,
            Contact.FirstName + ' ' + Contact.LastName AS [Ordered By],
            Location.Location,
            [Order].Note,
            OrgUnit.OrgUnit,
            Contact1.FirstName + ' ' + Contact1.LastName
                AS [Assigned To],
            CASE [Order].OrderTypeId
                When 1 then 'Req'
                When 2 then 'TRA'
                When 3 then 'SUP'
                When 4 then 'SCR'
                When 5 then 'RPR'
                When 6 then 'UPG'
            END,
            CASE [Order].OrderStatusid
                When 1 then 'Ord'
                When 2 then 'InP'
                When 3 then 'Cnl'
```

```
                When 4 then 'Cmp'
                When 5 then 'Dfr'
        END


FROM [Order] INNER JOIN
    Contact ON
    [Order].RequestedById = Contact.ContactId INNER JOIN
    Location ON
    [Order].DestinationLocationId = Location.LocationId INNER JOIN
    OrgUnit ON [Order].VendorOrgUnitId = OrgUnit.OrgUnitId AND
    Contact.OrgUnitId = OrgUnit.OrgUnitId INNER JOIN
    Contact Contact1 ON [Order].AssignedToId = Contact1.ContactId


return
```

# Exercise 4.10

Create a stored procedure that will return a recordset with the field names of the specified table. The stored procedure should have only one input parameter—table name.

## Exercise 4.10 Solution

Use the following code:

```
Create Procedure prListColumns
-- list columns of specified table
    (
        @chvTableName sysname,
        @debug int = 0
    )
As
set nocount on

declare @i tinyint,
  @ColName sysname

-- collect all columns in one table/recordset
Create Table #ColNames (ColName sysname)
```

```
Set @i = 1

-- loop through columns
while @i <= 255
begin
    -- get column name
    SELECT @ColName = COL_Name( OBJECT_ID(@chvTableName), @i)

    -- check that we looped through all columns
    if @ColName is null
        BREAK

    if @debug <> 0
        select @i i, @ColName ColName

    -- insert column into column
    insert into #ColNames (ColName)
    values (@ColName)

    set @i = @i + 1
end

-- display list of columns
select * from #ColNames

drop table #ColNames

return
```

# Exercise 4.11

Explain the problems associated with the use of cursors.

## Exercise 4.11 Solution

The nature of cursors is contrary to the spirit of SQL. Cursors are designed to work with a single record, and the basic idea behind SQL is to work with sets of records. If you use cursors, each operation has to be repeated for each record. This repetition is the reason you pay for their use with performance penalties. Some cursors also keep records in tables locked until they are released. Since the operations performed by cursors are longer than those performed with a set of records, such operations are more prone to concurrency problems. Solutions based on cursors are also more prone to errors because they are more complex and thus require more error handling.

# Exercise 4.12

Stored procedure sp_spaceused can return information about the space used by a database object. Collect the names of all tables in the Asset database using

```
select name from sysobjects where xtype = 'U'
```

Use a cursor to loop through the table names to display space information to users. This task is equivalent to Exercise 4.7. Compare the solutions.

## Exercise 4.12 Solution

This stored procedure uses a cursor to loop through tables:

```
Create Procedure prSpaceUsedByTables_Cursor
-- loop through table names in current database
    -- display info about amount of space used by each table
As
Set nocount on
Declare @TableName sysname

-- collect table names
Declare curTables CURSOR FOR
    select name
    from sysobjects
    where xtype = 'U'

Open curTables

-- get first table name
FETCH NEXT FROM curTables
    into @Tablename
```

```
exec sp_spaceused  @TableName

WHILE @@FETCH_STATUS = 0
BEGIN
    -- get next table
    FETCH NEXT FROM curTables
        into @TableName

    -- process next table
    exec sp_spaceused  @TableName
end


CLOSE curTables
DEALLOCATE curTables
```

## Exercise 4.13

Create two stored procedures that will return a resultset in the form of a denormalized Inventory table (see Figure B-3). All fields in the Inventory table that are links to other lookup tables should be replaced with values from those lookup tables.

Each stored procedure should use a different method to obtain information:

▼  Select statement with join

▲  Looping with cursor

### Exercise 4.13 Solution

The first solution uses a Select statement with many joined tables:

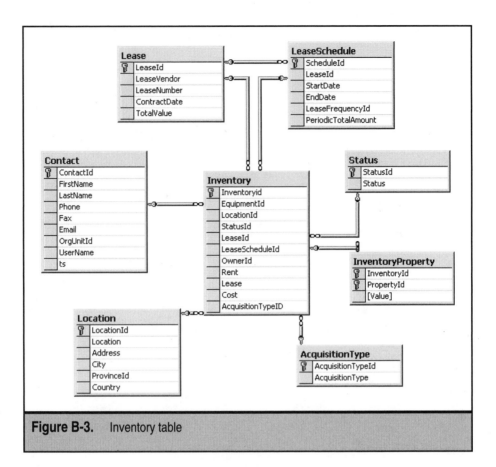

**Figure B-3.**    Inventory table

```
Create Procedure prReportInventory_SQL
-- return a report on assets in database
As
set nocount on

SELECT Inventory.Inventoryid, Equipment.Make, Equipment.Model,
    Location.Location, Status.Status, Lease.LeaseNumber,
    LeaseSchedule.StartDate, LeaseSchedule.EndDate,
    Contact.FirstName, Contact.LastName, Inventory.Rent,
    Inventory.Lease, Inventory.Cost,
    AcquisitionType.AcquisitionType,
    Inventory.AcquisitionDate
FROM AcquisitionType INNER JOIN Inventory
ON AcquisitionType.AcquisitionTypeId = Inventory.AcquisitionTypeID
    INNER JOIN Contact
    ON Inventory.OwnerId = Contact.ContactId
        INNER JOIN Equipment
```

```
            ON Inventory.EquipmentId = Equipment.EquipmentId
               INNER JOIN Lease
               ON Inventory.LeaseId = Lease.LeaseId
                  INNER JOIN LeaseSchedule
                  ON Inventory.LeaseScheduleId = LeaseSchedule.ScheduleId
                     INNER JOIN Location
                     ON Inventory.LocationId = Location.LocationId
                        INNER JOIN Status
                        ON Inventory.StatusId = Status.StatusId

Return
```

The solution using a cursor is far more complicated and executes more slowly:

```
Create Procedure prReportInventory_Cursor
-- return a report on assets in database
     @debug int = 0
As

declare    @Inventoryid int,
           @EquipmentId int,
           @LocationId int,
           @StatusId int,
           @LeaseId int,
           @LeaseScheduleId int,
           @OwnerId int,
           @Rent smallmoney,
           @Lease smallmoney,
           @Cost smallmoney,
           @AcquisitionTypeID int,
           @AcquisitionDate smalldatetime,
           @Make varchar(50),
           @model varchar(50),
           @Location varchar(50),
           @Status varchar(50),
           @LeaseNumber varchar(50),
           @StartDate smalldatetime,
           @EndDate smalldatetime,
           @FirstName varchar(30),
           @LastName varchar(30),
           @AcquisitionType varchar(20)

create table #InventoryDenormalized(
```

```
            InventoryId int,
            Make varchar(50),
            Model varchar(50),
            Location varchar(50),
            Status varchar(50),
            LeaseNumber varchar(50),
            StartDate smalldatetime,
            EndDate smalldatetime,
            FirstName varchar(30),
            LastName varchar(30),
            Rent smallmoney,
            Lease smallmoney,
            Cost smallmoney,
            AcquisitionType varchar(20),
            AcquisitionDate smalldatetime)

DECLARE @CrsrVar CURSOR

SET @CrsrVar = CURSOR FOR
    SELECT    Inventoryid, EquipmentId, LocationId,
              StatusId, LeaseId, LeaseScheduleId,
              OwnerId, Rent, Lease,
              Cost, AcquisitionTypeID, AcquisitionDate
    from Inventory

OPEN @CrsrVar

FETCH NEXT FROM @CrsrVar
INTO      @Inventoryid,
          @EquipmentId,
          @LocationId ,
          @StatusId,
          @LeaseId ,
          @LeaseScheduleId,
          @OwnerId,
          @Rent ,
          @Lease ,
          @Cost ,
          @AcquisitionTypeID,
          @AcquisitionDate

WHILE (@@FETCH_STATUS = 0)
BEGIN
```

```
if @debug <> 0
    select @Inventoryid,
           @EquipmentId,
           @LocationId ,
           @StatusId,
           @LeaseId ,
           @LeaseScheduleId,
           @OwnerId,
           @Rent ,
           @Lease ,
           @Cost ,
           @AcquisitionTypeID,
           @AcquisitionDate

-- get rest of info.
select    @Make = Make,
          @Model = Model
from Equipment
where Equipmentid = @EquipmentId

select @Location = Location
from Location
where LocationId = @Locationid

select @Status = Status
from Status
where StatusId = @Statusid


select @LeaseNumber = LeaseNumber
from Lease
where LeaseId = @Leaseid

select @StartDate = StartDate,
       @EndDate = EndDate
from LeaseSchedule
where ScheduleId = @Leasescheduleid

select    @FirstName = FirstName,
          @LastName = LastName
from Contact
where ContactId = @Ownerid
```

```
        select @AcquisitionType = AcquisitionType
        from AcquisitionType
        where AcquisitionTypeId = @AcquisitionTypeid

        -- insert everything
        insert into #InventoryDenormalized(
                InventoryId, Make, Model,
                Location, Status , LeaseNumber ,
                StartDate , EndDate , FirstName ,
                LastName, Rent, Lease ,
                Cost, AcquisitionType, AcquisitionDate)
        values ( @InventoryId, @Make, @Model,
                @Location, @Status, @LeaseNumber,
                @StartDate, @EndDate, @FirstName,
                @LastName, @Rent, @Lease,
                @Cost, @AcquisitionType, @AcquisitionDate)



        FETCH NEXT FROM @CrsrVar
            INTO      @Inventoryid,
                      @EquipmentId,
                      @LocationId ,
                      @StatusId,
                      @LeaseId ,
                      @LeaseScheduleId,
                      @OwnerId,
                      @Rent ,
                      @Lease ,
                      @Cost ,
                      @AcquisitionTypeID,
                      @AcquisitionDate


        END

CLOSE @CrsrVar
DEALLOCATE @CrsrVar

select * from #InventoryDenormalized

drop table #InventoryDenormalized

return 0
```

# CHAPTER 5. FUNCTIONS

## Exercise 5.1

Create a `Select` statement that returns the quarter from the current date in the following format: '3Q2000'.

### Exercise 5.1 Solution

Use the following code:

```
Select DATENAME(q, GETDATE()) + 'Q' + DATENAME(yyyy, GETDATE())
```

## Exercise 5.2

Create a table called ExpectedShippingDate that contains the following fields:

- ▼ ExpectedShippingDateId (offset from the starting date)
- ■ ExpectedShippingDate
- ■ ExpectedShippingDateOfMonth
- ■ ExpectedShippingMonth
- ■ ExpectedShippingYear
- ▲ ExpectedShippingQuarter

The table should be filled with one record for each date since 1/1/2000. Create a stored procedure Setup_ExpectedShippingDate to fill it.

### Exercise 5.2 Solution

Use the following statement to create the table:

```
CREATE TABLE [dbo].[ExpectedShipDate] (
    [ExpectedShipDateId] [smallint] NOT NULL ,
    [ExpectedShipDate] [smalldatetime] NULL ,
    [ExpectedShippingMonth] [tinyint] NULL ,
    [ExpectedShippingDay] [tinyint] NULL ,
    [ExpectedShippingYear] [smallint] NULL ,
```

```
    [ExpectedShippingQuarter] [char] (6) NULL
) ON [PRIMARY]
GO
```

The table can be filled using the following stored procedure:

```
CREATE PROCEDURE Setup_ExpectedShipDate
    @ExpectedShipDate smalldatetime = '1/1/2000',
    @day_number smallint = 5000
as

declare @ExpectedShipDateId              smallint
declare @ExpectedShippingMonth           tinyint
declare @ExpectedShippingDay             tinyint
declare @ExpectedShippingYear            smallint
declare @ExpectedShippingQuarter         char(6)         -- not (4) anymore
declare @ExpectedShipDatecurrent         smalldatetime
declare @intErrorCode                    int

set nocount on
select @intErrorCode = @@Error

If @intErrorCode = 0
begin
    select  @ExpectedShipDateId = 0,
            @ExpectedShipDatecurrent = @ExpectedShipDate
    select @intErrorCode = @@Error
end

while @intErrorCode = 0 and @day_number> 0
begin
    If @intErrorCode = 0
    begin
        select @ExpectedShipDateId =  @ExpectedShipDateId + 1,
            @ExpectedShippingMonth = datepart (mm,
@ExpectedShipDatecurrent),
            @ExpectedShippingDay = datepart (dd,
@ExpectedShipDatecurrent),
            @ExpectedShippingYear = datepart (yy,
@ExpectedShipDatecurrent)
        select @intErrorCode = @@Error
    end
```

```
        If @intErrorCode = 0
        begin
           Set @ExpectedShippingQuarter = dateName (qq, @ExpectedShipDate)
                           + 'Q' + dateName (yyyy, @ExpectedShipDate)
           select @intErrorCode = @@Error
        end
           -- insert row
        If @intErrorCode = 0
        begin
           insert into ExpectedShipDate (
                    ExpectedShipDateId, ExpectedShipDate,
                    ExpectedShippingMonth, ExpectedShippingDay,
                    ExpectedShippingYear, ExpectedShippingQuarter)

           values (@ExpectedShipDateId,   @ExpectedShipDatecurrent,
                  @ExpectedShippingMonth, @ExpectedShippingDay,
                  @ExpectedShippingYear,   @ExpectedShippingQuarter)

           Select @intErrorCode = @@Error
        End


        If @intErrorCode = 0
        Begin
           Select @day_number = @day_number - 1,
                  @ExpectedShipDatecurrent = @ExpectedShipDatecurrent + 1
           Select @intErrorCode = @@Error
        End

     End


     Return   @intErrorCode
     Go
```

## Exercise 5.3

Create a table to store contact information. The last column should
contain a binary checksum value so that you can later see if the
record has changed.

## Exercise 5.3 Solution

The following code snippet shows a new contact table with the BC field reserved for a binary checksum:

```
CREATE TABLE [Contact_with_BC] (
    [ContactId] [int] IDENTITY (1, 1) NOT NULL ,
    [FirstName] [varchar] (30) NOT NULL ,
    [LastName] [varchar] (30) NOT NULL ,
    [Phone] [typPhone] NULL ,
    [Fax] [typPhone] NULL ,
    [Email] [typEmail] NULL ,
    [OrgUnitId] [smallint] NOT NULL ,
    [UserName] [varchar] (50) NULL ,
    BC int null
) ON [PRIMARY]
GO
```

The value in the BC column can be managed from a trigger:

```
CREATE TRIGGER trContact_with_BC_IU ON [dbo].[Contact_with_BC]
FOR INSERT, UPDATE
AS

update Contact_with_BC
set BC = BINARY_CHECKSUM(FirstName, LastName, Phone,
                         Fax, Email, OrgUnitId, UserName)
where ContactId in (select ContactId from inserted)

GO
```

You can test the table, function, and trigger in the following manner:

```
insert Contact_with_BC (FirstName, LastName, Phone, OrgUnitId)
values('Tom', 'Jones', '123-4567', 1)

select * from Contact_with_BC
```

```
update Contact_with_BC
set Phone = '313-1313'
where ContactId = 1

select * from Contact_with_BC
```

# CHAPTER 6. COMPOSITE TRANSACT-SQL CONSTRUCTS—BATCHES, SCRIPTS, AND TRANSACTIONS

## Exercise 6.1

Create a database script for the Asset database.

### Exercise 6.1 Solution

1. Open Enterprise Manager.
2. Right-click the Asset database in the Console Tree pane.
3. Select All Tasks | Generate SQL Scripts.
4. Optionally make changes to default parameters, then click OK to accept.
5. When the application prompts you, specify a name for the script file to store the result.

## Exercise 6.2

Create a database script for a single stored procedure in the Asset database. Add a line of comment into the script and execute it.

### Exercise 6.2 Solution

1. Open Enterprise Manager.

2. Right-click the stored procedure in the Asset database for which you want to generate code.

3. Select All Tasks | Generate SQL Scripts.

4. The application displays a dialog box with a single stored procedure selected in the Objects To Be Scripted list (see Figure B-4). Click OK to accept the default parameters.

5. When the application prompts you, specify a name for the script file to be used to store the result.

6. Start Query Analyzer.

7. Open the script file (see the result of File | Open in Figure B-5).

8. Add a line of comment (place '--' at the beginning of the line).

9. Execute the script (Query | Execute).

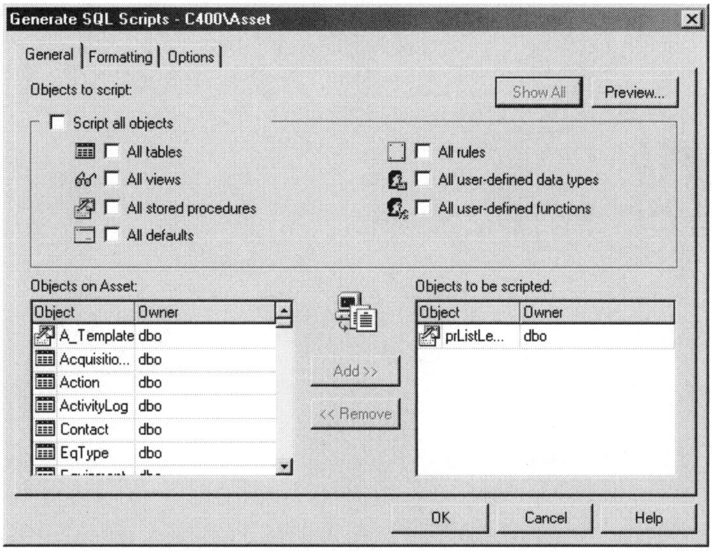

**Figure B-4.** Generating a script for a single stored procedure

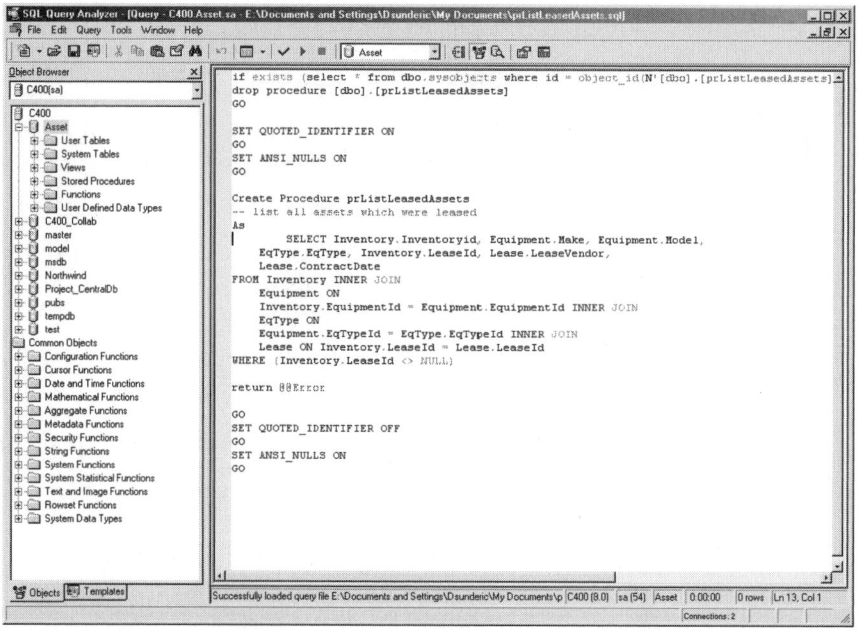

**Figure B-5.** A script for prListLeasedAssets

# Exercise 6.3

What is the problem with the following script?

```
select *
from Eq
/*
Go
delete Eq
where EqId > 100
Go
*/
select *
from EqType
```

How can you fix it?

## Exercise 6.3 Solution

The problem is that this script contains a comment that spans multiple batches. If you execute this script from Query Analyzer, it is divided into three batches. The first and the last batch do not execute because they contain incomplete comments. The second batch executes (contrary to expectations) and will purge a good portion of the Eq table.

You can fix the problem by changing the location of the comment markers:

```
select *
from Eq
Go
/*
delete Eq
where EqId > 100
*/
Go
select *
from EqType
```

You can also "comment-out" the Go command by placing two dashes at the beginning of the line with the Go statement:

```
select *
from Eq
/*
--Go
delete Eq
where EqId > 100
--Go
*/
select *
from EqType
```

# Exercise 6.4

How do the `Rollback Transaction` and `Commit Transaction` statements affect @@trancount?

## Exercise 6.4 Solution

`Commit Transaction` decreases @@trancount by one. If @@trancount then equals 1, it also commits changes to the database. `Rollback Transaction` discards all changes and sets @@trancount to 0.

# Exercise 6.5

Create a table with bank account information and then a stored procedure for transferring funds from one account to another. The stored procedure should contain transaction processing.

## Exercise 6.5 Solution

Use the following code:

```
CREATE TABLE [dbo].[Account] (
    [AccountId] [char] (10) NOT NULL ,
    [Balance] [money] NOT NULL ,
    [AccountTypeId] [int] NOT NULL
)
 GO


ALTER TABLE [dbo].[Account] WITH NOCHECK ADD
    CONSTRAINT [PK_Account] PRIMARY KEY  NONCLUSTERED
    (
        [AccountId]
    )
GO



CREATE PROCEDURE prTransferFunds
    @From char(20),
```

```
            @To char(20),
            @Amount money
    AS


    Begin Transaction

    update Account
    Set Balance = Balance - @Amount
    where AccountId = @From
    if @@Error <> 0 GOTO ERR


    update Account
    Set Balance = Balance + @Amount
    where AccountId = @To
    if @@Error <> 0 GOTO ERR


    Commit Transaction
    return 0


    ERR:
    Rollback Transaction
    Raiserror('Unable to transfer funds!', 16, 1)
    return 1
    GO
```

# Exercise 6.6

Is it okay to span a transaction over multiple batches?

## Exercise 6.6 Solution

Technically, it is possible to span a transaction over multiple batches, because SQL Server records them on the level of the user connection. However, it is not a recommended practice, because SQL Server blocks resources until the transaction is completed. It is important to complete the transaction as quickly as possible to release the blocked resources.

# CHAPTER 7. DEBUGGING AND ERROR HANDLING

## Exercise 7.1

Add debugging code to the following stored procedure:

```
Alter Procedure prSpaceUsedByTables_1
-- loop through table names in current database
    -- display info about amount of space used by each table
As
Set nocount on
declare @MaxCounter int,
        @Counter int,
        @TableName sysname

Create table #Tables (
    Id int identity(1,1),
    TableName sysname)

-- collect table names
insert into #Tables(TableName)
    select name
    from sysobjects
    where xtype = 'U'

-- prepare loop
Select @MaxCounter = Max(Id),
       @Counter = 1
from #Tables

while @Counter <= @MaxCounter
begin
    -- get table name
    select @TableName = TableName
    from #Tables
    where Id = @Counter

    -- display space used
```

```
        exec sp_spaceused  @TableName
        set @Counter = @Counter + 1
end


drop table #Tables
```

## Exercise 7.1 Solution

The new stored procedure is saved under a different name:

```
Create Procedure prSpaceUsedByTables_2
-- loop through table names in current database
        -- display info about amount of space used by each table
@debug int = 0
As
Set nocount on
declare @MaxCounter int,
        @Counter int,
        @TableName sysname


Create table #Tables (
        Id int identity(1,1),
        TableName sysname)


-- collect table names
insert into #Tables(TableName)
        select name
        from sysobjects
        where xtype = 'U'


if @debug <> 0
        select * from #Tables


-- prepare loop
Select @MaxCounter = Max(Id),
        @Counter = 1
from #Tables


if @debug <> 0
```

```
                   select @MaxCounter MaxCounter

         while @Counter <= @MaxCounter
         begin
              -- get table name
              select @TableName = TableName
              from #Tables
              where Id = @Counter

         if @debug <> 0
                   select @TableName TableName

              -- display space used
              exec sp_spaceused  @TableName
              set @Counter = @Counter + 1
         end

         Drop Table #Tables
```

# Exercise 7.2

Execute the stored procedure through Query Analyzer to review debugging information.

## Exercise 7.2 Solution

Use Query Analyzer, as shown in Figure B-6.

# Exercise 7.3

Run the stored procedure through TSQL Debugger to try debugging.

## Exercise 7.3 Solution

Right-click the procedure in the Object Browser of Query Analyzer. Click Debug and the program will prompt you to specify the parameters values, as shown in Figure B-7.

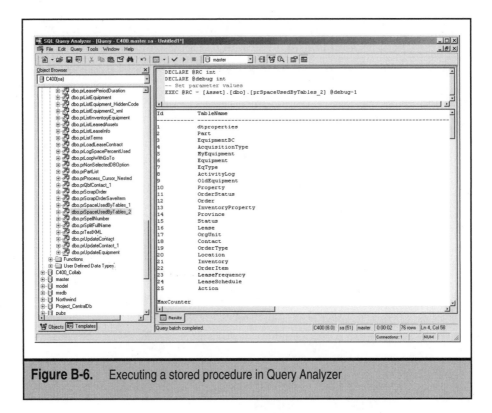

**Figure B-6.**    Executing a stored procedure in Query Analyzer

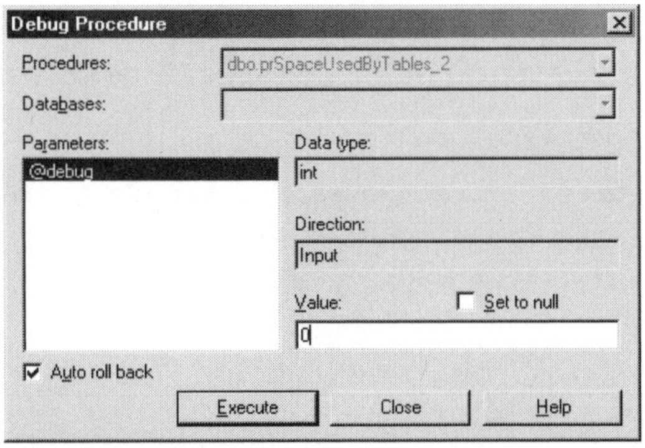

**Figure B-7.**    Debug Procedure dialog box

Set the value of @debug parameter to "0" and click on Execute. The program will launch the T-SQL Debugger window (see Figure B-8). You can now step through the procedure and investigate its local and global variables.

## Exercise 7.4

What is the problem with the following code snippet?

```
update LeaseSchedule
Set PeriodicTotalAmount = PeriodicTotalAmount + @mnyLease
where LeaseId = @intLeaseId
If @@Error <> 0
begin
    Print 'Unexpected error occurred: '
          + Convert(varchar, @@Error)
    Rollback transaction
    Return @@Error
end
```

### Exercise 7.4 Solution

The value of the @@Error global variable is set after every single Transact-SQL statement, including the If statement that is checking its value. Therefore, the Print statement cannot display the Error number as a part of the message. A better solution is the following:

```
Update LeaseSchedule
Set PeriodicTotalAmount = PeriodicTotalAmount + @mnyLease
Where LeaseId = @intLeaseId
Select @intErrorCode = @@Error

If @intErrorCode <> 0
Begin
    Print 'Unexpected error occurred: '
          + Convert(varchar, @intErrorCode)
    Rollback transaction
    Return @intErrorCode
End
```

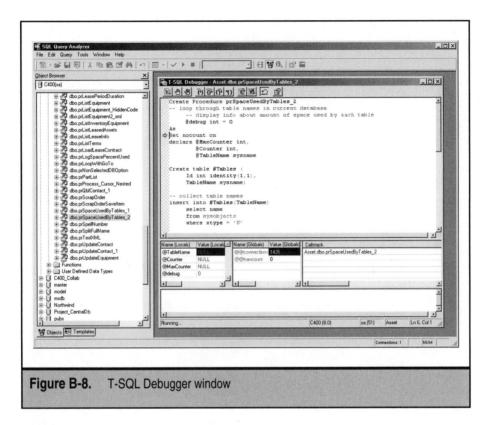

**Figure B-8.**   T-SQL Debugger window

# Exercise 7.5

Change the stored procedure from Exercise 6.5 so that it complies with the error handling solution proposed in this chapter.

## Exercise 7.5 Solution

Use the following code:

```
CREATE PROCEDURE prTransferFunds_2
    @From char(20),
    @To char(20),
    @Amount money,
    @debug int = 0
AS
```

```
set nocount on

Declare @intErrorCode int,
        @intTransactionCountOnEntry int,
        @chvProcedure sysname

Set @chvProcedure = 'prTransferFunds_2'

If @debug <> 0
    Select '**** '+ @chvProcedure + ' START ****'

Select @intErrorCode = @@Error

If @intErrorCode = 0
Begin
    Select @intTransactionCountOnEntry = @@TranCount
    BEGIN TRANSACTION
End

If @intErrorCode = 0
Begin
    update Account
    Set Balance = Balance - @Amount
    where AccountId = @From

    select @intErrorCode = @@Error
End

If @intErrorCode = 0
Begin
    Update Account
    Set Balance = Balance + @Amount
    Where AccountId = @To

    Select @intErrorCode = @@Error
End
```

```
If @@TranCount > @intTransactionCountOnEntry
Begin
    If @intErrorCode = 0
        COMMIT TRANSACTION
    Else
        ROLLBACK TRANSACTION
End


If @debug <> 0
    Select '**** '+ @chvProcedure + ' END ****'


Return @intErrorCode
```

# Exercise 7.6

Take the stored procedure from exercise 4.7 and wrap it in the error
handling solution described in this chapter.

## Exercise 7.6 Solution

Use the following code:

```
Create Procedure prSpaceUsedByTables_2
-- loop through table names in current database
    -- display info about amount of space used by each table
    @debug int = 0
As
set nocount on

Declare @intErrorCode int,
        @intTransactionCountOnEntry int,
        @chvProcedure sysname,
        @MaxCounter int,
        @Counter int,
        @TableName sysname

set @chvProcedure = 'prSpaceUsedByTables_2'
```

```
if @debug <> 0
    select '**** '+ @chvProcedure + ' START ****'


Select @intErrorCode = @@Error


If @intErrorCode = 0
Begin
    Create table #Tables (
        Id int identity(1,1),
        TableName sysname)


    Select @intErrorCode = @@Error
End



If @intErrorCode = 0
Begin
    -- collect table names
    insert into #Tables(TableName)
    select name
    from sysobjects
    where xtype = 'U'


    Select @intErrorCode = @@Error
End


If @intErrorCode = 0
Begin
    -- prepare loop
    Select @MaxCounter = Max(Id),
        @Counter = 1
    from #Tables


    Select @intErrorCode = @@Error
End
```

```
while @intErrorCode = 0 and @Counter <= @MaxCounter
begin
     If @intErrorCode = 0
     Begin
          -- get table name
          select @TableName = TableName
          from #Tables
          where Id = @Counter

          Select @intErrorCode = @@Error
     End

     If @intErrorCode = 0
          -- display space used
          exec @intErrorCode = sp_spaceused  @TableName

     set @Counter = @Counter + 1
end

drop table #Tables

if @debug <> 0
     select '**** '+ @chvProcedure + ' END ****'

return @intErrorCode
```

# CHAPTER 9. SPECIAL TYPES OF PROCEDURES

## Exercise 9.1

Create a function that returns the last date of a month containing a specified date.

### Exercise 9.1 Solution

Use the following code:

```
CREATE FUNCTION fnLastDateOfMonth
-- returns last date of the current month
    (
    @dtmDate datetime
    )
RETURNS datetime
AS
BEGIN
    declare @inyDay tinyint
    declare @dtmDateNew datetime

    set @inyDay = Day(@dtmDate)

    -- first day of the current month
    set @dtmDateNew = DateAdd( day, - @inyDay + 1, @dtmDate)
    -- first day of the next month
    set @dtmDateNew = DateAdd( month, 1, @dtmDateNew)
    -- last day of the current month
    set @dtmDateNew = DateAdd( day, - 1, @dtmDateNew)

    RETURN (@dtmDateNew)
END
```

You can test the function using a simple `Select` statement:

```
SELECT [Asset].[dbo].[fnLastDateOfMonth]('3/31/2000')
```

## Exercise 9.2

Create a function that returns a table containing the last days of months in a specified number of following years.

## Exercise 9.2 Solution

Use the following code:

```
CREATE FUNCTION dbo.fnListOfLastDatesMonth
(   @dtmStartDate datetime,
    @inyCountYears tinyint
)
RETURNS @tblDates table
    (
    LastDate datetime
    )
 AS
BEGIN

declare @dtmEndDate datetime
declare @dtmDate datetime

set @dtmEndDate = DATEADD(year, @inyCountYears, @dtmStartDate)
set @dtmDate = @dtmStartDate

while @dtmDate < @dtmEndDate
begin

    insert into @tblDates
    values(dbo.fnLastDateOfMonth(@dtmDate))

    set @dtmDate = DATEADD(month, 1, @dtmDate)

end
RETURN
END
```

You can test functions that return a table in any statement that uses a rowset provider, such as the From clause of a Select statement:

```
select * from dbo.fnListOfLastDatesMonth ('1/1/2000', 3)
```

# Exercise 9.3

Create a trigger on the Inventory table that will record in the ActivityLog table the user who is deleting assets from the database. The log should contain the user name of the person deleting records, the date of the deletion, and the IDs of the assets deleted.

## Exercise 9.3 Solution
Use the following code:

```
Create Trigger trInventory_D
On dbo.Inventory
For Delete
As

-- record in activity log each deletion of asset in Inventory table
Insert into ActivityLog( Activity,
                         LogDate,
                         UserName,
                         Note)
select   'ASSET DELETED',
         GetDate(),
         USER_NAME(),
         'InventoryId = ' + Convert(varchar, InventoryId)
from deleted
```

# Exercise 9.4

How can you disable nested and recursive triggers in SQL Server?

### Exercise 9.4 Solution

Execute sp_configure as follows:

```
exec sp_configure 'nested triggers', 0
exec sp_configure 'recursive triggers', 0
```

# Exercise 9.5

How can an administrator temporarily disable a trigger to allow the performance of administrative activities on a table?

### Exercise 9.5 Solution

Use the following command:

```
ALTER TABLE Order DISABLE TRIGGER trOrders_IU
```

# Exercise 9.6

Create a view for displaying denormalized information contained in the Inventory table. Design an instead-of insert trigger on the view to accommodate uploading of Inventory information from an external source.

### Exercise 9.6 Solution

You can use the Create View Wizard or any other tool to join tables and create the view:

```
SELECT Inventory.Inventoryid, Equipment.Make, Equipment.Model,
Location.Location, Status.Status, Contact.FirstName, Contact.LastName,
Inventory.Cost, AcquisitionType.AcquisitionType, Location.Address,
Location.City, Location.ProvinceId, Location.Country, EqType.EqType,
Contact.Phone, Contact.Fax, Contact.Email, Contact.UserName, Inventory.Rent,
Inventory.EquipmentId, Inventory.LocationId, Inventory.StatusId,
Inventory.OwnerId, Inventory.AcquisitionTypeID, Contact.OrgUnitId
```

```
FROM EqType RIGHT OUTER JOIN Equipment
  ON EqType.EqTypeId = Equipment.EqTypeId
  RIGHT OUTER JOIN Inventory
  INNER JOIN Status
  ON Inventory.StatusId = Status.StatusId
  LEFT OUTER JOIN AcquisitionType
  ON Inventory.AcquisitionTypeID = AcquisitionType.AcquisitionTypeId
  ON Equipment.EquipmentId = Inventory.EquipmentId
  LEFT OUTER JOIN Location
  ON Inventory.LocationId = Location.LocationId
  LEFT OUTER JOIN Contact
  ON Inventory.OwnerId = Contact.ContactId
GO
```

Only an instead-of trigger can be created on a view. This is a relatively complicated trigger. It first adds all missing information in the tables surrounding the Inventory table, and then it populates the Inventory table.

```
ALTER TRIGGER itr_vInventory_I
ON vInventory
instead of INSERT
AS

-- If the EQType is new, insert it
If exists(select EqType
          from inserted
          where EqType not in (select EqType
                                from EqType))
    -- we need to insert the new ones
    insert into EqType(EqType)
        select EqType
        from inserted
        where EqType not in (select EqType
                              from EqType)

-- now you can insert new equipment
If exists(select Make, Model, EqTypeId
          from inserted Inner Join EqType
          On inserted.EqType = EqType.EqType
          where Make + Model + Str(EqTypeId)
                not in (select Make + Model + Str(EqTypeId)
```

```
                                from Equipment))
            -- we need to insert the new ones
            Insert into Equipment(Make, Model, EqTypeId)
                select Make, Model, EqTypeId
                  from inserted Inner Join EqType
                  On inserted.EqType = EqType.EqType
                  where Make + Model + Str(EqTypeId)
                        not in (select Make + Model + Str(EqTypeId)
                                    from Equipment)


     -- if Location does not exist, insert it
     If exists(select Location
                from inserted
                    where Location not in (select Location
                                            from Location))
            -- we need to insert the new ones
            insert into Location(Location, Address,
                                    City, ProvinceId, Country)
                select Location, Address,
                        City, ProvinceId, Country
                from inserted
                where Location not in (select Location
                                        from Location)
     -- Status
     If exists(select Status
                from inserted
                    where Status not in (select Status
                                            from Status))
            -- we need to insert the new ones
            insert into Status(Status)
                select Status
                from inserted
                where Status not in (select Status
                                        from Status)


     -- AcquisitionType
     If exists(select AcquisitionType
                from inserted
                    where AcquisitionType not in (select AcquisitionType
                                                    from AcquisitionType))
            -- we need to insert the new ones
            insert into AcquisitionType(AcquisitionType)
```

```
                     select AcquisitionType
                     from inserted
                     where AcquisitionType not in (select AcquisitionType
                                                   from AcquisitionType)


     -- if Owner does not exist, insert it
     If exists(select Email
               from inserted
               where Email not in (select Email
                                   from Contact))
         -- we need to insert the new ones
         insert into Contact(FirstName, LastName,
                             Phone, Fax,
                             Email, UserName, OrgUnitId)
             select FirstName, LastName,
                    Phone, Fax,
                    Email, UserName, OrgUnitId
             from inserted
             where Email not in (select Email
                                 from Contact)


     Insert into Inventory(EquipmentId, LocationId, StatusId,
                           OwnerId, AcquisitionTypeId, Cost, Rent)
     Select  E.EquipmentId, L.LocationId, S.StatusId,  C.ContactId,
             A.AcquisitionTypeId, inserted.Cost, inserted.Rent
     From inserted inner join EqType
     on inserted.EqType =  EqType.EqType
        Inner Join Equipment E
        On inserted.Make = E.Make
        and inserted.Model = E.Model
        and EqType.EqTypeID = E.EqTypeID
           inner join Location L
           on inserted.Location = L.Location
              inner join Status S
              on inserted.Status = S.Status
                 inner join Contact C
                 on inserted.Email = C.Email
                    inner join AcquisitionType A
                    on inserted.AcquisitionType = A.AcquisitionType
     Go
```

To test the trigger, you have to insert a record into a view. Although the trigger does not need values for all fields (it ignores all "...Id" fields), you have to supply them:

```
INSERT INTO   [vInventory]([Inventoryid], [Make], [Model],
                           [Location], [Status], [FirstName],
                           [LastName], [Cost], [AcquisitionType],
                           [Address], [City], [ProvinceId],
                           [Country], [EqType], [Phone],
                           [Fax], [Email], [UserName],
                           [Rent], [EquipmentId], [LocationId],
                           [StatusId], [OwnerId], [AcquisitionTypeID],
                           [OrgUnitId])
VALUES(99, 'Brother', 'HPL-1700',
       ' Canadian Place', 'Active', 'Simon',
       'Maler', 695.00, 'Purchase',
       '1 Trigon Av.', 'Toronto', 'ON',
       'Canada', 'Monitor', '111-1231',
       '111-1121', 'SMaler@hotmail.com', 'SMaler',
       null, 99, 99,
       99, 99, 99,
       1)
```

# CHAPTER 10. ADVANCED STORED PROCEDURE PROGRAMMING

## Exercise 10.1

Create a pair of stored procedures that use optimistic locking to obtain and update a record in the Inventory table. Assume that the client application cannot handle the timestamp datatype and that you have to use the money datatype instead.

## Exercise 10.1 Solution

The record can be obtained using a stored procedure such as the following:

```
Create Procedure prGetInventory
-- get record with timestamp converted to money datatype
    (
        @intInventoryId int
    )
As
    set nocount on

    SELECT Inventoryid, EquipmentId, LocationId, StatusId, LeaseId,
        LeaseScheduleId, OwnerId, Rent, Lease, Cost,
        AcquisitionTypeID, AcquisitionDate,
        Convert(money, ts) mnyTimestamp
    FROM Inventory
    where InventoryId = @intInventoryId

return @@Error
```

The following stored procedure updates the record if it has not been changed since being read by the client application:

```
Create Procedure prUpdateInventory
-- update record from Inventory table
-- prevent user from overwriting changed record
    (
    @intInventoryid int,
    @intEquipmentId int,
    @intLocationId int,
    @intStatusId int,
    @intLeaseId int,
    @intLeaseScheduleId int,
    @intOwnerId int,
    @mnsRent smallmoney,
    @mnsLease smallmoney,
    @mnsCost smallmoney,
    @intAcquisitionTypeID int,
    @dtsAcquisitionDate smalldatetime,
    @mnyOriginalTS money
```

```
        )
As
set nocount on
declare @tsOriginalTS timestamp,
        @intErrorCode int

set @intErrorCode = @@Error

if @intErrorCode = 0
begin
    Set @tsOriginalTS = Convert(timestamp, @mnyOriginalTS)
    set @intErrorCode = @@Error
end

if @intErrorCode = 0
begin
    Update inventory
    Set EquipmentId = @intEquipmentId,
        LocationId = @intLocationId,
        StatusId = @intStatusId,
        LeaseId = @intLeaseId,
        LeaseScheduleId = @intLeaseScheduleId,
        OwnerId = @intOwnerId,
        Rent = @mnsRent,
        Lease = @mnsLease,
        Cost = @mnsCost,
        AcquisitionTypeID = @intAcquisitionTypeID,
        AcquisitionDate = @dtsAcquisitionDate
    where Inventoryid = @intInventoryid
    and TSEqual(ts, @tsOriginalTS)

    set @intErrorCode = @@Error
end

return @intErrorCode
```

# Exercise 10.2

Take a stored procedure from Exercise 4.7, 4.12, or 7.6 and return the results in a single resultset.

## Exercise 10.2 Solution

I have taken prSpaceUsedByTables_1 from Exercise 4.7 Solution and changed it into the following procedure:

```
Alter Procedure prSpaceUsedByTables_3
-- loop through table names in current database
     -- display info about amount of space used by each table
As
Set nocount on
declare @MaxCounter int,
         @Counter int,
         @TableName sysname

Create Table #SpaceInfo(name nvarchar(20),
                        rows char(11),
                        reserved varchar(18),
                        data varchar(18),
                        index_size varchar(18),
                        unused varchar(18))

Create table #Tables (
     Id int identity(1,1),
     TableName sysname)

-- collect table names
insert into #Tables(TableName)
     select name
     from sysobjects
     where xtype = 'U'

-- prepare loop
Select    @MaxCounter = Max(Id),
          @Counter = 1
from #Tables


while @Counter <= @MaxCounter
```

```
begin
     -- get table name
     select @TableName = TableName
     from #Tables
     where Id = @Counter

     -- display space used
     insert into #SpaceInfo(name, rows, reserved,
                            data, index_size, unused)
          exec sp_spaceused  @TableName

     set @Counter = @Counter + 1
end

select * from #SpaceInfo

drop table #Tables
drop table #SpaceInfo
```

The results from the sp_spaceused stored procedure are inserted into a temporary table.

```
insert into #SpaceInfo(name, rows, reserved,
                       data, index_size, unused)
     exec sp_spaceused  @TableName
```

#SpaceInfo has to have the same structure as the resultset from sp_spaceused. This requirement usually constitutes the biggest challenge in this kind of solution. It is easy if you can access the source code of the stored procedure or the structure of the resultset is published in the documentation, but such is not always the case.

```
Create Table #SpaceInfo(name nvarchar(20),
                        rows char(11),
                        reserved varchar(18) ,
                        data varchar(18) ,
                        index_size varchar(18) ,
                        unused varchar(18)  )
```

At the end of the stored procedure, results are sent to the caller:

```
select * from #SpaceInfo
```

## Exercise 10.3

Create a new version of the prGetInventoryProperties stored procedure that uses a `While` statement with a `Min()` function.

**NOTE:** Do not feel frustrated if you have trouble implementing the `While` loop in this case. This solution is complicated because three columns are read in each loop. The `aggregate` function `Min()` cannot be applied in a select list to one column without being applied to the others.

### Exercise 10.3 Solution

There are different solutions to this problem. One would be to use a subquery to extract the appropriate identifier field and then use that field to obtain the rest of the fields.

The original solution (prGetInventoryProperties) used an `aggregate` function in the select list. Since we removed the `aggregate` function from the select list, if no records qualify in the `Select` statement, the program does not set the values of variables to NULL. They simply retain their old values. The criteria in the `While` statement can never be satisfied, and the result is an endless loop. To prevent this, we set the values of the variables to NULL before each selection.

```
Alter Procedure prGetInventoryProperties_WhileLoop
-- Return comma-delimited list of properties
-- that are describing asset.
-- It uses While loop without temporary table
-- i.e.: Property = Value unit;Property = Value unit;Property = ...

    (
        @intInventoryId int,
        @chvProperties varchar(8000) OUTPUT,
        @debug int = 0
    )
```

```
As

declare @intCountProperties int,
        @chvProperty varchar(50),
        @chvValue varchar(50),
        @chvUnit varchar(50),
        @insLenProperty smallint,
        @insLenValue smallint,
        @insLenUnit smallint,
        @insLenProperties smallint,
        @chvOldProperty varchar(50)

-- identify Properties associated with asset
select    @chvProperty = Property,
          @chvValue = Value,
          @chvUnit = Unit
from InventoryProperty inner join Property
on InventoryProperty.PropertyId = Property.PropertyId
where InventoryProperty.InventoryId = @intInventoryId
and Property = (Select Min(Property)
          from InventoryProperty inner join Property
          on InventoryProperty.PropertyId = Property.PropertyId
          where InventoryProperty.InventoryId = @intInventoryId)

set @chvProperties = ''

-- loop through list of properties
while @chvProperty IS NOT NULL
begin
    if @debug <> 0
        select @chvProperty Property,
               @chvValue [Value],
               @chvUnit [Unit]

    -- check will new string fit
    select    @insLenProperty = DATALENGTH(@chvProperty),
              @insLenValue = DATALENGTH(@chvValue),
              @insLenUnit = DATALENGTH(@chvUnit),
              @insLenProperties = DATALENGTH(@chvProperties)

    if @insLenProperties + 2
```

```
                        + @insLenProperty + 1
                        + @insLenValue + 1
                        + @insLenUnit > 8000
              begin
                select 'List of properties is too long (over 8000 characters)!'
                return 1
              end

              -- assemble list
              set @chvProperties = @chvProperties
                                   + @chvProperty + '='
                                   + @chvValue + ' '
                                   + @chvUnit + '; '
              if @debug <> 0
                  select @chvProperties chvProperties

              -- set values to nulls to stop loop if record is not read
              -- but preserve the old value
  select      @chvOldProperty = @chvProperty,
              @chvProperty = NULL,
              @chvValue = NULL,
              @chvUnit = NULL

              -- let's go another round and get another property
  select      @chvProperty = coalesce(Property, ''),
              @chvValue = coalesce(Value, ''),
              @chvUnit = coalesce(Unit, '')
          from InventoryProperty inner join Property
          on InventoryProperty.PropertyId = Property.PropertyId
          where InventoryProperty.InventoryId = @intInventoryId
          and Property = (Select Min(Property)
                  from InventoryProperty inner join Property
                  on InventoryProperty.PropertyId = Property.PropertyId
                  where InventoryProperty.InventoryId = @intInventoryId
                  and Property > @chvOldProperty)
  end

  return 0
```

# CHAPTER 11. INTERACTION WITH THE SQL SERVER ENVIRONMENT

## Exercise 11.1

Create a trigger on the ActivityLog table that will send e-mail to the administrator when any record that contains the word 'Critical' as the first word of a Note is inserted.

### Exercise 11.1 Solution
Use the following code:

```
Create Trigger trActivityLog_CriticalNote_IU
On dbo.ActivityLog
For Insert, Update
As
if Exists(Select *
        from inserted
        where Left(Note,8) = 'Critical')
    Exec xp_sendmail
        @recipients = 'dejans; mirjanas',
        @subject = 'Critical activities recorded ' +
                    'in Activity Log of Asset database',
        @attach_results = 'TRUE'
```

## Exercise 11.2

Create a Transact-SQL batch that will compress files in the backup folder and transfer them to a drive on another machine.

### Exercise 11.2 Solution

The following statement uses PKZIP to compress all .dat files from the backup directory and place them on the C drive of the machine designated as P200:

```
xp_cmdshell 'c:\utl\pkzip -m \\p200\c\all.zip c:\mssql7\backup\*.dat'
```

# Exercise 11.3

Create a Transact-SQL batch that will create a scheduled job for compressing backup files. The job should be scheduled to run once a day.

### Exercise 11.3 Solution

Use the following code:

```
USE msdb
EXEC sp_add_job @job_name = 'ZIP Backup',
  @enabled = 1,
  @description = 'ZIP Backup files and put them on backup server',
  @owner_login_name = 'sa'

EXEC sp_add_jobstep @job_name = 'ZIP Backup',
    @step_name = 'ZIP',
    @subsystem = 'TSQL',
    @command = " exec xp_cmdshell " +
        "'c:\util\pkzip \\p200\c\all.zip c:\mssql7\backup\*.dat' "

EXEC sp_add_jobschedule @job_name = 'ZIP Backup',
    @name = 'Nightly ZIP',
    @freq_type = 4,    -- daily
    @freq_interval = 1,
    @active_start_time = '23:45'
```

# CHAPTER 12. XML SUPPORT IN SQL SERVER 2000

## Exercise 12.1

Create a stored procedure that returns an element-centric XML document and schema with information about a specified Order. Associated tables are shown in the following diagram:

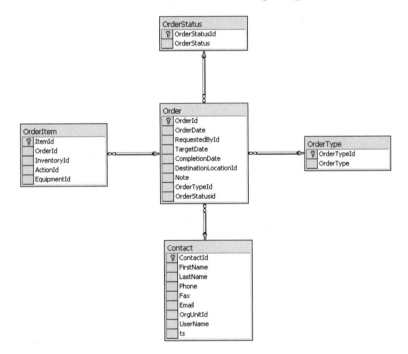

### Exercise 12.1 Solution

It is simple to create such a stored procedure. You can start by creating a `Select` statement that contains all these tables. Then you can add a `For XML` clause, and at the end, you can encapsulate everything in a stored procedure such as the following:

```
Create Procedure prOrderGetXML
    @intOrderId int
as

SELECT *
```

```
FROM dbo.Contact
  INNER JOIN [Order]
  ON Contact.ContactId = [Order].RequestedById
    INNER JOIN OrderItem
    ON [Order].OrderId = OrderItem.OrderId
      INNER JOIN OrderStatus
      ON [Order].OrderStatusid = OrderStatus.OrderStatusId
        INNER JOIN OrderType
        ON [Order].OrderTypeId = OrderType.OrderTypeId
where [Order].OrderId = @intOrderId
for XML Auto, elements, xmlData

return @@error
```

You can execute the stored procedure using the following code:

```
DECLARE @RC int
DECLARE @intOrderId int
-- Set parameter values
SET @intOrderId = 1
EXEC @RC = prOrderGetXML @intOrderId
```

SQL Server returns the following document containing both inline schema and Order data:

```
<Schema name="Schema" xmlns="urn:schemas-microsoft-com:xml-data"
                      xmlns:dt="urn:schemas-microsoft-com:datatypes">
   <ElementType name="dbo.Contact" content="eltOnly" model="closed"
order="many">
      <element type="dbo.Order" maxOccurs="*"/>
      <element type="ContactId"/>
      <element type="FirstName"/>
      <element type="LastName"/>
      <element type="Phone"/>
      <element type="Fax"/>
      <element type="Email"/>
      <element type="OrgUnitId"/>
      <element type="UserName"/>
      <element type="ts"/>
   </ElementType>
   <ElementType name="ContactId" content="textOnly"
              model="closed" dt:type="i4"/>
   <ElementType name="FirstName" content="textOnly"
```

```
                    model="closed" dt:type="string"/>
<ElementType name="LastName" content="textOnly"
                    model="closed" dt:type="string"/>
<ElementType name="Phone" content="textOnly"
                    model="closed" dt:type="string"/>
<ElementType name="Fax" content="textOnly"
                    model="closed" dt:type="string"/>
<ElementType name="Email" content="textOnly"
                    model="closed" dt:type="string"/>
<ElementType name="OrgUnitId" content="textOnly"
                    model="closed" dt:type="i2"/>
<ElementType name="UserName" content="textOnly"
                    model="closed" dt:type="string"/>
<ElementType name="ts" content="textOnly"
                    model="closed" dt:type="i8"/>
<ElementType name="dbo.Order" content="eltOnly"
                    model="closed" order="many">
   <element type="dbo.OrderItem" maxOccurs="*"/>
   <element type="OrderId"/>
   <element type="OrderDate"/>
   <element type="RequestedById"/>
   <element type="TargetDate"/>
   <element type="CompletionDate"/>
   <element type="DestinationLocationId"/>
   <element type="Note"/>
   <element type="OrderTypeId"/>
   <element type="OrderStatusid"/>
</ElementType>
<ElementType name="OrderId" content="textOnly"
                    model="closed" dt:type="i4"/>
<ElementType name="OrderDate" content="textOnly"
                    model="closed" dt:type="dateTime"/>
<ElementType name="RequestedById" content="textOnly"
                    model="closed" dt:type="i4"/>
<ElementType name="TargetDate" content="textOnly"
                    model="closed" dt:type="dateTime"/>
<ElementType name="CompletionDate" content="textOnly"
                    model="closed" dt:type="dateTime"/>
<ElementType name="DestinationLocationId" content="textOnly"
                    model="closed" dt:type="i4"/>
<ElementType name="Note" content="textOnly"
                    model="closed" dt:type="string"/>
```

```xml
<ElementType name="OrderTypeId" content="textOnly"
             model="closed" dt:type="i2"/>
<ElementType name="OrderStatusid" content="textOnly"
             model="closed" dt:type="ui1"/>
<ElementType name="dbo.OrderItem" content="eltOnly"
             model="closed" order="many">
   <element type="dbo.OrderStatus" maxOccurs="*"/>
   <element type="ItemId"/>
   <element type="OrderId"/>
   <element type="InventoryId"/>
   <element type="ActionId"/>
   <element type="EquipmentId"/>
</ElementType>
<ElementType name="ItemId" content="textOnly"
             model="closed" dt:type="i4"/>
<ElementType name="OrderId" content="textOnly"
             model="closed" dt:type="i4"/>
<ElementType name="InventoryId" content="textOnly"
             model="closed" dt:type="i4"/>
<ElementType name="ActionId" content="textOnly"
             model="closed" dt:type="i2"/>
<ElementType name="EquipmentId" content="textOnly"
             model="closed" dt:type="i4"/>
<ElementType name="dbo.OrderStatus" content="eltOnly"
             model="closed" order="many">
   <element type="dbo.OrderType" maxOccurs="*"/>
   <element type="OrderStatusId"/>
   <element type="OrderStatus"/>
</ElementType>
<ElementType name="OrderStatusId" content="textOnly"
             model="closed" dt:type="ui1"/>
<ElementType name="OrderStatus" content="textOnly"
             model="closed" dt:type="string"/>
<ElementType name="dbo.OrderType" content="eltOnly"
             model="closed" order="many">
   <element type="OrderTypeId"/>
   <element type="OrderType"/>
</ElementType>
```

```
        <ElementType name="OrderTypeId" content="textOnly"
                    model="closed" dt:type="i2"/>
        <ElementType name="OrderType" content="textOnly"
                    model="closed" dt:type="string"/>
</Schema>

<dbo.Contact xmlns="x-schema:#Schema">
    <ContactId>1</ContactId>
    <FirstName>Dejan</FirstName>
    <LastName>Sunderic</LastName>
    <Phone>111-1111</Phone>
    <Fax>111-1112</Fax>
    <Email>dejans@hotmail.com</Email>
    <OrgUnitId>1</OrgUnitId>
    <UserName>dejans</UserName>
    <ts>2503</ts>
    <dbo.Order>
        <OrderId>1</OrderId>
        <OrderDate>1999-01-10T00:00:00</OrderDate>
        <RequestedById>1</RequestedById>
        <TargetDate>2000-01-01T00:00:00</TargetDate>
        <OrderTypeId>3</OrderTypeId>
        <OrderStatusid>1</OrderStatusid>
        <dbo.OrderItem>
            <ItemId>2</ItemId>
            <OrderId>1</OrderId>
            <InventoryId>5</InventoryId>
            <dbo.OrderStatus>
                <OrderStatusId>1</OrderStatusId>
                <OrderStatus>Ordered</OrderStatus>
                <dbo.OrderType>
                    <OrderTypeId>3</OrderTypeId>
                    <OrderType>Scrap</OrderType>
                </dbo.OrderType>
            </dbo.OrderStatus>
        </dbo.OrderItem>
    </dbo.Order>
</dbo.Contact>
```

## Exercise 12.2

Create a stored procedure that returns an XML document based on the content of Order, OrderItem, and Equipment tables with the following structure:

```xml
<Order oid="1" OrderDate="1999-01-10T00:00:00">
  <OrderItem id="2" InventoryId="5">
    <Equipment EquipmentId="1" Make="Toshiba"
             Model="Portege 7020CT"/>
  </OrderItem>
  <OrderItem id="5" InventoryId="8">
    <Equipment EquipmentId="5" Make="Bang &amp; Olafson"
             Model="V4000"/>
  </OrderItem>
</Order>
<Order oid="6" OrderDate="2000-02-02T00:00:00">
  <OrderItem id="10" InventoryId="6">
    <Equipment EquipmentId="6" Make="NEC" Model="V90"/>
  </OrderItem>
  <OrderItem id="11" InventoryId="25">
    <Equipment EquipmentId="1" Make="Toshiba"
             Model="Portege 7020CT"/>
  </OrderItem>
  <OrderItem id="12" InventoryId="29">
    <Equipment EquipmentId="35" Make="NEC"
             Model="Multisync III"/>
  </OrderItem>
  <OrderItem id="13" InventoryId="27">
    <Equipment EquipmentId="34" Make="Toshiba"
             Model="Portege 7030CT"/>
  </OrderItem>
</Order>
<Order oid="7" OrderDate="2000-03-03T00:00:00"/>
...
```

## Exercise 12.2 Solution

We must use the `Explicit` mode of the `For XML` clause to control the content of the stored procedure precisely:

```
SELECT    1 as Tag, NULL as Parent,
          O.OrderID as [Order!1!oid],
          O.OrderDate as [Order!1!OrderDate],
          O.Note as [Order!1!Note],
          NULL as [OrderItem!2!id],
          NULL as [OrderItem!2!InventoryId],
          NULL as [Equipment!3!EquipmentId],
          NULL as [Equipment!3!Make],
          NULL as [Equipment!3!Model]
FROM [Order] O
UNION ALL
SELECT 2 as Tag, 1 as Parent,
          O.OrderID,
          NULL,
          NULL,
          OI.ItemID,
          OI.InventoryId,
          NULL,
          NULL,
          NULL
FROM      [Order] O, OrderItem OI
WHERE     O.OrderID = OI.OrderID
UNION ALL
SELECT    3 as Tag, 2 as Parent,
          O.OrderID,
          NULL,
          NULL,
          OI.ItemID,
          NULL,
          E.EquipmentID,
          E.Make,
          E.Model
FROM      [Order] O, OrderItem OI, Equipment E
WHERE     O.OrderID = OI.OrderID
```

```
AND       OI.EquipmentID = E.EquipmentID
ORDER BY [Order!1!oid], [OrderItem!2!id], [Equipment!3!EquipmentId]
FOR XML EXPLICIT
```

## Exercise 12.3

Create a stored procedure that receives Order information in the
form of an XML message, parses it, and stores it in tables.

### Exercise 12.3 Solution

You could use the OpenXML rowset provider to parse the content of
the XML document. Since Order.OrderId and OrderItem.ItemId
are identity fields, you need to ignore values provided in the XML
document.

The biggest problem that I had working with this stored
procedure was due to the fact that XML is case sensitive, unlike
Transact-SQL. You have to make column patterns in the OpenXML
rowset provider to match the names of the attributes.

```
Alter Procedure prOrderSave
-- Extract Order (and Order Items) info. from an XML document.
    @chvXMLDoc text,
    @debug int = 0
As
set nocount on

Declare @intErrorCode int,
        @intTransactionCountOnEntry int,
    @intRowCount int,
    @intDoc int,
    @intOrderId int

Select @intErrorCode = @@Error
If @debug <> 0
    select 'Load XML document.'
--Create an internal representation of the XML document.
If @intErrorCode = 0
    EXEC @intErrorCode = sp_xml_preparedocument @intDoc OUTPUT,
                                                @chvXMLDoc
```

```
If @intErrorCode = 0
Begin
    Select @intTransactionCountOnEntry = @@TranCount
    BEGIN TRANSACTION
    If @debug <> 0
        select 'Transaction started.'
End


-- extract order info
If @intErrorCode = 0
Begin
    Insert into [Order](OrderDate, RequestedById,
            TargetDate, CompletionDate, DestinationLocationId,
            Note, OrderTypeId, OrderStatusid)
    SELECT      OrderDate, RequestedById,
            TargetDate, CompletionDate, DestinationLocationId,
            Note, OrderTypeId, OrderStatusid
    FROM    OPENXML  (@intDoc, '/Order', 1)
            WITH  (OrderDate smalldatetime '@OrderDate',
                    RequestedById int '@RequestedById',
                    TargetDate smalldatetime '@TargetDate',
                    CompletionDate smalldatetime '@CompletionDate',
                    DestinationLocationId int '@DestinationLocationId',
                    Note text '@Note',
                    OrderTypeID int '@OrderTypeId',
                    OrderStatusId int '@OrderStatusid')
    Select @intErrorCode = @@Error,
       @intOrderId = @@identity
     If @debug <> 0
    Select 'OrderInserted:',
            @intErrorCode [Error],
            @intOrderId [identity]
End

-- extract OrderItem info
If @intErrorCode = 0
Begin
    Insert into OrderItem(OrderID, InventoryId, ActionId, EquipmentId)
    SELECT    @intOrderId, *
    FROM    OPENXML  (@intDoc, '/Order/OrderItem', 1)
            WITH    (InventoryId int '@InventoryId',
```

```
                              ActionId    int '@ActionId',
                              EquipmentId int '@EquipmentId')
       Select @intErrorCode = @@Error,
          @intRowCount = @@RowCount
       If @debug <> 0
       Select 'Order Item info inserted.',
               @intErrorCode Error,
               @intRowCount [RowCount]
   end


   If @@TranCount > @intTransactionCountOnEntry
   Begin
       If @intErrorCode = 0
       begin
           COMMIT TRANSACTION
           If @debug <> 0
         Select 'Transaction committed.'
       end
       Else
       begin
           ROLLBACK TRANSACTION
           If @debug <> 0
         Select 'Transaction rolled back.'
       end
   End


   If @intErrorCode = 0
       EXEC sp_xml_removedocument @intDoc


   return @intErrorCode
```

You can test the stored procedure using this code:

```
DECLARE @RC int
-- Set parameter values
EXEC @RC = [Asset].[dbo].[prOrderSave]
'<Order OrderId = "3" OrderDate = "1/1/2001"
       RequestedById = "1" TargetDate = "2/2/2001"
       CompletionDate = "3/3/2001" DestinationLocationId = "1"
       Note = "Special delivery." OrderTypeId = "1"
       OrderStatusid = "1">
   <OrderItem ItemId = "1" OrderID = "3"
             InventoryId = "5" ActionId = "1"
```

```
                EquipmentId = "1"/>
    <OrderItem ItemId = "2" OrderID = "3"
                InventoryId = "6" ActionId = "2"
                EquipmentId = "6"/>
</Order>', 1
select @RC Error
```

# Index

## ▼ E

## ▼ N

## ▼ O